AF372710

QURAN
MORAL COMPASS OF THE
BELIEVER

QURAN
MORAL COMPASS OF THE
BELIEVER

DR. ALI MOHAMED SALAH

Looh Press

2023

LOOH PRESS.
Copyright © Ali Mohamed Salah 2023
First Edition, First Print October 2023

PRINTED & DISTRIBUTED BY
Looh Press Ltd.
56 Lethbridge Close
Leicester, England. UK
www.LoohPress.com
LoohPress@gmail.com

A catalogue record of this title is available from the British Library.

Edited, Cover design & typeset by   Looh Press (Kusmin)

ISBN
978-1-912411-69-6   (Paperback)

TRANSLITERATION TABLE

(ء) = ʾ	(ا) = a / A / ā / Ā	(ب) = b / B
(ت) = t / T	(ث) = th / TH	(ج) = j / J
(ح) = ḥ / Ḥ	(خ) = kh / KH	(د) = d / D
(ذ) = dh / DH	(ر) = r / R	(ز) = z / Z
(س) = s / S	(ش) = sh / SH	(ص) = ṣ / Ṣ
(ض) = ḍ / Ḍ	(ط) = ṭ / Ṭ	(ظ) = ẓ / Ẓ
(ع) = ʿ / ʿ	(غ) = gh / GH	(ف) = f / F
(ق) = q / Q	(ك) = k / K	(ل) = l / L
(م) = m / M	(ن) = n / N	(ه) = h / H
(و) = w / W / ū / Ū	(ي) = y / Y / ī /	

 = Jalla Jallāluhu

 = Subḥānahu Wa Taʿālā

 = Sallalāhu ʿAlayhi Wasallam

 = Raḥimahu Allāh

 = Raḍiyallāhu ʿanhu

 = Raḍiyallāhu ʿanhā

 = Raḍiyallāhu ʿanhumā

CONTENTS

Dedication xii

Acknowledgment xiii

Introduction 1

Abstract 3

Definition of Morals 5

1.0   Chapter I: Moral and Ethics In Islam 9

1.1.   Section One: The Importance of Morals In Islam 10

1.2.   Section Two: Principles of Morals In The Quran 14

1.3.   Section Three: The Perfection of The Moral System In The Quran 19

1.4.   Section Four: Prophet Muḥammad (ﷺ) and His Role In Perfecting The Morals of Believers 23

1.5.   Section Five: Virtues of Good Morals In Islam 28

2.0   Chapter II: Faith and Morals In Islam 33

The Relationship Between Faith and Morals 34

2.1.   Section One: Etiquette and Behavior of The Believer Toward Allāh 38

2.1.1.   The Importance of A Beleiver's Good Behaviour Toward Allah 38

2.1.2.   Etiquette With Allāh Demands True Monotheism, Which Affirms His Oneness Without Any Partners. 39

2.1.3.   Denotation of Plyothiesim "Shirk". 41

2.1.4.   Atheism and Its Denotation 44

2.1.5.   Causes of Atheism 45

2.1.6.   Etiquette With Allāh Implies Worship and Obedience. 51

2.1.7.   The Meaning of Ibada (Worship) and The Purpose of Human Creation 53

2.1.8.   The Description of 'Ibādah Theologically 54

2.1.9.   The Difference Between ('Ibādah) Worship and (Ṭā'ah) Obedience 57

2.1.10.   Etiquette of Patience When Behaving With Allāh 58

2.1.11.   Obedience To The Commands of Allāh 59

2.1.12.   Restraining Oneself From Disobeying His Commands. 60

2.1.13.   Accepting The Decree, Fate, Or Destiny Written By Allāh 61

2.2.   Section Two: Etiquette and Behavior of The Believer Toward The Prophet Muhammed, ﷺ 63

2.2.1.   Showing Respect To Him When Drawing His Attention To An Important Matter. 63

2.2.2.   Manners of Calling The Prophet ﷺ 65

2.2.3.   Respect His Privacy, Time, Place, and Family. 66

2.2.4. Respect Him By Giving Preference To His Commandments Over Our Views and Opinions. 67

2.2.5. We Should Respect Him By Not Raising Our Voices Over His Voice During His Presence. 69

2.2.6. Conversations About Disobedience and Disloyalty To The Prophetﷺ Are Considered To Be Sinful. 71

2.2.7. Supporting The Prophetﷺ Means Honouring Him. 72

2.2.8. Betraying The Prophetﷺ Means Disloyalty. 72

2.2.9. Harming The Prophetﷺ In Any Form, By Word Or Action, Is A Very Heinous Sin. 73

2.2.10. Emulating Him and Following His (Sunnah) Prophetic Tradition As A Moral Ideal. 74

2.2.11. Denotation Meaning of Sunnah and Ḥadīth Mean 76

2.2.12. Sunnah Deniers 79

2.2.13. Similarities Between Sunnah Deniers and Orientalists 83

2.2.14. The Term Bid'ah, "Innovation," and Its Denotation 84

2.3. Section Three: Blasphemy Is Immorality 89

2.3.1. Insulting Allāh and The Messenger Is Immoral 90

2.3.1.1. Insulting Allāh (ﷻ). 90

2.3.1.2. Insulting The Prophet ﷺ 97

2.4. Section Four: Etiquette and Behaviour of The Believer Towards The Prophet's Companions ﷺ 100

2.4.1. The Status of The Companions In Islam 100

2.4.2. Virtues of The Companions In Islam 102

2.4.3. Shia's View of The Companions 105

3.0 CHAPTER III: SOCIAL MORALITY IN THE QURAN 109

3.1. Section One: Marriage and Morals In Islam 110

3.1.1. Part 1- Importance of Marriage: 110

3.1.2. Part 2: Moral Codes and Guidelines On Marital Harmony In Quran and Sunnah. 114

3.1.3. Part 3- Marital Conflict Resolution: Moral Guidelines 140

3.2. Section Two: Etiquette and Morality Toward Parents 186

3.2.1. The Significance of Etiquette and Morality Towards Parents In Islamic Teachings. 186

3.3. Section Three: Parental Moral Obligations Toward Children 199

3.3.1. Part 1: Islamic Perspective On Parent-Child Relationships 199

3.3.2. Part 2: Moral Parenting Compass In The Quran (Moral Codes) 217

3.3.3. Righteousness of Parents 234

3.3.4. Child Disciplining 237

3.4. Section Four: Moral Ettequites of The Believer With Relatives 242

3.5. Section Five
Moral Ettequites of The Believer With The Neighbors 247

4.0 CHAPTER IV: INDIVIDUAL MORALITY IN THE QURAN.......................................253

4.1. Section One: Importance of Good Manners
With People..254

    4.1.1. The Role of A Muslim's Morality In Achieving Salvation In The Hereafter ....
254

    4.1.2. The Significance of Individual Morality For The Society 256

    4.1.3. Individual Moral Qualities In The Quran 259

4.2. Section Two: The Most Significant Moral
Qualities In Islam 260

    4.2.1. Trust (Amaanah) 260

    4.2.2. Truth 268

    4.2.3. Modesty (Haya) 278

    4.2.4. Ḥilm (Forbearance) 287

    4.2.5. Ihsan 295

INDEX OF QURANIC VERSES...299

INDEX OF PROPHETIC NARRATIONS...314

BIBLIOGRAPHY 322

INDEX 330

DEDICATION

As a result, I dedicate this book to the souls of my beloved parents, who tirelessly invested their efforts in nurturing me, helping me realize my dreams, and shaping my career. May they be showered with the mercy of Allah and find eternal peace in the vast heavens of the Lord.

ACKNOWLEDGMENT

I would like to express my sincere gratitude to Allāh for His assistance in accomplishing this writing. Without Allāh's guidance and support, I would not have been able to complete this work.

I am deeply thankful to all those who supported and aided me throughout the process of writing my book. Their contributions, encouragement, and unwavering belief in my abilities have been invaluable, and I am immensely grateful for their presence in my life.

First and foremost, I extend my heartfelt appreciation to my family. Their unconditional patience and understanding during this journey have been immeasurable. They gave me time and space to immerse myself in my writing, even when sacrificing their needs. I am eternally grateful for their unwavering support.

I would also like to extend a special thanks to Abdirashid Hassan Ilmi for his technical expertise and guidance, which played a vital role in shaping the content and structure of this book. To Eng. Mohamed Abdulrahman Ismail, Najib Sayed Daher, Mohamed Isak, and Hussein Abdi Yusuf, I am deeply grateful for your contributions, patience, and technical support. Your assistance has made this book possible, and I am honored to have had you by my side throughout this journey.

To all those who have played a part, no matter how big or small, in helping me bring this book to fruition, I extend my heartfelt thanks. Their support has been invaluable, and I am truly humbled by your presence in my life.

With the most profound appreciation,

INTRODUCTION

Indeed, all praise and thanks are due to Allāh. We praise Him, we seek His assistance, we seek His forgiveness, and we seek His guidance. Whomsoever Allāh misguides, no one can guide, and whom Allāh guides, no one can misguide, and I bear witness that there is no one worthy of worship save Allāh, and Muḥammad is his final Messenger.

During my nearly quarter-century stay in the West, I have actively participated in Da'wa activities and have noticed an alarming trend among the second and third generations of Muslim communities in the West. Due to their Western upbringing, these generations increasingly move away from Islamic morals, ethics, and cultural values. As a result, their belief in Allāh and the Prophet Muḥammad has weakened, leading to doubts and misconceptions about Islam. The rise of atheism among the youth and the proliferation of distorted beliefs and ideologies further compound the situation.

Additionally, there has been a noticeable decline in moral values across various facets of life. Parent-child relationships have become strained, resulting in high divorce rates and a lack of understanding regarding marital morals and rights. Maintaining strong kinship ties is often overlooked, as the younger generation prioritizes personal aspirations over social issues and family matters. The neglect and mistreatment of older individuals and the growing disregard for young children due to the fast-paced nature of modern life are disconcerting trends.

The erosion of moral values can be attributed, in part, to the influence of Western ideals and misleading media portrayals. Traditional values and virtues gradually dissipate, giving rise to a more self-centered mindset. Society must recognize the significance of restoring moral values to address these issues. Encouraging young individuals to balance personal aspirations and social responsibilities is essential, fostering empathy and care for their families and the elderly. Preserving and celebrating cultural heritage can promote a comprehensive understanding of diverse perspectives. It is crucial to equip the youth with media literacy and critical thinking skills to help them discern between constructive and misleading influences.

In response to these challenges and deplorable circumstances and stances, the book "Quran: Moral Compass of the Believer-Nurturing Islamic Ethics in Western-Born Generations has been authored. Unlike previous works on morality, this book specifically caters to the West's second and third Muslim generations, aiming to compensate for the lack of an Islamic-cultural environment during their upbringing. By immersing readers in a Quranic atmosphere, the book addresses the pressing issues and offers solutions grounded in the Quran and Sunnah. Ultimately, society can reverse these disheartening trends through a collective commitment to moral values and cultivate a compassionate, respectful, and socially responsible community.

Author

Dr. Ali Mohamed Salah

September 2023

ABSTRACT

Indeed, All praise and thanks belong to Allāh.

This book delves into the profound moral system delineated in Islam as exemplified in the Holy Quran. It is a comprehensive effort to compile relevant Quranic verses and prophetic narrations that emphasize this aspect. The book aims to bridge the gap for second and third-generation Muslims born and raised in Western societies, often lacking sufficient knowledge of Islam and its cultural heritage.

Methodology

The methodology employed in this book involves a meticulous collection of Quranic verses and narrations pertinent to the topic, accompanied by an exploration of their applicability to the contemporary situations faced by the target reader and audience.

Objective

The primary objective of this book is to cater to the needs of Western-born and raised Muslims seeking to cultivate a deeper understanding of their faith and its moral framework. The book aims to empower these individuals with the necessary tools to navigate their lives following Islamic principles by addressing the dearth of the Islamic environment and education in their surroundings.

Unique Contribution

This book represents pioneering studies in nurturing Islamic ethics among Western-born Muslims, comprehensively examining the subject. Drawing upon my extensive experience in Da'wa (Islamic outreach) during my more than two-decade-long stay in the West, I have endeavored to provide unique insights and practical guidance tailored specifically for this audience.

By delving into the Quran as a moral compass, this book provides Western-born Muslims with the necessary guidance and insights to uphold Islamic ethics daily. Through a combination of profound Quranic teachings, practical applications, and real-life case studies, this book aims to empower and nurture the moral campus of the believer, thereby bridging the gap between Islamic teachings and the Western cultural context.

DEFINITION OF MORALS

Al-Jurjānī defined morals and said, "It is a firmly established disposition within oneself, from which actions easily and effortlessly emanate without the need for conscious thought and deliberation. If the actions emanating from it are virtuous, then the disposition is deemed to be good. However, if the actions emanating from it are vile, then the disposition from which it originates is deemed to be of bad character."[1]

Morals refer to principles or beliefs that guide individuals or societies in distinguishing right from wrong, good from evil, or desirable from undesirable behaviors or actions. Morals typically involve judgments about human behavior and its consequences regarding their impact on individuals, groups, or society. They often encompass fairness, justice, honesty, compassion, and respect.

The Difference between Morals, Morality, Ethics, Character, and Values:

A- Morals: Morals refer to the specific principles or beliefs that guide individuals or societies in determining right or wrong, good or bad. They are personal or collective standards of behavior that people adhere to and use as a basis for making ethical judgments. Cultural, social, religious, and personal factors often influence morals.

---

1   al-Jurjānī, ʿAlī b. Muḥammad al-Sayyid al-Sharīf (d. 816/1414). *Kitāb al-Taʿrīfāt*. (Beirut, Lebanon: Dār al-Kutub al-ʿilmiyyah, 1973), p. 136

B- Morality can be seen as the overarching concept encompassing the collective understanding of right and wrong, while morals represent the specific beliefs and principles derived from that understanding. Conversely, morality is a broader term encompassing the entire system or framework of principles, values, and beliefs governing human behavior concerning right or wrong. It is a more abstract and inclusive concept encompassing the overall understanding of morally acceptable behavior within a given society or ethical framework. In essence, morality provides the foundation or framework within which morals operate. It sets the broader guidelines and principles that shape and inform the specific moral beliefs and values individuals or societies hold.

C- Ethics: Ethics, as a branch of philosophy, studies moral principles, values, and judgments regarding right and wrong. It provides a framework for evaluating human actions and guiding decision-making based on moral principles. Ethics is a broader and more systematic approach to examining and understanding moral behavior. It explores different ethical theories and frameworks, such as consequentialism, deontological, and virtue ethics, to analyze ethical dilemmas and develop moral reasoning.

D- Values are broader and more abstract concepts that reflect an individual or society's beliefs about what is essential, desirable, or meaningful. They represent the core principles and ideals individuals or societies consider worthwhile and guide their behavior and choices. Values influence attitudes, shape personal and societal norms, and provide a foundation for making decisions across various aspects of life. Values can encompass moral principles but extend beyond them, including beliefs related to aesthetics, spirituality, personal fulfillment, and social dynamics.

Character refers to the combination of qualities, traits, and attributes that define an individual's moral and ethical nature. It represents the underlying values, beliefs, attitudes, and behaviors that shape a person's character and guide their actions and interactions with others. Character involves the cultivation of moral virtues, consistency in behavior, self-awareness, resilience, ethical decision-making, and other qualities that contribute to an individual's integrity and moral standing.[2]

---

2   Jennifer Gunner, What is the Difference Between Ethics, Morals, and Values? WF: Word Finder by your dictionary 1/20/2021; Dr. Alaa Aḥmad: Ethics, Morals, Principles, Values, Virtues, and Beliefs. What is the difference? Value Institute

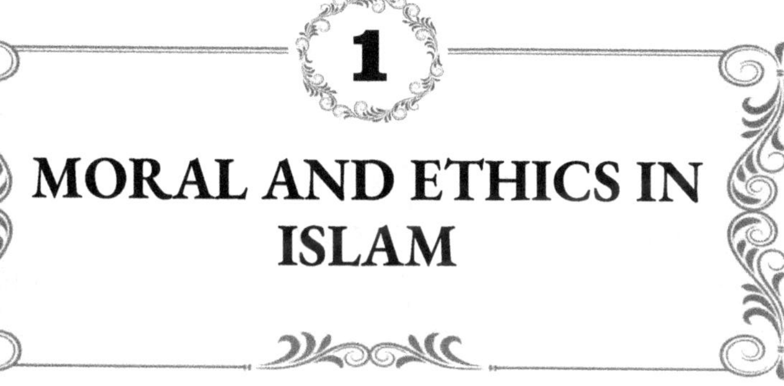

1

MORAL AND ETHICS IN ISLAM

SECTION ONE

THE IMPORTANCE OF MORALS IN ISLAM

Morality is the cornerstone of Islam, representing its essence and spirit in all aspects. All divine revelations have conveyed moral teachings to humanity throughout history, and all influential reformers, regardless of their affiliation or background, have advocated for moral values. As a result, Islamic philosophy, in general, is based on morals. Morality is the foundation of all civilizations, and its values are shared by all nations worldwide. It ensures that individuals within a society maintain harmonious relationships and interactions with each other. Therefore, the character is one of the fundamental sources of a nation's existence and strength, while immorality is the leading cause of a nation's decline.

A moral void can result in chaos, disharmony, disintegration, and division.

The Holy Quran emphasizes moral values in almost every aspect of life, from modesty in behavior to honesty in business, from being kind and dutiful to parents to taking care of animals and plants, and from treating neighbors well to treating wives with respect. Self-purification is at the core of Islamic morals, and Allāh has sent prophets and revealed holy scriptures to emphasize its significance and importance.

Islam supports morality and anything that leads to it while fighting corruption and issues that oppose it. Whatever leads to the welfare of the individual or society and does not contradict any aspect of the Religion is morally good, while anything harmful is ethically wrong. Allāh confirms this fact in the Quran, stating:

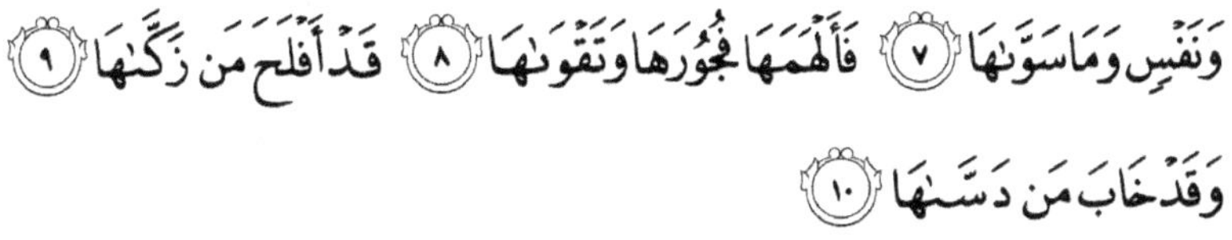

"AND [BY] THE SOUL AND HE WHO PROPORTIONED IT AND INSPIRED IT [WITH DISCERNMENT OF] ITS WICKEDNESS AND ITS RIGHTEOUSNESS, HE HAS SUCCEEDED WHO PURIFIES IT, AND HE HAS FAILED WHO INSTILLS IT [WITH CORRUPTION]."
[AL-SHAMS, 91:7-10]

Furthermore, morality is crucial to the Islamic system, and its values are essential for a healthy and harmonious society. The Quranic teachings emphasize the importance of morals in all aspects of life, and Muslims are encouraged to strive towards self-purification and uphold high moral values in their daily lives.

Sayyid Quṭub's interpretation of these verses suggests that Allāh has created humans with a dual nature and ability. Man can recognize good and evil in everything he encounters and directs himself towards one or the other. This dual ability is innate and deeply rooted within him. The two ingredients in man's makeup, i.e., earth's clay and Allāh's spirit, give rise to two equal tendencies to good and evil, to follow Divine guidance or to go astray. Divine messages and external factors can only awaken man's potential and help him develop in the chosen way. They do not create this potential. In addition to his innate ability, man has a conscious faculty that determines his line of action, making him responsible for his decisions and actions. Therefore, anyone who uses his conscious faculty to strengthen his inclinations towards what is good and weaken the evil drive within him will prosper.

On the other hand, anyone who suppresses the good tendency in him will be ruined. Man's freedom of choice adds to his responsibility; therefore, he is assigned a definite task related to the power given to him. According to Sayyid Quṭub's interpretation, man has the freedom to choose between his tendencies toward good and evil, but he is responsible for his actions and decisions. He must use his conscious faculty to strengthen his inclinations towards what is good and not suppress them to succeed in life.[3]

Sayyid Quṭub emphasizes that Allāh has given man the ability to think and differentiate between good and evil. This sense of morality distinguishes humans from animals and is essential for harmonious coexistence in society. Islam teaches us to follow a life of principles characterized by the best moral virtues and to avoid wrongful behavior. However, human reason needs to be tied to a higher authority to provide guidance in complex moral matters. This authority cannot be society, traditions, or customs but must be the Creator, who knows what would set our affairs right and what would corrupt us. By following Islamic values and teachings, we can fulfill our responsibilities towards ourselves and society and live a life of morality and righteousness. It is Allāh, Glory be to Him, who says,

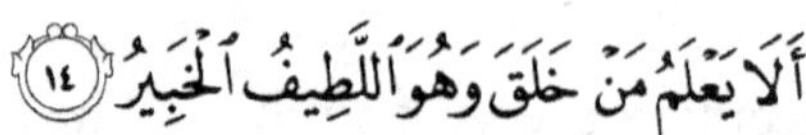

"DOES HE WHO CREATED NOT KNOW, WHILE HE IS THE SUBTLE, THE ACQUAINTED?"
[AL-MULK, 67:14]

Sayyid Quṭub's concept of duality should not be mistaken as suggesting that human reason and divine Revelation are two equal sources of moral obligation. Rather, divine Revelation is the ultimate legislator, and its rulings and commands become

---

3   Quṭub, 2015: 6:3917

understandable and binding only through the innate human power of reason, which is inherently mindful of God and accepts His existence as a true believer.

Therefore, it is the responsibility of human reason to submit to the commands of divine Revelation, as it receives a direct command from one's individual conscience, which orders one to submit to the divine commands.[4]

Islam rejects any belief or philosophy suggesting a source of moral obligation other than the divine Revelation of Allāh to His Messenger (ﷺ). This means that there is no higher authority than Allāh's guidance in matters of morality and ethics. Any other sources that humans may consider, such as personal inclinations or societal norms, are subject to the guidance of the divine Revelation and must conform to its principles. Therefore, the ultimate authority and source of moral obligation are found in the teachings of Islam, which provide a comprehensive and universal code of conduct for all humankind. Allāh says manifesting this:

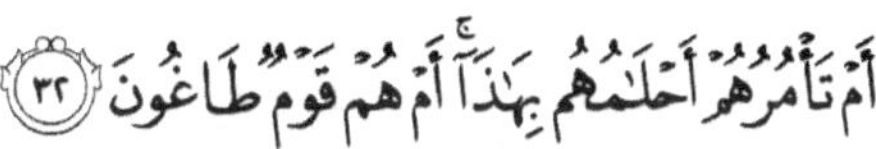

"OR DO THEIR MINDS COMMAND THEM TO [SAY] THIS, OR ARE THEY A TRANSGRESSING PEOPLE? [AT-TUR : 32]

---

4   Dastur al-akhlāq fil Quran by Dr. M. 'Abdalla Draz, pp.24-29

SECTION TWO

PRINCIPLES OF MORALS IN THE QURAN

Allāh sums up righteousness in the following verse:

۞ لَّيْسَ ٱلْبِرَّ أَن تُوَلُّوا۟ وُجُوهَكُمْ قِبَلَ ٱلْمَشْرِقِ وَٱلْمَغْرِبِ وَلَٰكِنَّ ٱلْبِرَّ مَنْ ءَامَنَ بِٱللَّهِ وَٱلْيَوْمِ ٱلْأَخِرِ وَٱلْمَلَٰٓئِكَةِ وَٱلْكِتَٰبِ وَٱلنَّبِيِّۦنَ وَءَاتَى ٱلْمَالَ عَلَىٰ حُبِّهِۦ ذَوِى ٱلْقُرْبَىٰ وَٱلْيَتَٰمَىٰ وَٱلْمَسَٰكِينَ وَٱبْنَ ٱلسَّبِيلِ وَٱلسَّآئِلِينَ وَفِى ٱلرِّقَابِ وَأَقَامَ ٱلصَّلَوٰةَ وَءَاتَى ٱلزَّكَوٰةَ وَٱلْمُوفُونَ بِعَهْدِهِمْ إِذَا عَٰهَدُوا۟ وَٱلصَّٰبِرِينَ فِى ٱلْبَأْسَآءِ وَٱلضَّرَّآءِ وَحِينَ ٱلْبَأْسِ أُو۟لَٰٓئِكَ ٱلَّذِينَ صَدَقُوا۟ وَأُو۟لَٰٓئِكَ هُمُ ٱلْمُتَّقُونَ ﴿١٧٧﴾

"RIGHTEOUSNESS IS NOT THAT YOU TURN YOUR FACES TOWARD THE EAST OR THE WEST, BUT [TRUE] RIGHTEOUSNESS IS [IN] ONE WHO BELIEVES IN ALLĀH, THE LAST DAY, THE ANGELS, THE BOOK, AND THE PROPHETS AND GIVES WEALTH, DESPITE THE LOVE FOR IT, TO RELATIVES, ORPHANS, THE NEEDY, THE TRAVELER, THOSE WHO ASK [FOR HELP], AND FOR FREEING SLAVES; [AND WHO] ESTABLISHES PRAYER AND GIVES ZAKAT; [THOSE WHO] FULFILL THEIR PROMISE WHEN THEY PROMISE; AND [THOSE WHO] ARE PATIENT IN POVERTY AND HARDSHIP AND DURING BATTLE. THOSE ARE THE ONES WHO HAVE BEEN TRUE, AND IT IS THOSE WHO ARE RIGHTEOUS". [AL-BAQARAH : 177]

This verse emphasizes that genuine and sincere faith is the foundation of righteousness. The key to virtuous behavior and good conduct is a strong relationship with God, who sees and knows all. A Muslim must maintain moral conduct in all circumstances because Allāh is aware of every action and intention, and deception is impossible. The love and awareness of God and the Day of Judgment enable a person to act with sincerity and devotion. The mention of turning one's face toward the East or the West is merely an illustration.

The verse's actual purpose is to emphasize that specific outward religious rites and conformist behavior do not constitute essential righteousness that earns God's recognition and approval.

Righteousness extends beyond performing familiar forms of piety and includes how one treats others. Being pious without performing deeds that demonstrate one's beliefs is insufficient. In summary, genuine faith is the foundation of righteousness and must be reflected in one's actions towards others, not just outward rituals.

The categories mentioned in the verse are the poor, orphans, travelers, and those in need. Therefore, the best way to demonstrate one's belief is by showing mercy and caring for them. As believers, we are called upon to act with compassion and kindness towards those who are less fortunate. This includes providing for the basic needs of the poor, supporting orphans, helping travelers, and assisting those in need. By doing so, we fulfill our duty as Muslims and demonstrate our faith through our actions. It is not enough to simply proclaim one's belief; it must be reflected in our deeds, especially towards those who require our assistance. Other verses add to confirm the previous verse by saying:

Allāh says in the Holy Quran:

وَٱعْبُدُوا۟ ٱللَّهَ وَلَا تُشْرِكُوا۟ بِهِۦ شَيْـًٔا ۖ وَبِٱلْوَٰلِدَيْنِ إِحْسَٰنًا وَبِذِى ٱلْقُرْبَىٰ وَٱلْيَتَٰمَىٰ وَٱلْمَسَٰكِينِ وَٱلْجَارِ ذِى ٱلْقُرْبَىٰ وَٱلْجَارِ ٱلْجُنُبِ وَٱلصَّاحِبِ بِٱلْجَنۢبِ وَٱبْنِ ٱلسَّبِيلِ وَمَا مَلَكَتْ أَيْمَٰنُكُمْ ۗ إِنَّ ٱللَّهَ لَا يُحِبُّ مَن كَانَ مُخْتَالًا فَخُورًا ﴿٣٦﴾

"SERVE GOD, AND JOIN NOT ANY PARTNERS WITH HIM, AND DO GOOD—TO PARENTS, ORPHANS, THOSE IN NEED, NEIGHBORS WHO ARE NEAR, NEIGHBORS WHO ARE STRANGERS; THE COMPANION BY YOUR SIDE, THE WAYFARER (YE MEET), AND WHAT YOUR RIGHT HANDS POSSESS: FOR GOD LOVETH NOT THE ARROGANT, THE VAINGLORIOUS" **[AL-NISA' : 36]**

The Quran also states:

لَن تَنَالُوا۟ ٱلۡبِرَّ حَتَّىٰ تُنفِقُوا۟ مِمَّا تُحِبُّونَ ۚ وَمَا تُنفِقُوا۟ مِن شَىۡءٍۢ فَإِنَّ ٱللَّهَ بِهِۦ عَلِيمٌ ۝

"NEVER WILL YOU ATTAIN THE GOOD [REWARD] UNTIL YOU SPEND [IN THE WAY OF ALLAH] FROM THAT WHICH YOU LOVE. AND WHATEVER YOU SPEND - INDEED, ALLAH IS KNOWING OF IT". **[AL-E-IMRAN : 92]**

Moreover, the Messenger of Allāh (ﷺ) illustrates the profound meaning of the verse said on the authority of Anas ibn Mālik:

«لَا يُؤْمِنُ أَحَدُكُمْ حَتَّى يُحِبَّ لِأَخِيهِ مَا يُحِبُّ لِنَفْسِهِ»

"One of you cannot be a true believer until he likes for his brother what he likes for himself." [Ṣaḥīḥ al-Bukhari, no. 13.]

The importance of being kind to others and treating them with the same kindness one desires for oneself is emphasized in various verses and narrations throughout the Quran. This responsibility is fulfilled by prioritizing one's own interests, but it is also highly rewarded to forego one's rights and show kindness to others.

An exemplary act of sacrifice by the Prophet's companions on the battlefield, where they passed water to their wounded comrade despite their own nearness to death, is an inspiring example of this noble principle.

Through its teachings, Islam instills discipline in our behavior and guides us toward controlling and refining our natural survival instincts, often leading us to prioritize our needs and desires. The Quranic moral compass directs us towards prioritizing the needs and desires of others when we genuinely love them. And when we love Allāh, our actions and choices reflect this love by sacrificing our own desires for His sake.

Moreover, the Quran commands us in several chapters to share these moral qualities and values with others, encouraging their wide application in all spheres and phases of life. Surat Al-Imran reads.

وَلْتَكُن مِّنكُمْ أُمَّةٌ يَدْعُونَ إِلَى الْخَيْرِ وَيَأْمُرُونَ بِالْمَعْرُوفِ وَيَنْهَوْنَ عَنِ الْمُنكَرِ ۚ وَأُولَٰئِكَ هُمُ الْمُفْلِحُونَ ﴿١٠٤﴾

"AND LET THERE BE [ARISING] FROM YOU A NATION INVITING TO [ALL THAT IS] GOOD, ENJOINING WHAT IS RIGHT AND FORBIDDING WHAT IS WRONG, AND THOSE WILL BE SUCCESSFUL." [AL-E-IMRAN, : 104]

Notably, the phrase "let there be" in this verse is strongly prescriptive and a must for Muslims to share these morals with others. And similarly, in the same chapter, it reads again.

كُنتُمْ خَيْرَ أُمَّةٍ أُخْرِجَتْ لِلنَّاسِ تَأْمُرُونَ بِالْمَعْرُوفِ وَتَنْهَوْنَ عَنِ الْمُنكَرِ وَتُؤْمِنُونَ بِاللَّهِ ۗ وَلَوْ ءَامَنَ أَهْلُ الْكِتَٰبِ لَكَانَ خَيْرًا لَّهُم ۚ مِّنْهُمُ الْمُؤْمِنُونَ وَأَكْثَرُهُمُ الْفَٰسِقُونَ ﴿١١٠﴾

"YOU ARE THE BEST NATION PRODUCED [AS AN EXAMPLE] FOR MANKIND. YOU ENJOIN WHAT IS RIGHT AND FORBID WHAT IS WRONG AND BELIEVE IN ALLĀH. IF ONLY THE PEOPLE OF THE SCRIPTURE HAD BELIEVED, IT WOULD HAVE BEEN BETTER FOR THEM. AMONG THEM ARE BELIEVERS, BUT MOST OF THEM ARE DEFIANTLY DISOBEDIENT". [AL-E-IMRAN : 110.]

The Quran often mentions commandments and prohibitions as two sides of the same coin in terms of the moral and spiritual development of the believer. It is stated in a verse of Surat Nahl as follows:

۞ إِنَّ ٱللَّهَ يَأْمُرُ بِٱلْعَدْلِ وَٱلْإِحْسَـٰنِ وَإِيتَآيِ ذِى ٱلْقُرْبَىٰ وَيَنْهَىٰ عَنِ ٱلْفَحْشَآءِ وَٱلْمُنكَرِ وَٱلْبَغْيِ ۚ يَعِظُكُمْ لَعَلَّكُمْ تَذَكَّرُونَ ﴿٩٠﴾

"INDEED, ALLĀH ORDERS JUSTICE AND GOOD CONDUCT, GIVING TO RELATIVES, AND FORBIDS IMMORALITY, BAD BEHAVIOR, AND OPPRESSION. HE ADMONISHES YOU THAT PERHAPS YOU WILL BE REMINDED" [AN-NAHL : 90].

This verse provides three commandments and three prohibitions that cover various aspects of a person's moral and spiritual development. On the positive side, it promotes justice, kindness towards others, and good treatment of relatives. On the negative side, it prohibits indecency, evil manifestation, and transgression. According to Abū al-A'lā al-Mawdūdī, Allāh has enjoined three essential things for a sound and healthy society: justice, which includes giving everyone their rightful moral, social, economic, legal, and political dues; Ihsan, which means being good, generous, sympathetic, tolerant, forgiving, polite, cooperative, selfless, etc.; and good treatment of one's relatives. These three virtues are necessary for a society to thrive and flourish.

The Quran also prohibits three vices that can ruin individuals and society as a whole: immodesty, universally recognized evils, and vices that transgress proper limits of decency and violate the rights of others.

One can see surprising cohesion and integrity through the Quran's topics, words, and concepts. The Book focuses on one aim: to guide people toward happiness and fulfillment. As Muḥammad Asad notes, no other book has been read with comparable intensity and veneration, nor has any other book provided such a comprehensive answer to the question of how to behave to achieve the good life in this world and the hereafter?[5]

---

5   Islamicity.org. "Ultimate Manifestation of God's Grace." IslamiCity, 30 July 2015, www.islamicity.org/3507/. Accessed 22 Aug. 2023.

SECTION THREE

THE PERFECTION OF THE MORAL SYSTEM IN THE QURAN

There are two primary common elements among all divine religions that are neither changed nor replaced: Creed and Good values. On the other hand, divine laws differ among all religions. Some laws abrogate others so that every religion can encompass a new set of rules. The new laws introduced to that particular religion aim to fit the time and the environment of that Prophet or Messenger of that religion. Abrogation of specific Sharia laws makes them consistent with people's different conditions and ways of life, ensuring the eternal validity of space and time. The Quran says regarding this:

$$\text{ثُمَّ جَعَلْنَاكَ عَلَىٰ شَرِيعَةٍ مِّنَ ٱلْأَمْرِ فَٱتَّبِعْهَا وَلَا تَتَّبِعْ أَهْوَآءَ ٱلَّذِينَ لَا يَعْلَمُونَ ﴿١٨﴾}$$

"THEN WE PUT YOU, [O MUḤAMMAD], ON AN ORDAINED WAY CONCERNING THE MATTER [OF RELIGION]; SO, FOLLOW IT AND DO NOT FOLLOW THE INCLINATIONS OF THOSE WHO DO NOT KNOW." [AL-JATHIYA : 18]

The virtues and vices that the Quran enjoins and forbids are common elements found in the divine messages brought to humankind by various prophets, including Prophet Abraham, Prophet Moses, and Prophet Jesus. May peace be upon them.

The Qur'an thus affirms the truth of the ways of guidance taught by the earlier prophets by saying:

۞ شَرَعَ لَكُم مِّنَ ٱلدِّينِ مَا وَصَّىٰ بِهِۦ نُوحًا وَٱلَّذِىٓ أَوْحَيْنَآ إِلَيْكَ وَمَا وَصَّيْنَا بِهِۦٓ إِبْرَٰهِيمَ وَمُوسَىٰ وَعِيسَىٰٓ أَنْ أَقِيمُوا۟ ٱلدِّينَ وَلَا تَتَفَرَّقُوا۟ فِيهِ كَبُرَ عَلَى ٱلْمُشْرِكِينَ مَا تَدْعُوهُمْ إِلَيْهِ ٱللَّهُ يَجْتَبِىٓ إِلَيْهِ مَن يَشَآءُ وَيَهْدِىٓ إِلَيْهِ مَن يُنِيبُ ﴿١٣﴾

"HE HAS ORDAINED FOR YOU OF RELIGION WHAT HE ENJOINED UPON NOAH AND THAT WHICH WE HAVE REVEALED TO YOU, [O MUḤAMMAD], AND WHAT WE ENJOINED UPON ABRAHAM AND MOSES AND JESUS - TO ESTABLISH THE RELIGION AND NOT BE DIVIDED THEREIN. DIFFICULT FOR THOSE WHO ASSOCIATE OTHERS WITH ALLĀH IS THAT TO WHICH YOU INVITE THEM. ALLĀH CHOOSES FOR HIMSELF WHOM HE WILLS AND GUIDES TO HIMSELF WHOEVER TURNS BACK [TO HIM]"
[ASH-SHURA : 13]

Thus, we understand from these verses that the Qur'an encompasses the meanings and teachings of all divine books revealed before it and adds to and completes them. Therefore, everything a man needs, spiritual or social life, is contained and explained in the Qur'an.

The Quran is distinguished from other scriptures in that it offers a comprehensive code of life that covers both secular and spiritual matters, mundane and celestial. Its system of morality is characterized by balance and proportion, assigning each moral virtue a fitting place and function within the broader scheme of life. The Quran's application is extensive, addressing every aspect of individual and collective human life, from birth to death.[6] The following four verses affirm:

مَّا فَرَّطْنَا فِى ٱلْكِتَٰبِ مِن شَىْءٍ ثُمَّ إِلَىٰ رَبِّهِمْ يُحْشَرُونَ ﴿٣٨﴾

"WE HAVE NOT NEGLECTED IN THE REGISTER A THING. THEN UNTO THEIR LORD, THEY WILL BE GATHERED" [AL-AN'AM : 38.]

---

6   E-Journal of Al-Azhar Al-Sharif, Sun, Jan 2020

The Quran also teaches us about the completion and perfection of Sharia, indicating that it is free from contradiction and inconsistency, and has eternal validity across all times and spaces. It says:

$$\text{أَكْمَلْتُ لَكُمْ دِينَكُمْ وَأَتْمَمْتُ عَلَيْكُمْ نِعْمَتِي وَرَضِيتُ لَكُمُ ٱلْإِسْلَٰمَ دِينًا}$$

THIS DAY I HAVE PERFECTED FOR YOU YOUR RELIGION AND COMPLETED MY FAVOR UPON YOU AND HAVE APPROVED FOR YOU ISLAM AS RELIGION. [AL-MAIDAH : 3]

$$\text{ذَٰلِكَ ٱلدِّينُ ٱلْقَيِّمُ وَلَٰكِنَّ أَكْثَرَ ٱلنَّاسِ لَا يَعْلَمُونَ ﴿٣٠﴾}$$

"THAT IS THE CORRECT RELIGION, BUT MOST PEOPLE DO NOT KNOW." [AR-RUM : 30]

$$\text{إِنَّ هَٰذَا ٱلْقُرْءَانَ يَهْدِي لِلَّتِي هِيَ أَقْوَمُ وَيُبَشِّرُ ٱلْمُؤْمِنِينَ ٱلَّذِينَ يَعْمَلُونَ ٱلصَّٰلِحَٰتِ أَنَّ لَهُمْ أَجْرًا كَبِيرًا ﴿٩﴾}$$

"INDEED, THIS QUR'AN GUIDES TO THAT WHICH IS MOST SUITABLE AND GIVES GOOD TIDINGS TO THE BELIEVERS WHO DO RIGHTEOUS DEEDS THAT THEY WILL HAVE A GREAT REWARD." [AL-ISRA' : 9]

The Quran addresses the down-to-earth and practical aspects of day-to-day living, clearly articulating Allāh's expectations for believers as they traverse daily life in the community. Allāh has revealed the Quran to the Prophet. ﷺ, piecemeal to cover all humanity's needs. Gradually revealing the Quran was to keep its guidance eternal so that it echoes for generations until the end of the world. The coverage of the Quran ranges from answering their questions regarding the existential crises of individuals to outlining precious and divinely ordained laws concerning ecological stewardship to making clear what is right and wrong.

The verse proves that the Quran shows man how to realize his goal on earth, describing this path in complete terms. It is a way of correctly viewing the reality of things, a vision - personal, social, and cosmic - based on correct behavior and precise interaction between men. Considering these Quranic verses, there is no doubt that the moral system in Islam is the right and most suitable one that can keep humankind within the scope of today and the new challenges of the contemporary world while holding to the rope of morality and manners. Imam al-Shāṭibī (d. 790/1388) sheds light on this, stating that the intended completion is the completion of the broad fundamental basis.

Therefore, no needed base of the Religion related to the essentials, necessities, or complements was ever left out without being fully explained. Some particular aspects may not be mentioned directly but are left for the Mujtahid to derive its rulings based on these broad fundamental bases because the Ijtihād base is guaranteed by the Quran and the Sunnah and must be put into practice and not be abandoned.[7]

Ziauddin Saradar wrote in an article: "The Qur'an is an "open" book—a spiritual and moral resource that, if properly understood, provides Muslims with useful guidance through the complexities of modern life. It came to speak to all of humanity. However, it came to speak not in a vacuum, but within a historical context".[8]

The Quran's perfection and eternal nature are rooted in the fact that it is the final and ultimate guidance for humanity, revealed by Allāh. As such, Allāh has revealed the Quran as a complete and perfect guide to meet all of humanity's needs, both in this life and the Hereafter.

---

7   Abū Isḥāq Ibrāhīm b. Mūsā al-Shāṭibī (d. 720/1388), al-I'tiṣām, chapter 1, section 1, page 39.

8   KM, Kashmir Monitor "Rereading the Quran" Feb-23-201

SECTION FOUR

PROPHET MUḤAMMAD (ﷺ) AND HIS ROLE IN PERFECTING THE MORALS OF BELIEVERS

A noble character holds a prominent position in Islam, evident in all its rules and regulations. The Prophet was chosen as a messenger to perfect high moral standards among his followers. The primary mission of Prophet Muḥammad (ﷺ) was to instill good character and morality within the believers, guiding them in every aspect of their lives. In pursuit of this mission, Prophet Muḥammad (ﷺ) declared in an authentic narration:

«إِنَّمَا بُعِثْتُ لِأُتَمِّمَ صَالِحَ الأَخْلاقِ»

On the authority of Abū Huraira, Allāh's Messenger said: "I have only been sent to perfect good moral character."[9]

This report is graded as authentic (ṣaḥīḥ) by Hakim and was agreed upon by Al-zahabi.

Two keywords, "Akhlāq" and "perfection," are of great significance in the text and deserve to be highlighted to fully grasp the depth of what the context demonstrates.

---

9   Al-Beihaki. (n.d.). Al-Sunan. Vol. 4, p. 323.

Firstly, '*Akhlāq*' is an Arabic term that refers to practicing virtue, morality, good manners, and character in Islam. In simpler terms, Akhlāq pertains to a person's ethics, good conduct, and moral character. The "good moral" in this context is comprehensive and inclusive, meaning that it pertains to adhering to the sound creed ('Aqīdah) and performing acts of worship ('Ibādah) concerning Allāh. As for people, good character means being just, merciful, forgiving, and patient in our interactions with others (mu'āmalāt).

Secondly, the word "perfection" implies that there are two types of good moral conduct. The first type is common knowledge which all people know instinctively. The second type is that which completes and perfects it. The latter can only be known through Revelation by Allāh's guidance. Therefore, the Prophet was sent to teach it to the people as part of the Message he brought. The Prophetic Message contains a set of manners and moralities that are comprehensive of worldly matters, religious matters, worship, and dealings – dealings with one's family, children, acquaintances, and strangers. The Prophet's mission was to illuminate people's lives with the light of virtue and good manners, creating brightness of character in them and filling their laps with the pearls of good conduct.

The Prophet, ﷺ embodied and exemplified the moral, qualities that the Quran enjoined. His words and actions guided us toward perfecting our characters, morals, and manners to lead our lives accordingly. The mission of perfection was to transmit these eternal meanings through words and actions, guiding us toward the path of righteousness.

It is mentioned in the long story about Sa'd ibn Hesham ibn 'Aamir when he came to Madinah and went to 'A'isha (ﷺ) and asked her about some matters. He said: I said: "O Mother of the believers, tell me about the character of the Messenger of Allāh ﷺ. She said: Do you not read the Quran? I said: Of course. She said: The character of the Prophet of Allāh ﷺ was the Quran. I wanted to get up and not ask about anything else until I died"[10]. According to another report by the same narrator: "I said: O Mother of the believers, tell me about the character of the Messenger of Allāh (ﷺ). She said: O my son, do you not read the Quran? Allāh says in the Quran:

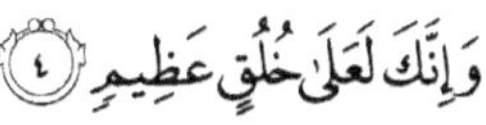

"AND INDEED, YOU ARE OF A GREAT MORAL CHARACTER." [AL-QALAM : 4]

The character of Muḥammad was the Quran".[11]

Al-Nawawi (رحمه الله) explained in Sharḥ Muslim that following the Quran means acting according to its teachings, adhering to its limits, observing its etiquette, reflecting on its lessons and parables, pondering its meanings, and reciting it correctly[12]. Similarly, Ibn Rajab stated in Jamie' al-'Uloom wa'l-Hikam that following the Quran requires adopting its attitudes and pleasing Allāh by approving what He praises in the Quran and disapproving what He condemns in it.[13] Al-Munaawi added in Fayd al-Qadeer that following the Quran encompasses all its commands, prohibitions, promises, warnings, and so on.[14] Therefore, the Prophet's attitude embodied everything in the Quran, and he avoided whatever it regarded as evil and promoted what it regarded as good.

---

10 Muslim (746)

11 Abū Ya'la (8/275) with a ṣaḥīḥ isnad.

12 3/268

13 1/148

14 5/170

By committing to the morals and etiquette of the Quran, the Prophet (ﷺ) qualified for Allāh's praise and exaltation. The Quran thoroughly describes his character, and Allāh made him an example for all believers.

However, concerning verse 4 of Surah Al-Qalam, Aisha (﵂) mentioned in a hadith that the "great moral character" mentioned in this verse refers to the Quran, the Prophet, and the religion of Islam as a whole. Commentators have also explained that the Prophet emulated the Quran in its commands and prohibitions, making it his temperament. His character became accustomed to it, and he abandoned his visceral carnal nature, doing whatever the Quran commanded and abstaining from what was prohibited. Furthermore, Allāh ingrained within him great character traits such as modesty, generosity, courage, forgiveness, forbearance, and every beautiful quality. Ibn Kathir, a prominent Islamic scholar, commented on this verse in his Tafsir, affirming that the Prophet was the best role model for humankind as he embodied all the teachings of the Holy Quran through his words and actions."[15]

However, attentively going through the biography of the prophet, ﷺ, we find that his character was marked by several outstanding qualities, making him an excellent role model for all humanity. These qualities include:

1- **Honesty and truthfulness:** The Prophet was known for his impeccable honesty, earning him the title of "Al-Amin" (the trustworthy) among his community even before he received his prophethood. He never told a lie or deceived anyone.

---

15 Tafsīr Ibn Kathīr, 68:4.

2- **Compassion and empathy:** The Prophet was very kind and compassionate and empathize with everyone, regardless of their social status or religion. He always went out of his way to help the poor, the needy, and the oppressed.

3- **Humility:** The Prophet was humble and never arrogant or conceited. He treated everyone with respect and dignity, regardless of their social status.

4- **Forgiveness**: The Prophet was forgiving and never held grudges or sought revenge. He always forgave those who wronged him and encouraged his followers to do the same.

5- **Justice and fairness:** The Prophet was a just and fair person who never discriminated against anyone based on race, ethnicity, or social status. He treated everyone equally and ensured that justice was served to all.

6- **Modesty:** The Prophet was modest and never sought personal fame or fortune. He lived a simple life and encouraged his followers to do the same.

7- **Patience and perseverance:** The Prophet faced many challenges and obstacles during his life, but he always remained patient and persevered through difficult times. He encouraged his followers to do the same and reminded them that Allāh is with those who are patient.

Finally, the character of Prophet Muḥammad (ﷺ) was characterized by excellent moral and ethical qualities that make him an ideal role model for all humanity.

SECTION FIVE

VIRTUES OF GOOD MORALS IN ISLAM

Islam encourages individuals to cultivate good morals and ethical behavior, discouraging them from engaging in bad habits and traits. The Quran and Sunnah reference numerous virtues and principles essential for leading a virtuous life. The Sunnah provides a comprehensive guide to the life of Prophet Muḥammad, ﷺ, including his actions, words, and attitudes.

Islam enumerates a range of virtues and principles and encourages believers to integrate them into their lives. To illustrate the importance of these virtues, consider some examples of how strongly and emphatically Islam calls upon people to adopt good moral character.

Among the countless virtues the Prophet promised the highest to those who refine themselves morally are:

A- The privilege of being close to the Prophet, ﷺ on the day of judgment. In this regard, Jabir narrated that the Messenger of Allāh said:

«إِنَّ مِنْ أَحَبِّكُمْ إِلَيَّ وَأَقْرَبِكُمْ مِنِّي مَجْلِسًا يَوْمَ الْقِيَامَةِ أَحَاسِنَكُمْ أَخْلَاقًا وَإِنَّ أَبْغَضَكُمْ إِلَيَّ وَأَبْعَدَكُمْ مِنِّي مَجْلِسًا يَوْمَ الْقِيَامَةِ الثَّرْثَارُونَ وَالْمُتَشَدِّقُونَ وَالْمُتَفَيْهِقُونَ». قَالُوا يَا رَسُولَ اللَّهِ قَدْ عَلِمْنَا الثَّرْثَارُونَ وَالْمُتَشَدِّقُونَ فَمَا الْمُتَفَيْهِقُونَ قَالَ: «الْمُتَكَبِّرُونَ»

"Indeed, the most beloved among you to me, and the nearest to sit with me on the Day of Judgment is the best of you in character. And indeed, the most disliked among you to me, and the one sitting furthest from me on the Day of Judgement is the Thartharun, and the Mutashaddiqun and the Muthafaihiqun." They said: "O Messenger of Allāh! We know about the Thartharun and the Mutashaddiqun, but what about the Muthafaihiqun?"' He said: "The arrogant."[16]

B- Good morals will hold great weight on the scale of deeds, even though they cannot be quantified numerically.

«لا شيء أثقل في ميزان المؤمن يوم القيامة من حسن الخلق، وإن الله يبغض الفاحش البذئ»

"Nothing weighs heavier in the balance on the Day of Judgment than good character. God hates that which is wanton and base." [17]

The Hadith highlights the unique aspect that a good character holds the greatest weight on the scale of deeds on the Day of Judgment, even though the character is not quantifiable. While deeds are tangible actions, a character is an intangible quality that cannot be physically weighed.

However, some scholars argue that just as advancements in science have allowed for the measurement of things like temperature, Allāh's scale on the Day of Judgment is precise and sensitive enough to measure qualities that are not material or quantifiable for us. Thus, while we may not be able to comprehend the measurement of character, Allāh's scale can accurately weigh and evaluate it.

---

16 Al-Tirmidhi (1/4)

17 Tirmidi 2004, Ibnu majah 4246

C- The most excellent person is the one who possesses the finest character.

When asked about the best of the believers, the Prophet, ﷺ, replied, as reported by Abū Huraira:

«اكمل المؤمنين إيمانا أحسنهم خلقا»

"They are those who have the best character and manners."[18]

D- Good morals aid in achieving the elevated status of those who frequently fast and pray at night.

The Prophet (ﷺ) mentioned that a person could reach the level of the one who is praying at night (performing qiyāmul layl) and fasting all day just by having good character. As mentioned in the narration on the authority of Aisha (ﷺ) and other companions (may Allāh be pleased with them).

Aisha reported that the Messenger of Allāh (ﷺ) said:

«إِنَّ الْمُؤْمِنَ لَيُدْرِكُ بِحُسْنِ خُلُقِهِ دَرَجَةَ الصَّائِمِ الْقَائِمِ»

"Verily, the believer may reach by his good character the rank of one who regularly fasts and stands for prayer at night."[19]

Ibn al-Qayyim ﵀, said, "The religion itself is an entirely good character, so whoever surpasses you in character has surpassed you in Religion. Likewise, it is such with spirituality (al-taṣawwuf). Al-Kanani said: Spirituality is a good character, so whoever surpasses you in character has surpassed you in spirituality." And he said, " Good manners itself is the religion in its entirety."[20]

---

18 Sunan At-Tirmidhi: 1162; Sunan Abū Daawood: 4682

19 Sunan Abū Dawood 4798

20 Ibn al-Qayyim Madārij al-Sālikīn. volume 2, page 294.

E- Possessing good morals can serve as a means of protection from Hellfire.

«قِيلَ لِلنَّبِيِّ ﷺ يَا رَسُولَ اللهِ إِنَّ فُلَانَةَ تَقُومُ اللَّيْلَ وَتَصُومُ النَّهَارَ وَتَفْعَلُ وَتَصَّدَّقُ وَتُؤْذِي جِيرَانَهَا بِلِسَانِهَا فَقَالَ رَسُولُ اللهِ صَلَّى اللَّهُ عَلَيْهِ وَسَلَّمَ«لَا خَيْرَ فِيهَا هِيَ مِنْ أَهْلِ النَّارِ»

On the authority of Abū Hurairah, The Prophet, ﷺ, was asked: O Messenger of Allāh! A certain woman always prays late at night, fasts the days, acts righteously, and gives charity, but she hurts her neighbors with her sharp tongue, then the Messenger of Allāh, ﷺ, said, "There is no goodness in her. She is one of the people of Hellfire".[21]

This narration emphasizes the significance and excellence of good character. The Prophet, ﷺ, narrates a story about a woman who exceeded the obligatory acts of prayer, fasting, and charity but was still considered among the inhabitants of Hell because she could not control her speech and spoke harshly to her neighbors. This highlights the importance of good character in Islam and the weight it carries in determining a person's standing in the Hereafter.

---

21 Al-Albani, Ṣaḥīḥ Al-Ādab al-Mufrad by Al-Bukhari, published by Darul-Sadiqin in 1421 AH, on page 117

FAITH AND MORALS IN ISLAM

The principal moral codes:

1- 1-ETIQUETTES AND MORALS TOWARDS ALLĀH ﷻ

2- 2-ETIQUETTES AND MORALS TOWARDS THE PROPHET ﷺ.

3- 3-ETIQUETTES AND MORALS TOWARDS COMPANIONS OF THE PROPHET ﷺ.

In the previous chapter, we attempted to emphasize several introductory themes that form the foundation of the subject matter. This paved the way to present a comprehensive Quranic code of morals that deals with almost all aspects of our moral behavior, which is a reflection of our faith as depicted in the Quran.

The Quran is a divine revelation consisting of 6,236 verses (ayahs) divided into 114 chapters or surahs, each named after a significant event, theme, or topic relevant to the chapter. Notably, one-fourth of the total Quranic verses, i.e., 1504, is dedicated to addressing issues directly pertinent to the morals and characters that are incumbent upon all believers to exhibit.

Accordingly, the most prevalent theme related to the refinement of morals in the Quran is 'enjoining good and forbidding evil.' These moral themes are introduced within the context of faith and belief in Allāh and the Hereafter.

THE RELATIONSHIP BETWEEN FAITH AND MORALS

Faith and morals are deeply connected and interdependent. Faith serves as the root of a tree, and good deeds are like the branches, leaves, and fruits of that tree. Without the effects of deeds, faith, and belief in conscience are incomplete. Faith is reflected in one's behavior, manners, and character, and good deeds are the medium through which people can measure and scale the strength or weakness of faith. Misbehavior or rude treatment towards others signifies the superficiality of faith and its mere appearance on the tongue rather than its actual existence in the heart.

The Quran and Sunnah provide ample evidence to demonstrate the interconnection of morals to fundamental beliefs in Islam, specifically the belief in Allāh, His Messenger, and the Hereafter. Allāh has mentioned 811 times in various verses that belief in Him, and the hereafter is the foundation of good morals and behaviors. Among these faith-moral-based verses, there are almost 99 verses in which Allāh always uses the term "O you who believe" before giving commands for good or forbidding bad character. The purpose of this Divine call to the believers by the title of faith is to instill good manners in their souls and hearts, connecting their faith with high morals.

Similarly, the Prophet (ﷺ) consistently links faith to a noble character when teaching the believers some noble characteristics. Below are some examples of verses from the Quran and Sunnah that illustrate the influence of faith on our morals and behaviors. Allāh says in the following two verses of the Quran:

ذَٰلِكَ يُوعَظُ بِهِۦ مَن كَانَ مِنكُمْ يُؤْمِنُ بِٱللَّهِ وَٱلْيَوْمِ ٱلْآخِرِ ذَٰلِكُمْ أَزْكَىٰ لَكُمْ وَأَطْهَرُ وَٱللَّهُ يَعْلَمُ وَأَنتُمْ لَا تَعْلَمُونَ ﴿٢٣٢﴾

"THAT IS INSTRUCTED TO WHOEVER OF YOU BELIEVES IN ALLĀH AND THE LAST DAY. THAT IS BETTER FOR YOU AND PURER, AND ALLĀH KNOWS AND YOU KNOW NOT".
[AL-BAQARAH : 232]

فَإِذَا بَلَغْنَ أَجَلَهُنَّ فَأَمْسِكُوهُنَّ بِمَعْرُوفٍ أَوْ فَارِقُوهُنَّ بِمَعْرُوفٍ وَأَشْهِدُوا۟ ذَوَىْ عَدْلٍ مِّنكُمْ وَأَقِيمُوا۟ ٱلشَّهَٰدَةَ لِلَّهِ ذَٰلِكُمْ يُوعَظُ بِهِۦ مَن كَانَ يُؤْمِنُ بِٱللَّهِ وَٱلْيَوْمِ ٱلْآخِرِ

"THEY HAVE [NEARLY] FULFILLED THEIR TERM, EITHER RETAIN THEM ACCORDING TO ACCEPTABLE TERMS OR PART WITH THEM ACCORDING TO ACCEPTABLE TERMS. AND BRING TO WITNESS TWO JUST MEN FROM AMONG YOU AND ESTABLISH THE TESTIMONY FOR [THE ACCEPTANCE OF] ALLĀH. THAT IS INSTRUCTED TO WHOEVER SHOULD BELIEVE IN ALLĀH AND THE LAST DAY". **[AT-TALAQ : 2]**

The aforementioned verses emphasize the importance of treating one's spouse with kindness and avoiding harm, even in the event of marital breakdown and divorce, linking this behavior to one's belief in Allāh and the hereafter. Another example is found in verse 232 of Surah Al-Baqara, where the word "azka" is used, derived from the root verb "tazkiya," which means purification and denotes refinement in one's inward and outward conduct and manners. In the following three narrations by Abū Huraira, the Prophet ﷺ says :

A-

«لاَ يَزْنِي الزَّانِي حِينَ يَزْنِي وَهُوَ مُؤْمِنٌ وَلاَ يَشْرَبُ الْخَمْرَ شَارِبُهَا حِينَ يَشْرَبُهَا وَهُوَ مُؤْمِنٌ وَلاَ يَسْرِقُ السَّارِقُ حِينَ يَسْرِقُ وَهُوَ مُؤْمِنٌ وَلاَ يَنْتَهِبُ نُهْبَةً يَرْفَعُ النَّاسُ إِلَيْهِ فِيهَا أَبْصَارَهُمْ حِينَ يَنْتَهِبُهَا وَهُوَ مُؤْمِنٌ»

'The adulterer is not a believer at the moment when he is committing adultery, and the wine drinker is not a believer at the moment when he is drinking wine, and the thief is not a believer at the moment when he is stealing, and the robber is not a believer at the moment when he is robbing, and people are looking on."[22]

B-

«مَنْ كَانَ يُؤْمِنُ بِاللَّهِ وَالْيَوْمِ الآخِرِ فَلْيَقُلْ خَيْرًا، أَوْ لِيَصْمُتْ، وَمَنْ كَانَ يُؤْمِنُ بِاللَّهِ وَالْيَوْمِ الآخِرِ فَلاَ يُؤْذِ جَارَهُ، وَمَنْ كَانَ يُؤْمِنُ بِاللَّهِ وَالْيَوْمِ الآخِرِ فَلْيُكْرِمْ ضَيْفَهُ»

"Whoever believes in Allāh and the Last Day should talk about what is good or keep quiet, and whoever believes in Allāh and the Last Day should not hurt (or insult) his neighbor; and whoever believes in Allāh and the Last Day should entertain his guest generously."[23]

C-

«وَاللّه لا يؤمن، واللّه لايؤمن، واللّه لا يؤمن!» قيل: من يا رسول اللّه؟ قال: «الذي لا يأمن جاره بوائقه». وفي رواية لمسلم:«لايدخل الجنة من لا يأمن جاره بوائقه»

The Prophet (ﷺ) said, "By Allāh, he is not a believer! By Allāh, he is not a believer! By Allāh, he is not a believer." It was asked, "Who is that, O Messenger of Allāh?" He said, "One whose neighbor does not feel safe from his evil."[24] Another narration of Imam Muslims is: that the Messenger of Allāh (ﷺ) said, "He will not enter Jannah whose neighbor is not secure from his wrongful conduct."[25]

---

22 Bukhari 6475 vol:8 Book 76 Hadith 482.

23 Bukhar 6475 vol: 81 Hadith 64

24 Bukhari 6016.

25 Muslim 65.

The texts above have established a strong link between a person's belief in Allāh and the hereafter and their morals and ethics. Only when a person confirms the essence of this 'Aqīdah can they behave nicely. Furthermore, it is remarkable that any practicing believer with solid faith would even consider committing sins like theft and fornication or deliberately harming their neighbor. Faith can potentially refine a person's behavior and prevent them from falling into heinous sins. Thus, the following sections of the book will explore the significance of faith and its fundamental elements and components that reflect our conduct.

SECTION ONE

ETIQUETTE AND BEHAVIOR OF THE BELIEVER TOWARD ALLĀH

2.1.1. THE IMPORTANCE OF A BELEIVER'S GOOD BEHAVIOUR TOWARD ALLAH

In Islam, good manners and ethics are highly valued and given priority over other principles. This is evident in the contents of the Quran and the Prophetic narrations about Akhlāq (morals), which emphasize the importance of character as an integral part of faith. The moral system of Islam encompasses every aspect of life, including one's relationship with oneself, others, and ultimately with The Creator. It is through having good morals that we strengthen our faith.

While discussions on morals and manners usually center around our behaviors and dealings with others, it is essential to highlight that our conduct with Allāh (ﷻ) forms the basis of our manners. Imam Al-Ghazali (May God Bless Him) emphasized this point in his book 'The Beginning of Guidance,' stating that observing Ādab (etiquette) in our conduct with Allāh means refraining from any disobedience in our actions and sayings. "Know that your disobedience against Allāh. with your physical body, while it is a bounty from Allāh and a trust to you, and using it to disobey Him is the ultimate ingratitude. And your betrayal of Him entrusting you (with your physical body) that he has placed on you is the ultimate transgression. Indeed, the parts of your body are your subjects, so pay attention to how you govern them."[26]

This includes fulfilling our obligations and duties towards Him, such as prayer, fasting, giving charity, and avoiding anything that displeases Him, such as lying, backbiting, and cheating.

Furthermore, showing gratitude and humility towards Allāh is an important aspect of Ādab. This involves recognizing His blessings and acknowledging our weaknesses and shortcomings. It also means being patient during difficult times and trusting in Allāh's plan for us.

In summary, the etiquette and behavior of the believer towards Allāh are fundamental aspects of good morals in Islam.

Muslims' behavior towards the Creator is paramount as it sets the tone for all other aspects of morality. Ādab with Allāh is the foundation upon which all other manners are built, and it should be the ultimate goal of every believer. To achieve this, one must fulfill the rights of Allāh as prescribed in Islam and understand the true essence of Ādab.

2.1.2. ETIQUETTE WITH ALLĀH DEMANDS TRUE MONOTHEISM, WHICH AFFIRMS HIS ONENESS WITHOUT ANY PARTNERS.

The Quran describes Shirk as the ultimate injustice and transgression that goes against the very essence of Tawḥīd (Oneness of Allāh). Therefore, etiquette with Allāh demands true monotheism, which affirms His Oneness without any partners and is the foundation of Islam. This belief in Tawḥīd shapes our

---

26 Ihya ulumudeen al-Ghazali, p. 72-73

relationship with Allāh and is the fundamental element of our faith, as it determines our status in the hereafter. As believers, we must strive to uphold this belief and avoid any acts that may lead us to commit Shirk, which is the greatest sin and a cause for eternal punishment.

In the Quran, Allāh Almighty stated that Shirk is a big sin that He will never forgive. As many as 170 Quranic verses warn against Shirk, associating with Allāh others. Allāh says in the Holy Quran:

A-

فَلَا تَجْعَلُوا لِلَّهِ أَندَادًا وَأَنتُمْ تَعْلَمُونَ ﴿٢٢﴾

"SO DO NOT ATTRIBUTE TO ALLĀH EQUALS WHILE YOU KNOW [THAT THERE IS NOTHING SIMILAR TO HIM." [AL-BAQARAH : 22]

B-

وَٱعْبُدُوا۟ ٱللَّهَ وَلَا تُشْرِكُوا۟ بِهِۦ شَيْـًٔا

"WORSHIP ALLĀH AND ASSOCIATE NOTHING WITH HIM" [AN-NISA' : 36]

إِنَّ ٱللَّهَ لَا يَغْفِرُ أَن يُشْرَكَ بِهِۦ وَيَغْفِرُ مَا دُونَ ذَٰلِكَ لِمَن يَشَآءُ وَمَن يُشْرِكْ بِٱللَّهِ فَقَدِ ٱفْتَرَىٰٓ إِثْمًا عَظِيمًا ﴿٤٨﴾

"INDEED, ALLĀH DOES NOT FORGIVE ASSOCIATION WITH HIM, BUT HE FORGIVES WHAT IS LESS THAN THAT FOR WHOM HE WILLS. AND HE WHO ASSOCIATES OTHERS WITH ALLĀH HAS CERTAINLY FABRICATED A TREMENDOUS SIN". [AN-NISA' : 48]

C-

قُلْ تَعَالَوْا۟ أَتْلُ مَا حَرَّمَ رَبُّكُمْ عَلَيْكُمْ أَلَّا تُشْرِكُوا۟ بِهِۦ شَيْـًٔا

"SAY, "COME, I WILL RECITE WHAT YOUR LORD HAS PROHIBITED TO YOU. [HE COMMANDS] THAT YOU NOT ASSOCIATE ANYTHING WITH HIM". [AL-AN'AM : 151]

D-

وَإِذْ قَالَ لُقْمَٰنُ لِٱبْنِهِۦ وَهُوَ يَعِظُهُۥ يَٰبُنَيَّ لَا تُشْرِكْ بِٱللَّهِ إِنَّ ٱلشِّرْكَ لَظُلْمٌ عَظِيمٌ ﴿١٣﴾

"AND [MENTION, O MUHAMMAD], WHEN LUQMAN SAID TO HIS SON WHILE HE WAS INSTRUCTING HIM, "O MY SON, DO NOT ASSOCIATE [ANYTHING] WITH ALLĀH. INDEED, ASSOCIATION [WITH HIM] IS GREAT INJUSTICE." [LUQMAN : 13]

E-

ذَٰلِكَ وَمَن يُعَظِّمْ حُرُمَٰتِ ٱللَّهِ فَهُوَ خَيْرٌ لَّهُۥ عِندَ رَبِّهِۦ وَأُحِلَّتْ لَكُمُ ٱلْأَنْعَٰمُ إِلَّا مَا يُتْلَىٰ عَلَيْكُمْ فَٱجْتَنِبُوا ٱلرِّجْسَ مِنَ ٱلْأَوْثَٰنِ وَٱجْتَنِبُوا قَوْلَ ٱلزُّورِ ﴿٣٠﴾ حُنَفَآءَ لِلَّهِ غَيْرَ مُشْرِكِينَ بِهِۦ وَمَن يُشْرِكْ بِٱللَّهِ فَكَأَنَّمَا خَرَّ مِنَ ٱلسَّمَآءِ فَتَخْطَفُهُ ٱلطَّيْرُ أَوْ تَهْوِي بِهِ ٱلرِّيحُ فِي مَكَانٍ سَحِيقٍ ﴿٣١﴾

"THAT [HAS BEEN COMMANDED], AND WHOEVER HONORS THE SACRED ORDINANCES OF ALLĀH - IT IS BEST FOR HIM IN THE SIGHT OF HIS LORD. AND PERMITTED TO YOU ARE THE GRAZING LIVESTOCK, EXCEPT WHAT IS RECITED TO YOU. SO AVOID THE UNCLEANLINESS OF IDOLS AND AVOID FALSE STATEMENT". [AL-HAJJ : 30]

"INCLINING [ONLY] TO ALLĀH, NOT ASSOCIATING [ANYTHING] WITH HIM. AND HE WHO ASSOCIATES WITH ALLĀH - IT IS AS THOUGH HE HAD FALLEN FROM THE SKY AND WAS SNATCHED BY THE BIRDS OR THE WIND CARRIED HIM DOWN INTO A REMOTE PLACE".

[AL-HAJJ : 31]

The verses mentioned above, and many others from various chapters of the Holy Quran, urge humanity to believe in Allāh as the Creator and submit to Him alone. Furthermore, the verses denounce the act of associating partners with Allāh or worshiping Him in the form of an image. As a result, it is disrespectful and audacious to undermine the significance of Monotheism "Tawḥīd" or disregard Allāh's rights over His servants.

2.1.3. DENOTATION OF PLYOTHIESIM "SHIRK".

The term "Shirk" refers to the act of assigning a portion or share of worship to a partner. Specifically, it means invoking someone or something besides Allāh in the context of worship ('Ibādah). This can take the form of directing worship towards an angel, prophet, righteous person, building, or any other created being. It is important to note that directing any form of worship to anyone or anything besides Allāh is the most significant act Allāh has prohibited.[27]

Shirk refers to attributing Allāh's rights to someone or something else, which ascribes a partner or rival to Allāh in Lordship. On the other hand, Tawḥīd (Monotheism) asserts that only Allāh has the right to be worshiped and revered by His servants. Hence, Shirk is a significant issue in religion, and the Quran indicates that it is a hazardous act that can lead a person out of Islam. However, the degree or type of Shirk determines whether a person is considered a disbeliever (kāfir). Major Shirk involves ascribing to someone or something that belongs solely to Allāh, such as Lordship (rubūbiyyah), Divinity (ulūhiyyah), and the Divine Names and Attributes of God (Al-Asmā' Wa-sifāt). It is considered an act that removes a person from the fold of Islam.

In contrast, Minor Shirk (Shirk Al-Asghar) does not make the doer a disbeliever but is still considered a heinous sin. Minor Shirk includes any action to gain praise, fame, or otherworldly purposes. These actions are considered Shirk because the individual is doing the act for other people instead of for the sake of God. Examples of Minor Shirk can include praying to God in front of others to gain praise, donating to a charity to show off, gaining fame, or for any worldly purpose. When one commits such an action, the excellent deed becomes nullified, and the doer receives no reward.

The Messenger of Allāh gave a clear example of the latter type of Minor Shirk in the following Hadith:

On the authority of Mohamud bin labeled, as recorded in Musnad Aḥmad, the Prophet said:

---

27 Fawzan, S. (2006). Sharḥ Usool Ulthalatha [Explanation of the Three Fundamental Principles. Mu'sast Al-Risalah. (1st ed.). pp. 35-39.

»إِنَّ أَخْوَفَ مَا أَخَافُ عَلَيْكُمْ اَلشِّرْكُ اَلْأَصْغَرُ: اَلرِّيَاءُ. وزاد أحمد: " يقول الله -عز وجل- لهم يوم القيامة -إذا جزى الناس بأعمالهم-: اذهبوا إلى الذين كنتم تراءون في الدنيا فانظروا هل تجدون عندهم جزاء«

"The thing I fear most for you is minor Shirk.' They (the Companions) said, 'O Messenger of Allāh, what is Minor Shirk?' He (ﷺ) said, ‹Riya.› Imam Aḥmad added saying: Indeed, Allāh (Blessed and Exalted be He) shall say on the Day of Resurrection to the people who used to do good deeds for show: Go to those for whom you were showing off with your acts in worldly life and see if you can find with them recompense."[28]

The sin of Shirk, being punishable and unforgivable, highlights the significance of Tawḥīd, which is the believer's duty to affirm the Oneness of Allāh without any association of partners. Shirk is an unforgivable sin because it contradicts the belief that Allāh alone is worthy of worship. As such, it is considered the greatest sin in the sight of Allāh and can only be forgiven through sincere repentance and turning to Allāh.[29]

The belief in Allāh should be certain, recognizing Him as the Lord who created all things and possesses the Attributes of Lordship such as being the Maker, Shaper, All-Powerful, and Sustainer. It is also important to recognize that only Allāh is described with all the Attributes of Perfection and that any reproachable names or attributes cannot be attributed to Him. Additionally, Allāh alone is worthy of worship, and nothing should be worshipped besides Him. These concepts are known as the unity of Lordship (Tawḥīd al-Rubūbiyyah) and the unity of divinity (Tawḥīd al-Ulūhiyyah)[30]

---

28 Musnad Aḥmad: 24350, Albeihaki 6831, Albani: alsilsilah alsaheeha 901

29 Kitab Tawḥīd, Chapter 4-5, pages 16-19.

30 The article "Sincere Seeker: Shirk (Polytheism) in Islam" was published on February 13, 2019

2.1.4. ATHEISM AND ITS DENOTATION

The term "Atheism" is derived from the Greek prefix "a-," meaning "no" or "non," and the word for God, "Theos," which essentially defines itself as a belief that there exists positive evidence that there is no God. According to Josh McDowell and Don Stewart's Handbook of Today's Religions, an atheist is convinced that all religious beliefs, evidence, and faith are false.[31]

In Arabic, the term "Ilhad" is associated with the modern meaning of atheism, but its Quranic denotation and roots have a different meaning. In the Quran, "Ilhad" and its derivatives mean "to be inclined to something negative or blasphemy," "to deviate from something good," or "to tend to something negative or blasphemy." These basic meanings occur in various forms.[32]

The word "Atheism" in the Quran is lacking because humanity in its early ages believed in the existence of God and supernatural power but with different approaches and ways. Disbelievers during that time, whom the Quran referred to and refuted their stances and ideologies, were not categorized or known as Atheists. Their disbelief was based on the denial of monotheism, the Oneness of God, as they believed in other Gods besides partners and interceptions.

Stephen Nichols, History of Atheism, In an article on the history of Atheism, Stephen Nichols notes that the term "Atheism" first appeared in the middle of the 1500s but was more prevalent in the

---

31 Josh McDowell and Don Stewart, *Handbook of Today's Religions* (San Bernadino, CA: Here's Life, 1983), 413-14

32 Quranic Terminology: (Ilhad – Root: l/h/d) was published in Arabic on December 26, 2015

nineteenth and twentieth centuries modern world. According to a poll from 2014, Atheism remains a significant belief system in the current landscape.[33]

2.1.5. CAUSES OF ATHEISM

Many people experience doubts and confusion about religion during adolescence and young adulthood due to societal pressures, popular culture, and peer influence. These doubts and confusion can provide a justification for rejecting God and embracing immorality. Over time, this can lead to a rejection of values and spirituality, resulting in a spiritual void that may be filled with immoral behavior. In response to this, atheists have popularized various forms and methods of atheism, often attacking religion as irrational and harmful.

There is a religious perspective that suggests that the main reason for Atheism to exist is "Moral Rebellion." According to this view, doubts and confusion about religion can lead individuals to reject God and embrace immorality, ultimately rebelling against values and spirituality.

Jarl Waggoner argues that Atheism is not based on a lack of evidence but on moral rebellion. This means that presenting evidence against Atheism may not effectively change the beliefs of those who reject God for moral reasons. If the evidence did not lead individuals to become Atheists in the first place, it is unlikely that evidence alone will convince them to abandon Atheism."[34]

---

33 An article of 5minites in church "History of Atheism" September 23, 2020

34 Jarl Waggoner, M.Div., Responding Biblically to Atheism, publisher July 12, 2022.

Jarl Waggoner raises an important point that while there may not always be one specific immoral act that leads a person to reject belief in God, it could be a combination of various moral failures or a desire to live without the restraints and judgment of a holy God. These thoughts and desires may not be easy to detect but are still immoral in nature. This aligns with the idea that Atheism is not necessarily based on a lack of evidence but rather a moral rebellion against God.[35]

Second, while most atheists present their decision to reject belief in God in terms of intellect and reasoning, some are quite forthright and explicit in confirming that their journey began with immortality. For instance, former Church of Christ minister John Loftus admits that his turn to atheism started with an adulterous affair.[36]

Spiegel argues that Atheism is not the result of an objective assessment of evidence but rather a product of stubborn disobedience and wilful rebellion. He asserts that Atheism arises from the suppression of truth by wickedness, the cognitive consequence of immorality, and ultimately, it is a sin that is the mother of unbelief. Aldous Huxley, a prominent figure in the realm of Atheism, has confessed that his rejection of morality stemmed from a desire for sexual freedom.[37]

Huxley's statement supports the idea that, for some, moral rebellion is a driving force behind their rejection of God.

It is worth noting that Huxley's statement was not explicitly about rejecting belief in God, but the point about choosing to reject morality is still relevant. As mentioned earlier in this discussion,

---

35 ibid

36 ibid

37 Spiegel, The Making of an Atheist, 18, 73.

while the Quran does not mention contemporary atheists by name, it does address their behavior and the reasons for their disbelief in the existence of the Creator. The Quran identifies those who worship their desires, whims, and lusts as their God instead of worshipping the Creator, who is the only one deserving of worship.

The Quran recorded this fact 1500 years ago and says:

أَرَءَيْتَ مَنِ ٱتَّخَذَ إِلَـٰهَهُۥ هَوَىٰهُ أَفَأَنتَ تَكُونُ عَلَيْهِ وَكِيلًا ﴿٤٣﴾

أَمْ تَحْسَبُ أَنَّ أَكْثَرَهُمْ يَسْمَعُونَ أَوْ يَعْقِلُونَ إِنْ هُمْ إِلَّا كَٱلْأَنْعَـٰمِ بَلْ هُمْ أَضَلُّ سَبِيلًا ﴿٤٤﴾

"OR DO YOU THINK THAT MOST OF THEM HEAR OR REASON? THEY ARE NOT EXCEPT LIKE LIVESTOCK. RATHER, THEY ARE [EVEN] MORE ASTRAY IN [THEIR] WAY". [AL-FURQAN : 43]

"HAVE YOU SEEN THE ONE WHO TAKES AS HIS GOD HIS OWN DESIRE? THEN WOULD YOU BE RESPONSIBLE FOR HIM"? [AL-FURQAN : 44]

The verse in Zilal al-Qur'ān titled "When Desire is Worshipped," comments on a person who makes their desires their deity. The verse asks, "Have you considered the one who makes his desires his deity? Could you, then, be held responsible for him?" The verse is carefully phrased to depict the psychological state of a person who disregards accepted standards and values and submits only to their own desires. Such a person applies no standard, recognizes no value, and acknowledges no logic. When their desire moves in a particular direction, they follow it like slaves submitting to a powerful master. Allāh, who is limitless in His glory, addresses His servant and Messenger in a kind and compassionate manner and refers to this type of person. Allāh draws a picture of a man who pays no regard to truth, logic, or sound argument and comforts the Prophet so that he does not feel too disappointed at having failed to guide someone who has no propensity to follow the guidance. Hence, the Prophet need not concern himself with such people.

The surah hurls further ridicule on those who submit to their lust and worship their desire, turning a blind eye to the truth. It puts them on the same level as animals which are devoid of hearing or logic.

This is followed by even more ridicule, which shows such people as inferior to animals: "Or do you think that most of them listen and use their reason? They are but like cattle. Nay, they are even far worse astray." [38]

The comment adds that this very clear statement that maintains accuracy applies, as the surah says, to 'most of them' because only a minority of unbelievers showed any inclination to accept guidance or reflect on what they heard. The majority, who took their desires as their gods, which they blindly obeyed, ignored all the signs they heard and saw and were indeed like cattle. Indeed, man is distinguished from animals by his propensity to reflect and understand, as well as by his ability to mould his life in accordance with the truth he accepts upon consideration and reflection. His great human quality is that he is able to change course on being convinced by sound argument. An animal is guided to what suits it by the abilities and susceptibilities God has placed within it. When man deliberately abandons such qualities, he puts himself in a position worse than that of animals.

The surah uses strong language to condemn those who prioritize their desires over the truth and worship their own pleasure. Such people are depicted as being on the same level as animals, devoid of hearing or logic. The condemnation intensifies as the surah paints them as even inferior to animals, stating that they are far worse astray than cattle. This accurate statement applies to the majority of unbelievers who ignore all signs and blindly follow

______

38 (Verse 44). Zilal al-Qur'ān, p. 322.

their desires. Man is distinguished from animals by his ability to reflect and understand, as well as to change his course on being convinced by sound argument. When he deliberately abandons these qualities, he puts himself in a position worse than that of animals. An animal is guided to what suits it by the abilities and susceptibilities God has placed within it.[39]

Quran highlights the severity of denying the existence of Allāh, the Creator, and refusing to acknowledge Him. Such denial is a form of blasphemy and constitutes blatant atheism, which is considered even worse than shirk (polytheism) and kufr.

However, Scholars have compared the three groups of mushrik (polytheists), kāfir (disbelievers), and atheists and have noted that despite their shared state of kufr, the atheist is considered the worst of the three. In various parts of his book, Ibn Taymiyyah draws a comparison between them and emphasizes the severity of atheism as it involves a complete rejection of the concept of a higher power. He said in these quotations as follows: He said: "Kufr, or disbelief, can take many forms such as outright rejection of Allāh and His Messengers, doubt, and uncertainty about the existence of Allāh, or ignoring the issue altogether due to envy, arrogance, or following one's desires that distract a person from following the message.

However, those who actively reject and disbelieve in Allāh and His Messengers are in a state of greater Kufr compared to those who reject out of envy or other reasons, even if they acknowledge that the Messengers brought the message of truth. It is important to note that the sin of disbelief is severe and should not be taken lightly."[40]

---

39 (Verse 44). Zilal al-Qur'ān, p. 322.

40 Majmoo al-fatawa 17/291

He added, " It is stated that a person who denies the Hereafter but acknowledges that the universe was created is considered a Kaafir by Allāh. However, the level of Kufr is even greater for someone who denies the Hereafter and claims that the universe has existed eternally. According to this view, denying the Hereafter is a form of Kufr regardless of whether or not the person believes in the creation of the universe".[41]

In another volume, he noted saying:

"Allāh describes the one who denies the Hereafter but believes that this universe is created as a kāfir. However, the one who denies the Hereafter and claims that the universe has existed from eternity is regarded as an even worse kāfir in the sight of Allāh. May Allāh be exalted.".[42]

Furthermore, Islam does not view atheism positively and considers it a deviation from the truth. According to Islamic teachings, belief in God is a fundamental part of one's identity as a Muslim. The Islamic concept of Tawḥīd, or the oneness of God, is a central tenet of the faith, and denying this belief is considered a major sin. In Islamic theology, the existence of God is seen as self-evident and is not subject to debate or questioning.

As a result, atheism is a rejection of the truth and a misguided way of life. Atheists lack morals, guidance, or being influenced by the devil. However, in recent years, there have been efforts within the Muslim community to engage in dialogue with atheists and to find common ground. Some Muslim scholars and thinkers have argued that Islam has a rich tradition of critical thinking and intellectual inquiry and that atheists can engage in these activities without necessarily rejecting belief in God.

---

41 ibid

42 ibid 6/633

In conclusion, this discourse highlights the immorality of atheism and the fact that it represents blind faith in the face of overwhelming evidence of the existence of the Creator. Therefore, believers must resist this trend and refute its false and baseless arguments using reason and rationality. We must work together to counter this misleading trend that seeks to influence the minds of young people. Scholars should engage in giving talks and speeches from pulpits, classrooms, and public forums, aimed at eradicating this immoral behavior toward God, the Creator.

2.1.6. ETIQUETTE WITH ALLĀH IMPLIES WORSHIP AND OBEDIENCE.

The right of Allāh Almighty over His slaves is that they affirm His Oneness and not associate anything with Him. It is also His right (Noble & Sublime) over His slaves that they worship Him Alone (Noble & Sublime) and obey none but Him.

They must not associate any partners in their worship of Allāh Almighty. They must obey His commands and avoid His prohibitions, thereby seeking His mercy and good pleasure (Blessed & Exalted) upon them and that He removes His punishment and torment from them.

Etiquette with Allāh is a crucial aspect of the Islamic faith that involves showing utmost respect, love, and devotion to the Creator. Central to this etiquette is the affirmation of Allāh's Oneness, which means that Muslims believe in the existence of only one true God without associating any partners with Him. This is known as the concept of Tawḥīd in Islam, forming the basis of the Islamic faith.

Muslims believe that Allāh is the only deity worthy of worship and that all forms of worship should be directed toward Him alone. This includes acts such as prayer, fasting, charity, and pilgrimage, which are all considered ways to seek Allāh's pleasure and draw closer to Him.

In order to seek Allāh's mercy and good pleasure (Blessed & Exalted) upon them and to avoid His punishment and torment, Muslims must refrain from associating any partners with Him. This means that they must not attribute any of Allāh's attributes or characteristics to any other being, nor should they seek help or guidance from any other entity besides Allāh.

Furthermore, Muslims must obey Allāh's commands while abstaining from His prohibitions. This involves following the teachings of the Quran and the example of the Prophet Muḥammad (ﷺ), who was sent as a mercy to all of humanity. Muslims believe that by obeying Allāh's commands and avoiding His prohibitions, they will attain success in this life and the hereafter, as well as the pleasure of Allāh. The above fact is stated in a narration by Narrated Mu'adh bin Jabal that The Prophet, ﷺ, said:

«يَا مُعَاذُ أَتَدْرِي مَا حَقُّ اللَّهِ عَلَى الْعِبَادِ» قَالَ اللَّهُ وَرَسُولُهُ أَعْلَمُ. قَالَ: «أَنْ يَعْبُدُوهُ وَلَا يُشْرِكُوا بِهِ شَيْئًا، أَتَدْرِي مَا حَقُّهُمْ عَلَيْهِ» قَالَ اللَّهُ وَرَسُولُهُ أَعْلَمُ. قَالَ «أَنْ لَا يُعَذِّبَهُمْ»

"O Mu'adh! Do you know what Allāh's Right upon His slaves is?" I said, "Allāh and His Apostle know best." The Prophet ﷺ said, "To worship Him الله Alone and to join none in worship with Him (الله). Do you know what their right upon Him is?" I replied, "Allāh and His Apostle know best." The Prophet ﷺ said, "Not to punish them (if they do so)[43].

---

43 Al-Bukhari, book of Al-Tawḥīd 7373 and Muslim hadith no: 30

2.1.7. THE MEANING OF IBADA (WORSHIP) AND THE PURPOSE OF HUMAN CREATION

Before delving into the definition of "IBĀDAH," it is crucial to understand the purpose behind the creation of humankind. The Islamic belief holds that Allāh, the Almighty, created human beings with a specific purpose. According to this belief, the primary objective of human existence is to affirm Allāh's Oneness (Tawḥīd) and worship Him alone without any partner or associate.

This concept is clearly stated in Islamic scripture, where Allāh explicitly mentions the purpose of human creation. As the Quran says:

$$\text{﴿٥٧﴾ وَمَا خَلَقْتُ الْجِنَّ وَالْإِنسَ إِلَّا لِيَعْبُدُونِ ﴿٥٦﴾ مَا أُرِيدُ مِنْهُم مِّن رِّزْقٍ وَمَا أُرِيدُ أَن يُطْعِمُونِ}$$

$$\text{﴿٥٨﴾ إِنَّ اللَّهَ هُوَ الرَّزَّاقُ ذُو الْقُوَّةِ الْمَتِينُ}$$

AND I DID NOT CREATE THE JINN AND MANKIND EXCEPT TO WORSHIP ME. THEREFORE, I DO NOT WANT FROM THEM ANY PROVISION, NOR DO I WANT THEM TO FEED ME. INDEED, IT IS ALLĀH WHO IS THE [CONTINUAL] PROVIDER, THE FIRM POSSESSOR OF STRENGTH.
[ADH-DHARIYAT : 56 - 58]

This verse highlights that Allāh created humankind solely to worship Him, the ultimate goal every human should strive to achieve.

Ibn Kathir (ﷺ), commenting on the verse, said:

"I.e., I have created them so that I may command them to worship Me, not because I have any need of them. 'Ali ibn Abi Talha said, narrating from Ibn' Abbas: "except that they should worship Me (alone)" willingly or unwillingly.

This is the view favored by Ibn Jarir. Ibn Jurayj said: i.e., except that they should know Me. Al-Rabi' ibn Anas said: "Except that they should worship Me," i.e., for the purpose of worship."[44]

However, the term "'IBĀDAH" in Islam refers to the act of worship that a Muslim performs to show their submission and devotion to Allāh. Similarly, the purpose of human creation in Islam is to affirm Allāh's Oneness and worship Him alone. 'IBĀDAH plays a crucial role in fulfilling this purpose, as it allows individuals to show their devotion and submission to Allāh in various ways

2.1.8. THE DESCRIPTION OF 'IBĀDAH THEOLOGICALLY

The term "'IBĀDAH" in Islam has a rich linguistic history that sheds light on its meaning and significance. While it is true that one of the original meanings of "'IBĀDAH" is "to lower oneself," it is important to note that this definition alone does not fully capture the essence of the concept in an Islamic context.

In fact, the term "'IBĀDAH" in Islam encompasses a much broader range of meanings and practices. It refers to all acts of worship and devotion a Muslim performs to please Allāh and gain His favor. These acts can take various forms, including prayer, fasting, giving charity, and performing pilgrimage.

While lowering oneself before Allāh is certainly a central aspect of 'IBĀDAH, it is not the only one. The concept of 'IBĀDAH is also closely linked to the idea of submission and obedience to Allāh's will. Muslims believe they express their submission and devotion to Him by worshiping and following Allāh's commands.

---

44 (Tafsir Ibn Kathir, 4/239)

Nevertheless, while the linguistic roots of the term "'IBĀDAH" may suggest a narrow definition, the concept has much broader implications and encompasses a range of practices and beliefs in Islam. It represents the idea of submission, devotion, and worship to Allāh, and it is a fundamental aspect of the Muslim faith and practice.

However, Islam's traditional definition of worship is much more comprehensive and includes almost everything in an individual's activities. Worship encompasses all external and internal sayings and actions that God loves. In other words, worship is everything one says or does for the pleasure of Allāh, including rituals, beliefs, social activities, and personal contributions to the welfare of society.

Here are the various definitions of 'Ibādah:

Ar-Raghib al-Asfahani described worship as a wilfully chosen action devoid of bodily desires, which is carried out to seek nearness to Allāh and obedience to the Shariah[45]

al-Baghawī, stated that worship involves obedience with lowering oneself and submission, and the slave is called "'Abd" due to his submission and obedience.[46]

Ibn Taymiyyah defined worship as obedience to Allāh by carrying out what He commanded on His messengers' tongues.[47]

---

45 (Tafseel an-Nash'atayn wa Tahseel as-Sa'aadatayn p. 157).

46 (Sharḥ us-Sunnah 1/53)

47 (Majmoo'ul-Fataawaa 10/149)

Ibn al-Qayyim described worship as gratefulness to Allāh, love of Him, and awe of Him. Ibn Kathir explained that "'Ibādah" in the language means humbleness and is an expression of what brings together the perfection of love, fear, and hope in Allāh's service[48]

For the 'Ibādah of the believer to abide by etiquettes and morals outlined by Allāh, it should -based on scholarly opinion- meet the mandatory conditions of worship. These conditions are as follows:

Firstly: Sincere determination is a condition that goes with worship itself. On the authority of Umar bin Khattab, the Prophet, ﷺ, said:

«إِنَّمَا الْأَعْمَالُ بِالنِّيَّاتِ وَإِنَّمَا لِكُلِّ امْرِئٍ مَا نَوَى فَمَنْ كَانَتْ هِجْرَتُهُ إِلَى اللَّهِ وَرَسُولِهِ فَهِجْرَتُهُ إِلَى اللَّهِ وَرَسُولِهِ وَمَنْ كَانَتْ هِجْرَتُهُ لِدُنْيَا يُصِيبُهَا أَوِ امْرَأَةٍ يَنْكِحُهَا فَهِجْرَتُهُ إِلَى مَا هَاجَرَ إِلَيْهِ»

"Actions are not but intentions; Thus, he whose migration was for Allāh and his Messenger, his migration was for Allāh and his Messenger, and he whose migration was for some worldly benefit or took the hand of a woman in marriage, his migration was for that which he migrated."[49]

Secondly: Compatibility with Islam law (شريعة) as ordained by Allāh. A'isha related that The Prophet, ﷺ, said:

«قَالَ رَسُولُ اللَّهِ ﷺ «مَنْ أَحْدَثَ فِي أَمْرِنَا هَذَا مَا لَيْسَ فِيهِ فَهُوَ رَدٌّ» وفي رواية أخرى قال «مَنْ عَمِلَ عَمَلًا لَيْسَ عَلَيْهِ أَمْرُنَا فَهُوَ رَدٌّ»

"Whoever innovates into this affair of ours that which is not from it shall have it rejected."[50] In another narration, he also said: " Whoever does an action that is not from this affair of ours will have it rejected." Therefore, it should not oppose, add, or remove anything from how the Prophet (ﷺ) performed it.

---

48 (Madaarij as-Saalikeen 1/74)

49 (Bukhari 54, Muslim 1907)

50 (Bukhari 2697 and Muslim 1718)

If it is not following the Sunnah of the Prophet (ﷺ), it will be rejected, even if the individual had good intentions. Due to the testification, ‹Muḥammad is the Messenger of Allāh,' which entails that one worships Allāh only with what the Prophet (ﷺ) prescribed.

2.1.9. THE DIFFERENCE BETWEEN ('IBĀDAH) WORSHIP AND (ṬĀ'AH) OBEDIENCE

We can gain insight into the distinctions between Worship ('Ibādah) and Obedience (Ṭā'ah) by examining the writings of Ibn Taymiya and Bin Baz in the following main points that draw the lines of differences between them:

1- The concept of obedience (ṭā'ah) encompasses a broader scope than worship ('Ibādah).

2- Worship involves inward acts of submission to Allāh, while obedience involves outward acts demonstrating loyalty to the Creator.

3- Based on this understanding, every act of worship that complies with Allāh's sharia is also an act of obedience.

4- Worship is exclusively ascribed to Allāh, whereas obedience can refer to obeying Allāh or others.

5- Obedience to someone other than Allāh may be rewarded or punished, depending on whether it aligns with Allāh's commands or goes against them. However, there are also permissible forms of obedience that are not subject to reward or punishment.[51]

---

51 Fatwah Ibn Taymiya 1/17 and 3/108, Majmu' fatwaa and wamaqalat mutanwi'ah by Ibn Baz 5/17-18.

2.1.10. ETIQUETTE OF PATIENCE WHEN BEHAVING WITH ALLĀH

Sabr is a word that encompasses a range of emotions and states beyond patience, such as endurance, restraint, acceptance, sincerity in obedience, and submission to the plans of The Most Loving. While sabr is often associated with practicing patience during difficult times, exhibiting it during times of abundance and blessings is equally vital. In such situations, sabr takes the form of steadfastness, involving increasing in gratitude, remaining disciplined, and staying connected to Allāh.

Sabr can be categorized into two main types: physical and spiritual. Physical sabr involves being patient during times of pain, illness, or physical affliction, while spiritual sabr requires actively resisting one's nafs or impulses of the ego. Humans can feel dissatisfaction and frustration when their experiences do not align with their mental timelines. However, Allāh controls the timing of everything, including when to test His servants with abundance or restriction. As such, we must always strive to remain in a state of sabr.

Additionally, sabr, which is the most virtuous trait of morality when it comes to our behavior towards Allāh and His creatures, can be categorized into three types: demonstrating obedience to Allāh's commands, restraining oneself from disobeying those commands, and accepting Allāh's decree, fate, or destiny. By acknowledging the multifaceted nature of sabr, we can improve our comprehension and development of this important quality in our lives.

2.1.11. OBEDIENCE TO THE COMMANDS OF ALLĀH

Obeying Allāh's commands, as enshrined in the Quran and Sunnah, requires strong patience to fulfill and implement them in our daily lives. Although these obligations are within our capacity and ability, human nature may lead to feelings of laziness when it comes to following divine orders. It is natural for some people to find these obligations heavy when they first attempt to carry them out. However, with the passage of time and diligent practice, one can become accustomed to them and integrate them into their routines and daily lives.

To reach this level, one needs to cultivate and employ the virtuous quality of sabr, which enables us to find enjoyment in fulfilling our obligations and helps us to please our Lord. Allāh says:

$$وَٱسۡتَعِينُوا۟ بِٱلصَّبۡرِ وَٱلصَّلَوٰةِ ۚ وَإِنَّهَا لَكَبِيرَةٌ إِلَّا عَلَى ٱلۡخَـٰشِعِينَ ﴿٤٥﴾$$

"AND SEEK HELP THROUGH PATIENCE AND PRAYER, AND INDEED, IT IS DIFFICULT EXCEPT FOR THE HUMBLY SUBMISSIVE [TO ALLĀH]." **[AL-BAQARAH : 45]**

Allāh has promised great rewards for those who remain patient in upholding His orders and commandments. He said:

$$وَٱلَّذِينَ صَبَرُوا۟ ٱبۡتِغَآءَ وَجۡهِ رَبِّهِمۡ وَأَقَامُوا۟ ٱلصَّلَوٰةَ وَأَنفَقُوا۟ مِمَّا رَزَقۡنَـٰهُمۡ سِرࣰّا وَعَلَانِيَةࣰ وَيَدۡرَءُونَ بِٱلۡحَسَنَةِ ٱلسَّيِّئَةَ أُو۟لَـٰٓئِكَ لَهُمۡ عُقۡبَى ٱلدَّارِ ﴿٢٢﴾$$

$$جَنَّـٰتُ عَدۡنࣲ يَدۡخُلُونَهَا وَمَن صَلَحَ مِنۡ ءَابَآئِهِمۡ وَأَزۡوَٰجِهِمۡ وَذُرِّيَّـٰتِهِمۡ ۖ وَٱلۡمَلَـٰٓئِكَةُ يَدۡخُلُونَ عَلَيۡهِم مِّن كُلِّ بَابٍ ﴿٢٣﴾$$

$$سَلَـٰمٌ عَلَيۡكُم بِمَا صَبَرۡتُمۡ ۚ فَنِعۡمَ عُقۡبَى ٱلدَّارِ ﴿٢٤﴾$$

AND THOSE WHO ARE PATIENT, SEEKING THE COUNTENANCE OF THEIR LORD, AND ESTABLISH PRAYER AND SPEND FROM WHAT WE HAVE PROVIDED FOR THEM SECRETLY AND PUBLICLY AND PREVENT EVIL WITH GOOD - THOSE WILL HAVE THE GOOD CONSEQUENCE OF [THIS] HOME.

GARDENS OF PERPETUAL RESIDENCE; THEY WILL ENTER THEM WITH WHOEVER WERE RIGHTEOUS AMONG THEIR FATHERS, THEIR SPOUSES, AND THEIR DESCENDANTS. AND THE ANGELS WILL ENTER UPON THEM FROM EVERY GATE, [SAYING]", "PEACE BE UPON YOU FOR WHAT YOU PATIENTLY ENDURED. AND EXCELLENT IS THE FINAL HOME." [AR-RA'D : 22 - 24]

2.1.12. RESTRAINING ONESELF FROM DISOBEYING HIS COMMANDS.

Disobeying the Creator is a serious sin that must be avoided as it contradicts one's claim of faith and belief in Allāh. The sinful soul is inclined to fall into whims and desires that can distance it from Allāh. Therefore, Muslims must not allow their ego to be free to do whatever they want, which is against the Divine law. Instead, they should strive to reconcile themselves with obeying Allāh and cultivate the quality of restraint to prevent themselves from falling into disobedience.

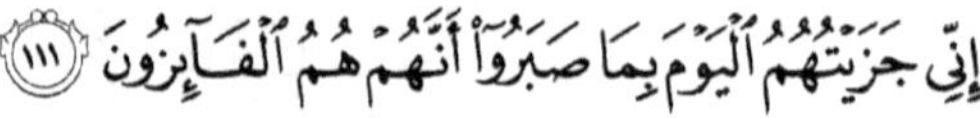

"INDEED, I HAVE REWARDED THEM THIS DAY FOR THEIR PATIENT ENDURANCE - THAT THEY ARE THE ATTAINERS [OF SUCCESS." [AL-MU'MINŪN : III]

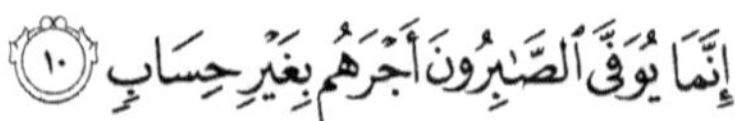

"INDEED, THE PATIENT WILL BE GIVEN THEIR REWARD WITHOUT ACCOUNT." [AZ-ZUMAR : IO]

وَٱللَّهُ يُحِبُّ ٱلصَّابِرِينَ ﴿١٤٦﴾

"AND ALLĀH LOVES THE STEADFAST." [AL-E-IMRAN : I46]

The verses above declare that those who strive for the cause of Allāh by restraining their souls from disobedience will be successful and beloved by Allāh. They will receive their rewards without any reckoning.

2.1.13. ACCEPTING THE DECREE, FATE, OR DESTINY WRITTEN BY ALLĀH

The third type of Sabr, the sixth pillar of faith, is the most significant and difficult one as it requires total submission and contentment with Allāh's prescription and predomination in all life situations.

A person who loves Almighty Allāh finds it easier to exhibit patience and perseverance in the face of any changes in their life, whether good or bad. This is because they understand that everything comes from Allāh and that there must be a reason for it. A person who loves wants to be seen by their Beloved in the best of states, and therefore they exhibit the best of patience.

Something happens to us in our lives, and we feel it is the worst thing that could happen. But after the trial, when relief and ease come, we realize that the difficult times had happened for good to come. Believers need to be patient and remember that Allāh has already predetermined and prescribed these tests and calamities, and we can do nothing about them. Allāh is sufficient for us and the best arranger of all our affairs. He will guide us to what is good for us in this life and the Hereafter. Allāh says:

$$وَلَنَبْلُوَنَّكُم بِشَىْءٍ مِّنَ ٱلْخَوْفِ وَٱلْجُوعِ وَنَقْصٍ مِّنَ ٱلْأَمْوَٰلِ وَٱلْأَنفُسِ وَٱلثَّمَرَٰتِ ۗ وَبَشِّرِ ٱلصَّٰبِرِينَ ﴿١٥٥﴾$$

$$ٱلَّذِينَ إِذَآ أَصَٰبَتْهُم مُّصِيبَةٌ قَالُوٓاْ إِنَّا لِلَّهِ وَإِنَّآ إِلَيْهِ رَٰجِعُونَ ﴿١٥٦﴾$$

$$أُوْلَٰٓئِكَ عَلَيْهِمْ صَلَوَٰتٌ مِّن رَّبِّهِمْ وَرَحْمَةٌ ۖ وَأُوْلَٰٓئِكَ هُمُ ٱلْمُهْتَدُونَ ﴿١٥٧﴾$$

"AND WE WILL SURELY TEST YOU WITH SOMETHING OF FEAR AND HUNGER AND A LOSS OF WEALTH AND LIVES AND FRUITS, BUT GIVE GOOD TIDINGS TO THE PATIENT, WHO, WHEN DISASTER STRIKES THEM, SAY, "INDEED WE BELONG TO ALLĀH, AND INDEED TO HIM WE WILL RETURN."

THOSE ARE THE ONES UPON WHOM ARE BLESSINGS FROM THEIR LORD AND MERCY. AND IT IS THOSE WHO ARE THE [RIGHTLY] GUIDED" : [AL-BAQARAH : 155- 157]

وَٱصۡبِرۡ عَلَىٰ مَآ أَصَابَكَۖ إِنَّ ذَٰلِكَ مِنۡ عَزۡمِ ٱلۡأُمُورِ ﴿١٧﴾

"AND BE PATIENT OVER WHAT BEFALLS YOU. INDEED, [ALL] THAT IS OF THE MATTERS [REQUIRING] DETERMINATION". [LUQMAN : 17]

SECTION TWO

ETIQUETTE AND BEHAVIOR OF THE BELIEVER TOWARD THE PROPHET MUHAMMED, 

Throughout the Qur'an, Allāh (ﷻ) commands humanity to fear Him and hold the Prophet ﷺ in high esteem. In addition to instructing us to adhere to a code of respect and reverence for the Prophet ﷺ, Allāh (ﷻ) provides practical demonstrations of how to approach and interact with him.

While respect generally refers to treating someone with reverence, the Quran distinguishes respect for the Prophet ﷺ from that of other human beings. Several verses in different chapters of the Quran emphasize the importance of showing reverence to the Prophet Muhammed ﷺ. These verses contain divine teachings that direct believers to demonstrate respect in their interactions with the Messenger. The verses and what they demonstrate are as follows:

2.2.1. SHOWING RESPECT TO HIM WHEN DRAWING HIS ATTENTION TO AN IMPORTANT MATTER.

Allāh says in the Quran:

يَٰٓأَيُّهَا ٱلَّذِينَ ءَامَنُوا۟ لَا تَقُولُوا۟ رَٰعِنَا وَقُولُوا۟ ٱنظُرْنَا وَٱسْمَعُوا۟ وَلِلْكَٰفِرِينَ عَذَابٌ أَلِيمٌ ﴿١٠٤﴾

"O YOU WHO HAVE BELIEVED, SAY NOT [TO ALLĀH'S MESSENGER], "RA'INA" BUT SAY, "UNTHURNA" AND LISTEN. AND FOR THE DISBELIEVERS IS A PAINFUL PUNISHMENT".

[AL-BAQARAH : 104]

In the first place, the verse above draws attention to the importance of respecting Allāh's Messenger, peace and blessings be upon him; according to some scholars, even the slightest disrespect when addressing the Prophet (ﷺ) can harm one's faith and deeds. This is because the Jews, when visiting the Prophet (ﷺ), would use ambiguous words or twist the terms to insult him while pretending to show respect. For instance, they would use the term "ra'ina" to draw his attention, which could also mean "Listen, may you become deaf" in Hebrew or "If you listen to us, then we will listen to you" in colloquial Arabic. The word could also be easily twisted into "ra'inaa," which means "our shepherd." Therefore, Allāh commands believers to use a different term, such as "und-ur nii," when seeking the Prophet's attention.

Throughout history, scholars and learned men have engaged in discussions about the life of the Prophet (ﷺ) through speeches or written works. Therefore, they should be mindful of showing reverence and respect to the Prophet (ﷺ) and carefully choose their words and phrases when describing him. In other words, they should refrain from using words that may be honorific in one language but derogatory in another or ambiguous words that could be easily twisted to insult the Prophet (ﷺ). Furthermore, they should avoid using words that imply respect and reverence but have slightly different pronunciations that convey disrespect to him and paying heed to his teachings.'52

---

52 (Raḥīm Ebrahim, Major themes in Surat alhujurat; Chapter 49 of the Quran. Pages:33-34)

Regarding the command to "listen," it should be noted that listening is an involuntary sense as long as hearing is not impaired. Therefore, the direct meaning of the command to "listen" here may not be applicable. Rather, "listening" can be interpreted in one of the following three ways:

Firstly, it means to dedicate one's attention and listen attentively to what the Prophet (ﷺ) is saying so that there is no need for repetition.

Secondly, it means to listen with acceptance and obedience, unlike the Jews who would say, "We listen and disobey.

Thirdly, it means to listen to what one is ordered to do so that they do not revert to what they were prohibited from doing as a form of affirmation.

2.2.2. MANNERS OF CALLING THE PROPHET ﷺ

In the Quran:

لَّا تَجْعَلُوا دُعَآءَ الرَّسُولِ بَيْنَكُمْ كَدُعَآءِ بَعْضِكُم بَعْضًا قَدْ يَعْلَمُ اللَّهُ الَّذِينَ يَتَسَلَّلُونَ مِنكُمْ لِوَاذًا فَلْيَحْذَرِ الَّذِينَ يُخَالِفُونَ عَنْ أَمْرِهِ أَن تُصِيبَهُمْ فِتْنَةٌ أَوْ يُصِيبَهُمْ عَذَابٌ أَلِيمٌ ۝

DO NOT MAKE [YOUR] CALLING OF THE MESSENGER AMONG YOURSELVES AS THE CALL OF ONE OF YOU TO ANOTHER. ALREADY ALLĀH KNOWS THOSE OF YOU WHO SLIP AWAY, CONCEALED BY OTHERS. SO LET THOSE BEWARE WHO DISSENT FROM THE PROPHET'S ORDER, LEST FITNAH STRIKE THEM OR A PAINFUL PUNISHMENT. [AN-NUR : 63]

It is important to recognize that our love for the Prophet ﷺ is paramount and carries significant obligations and duties. One of these duties is to show respect to him. As Muslims, when addressing the Prophet ﷺ, we should not refer to him by name or mention him without a title. How we address each other should differ from how we address the Prophet ﷺ.

The directive in verse is to hold the Prophet ﷺ in high esteem and address him with respect. Despite the Prophet's modesty and approachability, it was not appropriate for his Companions to forget that he was their leader. He educated and refined their manners, and they should address him with the appropriate level of respect, not as they would address one another. The verse serves as a reminder to Muslims and prohibits them from referring to the Messenger ﷺ by his name or nickname in the same way they address one another.

2.2.3. RESPECT HIS PRIVACY, TIME, PLACE, AND FAMILY.

In Surat Al-ahzab comes this Command from Allāh saying:

يَـٰٓأَيُّهَا ٱلَّذِينَ ءَامَنُوا۟ لَا تَدْخُلُوا۟ بُيُوتَ ٱلنَّبِيِّ إِلَّآ أَن يُؤْذَنَ لَكُمْ إِلَىٰ طَعَامٍ غَيْرَ نَـٰظِرِينَ إِنَىٰهُ

وَلَـٰكِنْ إِذَا دُعِيتُمْ فَٱدْخُلُوا۟ فَإِذَا طَعِمْتُمْ فَٱنتَشِرُوا۟ وَلَا مُسْتَـْٔنِسِينَ لِحَدِيثٍ إِنَّ ذَٰلِكُمْ كَانَ

يُؤْذِى ٱلنَّبِيَّ فَيَسْتَحْىِۦ مِنكُمْ وَٱللَّهُ لَا يَسْتَحْىِۦ مِنَ ٱلْحَقِّ وَإِذَا سَأَلْتُمُوهُنَّ مَتَـٰعًا

فَسْـَٔلُوهُنَّ مِن وَرَآءِ حِجَابٍ ذَٰلِكُمْ أَطْهَرُ لِقُلُوبِكُمْ وَقُلُوبِهِنَّ وَمَا كَانَ لَكُمْ أَن تُؤْذُوا۟

رَسُولَ ٱللَّهِ وَلَآ أَن تَنكِحُوٓا۟ أَزْوَٰجَهُۥ مِنۢ بَعْدِهِۦٓ أَبَدًا إِنَّ ذَٰلِكُمْ كَانَ عِندَ ٱللَّهِ عَظِيمًا ﴿٥٣﴾

"O YOU WHO HAVE BELIEVED, DO NOT ENTER THE HOUSES OF THE PROPHET EXCEPT WHEN YOU ARE PERMITTED FOR A MEAL, WITHOUT AWAITING ITS READINESS. BUT WHEN YOU ARE INVITED, THEN ENTER; AND WHEN YOU HAVE EATEN, DISPERSE WITHOUT SEEKING TO REMAIN FOR CONVERSATION. INDEED, THAT [BEHAVIOR] WAS TROUBLING THE PROPHET, AND HE IS SHY OF [DISMISSING] YOU. BUT ALLĀH IS NOT SHY OF THE TRUTH. AND WHEN YOU ASK [HIS WIVES] FOR SOMETHING, ASK THEM FROM BEHIND A PARTITION. THAT IS PURER FOR YOUR HEARTS AND THEIR HEARTS. AND IT IS NOT [CONCEIVABLE OR LAWFUL] FOR YOU TO HARM THE MESSENGER OF ALLĀH OR TO MARRY HIS WIVES AFTER HIM, EVER. INDEED, THAT WOULD BE IN THE SIGHT OF ALLĀH AN ENORMITY." [AL-AHZAB : 53.]

According to commentators of the Quran, the verse highlights specific manners for entering people's homes that were not customary in pre-Islamic Arabia. In the past, it was common for people to enter a home without seeking permission first.

In the nomadic culture prevalent among the Arabs, it was not uncommon for visitors to arrive unannounced, sometimes during mealtimes, and extend their stay until mealtime approached. This practice was particularly evident in the Prophet's homes, a source of knowledge and wisdom. Some guests would arrive and, upon seeing food being prepared, would wait for the meal without being invited. Others would stay to chat even after the meal was over, despite not being invited in the first place. They were often oblivious to the inconvenience their behavior caused the Prophet and his family.[53]

2.2.4. RESPECT HIM BY GIVING PREFERENCE TO HIS COMMANDMENTS OVER OUR VIEWS AND OPINIONS.

The Quranic teachings regarding honouring our Messenger ﷺ continue by saying:

يَـٰٓأَيُّهَا ٱلَّذِينَ ءَامَنُوا۟ لَا تُقَدِّمُوا۟ بَيْنَ يَدَيِ ٱللَّهِ وَرَسُولِهِۦ وَٱتَّقُوا۟ ٱللَّهَ إِنَّ ٱللَّهَ سَمِيعٌ عَلِيمٌ ﴿١﴾

"O YOU WHO HAVE BELIEVED, DO NOT PUT [YOURSELVES] BEFORE ALLĀH AND HIS MESSENGER BUT FEAR ALLĀH. INDEED, ALLĀH IS HEARING AND KNOWING".

[AL-HUJURAT 1.]

The verse above is elaborated by that of Surat AL-Ahzab which says:

____
53 Zilalul Quran, tafseer Surat Alhzab, page 83.

وَمَا كَانَ لِمُؤْمِنٍ وَلَا مُؤْمِنَةٍ إِذَا قَضَى اللَّهُ وَرَسُولُهُ أَمْرًا أَن يَكُونَ لَهُمُ الْخِيَرَةُ مِنْ أَمْرِهِمْ وَمَن يَعْصِ اللَّهَ وَرَسُولَهُ فَقَدْ ضَلَّ ضَلَالًا مُّبِينًا ﴿٣٦﴾

"IT IS NOT FOR A BELIEVING MAN OR A BELIEVING WOMAN, WHEN ALLĀH AND HIS MESSENGER HAVE DECIDED A MATTER, THAT THEY SHOULD [THEREAFTER] HAVE ANY CHOICE ABOUT THEIR AFFAIR. AND WHOEVER DISOBEYS ALLĀH AND HIS MESSENGER HAS CERTAINLY STRAYED INTO CLEAR ERROR". [AL-AHZAB : 36]

The verses above highlight fundamental principles of morals and manners that were revealed to lay the foundation for this issue. These principles are as follows:

A- A believer should not prioritize their own opinions and views over the decisions of Allāh and His Messenger, as doing so contradicts one's faith and shows an attitude of independence against them.

B- A believer should be subordinate to Allāh and His Messenger (ﷺ) and should not surpass them in any matter in which they have already given guidance.

C- A believer should not act independently based on their own rational thinking, as this may not align with Allāh's laws and guidance.

D- Regarding legislation, it is the duty of every Muslim to conform to it without subjecting it to personal interpretation or attempts to serve their own interests.

By following these principles, believers can maintain a strong faith and respect for Allāh and His Messenger and uphold moral and ethical behavior in their daily lives. In his comments on this verse, Ibn Kathir mentions: (meaning, do not rush in making decisions before him; instead, follow his lead in all matters.

Ali bin Abi Talha reported that Ibn Abbas, may Allāh be pleased with him, commented (Make not [a decision] in advance before Allāh and His Messenger),

"Do not say anything that contradicts the Qur'an and Sunnah.")

Ibn Kathir added by quoting a statement, elaborating the verse further, from Qatada and said: (We were told that some people used to say, 'Revelation should be sent down about such and such matters,' and 'such and such practices should be rendered allowed.' Allāh the Exalted disliked this attitude).[54]

2.2.5. WE SHOULD RESPECT HIM BY NOT RAISING OUR VOICES OVER HIS VOICE DURING HIS PRESENCE.

In the same chapter, a new command is given, with a firm directive from Allāh that prohibits Muslims from raising their voices above that of the Prophet ﷺ. Such behavior is considered inappropriate and disrespectful towards the Prophet's personality and prophethood. The Quranic verse straightforward gives this clear commandment:

$$\text{يَـٰٓأَيُّهَا ٱلَّذِينَ ءَامَنُوا۟ لَا تَرْفَعُوٓا۟ أَصْوَٰتَكُمْ فَوْقَ صَوْتِ ٱلنَّبِىِّ وَلَا تَجْهَرُوا۟ لَهُۥ بِٱلْقَوْلِ كَجَهْرِ بَعْضِكُمْ لِبَعْضٍ أَن تَحْبَطَ أَعْمَـٰلُكُمْ وَأَنتُمْ لَا تَشْعُرُونَ ٢}$$

$$\text{إِنَّ ٱلَّذِينَ يَغُضُّونَ أَصْوَٰتَهُمْ عِندَ رَسُولِ ٱللَّهِ أُو۟لَـٰٓئِكَ ٱلَّذِينَ ٱمْتَحَنَ ٱللَّهُ قُلُوبَهُمْ لِلتَّقْوَىٰ لَهُم مَّغْفِرَةٌ وَأَجْرٌ عَظِيمٌ ٣}$$

$$\text{إِنَّ ٱلَّذِينَ يُنَادُونَكَ مِن وَرَآءِ ٱلْحُجُرَٰتِ أَكْثَرُهُمْ لَا يَعْقِلُونَ ٤}$$

$$\text{وَلَوْ أَنَّهُمْ صَبَرُوا۟ حَتَّىٰ تَخْرُجَ إِلَيْهِمْ لَكَانَ خَيْرًا لَّهُمْ وَٱللَّهُ غَفُورٌ رَّحِيمٌ ٥}$$

---

54 Ibn Kathir, Vol: 10, page 515.

"O YOU WHO HAVE BELIEVED, DO NOT RAISE YOUR VOICES ABOVE THE VOICE OF THE PROPHET OR BE LOUD TO HIM IN SPEECH LIKE THE LOUDNESS OF SOME OF YOU TO OTHERS, LEST YOUR DEEDS BECOME WORTHLESS WHILE YOU PERCEIVE NOT." "INDEED, THOSE WHO LOWER THEIR VOICES BEFORE THE MESSENGER OF ALLĀH - THEY ARE THE ONES WHOSE HEARTS ALLĀH HAS TESTED FOR RIGHTEOUSNESS. FOR THEM IS FORGIVENESS AND A GREAT REWARD". "INDEED, THOSE WHO CALL YOU, [O MUḤAMMAD], FROM BEHIND THE CHAMBERS - MOST OF THEM DO NOT USE REASON." "AND IF THEY HAD BEEN PATIENT UNTIL YOU [COULD] COME OUT TO THEM, IT WOULD HAVE BEEN BETTER FOR THEM. BUT ALLĀH IS FORGIVING AND MERCIFUL".[AL-ḤUJURAT : 2-5]

Drawing a practical lesson to the situations that we live in, Abūl A'la Almoududi says in Tafheem ul Quran:

"Although this etiquette was taught for sitting in the Prophet's (ﷺ) assembly and its addressees were the people who were living in his time, the people of the later ages should also observe the same respect and reverence on the occasion when the Prophet›s name is mentioned, or command of his is stated, or his sayings are explained. Besides, this verse also points out what attitude the people should adopt when talking to persons of a higher rank and status than themselves. A person's talking before the men of a higher rank in a way as he talks before his friends or the common men is in fact a sign that he has no respect for them in his heart and he does not recognize any difference between them and the common people".[55]

Thus, Islamic scholars, having realized the extent of this injunction, state that it is reprehensible to raise one's voice near the Prophet's grave in the same way as it was disagreeable to do so in his presence. In this way, Muslims demonstrate their respect for the Prophet in all situations.

Again, Allāh states another situation in verses 4 and 5, where He, Allāh, the Almighty, dispraises those who call the Prophet from behind the chambers, i.e., the residences of his wives, like some nomad Arabs used to do. Allāh describes them as: "...most of them do not use reason." It was reported that this verse was revealed about al-Aqra' ibn Habis At-Tamimi. May Allāh be pleased with Him, according to more than one source. Imam Aḥmad recorded that Al-Aqra' ibn Habis said that he called the Messenger of Allāh from

---

55 Tafsīr Surat al-Hujurat verse 2.

behind his dwellings, saying, "O Muḥammad! O, Muḥammad!" "O Allāh's Messenger!" according to another narration, but the Messenger did not answer him. Al-Aqra' then said, "O Messenger of Allāh, praising me is good, and dispraising me is bad." He said, "That is due to Allāh Almighty."[56] Hence, Almighty Allāh taught them good manners in addressing the Prophet.

2.2.6. CONVERSATIONS ABOUT DISOBEDIENCE AND DISLOYALTY TO THE PROPHET ﷺ ARE CONSIDERED TO BE SINFUL.

Talks and conversations about being disobedient to the Prophet ﷺ are deemed, by and large, sinful in the Quran. Allāh says in this regard:

أَلَمْ تَرَ إِلَى ٱلَّذِينَ نُهُوا عَنِ ٱلنَّجْوَىٰ ثُمَّ يَعُودُونَ لِمَا نُهُوا عَنْهُ وَيَتَنَٰجَوْنَ بِٱلْإِثْمِ وَٱلْعُدْوَٰنِ وَمَعْصِيَتِ ٱلرَّسُولِ وَإِذَا جَآءُوكَ حَيَّوْكَ بِمَا لَمْ يُحَيِّكَ بِهِ ٱللَّهُ وَيَقُولُونَ فِىٓ أَنفُسِهِمْ لَوْلَا يُعَذِّبُنَا ٱللَّهُ بِمَا نَقُولُ حَسْبُهُمْ جَهَنَّمُ يَصْلَوْنَهَا فَبِئْسَ ٱلْمَصِيرُ ٨

يَٰٓأَيُّهَا ٱلَّذِينَ ءَامَنُوٓا إِذَا تَنَٰجَيْتُمْ فَلَا تَتَنَٰجَوْا بِٱلْإِثْمِ وَٱلْعُدْوَٰنِ وَمَعْصِيَتِ ٱلرَّسُولِ وَتَنَٰجَوْا بِٱلْبِرِّ وَٱلتَّقْوَىٰ وَٱتَّقُوا ٱللَّهَ ٱلَّذِىٓ إِلَيْهِ تُحْشَرُونَ ٩

"HAVE YOU NOT CONSIDERED THOSE WHO WERE FORBIDDEN FROM PRIVATE CONVERSATION, THEN THEY RETURN TO THAT WHICH THEY WERE FORBIDDEN AND CONVERSE AMONG THEMSELVES ABOUT SIN AND AGGRESSION AND DISOBEDIENCE TO THE MESSENGER? AND WHEN THEY COME TO YOU, THEY GREET YOU WITH THAT [WORD] BY WHICH ALLĀH DOES NOT GREET YOU AND SAY AMONG THEMSELVES, "WHY DOES ALLĀH NOT PUNISH US FOR WHAT WE SAY?" SUFFICIENT FOR THEM IS HELL, WHICH THEY WILL [ENTER TO] BURN, AND WRETCHED IS THE DESTINATION. O YOU WHO HAVE BELIEVED, WHEN YOU CONVERSE PRIVATELY, DO NOT CONVERSE ABOUT SIN AND AGGRESSION AND DISOBEDIENCE TO THE MESSENGER BUT CONVERSE ABOUT RIGHTEOUSNESS AND PIETY. AND FEAR ALLĀH, TO WHOM YOU WILL BE GATHERED". [AL-MUJADILA : 8 - 9.]

---

56 Musnad Aḥmad Vol: 4, pages 4,6, 227.

The term "Najwa" refers to whispering, secret talks, and confidential consultations. According to the Quranic passage, as noted by Abū Ala in Tafheem ul Quran, it can be inferred that Najwa is not inherently forbidden. However, its lawfulness or unlawfulness depends on the character of the people involved and the circumstances under which such talks are held. The nature of the consultations also plays a role; if people known for their sincerity, righteousness, and purity of character are seen talking secretly together, it would not raise suspicions of mischief. However, if people notorious for their evil character engage in whispering and secret consultations, it produces suspicion that they are plotting a new conspiracy. The prohibition mentioned in these verses is specifically related to situations when Najwa is used to disobey or be disloyal to the Prophet.[57]

2.2.7. SUPPORTING THE PROPHET ﷺ MEANS HONOURING HIM.

The following verse points to the fact above:

فَٱلَّذِينَ ءَامَنُوا۟ بِهِۦ وَعَزَّرُوهُ وَنَصَرُوهُ وَٱتَّبَعُوا۟ ٱلنُّورَ ٱلَّذِىٓ أُنزِلَ مَعَهُۥٓ أُو۟لَٰٓئِكَ هُمُ ٱلْمُفْلِحُونَ ﴿١٥٧﴾

"SO THEY WHO HAVE BELIEVED IN HIM HONORED HIM, SUPPORTED HIM, AND FOLLOWED THE LIGHT WHICH WAS SENT DOWN WITH HIM - IT IS THOSE WHO WILL BE THE SUCCESSFUL." [AL-A'RAF : 157]

2.2.8. BETRAYING THE PROPHET ﷺ MEANS DISLOYALTY.

Allāh, strongly condemns any form of disloyalty by declaring as follows:

---

57 Tafheemul Quran, tafseer verses 8-9 of AlMujadala

يَـٰٓأَيُّهَا ٱلَّذِينَ ءَامَنُوا۟ لَا تَخُونُوا۟ ٱللَّهَ وَٱلرَّسُولَ وَتَخُونُوٓا۟ أَمَـٰنَـٰتِكُمْ وَأَنتُمْ تَعْلَمُونَ ﴿٢٧﴾

"O YOU WHO HAVE BELIEVED, DO NOT BETRAY ALLĀH AND THE MESSENGER OR BETRAY YOUR TRUSTS WHILE YOU KNOW [THE CONSEQUENCE]." [AL-ANFAL : 27]

The Quran follows that in no way must a believer be disloyal to the Prophet (ﷺ) because disloyalty to him is, in effect, disloyalty to Allāh (ﷻ). Therefore, if a believer is unfaithful to the Prophet ﷺ, there is a defect within his innermost self, and his (faith) would be questioned.

2.2.9. HARMING THE PROPHET ﷺ IN ANY FORM, BY WORD OR ACTION, IS A VERY HEINOUS SIN.

The following injunction is another example wherein Allāh warns humankind of the severe consequences of disrespecting the Prophet ﷺ. The verse reads as follows:

إِنَّ ٱلَّذِينَ يُؤْذُونَ ٱللَّهَ وَرَسُولَهُۥ لَعَنَهُمُ ٱللَّهُ فِى ٱلدُّنْيَا وَٱلْءَاخِرَةِ وَأَعَدَّ لَهُمْ عَذَابًا مُّهِينًا ﴿٥٧﴾

"INDEED, THOSE WHO ABUSE ALLĀH AND HIS MESSENGER - ALLĀH HAS CURSED THEM IN THIS WORLD AND THE HEREAFTER AND PREPARED FOR THEM A HUMILIATING PUNISHMENT." [AL-AHZAB : 57]

This verse demonstrates that Allāh will always protect the Messenger ﷺ in all situations throughout His eternal life. Besides, Allāh assures Him that however vehement his opponents might be in rejecting his call and how insulting they might be in taunting him, they can never inflict harm on him or his mission. Allāh has exalted his honor and has granted him ﷺ the highest position amongst all created beings. ﷺ

2.2.10. EMULATING HIM AND FOLLOWING HIS (SUNNAH) PROPHETIC TRADITION AS A MORAL IDEAL.

A thorough study of human history reveals that the emergence of prophets and messengers marked the beginning of life. Undeniably, no religion can be comprehended and implemented without the guidance of a messenger who interprets and clarifies it. For this reason, Allāh has sent a messenger to guide every nation.

As with other prophets, Allāh sent Prophet Muḥammad ﷺ with the message of perfecting people's morals and behaviors, leading them to the straight path. Allāh made his prophethood eternal until the Day of Judgment and universal for everyone. Therefore, all Muslims are responsible for obeying, respecting, and loving him, following his way of life, and following His Sunnah.

In the Quran, obedience to the Prophet ﷺ is considered as important as obedience to Allāh. Allāh made obeying His Messenger tantamount to obeying Himself and placed obedience to Himself alongside obedience to His Messenger. As a result, Allāh promises an abundant reward for those who follow and respect the Prophet, while severe punishment is threatened for those who oppose and disobey him.

Therefore, following whatever the Prophet ﷺ commanded is mandatory, and refraining from what he prohibited.

Examining the lives, governance, and accomplishments of the al-Khalifa' al-Rashida (Rightly Guided Caliphs) reveals that none of these pious caliphs claimed to be a new source of legislation. Abū

Bakr ﷺ refused to use any authority other than that prescribed by the Quran or the Hadith. He sought counsel from the companions of the Prophet ﷺ only in certain unique matters.[58]

In a letter addressed to Qadi (judge) Shurayh ﷺ, Umar ﷺ advised him to follow a specific method of judgment. He wrote, "If you find anything in the Quran pertaining to the matter at hand, then judge accordingly. If there is no direction to be found, consult the Sunnah of the Prophet ﷺ and decide accordingly. And if neither the Quran, the Sunnah, or any subordinate authority addresses the issue, then use personal judgment, but only as a last resort." [59]

To fulfill their duties as Allāh's servants, Muslims must study the practices of the Prophet ﷺ. Accessing the Sunnah and its sources requires utilizing the golden treasure of books preserved by predecessors who devoted themselves to keeping the Sunnah intact and reliable. The primary source of information for the Sunnah is the excellent hadith compilations of scholars such as Imam al-Bukhari, Imam Muslim, and other classical-era ḥadīth scholars. They collected, classified, and organized the Hadeeths based on their ranks and themes in Islamic references of Ḥadīth. Furthermore, the vast collections of the Prophet's words, deeds, and personal attributes, particularly those displayed during his prophethood, were collected with great care by reliable narrators or reporters, as recognized by all Sunni scholars.

---

58 *Council of Elders,"* who represented the will of the people. Naz. Abū Bakar. Lahore. Ferozsons Ltd. 1970, pp.104-105

59 Numani, Maulana Shibli. Al-Farooqui. Tran. By Sayed Abū Zafar. Karachi. Educational Press. 1975, 201.

In order to fully understand the meaning of the terms "Sunnah and Ḥadīth," which are crucial in this regard, it is necessary to provide more illustrations to clarify their linguistic and technical meanings when used together or separately.

2.2.11. DENOTATION MEANING OF SUNNAH AND ḤADĪTH MEAN

Linguistically: According to Arabic lexicographers, the term Sunnah originates from the root word 'sunnah". This root word means to make a path easy to traverse or to pave the way and make following it straightforward. Therefore, Sunnah can refer to a street, path, or road. It can also denote how Allāh's Prophets explained Divinely revealed scriptures and laws.

Technically, Sunnah means all narrated and connected to Muḥammad (ﷺ), Allāh's final Prophet. It includes everything authentically narrated of the Prophet's (ﷺ) actions, sayings, tacit approvals, and characteristics.

Ḥadīth: (The Arabic word "Ḥadīth" basically means "an item of news, conversation, a tale, a story, or a report," whether historical or legendary, true or false, relating to the present or the past. Its secondary meaning as an adjective is "new" as opposed to "Qadim" or "old." However, like other Arabic words (e.g., salah, zakat), its meaning changed in Islam. From the time of the Prophet ﷺ, his stories and communications dominated all other forms of communication.

Consequently, the term "ḥadīth" began to be used almost exclusively for reports that spoke of his actions and sayings).[60]

---

60 Ḥadīth literature, p. 1 and Studies in Ḥadīth Methodology and literature, Pp. 1-3.

Therefore. The Ḥadīth represents a personal source of divine guidance that Allāh granted His Prophet ﷺ, similar to the Quran. The Prophet ﷺ reiterated this point in his recorded statements, "Indeed, I was given the Quran and something similar to it along with it."[61]

Since Revelation guided the Prophet personally, his character and social interactions became prime examples of moral conduct for Muslims until the last day.

Allāh draws our attention to this fact in the following Quranic verses to show that his daily life represents and ideal code of good conduct since his character was the Quran:

لَّقَدْ كَانَ لَكُمْ فِي رَسُولِ ٱللَّهِ أُسْوَةٌ حَسَنَةٌ لِّمَن كَانَ يَرْجُواْ ٱللَّهَ وَٱلْيَوْمَ ٱلْأَخِرَ وَذَكَرَ ٱللَّهَ كَثِيرًا ﴿٢١﴾

".THERE HAS CERTAINLY BEEN FOR YOU IN THE MESSENGER OF ALLĀH AN EXCELLENT PATTERN FOR ANYONE WHOSE HOPE IS IN ALLĀH AND THE LAST DAY AND [WHO] REMEMBERS ALLĀH OFTEN". [AL-AHZAB : 21]

قُلْ إِن كُنتُمْ تُحِبُّونَ ٱللَّهَ فَٱتَّبِعُونِي يُحْبِبْكُمُ ٱللَّهُ وَيَغْفِرْ لَكُمْ ذُنُوبَكُمْ وَٱللَّهُ غَفُورٌ رَّحِيمٌ ﴿٣١﴾

"SAY, [O MUHAMMAD], "IF YOU SHOULD LOVE ALLĀH, THEN FOLLOW ME, [SO] ALLĀH WILL LOVE YOU AND FORGIVE YOU YOUR SINS. AND ALLĀH IS FORGIVING AND MERCIFUL." [AL-E-IMRAN : 31]

وَمَآ ءَاتَىٰكُمُ ٱلرَّسُولُ فَخُذُوهُ وَمَا نَهَىٰكُمْ عَنْهُ فَٱنتَهُواْ وَٱتَّقُواْ ٱللَّهَ إِنَّ ٱللَّهَ شَدِيدُ ٱلْعِقَابِ ﴿٧﴾

"AND WHATEVER THE MESSENGER HAS GIVEN YOU - TAKE; AND WHAT HE HAS FORBIDDEN YOU - REFRAIN FROM. AND FEAR ALLĀH; INDEED, ALLĀH IS SEVERE IN PENALTY". [AL-HASHR : 7]

The three verses above constitute the cornerstone of our topic, which is the importance of following and adhering to the Sunnah of the Prophet Muḥammad ﷺ. The verses highlight the significance of loving the Prophet ﷺ and Sunnah's role in

---

61 Dr. Abū Ameena Bilal Philips, Usool Al-Ḥadīth pp 13, 16 and 20

the divine law. We can infer from the verses that merely declaring love for the Prophet ﷺ with our tongues is not enough; rather, it must come from the depths of our hearts. Failure to do so would call into question one's faith or Īmān. The Sunnah of the Prophet encompasses his character, etiquettes, habits, and legislative obligations that he performed to bring Muslim believers closer to Allāh as the walking Quran, following the Prophet ﷺ, is the right path that leads to ultimate satisfaction. Therefore, it is crucial to follow especially the obligatory and compulsory aspects of the Sunnah. Following and imitating the Prophet's daily actions are highly praiseworthy and beneficial for personal and social life and all of humankind. Those who love Allāh will strive to emulate the person Allāh loves and is pleased with and replicate his deeds. While not everyone can act according to the complete Sunnah, everyone can at least intend to act according to certain aspects of it and give preference to the Sunnah.

Before we delve into new topics, it is crucial to elaborate further on the significance of the Sunnah. As previously noted, Allāh commands strict obedience to His Prophet in His verses. Therefore, Islam can only be lived by practicing the Sunnah and the Quran. The Sunnah is inseparable from the Quran as it represents the living interpretation of the Quran by the Prophet ﷺ. It is impossible to fully comprehend and practice the Quran's commands without following the Sunnah of the Prophet of Allāh. Hence, our religion is only complete by integrating the Quran and the Sunnah. It is essential to highlight the significance of the Sunnah and provide evidence to support this fact.

A- The companions of the Prophet ﷺ learned and practiced the commands of the Religion by observing the Prophet's examples.

B-   To fully understand the Quran's meanings, one must consider the Prophet's actions and statements regarding it. For instance, the Quran instructs believers to offer salah (formal prayer) and pay zakat (obligatory charity) in Surah Al-Baqarah (2:3). However, to perform these instructions correctly, we must study the methodology of the Prophet ﷺ in this regard. The Prophet ﷺ instructed his followers to "Pray as you saw me pray" and specified that 2.5% of surplus wealth, unused for a year, should be given as zakat. The Quranic verses give general information on prayer and ablution, but to understand the details of how to perform prayers, the correct way to do ablution, and what nullifies or invalidates prayer and ablution, we must refer to the Sunnah of the Prophet ﷺ. Therefore, studying the Sunnah is necessary to follow the correct methodology of performing the commands of Allāh in the Quran.[62]

2.2.12. SUNNAH DENIERS

Although the Sunnah holds great importance in Islam, there are individuals who reject it. The Prophet ﷺ forewarned his companions during his time that there would be those who hold negative views towards the Sunnah, motivated by their desire to eliminate Islamic law.

Therefore, the Messenger of Allāh alerted on this as noted in the books of Ḥadīth: On the authority of Al-Miqdam, the Prophet ﷺ said:

«يوشِكُ أَنْ يقعُدَ الرجلُ مُتَّكِئًا على أَريكَتِهِ ، يُحَدَّثُ بحديثٍ مِنْ حديثي ، فيقولُ : بينَنَا وبينَكُمْ كتابُ اللهِ ، فما وجدْنا فيه مِنْ حلالٍ اسْتَحْلَلْناهُ ، وما وجدْنا فيه مِنْ حرامٍ حرَّمْناهُ ، أَلا وإنَّ ما حرَّمَ رسولُ اللهِ مثلَ ما حرَّمَ اللهُ»

---

62 Dr. Abū Ameena Bilal Philips, Usool Al-Ḥadīth, p: 17.

> "The time will come when a man leaning on his couch will say, "Follow the Qur'an only; what you find in it as halaal, take it as ḥalāl; and what you find in it as ḥarām, take it as ḥarām." But truly, what the Messenger of God has forbidden is like what God has forbidden."[63]

The Prophet ﷺ, in light of this Ḥadīth, mentioned that there would arise a group Claiming that the Quran is the only source of guidance and that the Sunnah is a human invention with no basis in Islam. This viewpoint is known as Quranism or sometimes as Ahl al-Qur'ān (People of the Quran).

Those who deny the Sunnah often reject the authority of hadith, which are the narrations of the Prophet's sayings and actions. They argue that hadiths are unreliable and may have been fabricated by later generations. Some also claim that the Quran is sufficient for guidance and that following the Sunnah is unnecessary.

Muslims believe that the Quran and the Sunnah are interlinked and that the Sunnah is necessary for understanding the Quran and implementing its teachings in daily life.

However, it is not uncommon to witness certain members of the so-called liberal elite in our contemporary world boldly proclaim that "The Book of Allāh (the Qur'an) is sufficient, and there is no need for the Sunnah of the Prophet ﷺ." Such claims are not only in opposition to the Quran but also show a lack of respect toward the Prophet ﷺ. Moreover, they stem from deep-seated ignorance.

Embracing the Sunnah is crucial, as it can lead to salvation. In an analogy presented by Muḥammad Asad, those who hold such a view are akin to individuals who want to enter a palace but refuse to use the key that unlocks its door. As Dahhak puts it, "Paradise

---

63 Tirmidhi, sharh Ibn Al-Arabi vo:10, pp:132 Al-fat-h Al-Kabeer vol:3. Pp: 438.

and the Sunnah are intertwined, for those who follow the Sunnah in this world will be saved, just as those who enter Paradise in the Hereafter."[64]

It is unthinkable for any true Muslim to defy the teachings of the Qur'an and Sunnah. However, those who attempt to reject the Sunnah risk disbelief in the Qur'an. Allāh, the Almighty, has emphasized the significance of the Sunnah in various verses, as shown below.

يَـٰٓأَيُّهَا ٱلَّذِينَ ءَامَنُوٓاْ أَطِيعُواْ ٱللَّهَ وَأَطِيعُواْ ٱلرَّسُولَ وَأُوْلِى ٱلْأَمْرِ مِنكُمْ فَإِن تَنَـٰزَعْتُمْ فِى شَىْءٍ فَرُدُّوهُ إِلَى ٱللَّهِ وَٱلرَّسُولِ إِن كُنتُمْ تُؤْمِنُونَ بِٱللَّهِ وَٱلْيَوْمِ ٱلْأَخِرِ ذَٰلِكَ خَيْرٌ وَأَحْسَنُ تَأْوِيلًا ﴿٥٩﴾

"O YOU WHO HAVE BELIEVED, OBEY ALLĀH AND OBEY THE MESSENGER AND THOSE IN AUTHORITY AMONG YOU. AND IF YOU DISAGREE OVER ANYTHING, REFER IT TO ALLĀH AND THE MESSENGER, IF YOU SHOULD BELIEVE IN ALLĀH AND THE LAST DAY. THAT IS THE BEST [WAY] AND BEST IN RESULT". [AN-NISA' : 59.]

In the verse above, Believers are told to take the Quran and the Sunnah as their guides in matters on which they disagree.

He also said in another verse:

لَقَدْ مَنَّ ٱللَّهُ عَلَى ٱلْمُؤْمِنِينَ إِذْ بَعَثَ فِيهِمْ رَسُولًا مِّنْ أَنفُسِهِمْ يَتْلُواْ عَلَيْهِمْ ءَايَـٰتِهِۦ وَيُزَكِّيهِمْ وَيُعَلِّمُهُمُ ٱلْكِتَـٰبَ وَٱلْحِكْمَةَ وَإِن كَانُواْ مِن قَبْلُ لَفِى ضَلَـٰلٍ مُّبِينٍ ﴿١٦٤﴾

"CERTAINLY, DID ALLĀH CONFER [GREAT] FAVOR UPON THE BELIEVERS WHEN HE SENT AMONG THEM A MESSENGER FROM THEMSELVES, RECITING TO THEM HIS VERSES, PURIFYING THEM AND TEACHING THEM THE BOOK AND WISDOM, ALTHOUGH THEY HAD BEEN BEFORE IN MANIFEST ERROR." [AL-E-IMRAN : 164]

After carefully examining the various verses of the Quran and relevant Hadeeths that emphasize the importance of the Sunnah, it is crucial to understand how Muslim scholars view those who reject it in light of divine law. It should be noted that there is a

---

64 (Tafsir al-Qurtubi, XII, 365.

unanimous agreement among scholars that anyone who denies the Sunnah as evidence for Sharia law in general or rejects a Ḥadīth of the Prophet ﷺ despite knowing it to be his words is considered a disbeliever. According to scholars, such an individual has not even reached the lowest level of Islam and submission to Allāh and His Messenger.[65]

Imam Maalik ﵁, was one of the most outstanding Muslim scholars who compared the Sunnah of the Prophet ﷺ to the Ark of Noah and said: "The Sunnah of the Prophet Muḥammad ﷺ is like the Ark of Noah. Whoever embarks upon it reaches salvation, and whoever refuses it gets drowned."[66]

According to Ibn al-Wazir, ﵁, rejecting the ḥadīth of the Messenger of Allāh ﷺ when one is aware that it is his ḥadīth constitutes blatant disbelief.[67]

As-Suyooti, ﵁, said that whoever denies that the ḥadīth of the Prophet ﷺ constitutes sharia evidence, whether he denies a report that speaks of something that the Prophet ﷺ said or did if that ḥadīth fulfills the conditions stipulated in usool al-hadith, has committed an act of disbelief that puts him beyond the bounds of Islam. He will be gathered (on the Day of Resurrection) with the Jews and Christians or whomever Allāh wills of the disbelieving groups.[68]

Ibn Taymiyyah emphasized that it is obligatory to believe in whatever the Prophet narrated from Allāh, whether we understand it or not because He is a reliable truth-teller.[69]

---

65 Majmuu'ul Fatawaa, vol:3. Pp: 268,269 and 273
66 Tarikh Bagdad 3850, Tarikh ibn asakir 14, Majmuual Fatawaa, vol: 4, pp: 137.
67 Al-'Awaasim wa'l-Qawaasim, 2/274.
68 Miftah al-Jannah fi'l-Ihtijaaj bi's-Sunnah, p 14.
69 Majmuu'ul fatawa, vol:3, p:41.

Imam Al-Barbahārī stated that Allāh would not accept anything of the Sunnah from a person while he abandons some of it, and whoever rejects anything from the Sunnah has denied all of it. So, upon us is to accept it all. Leave off contending and disputing, for that is not from the Religion at all.[70]

Imam Is-haaq ibn Raahawayh, رحمه الله, stated that whoever hears a report from the Messenger of Allāh ﷺ that he accepts as being sound, then rejects it, not by way of dissimulation (when he has no choice because of a threat), is a disbeliever.[71]

In short, those various statements by scholars point to the fact that denying the Sunnah can lead to misguided practices and beliefs. Without the guidance of the Sunnah, Muslims may misunderstand or misapply the teachings of the Quran.

Allāh has obligated all His slaves to enter Islam completely by adhering firmly to its legislation and shunning anything that contradicts it. Disrespecting the Prophet (ﷺ), denying his Sunnah, undermining his status in Islam, and introducing innovation in the Religion are all forbidden in Islam.

2.2.13. SIMILARITIES BETWEEN SUNNAH DENIERS AND ORIENTALISTS

The view of the so-called Muslims who deny the Sunnah is indifferent to that of the orientalists who have criticized the Sunnah as being unreliable and unauthentic or have viewed it as a source of historical and cultural information.

---

70 Sharḥ Al-sunnah, 113-119.

71 ibid

The standard views shared by the two groups is that both level against the Sunnah on the issue of its authenticity. The sunnah deniers and Orientalists question the reliability of the hadiths, narrating the Prophet's sayings and actions. They argued that the hadiths were transmitted orally for many years before being recorded in writing, and this process may have led to errors and inaccuracies. Their views on Sunnah also suggest that hadiths were fabricated to serve particular groups' political and social agendas.

It is recognizable that the views of Muslims who deny the Sunnah and Orientalists who study Islamic texts may differ significantly in many areas concerning Islamic teachings and their approaches to interpreting the Islamic legacy.

While there may be some similarities in the criticisms leveled against the Sunnah by both groups, it is crucial to recognize that their motivations and perspectives differ vastly. Despite that difference in terms of their methodologies, one area of agreement between these two groups is their criticism of the authenticity of the Sunnah. Both groups have questioned the reliability of the hadiths, which are the narrations of the Prophet's sayings and actions. They argue that the hadiths were transmitted orally for many years before being recorded in writing, which may have led to errors and inaccuracies. Some have also suggested that hadiths were fabricated for political or social purposes.

2.2.14. THE TERM BID'AH, "INNOVATION," AND ITS DENOTATION

As opposed to Sunnah, something called bid'ah is also necessary to shed light on it " By their opposites are things made." Therefore, in this section, we will delve more into the meaning of Bid'ah and its implications.

1.Definition of bid'ah.

The definition of the Arabic word "bid'ah" (بدعة) implies the act of initiating something without any precedent. In Islamic jurisprudence, "bid'ah" refers to introducing new practices into the religion of Allāh that have no basis in the Quran or Sunnah - i.e., no evidence from Islamic scripture to support them. In fact, Allāh revealed to the Prophet Muḥammad (ﷺ) towards the end of his life that the religion of Islam had been completed, as stated in the following verse:

$$\text{ٱلْيَوْمَ أَكْمَلْتُ لَكُمْ دِينَكُمْ وَأَتْمَمْتُ عَلَيْكُمْ نِعْمَتِي وَرَضِيتُ لَكُمُ ٱلْإِسْلَٰمَ دِينًا}$$

"THIS DAY, I HAVE PERFECTED FOR YOU YOUR RELIGION AND COMPLETED MY FAVOR UPON YOU AND HAVE APPROVED FOR YOU 'ISLAM AS RELIGION." [AL-MA'IDAH : 3]

Thus, any new practices or innovations introduced into Islam's religion after the time of the Prophet Muḥammad (ﷺ) are considered "bid'ah" and are not recognized as legitimate parts of Islamic tradition. It is important for Muslims to follow the Quran and Sunnah and avoid introducing new practices that have no basis in Islamic scripture.

The verse in question unequivocally declares that Allāh has completed and perfected His Revelation, making it clear that no addition or deletion is permissible by anyone. As a result, it is imperative for every Muslim to understand that any changes in matters of worship are strictly prohibited. There are several reasons why any additions or modifications made by humans are not allowed:

A- It is a sign of disrespect towards Allāh and His Messenger. Introducing new practices implies that Allāh's religion was not perfect or complete when it was revealed or that the Prophet (ﷺ) did not convey the message as required.

B- Any human being, even one under the influence of Satan, can add something that they think is beneficial. However, these additions can ultimately lead to the degradation of the completed and perfected Religion established by Allāh.

C- All innovations in matters of religion lead to deviation, and all deviation leads to Hellfire. Therefore, it is essential to avoid any deviation in matters of worship, no matter how minor they may seem.

D- If changes are allowed, no matter how small, they will lead to further deviations that accumulate over time. This will result in a new man-made religion, not Islam, as Allāh perfected it.

However, the completion and perfection of Allāh's Revelation mean that modifications or innovations in worship matters are prohibited. Muslims must adhere strictly to the Quran and Sunnah and avoid any deviation that could lead to the creation of a new religion.

Moreover, authentic narrations of the prophet ﷺ clarify what Bid'ah means in Islam. On the authority of Aisha, the prophet ﷺ said:

«مَنْ أَحْدَثَ فِي أَمْرِنَا هَذَا مَا لَيْسَ مِنْهُ فَهُوَ رد» وَفِي رِوَايَةٍ لِمُسْلِمٍ: «مَنْ عَمِلَ عَمَلًا لَيْسَ عَلَيْهِ أَمْرُنَا فَهُوَ رَدٌّ»

" If anyone introduces in our matter something which does not belong to it, it will be rejected, »[72] The narration in Muslim says: « If anyone introduces a practice which I do not authenticate, it is to be rejected.»[73]

Sheikh Muḥammad bin Uthaymeen provided a clear and concise definition of bid'ah in accordance with Sharia law. He stated that bid'ah refers to "worshipping Allāh in ways Allāh has

---

72 al-Ṣaḥīḥ al-Bukhari 2697 and Ṣaḥīḥ al-Muslim 1718

73 Ṣaḥīḥ al-Muslim 1718

not prescribed" or "worshipping Allāh in ways that are not in accordance with the Prophet (ﷺ) or his rightly guided successors (al-Khalifa' al-raashidoon)."

The Quranic verse supports these two definitions: "Or have they partners with Allāh (false gods) who have instituted for them a religion which Allāh has not ordained?"[74] and by the ḥadīth of the Prophet (ﷺ) which advises his followers to adhere to his way (Sunnah) and the way of the rightly-guided successors who come after him; The prophet ﷺ said: "I urge you to adhere to my way (Sunnah) and the way of the rightly-guided successors (al-khulafa' al-raashidoon) who come after me. Therefore, hold fast to it and bite onto it with your eyeeeth [i.e., cling firmly to it], and beware of newly invented matters."

It is important to note that anyone who worships Allāh in a manner that Allāh has not prescribed or in a way that is not in accordance with the way of the Prophet (ﷺ) or his rightly guided successors (al-khulafa' al-Rāshidoon), is an innovator. This includes innovations in matters related to the names and attributes of Allāh, as well as His rulings and laws.

However, it is important to distinguish between innovations in matters of worship and those related to habit and custom. These are not innovations in the religious sense, and they are not the things that the Prophet (ﷺ) warned us about. Although they may be described similarly in linguistic terms, ordinary matters of habit and custom are not considered bid'ah in Islam. And there is no such thing in Islam as bid'ah ḥasanah (good innovation)."[75]

---

74 [al-Shooraa 42:21]

75 Majmoo' Fataawa Ibn 'Uthaymeen, vol. 2, p. 291.

The definition of bid'ah provided by Sheikh Hafiz al-Hakami states that the kind of bid'ah that constitutes kufr is when one denies a matter that is widely known and on which there is scholarly consensus, such as denying something obligatory or making something ḥarām ḥalāl. This type of bid'ah implies the rejection of the Qur'an and the message of Allāh. Examples include the bid'ah of the Jahamiyyah, who denied the attributes of Allāh, or the Qadariyyah, who denied the knowledge and actions of Allāh. On the other hand, the second category of bid'ah, which does not constitute kufr, does not imply a rejection of the Qur'an or anything with which Allāh sent His Messengers. Examples of this type of bid'ah include the Marwaani bid'ahs, such as delaying some of the prayers until the end of the due times or delivering the khutbah while sitting down on Fridays. Although the greatest Sahaabah denounced these practices, they were not considered as kaafirs or refused allegiance. [76]

However, according to Al-Hakami, Bid'ah may be divided into two categories: A-Bid'ah, which constitutes kufr (disbelief), and B-Bid'ah, which does not constitute kufr.

In conclusion, respect for the prophet (ﷺ) should be that we treat him with great reverence, adoration, and honor. To realize that, we should, therefore:

A- Concentrate on its study and conformity.

B- Moreover, respect for the Prophet ﷺ must be sustained and perpetuated so that future generations would adopt his teachings and thus make his followers conscious of his everlasting Message.

---

76 Ma'aarij al-Qubool, 2,503-504.

SECTION THREE

BLASPHEMY IS IMMORALITY

In Islamic jurisprudence, blasphemy refers to any verbal expression that suggests apostasy (riddah). Unlike Christianity, which restricts the term blasphemy to the mockery of God, Islam employs the term in various disciplines with different meanings, all of which aim to protect the sacred belief from violation. In the Quran, the phrase "kalimat al-kufr" is used interchangeably with blasphemy. Theologically, blasphemy overlaps with infidelity (kufr) and includes atheism, which is the deliberate rejection of God and revelation. In this sense, expressing religious views that differ from standard Islamic beliefs can also be considered blasphemous.

Additionally, blasphemy can be seen as equivalent to heresy (zandaqah), a term originating from pre-Islamic Persia and used to refer to the revolutionary teachings of Mani and Mazdak. Thus, defining blasphemy in Islam extends beyond insulting language aimed at God, the Prophet, or the revelation, to include any form of behavior deemed blasphemous.[77]

While Wikipedia's definition of blasphemy in Islam is generally accurate, it is essential to note that the concept of blasphemy in Islam goes beyond impious utterances or actions directed toward

---

77 Carl W. Ernst discusses this in his article "Blasphemy: Islamic Concept," found in Encyclopedia.com (1987).

God alone. It also includes actions or speech that are deemed disrespectful or offensive towards the Prophet Muḥammad, other Prophets, companions, or the religion of Islam as a whole. This can include denying any of the fundamental beliefs of the religion, insulting an angel, or maintaining that God had a son. Overall, the concept of blasphemy in Islam encompasses a broad range of actions and behaviors that are seen as disrespectful toward the religion and its beliefs.

Blasphemy in Islam encompasses disrespect towards Islam and all its principles and values in general. However, the most severe form of blasphemy is when it relates to Allāh, the Prophet ﷺ, and his companions. Understanding Islamic rulings and how Muslim scholars view such acts is important.

Thus, we will have an insight into the rulings of Islam on that and how Muslim scholars view it.

2.3.1. INSULTING ALLĀH AND THE MESSENGER IS IMMORAL

2.3.1.1. INSULTING ALLĀH (ﷻ)

As mentioned earlier, demonstrating respect for Allāh encompasses various aspects, such as believing in His existence, affirming His Oneness, and refraining from associating any partners with Him. This respect can be expressed through venerating all His sacred symbols, remaining vigilant in upholding His boundaries, and speaking positively about Him and the Religion He has bestowed upon us through His prophet (ﷺ).

On the contrary, insulting or speaking insolently about Allāh or His messenger, displaying contemptuous rudeness, or showing any form of disrespect that contradicts our faith or may lead to disbelief is strictly warned against in Islam. This is because belief in Allāh and His messenger is rooted in respect, reverence, submission to Allāh, and obedience to both. Therefore, any form of disrespect towards Allāh or the prophet (ﷺ), whether through words or actions, undermines one's faith and nullifies Islam, consequently placing a person outside the fold of Islam.

Allāh invites humanity to acknowledge Him and censures those who engage in polytheism by neglecting His attributes, lordship, and obligation to recognize His authority and rights over His servants. Hence, disregarding Allāh, His position, and His rights constitutes a blatant act of blasphemy and disbelief.

In the Holy Quran, Allāh says:

وَمَا قَدَرُوا۟ ٱللَّهَ حَقَّ قَدْرِهِۦٓ إِذْ قَالُوا۟ مَآ أَنزَلَ ٱللَّهُ عَلَىٰ بَشَرٍ مِّن شَىْءٍۗ قُلْ مَنْ أَنزَلَ ٱلْكِتَٰبَ ٱلَّذِى جَآءَ بِهِۦ مُوسَىٰ نُورًا وَهُدًى لِّلنَّاسِۖ تَجْعَلُونَهُۥ قَرَاطِيسَ تُبْدُونَهَا وَتُخْفُونَ كَثِيرًاۖ وَعُلِّمْتُم مَّا لَمْ تَعْلَمُوٓا۟ أَنتُمْ وَلَآ ءَابَآؤُكُمْۖ قُلِ ٱللَّهُۖ ثُمَّ ذَرْهُمْ فِى خَوْضِهِمْ يَلْعَبُونَ ﴿٩١﴾

"AND THEY DID NOT APPRAISE ALLĀH WITH TRUE APPRAISAL WHEN THEY SAID, " ALLĀH DID NOT REVEAL TO A HUMAN BEING ANYTHING." SAY, "WHO REVEALED THE SCRIPTURE THAT MOSES BROUGHT AS LIGHT AND GUIDANCE TO THE PEOPLE? YOU [JEWS] MAKE IT INTO PAGES, DISCLOSING [SOME OF] IT AND CONCEALING MUCH. AND YOU WERE TAUGHT THAT WHICH YOU KNEW NOT - NEITHER YOU NOR YOUR FATHERS." SAY, " ALLĀH [REVEALED IT]." THEN LEAVE THEM IN THEIR [EMPTY] DISCOURSE, AMUSING THEMSELVES." [AL-AN'AM : 91]

Again, it reads in the Quran:

وَمَا قَدَرُوا۟ ٱللَّهَ حَقَّ قَدْرِهِۦ وَٱلْأَرْضُ جَمِيعًا قَبْضَتُهُۥ يَوْمَ ٱلْقِيَٰمَةِ وَٱلسَّمَٰوَٰتُ مَطْوِيَّٰتٌۢ بِيَمِينِهِۦۚ سُبْحَٰنَهُۥ وَتَعَٰلَىٰ عَمَّا يُشْرِكُونَ ﴿٦٧﴾

"THEY HAVE NOT APPRAISED ALLĀH WITH TRUE APPRAISAL, WHILE THE EARTH ENTIRELY WILL BE [WITHIN] HIS GRIP ON THE DAY OF RESURRECTION, AND THE HEAVENS WILL BE FOLDED IN HIS RIGHT HAND. EXALTED IS HE AND HIGH ABOVE WHAT THEY ASSOCIATE WITH HIM." [AZ-ZUMAR : 67.]

In the verses mentioned above, Allāh emphasizes that the polytheists failed to honestly acknowledge and glorify Him in accordance with His immense greatness. The first verse highlights how the disbelievers claimed that Allāh had not sent any revelations to any human being. This assertion aimed to deny the messages and Messengers of Allāh, thereby providing them with an excuse for not understanding the purpose of their creation.

Moreover, the second verse reveals that instead of recognizing Allāh's greatness and worshipping Him alone, the polytheists committed the grave error of associating partners with Him in worship. These partners, however, possess deficient qualities and abilities. They are incapable of bringing about any benefit or harm, granting or withholding anything, or having ownership over anything. Yet, the polytheists consider these created beings, who are fundamentally lacking, as equal to the Creator—the Almighty Lord—whose magnificence is evident and whose power is irresistible. On the Day of Resurrection, the entire earth will be within the grasp of al-Raḥmān (the Most Merciful), and even the vast heavens will be folded up in His right hand. Therefore, anyone who regards anyone or anything as equal to Allāh fails to exalt Him as He truly deserves. Such a person engages in the greatest injustice.

Allāh calls upon humanity not to fall behind other creatures in recognizing and worshipping Him as their Lord. The heavens and the angels glorify Allāh with a sense of awe and reverence whenever His name is mentioned. It is incumbent upon humankind to demonstrate similar devotion and admiration for Allāh, acknowledging His greatness and submitting to His will.

تَكَادُ ٱلسَّمَٰوَٰتُ يَتَفَطَّرْنَ مِن فَوْقِهِنَّ وَٱلْمَلَٰٓئِكَةُ يُسَبِّحُونَ بِحَمْدِ رَبِّهِمْ وَيَسْتَغْفِرُونَ لِمَن فِي ٱلْأَرْضِ أَلَآ إِنَّ ٱللَّهَ هُوَ ٱلْغَفُورُ ٱلرَّحِيمُ ۝

"THE HEAVENS ALMOST BREAK FROM ABOVE THEM, AND THE ANGELS EXALT [ALLĀH] WITH PRAISE OF THEIR LORD AND ASK FORGIVENESS FOR THOSE ON EARTH. UNQUESTIONABLY, IT IS ALLĀH WHO IS THE FORGIVING, THE MERCIFUL" [AL-SHURA : 5]

Quranic verses keep on warning humanity against being disrespectful and abusive to Allāh and His messenger. For example, the following verse clearly states the punishment they deserve for those who attempt to humiliate them by violating their teachings:

إِنَّ ٱلَّذِينَ يُؤْذُونَ ٱللَّهَ وَرَسُولَهُۥ لَعَنَهُمُ ٱللَّهُ فِى ٱلدُّنْيَا وَٱلْءَاخِرَةِ وَأَعَدَّ لَهُمْ عَذَابًا مُّهِينًا ﴿٥٧﴾

"INDEED, THOSE WHO ABUSE ALLĀH AND HIS MESSENGER - ALLĀH HAS CURSED THEM IN THIS WORLD AND THE HEREAFTER AND PREPARED FOR THEM A HUMILIATING PUNISHMENT." [AHZAB : 57.]

The term "abuse" used in the verse has a broader meaning than just "insult." While "insult" refers to intentionally rude actions or speech, "abuse" encompasses improper treatment, wrongful practices, or any action that goes against the sanctity of Allāh's symbols revered in Islam, such as the Quran, the Prophet, the angels, and places of worship. In various English translations of the Quran, commentators may use verbs like "annoy," "cause annoyance," or "trouble" instead of "abuse." Although the wording may vary, the intention is to highlight the same point: any action that violates Allāh's sanctuaries and religious symbols held in high esteem by Islam is considered an offense and annoyance to Allāh.

Abusing Allāh can manifest in acts such as burning or disrespecting the Quran, mocking the Prophet, or showing contempt towards any religious symbol. All such acts constitute abuse and offense towards Allāh, causing Him annoyance.

Abūl-Ala Maududi, in his commentary on the verse, explains that "to trouble Allāh" implies two things: first, disobedience towards Allāh by adopting an attitude of disbelief, associating partners with Him, or rejecting His laws, and second, troubling His Messenger, as obedience to the Messenger is obedience to Allāh, and opposition to the Messenger is opposition to Allāh.[78]

It is important to note that humans are incapable of truly offending or harming Allāh. However, what causes annoyance or trouble to Allāh is what affects His beloved ones, such as the Prophet and his companions. When Allāh honors and praises the Prophet, it is deeply inappropriate and absurd for humans to offend him. While humans cannot truly offend or harm Allāh, the expression emphasizes the sensitivity towards any offense committed against the Prophet, considering it an offense against Allāh Himself.[79]

Undoubtedly, insulting Allāh is the gravest and most detestable form of verbal nullification of faith. Whether the offender accepts their act as de-Islamizing or not, insulting Allāh results in de-Islamization. In that case, it is logical to consider that cursing Allāh and His Prophet (ﷺ) also leads to de-Islamization. On the authority of Abū Hurayrah ؓ, He reported that the Prophet (may Allāh's peace and blessings be upon him) said that Allāh said:

«قالَ اللَّهُ: كَذَّبَني ابنُ آدَمَ ولَمْ يَكُنْ له ذلكَ، وشَتَمَني ولَمْ يَكُنْ له ذلكَ، فأمَّا تَكْذيبُهُ إيَّايَ فقَوْلُهُ: لَنْ يُعِيدَني، كما بَدَأني، وليسَ أوَّلُ الخَلْقِ بأهْوَنَ عَلَيَّ مِن إعادَتِهِ، وأمَّا شَتْمُهُ إيَّايَ فقَوْلُهُ: اتَّخَذَ اللَّهُ ولَدًا وأنا الأحَدُ الصَّمَدُ، لَمْ ألِدْ ولَمْ أُولَدْ، ولَمْ يَكُنْ لي كُفْئًا أحَدٌ»

"The son of Adam tells a lie against Me, and he has no right to do so, and he insults Me and has no right to do so. His lying against Me is his saying that I will not resurrect him as I created him for the first time. The first creation was not easier for Me than resurrecting him again (they are both easy for Me). His

---

78 Tafheemul Quran, p. 426

79 Zilalul Quran, Surah Al-Ahzab

insult to Me is his saying that Allāh has begotten a son, while I am The One, The Eternal Refuge, Who begets not nor was He begotten, and there is none like unto Me.[80]

In a sacred narration, the Prophet Muḥammad (may Allāh's peace and blessings be upon him) conveys to us a message from Allāh addressing two categories of people.

The first category consists of those who deny the resurrection after death. This category includes polytheists, idol worshippers, and Christians who falsely claimed things about Allāh that they should not have. Denying the resurrection is equivalent to disbelief and denial of Allāh's power. By denying the resurrection, they essentially claim that Allāh will not bring mankind back to life after creating them from nothing. However, Allāh refutes their claim by emphasizing that starting creation from nothingness and resurrecting the dead are equally easy for Him. In fact, resurrection is often considered easier since the basic components of the body already exist.

The second category, relevant to the discourse, pertains to those who insult Allāh by attributing imperfections to Him, ascribing a son to Him, or claiming that angels are His daughters. According to the Hadith, insulting Allāh by human beings is to attribute offspring to Him. All such claims constitute a blatant insult to Allāh because they involve attributing imperfections and deficiencies to Him and treating Him as if He were a creation.

In the Quran, Allāh prohibits Muslims from insulting the gods of the polytheists, as doing so may lead to Allāh being offended or insulted. He said:

---

80 Al-Bukhari 4974 and Al-Nasa' 2078

وَلَا تَسُبُّوا۟ ٱلَّذِينَ يَدْعُونَ مِن دُونِ ٱللَّهِ فَيَسُبُّوا۟ ٱللَّهَ عَدْوًۢا بِغَيْرِ عِلْمٍ ۗ كَذَٰلِكَ زَيَّنَّا لِكُلِّ أُمَّةٍ عَمَلَهُمْ ثُمَّ إِلَىٰ رَبِّهِم مَّرْجِعُهُمْ فَيُنَبِّئُهُم بِمَا كَانُوا۟ يَعْمَلُونَ ﴿١٠٨﴾

"AND DO NOT INSULT THOSE THEY INVOKE OTHER THAN ALLĀH, LEST THEY INSULT ALLĀH IN ENMITY WITHOUT KNOWLEDGE. THUS WE HAVE MADE PLEASING TO EVERY COMMUNITY THEIR DEEDS. THEN TO THEIR LORD IS THEIR RETURN, AND HE WILL INFORM THEM ABOUT WHAT THEY USED TO DO". [AL-AN'AM : 108]

The previous verse commands believers not to cause Allāh to be insulted. While idol worship is considered shirk (polytheism) and forbidden in Islam, insulting these idols could provoke anger from the polytheists who consider them gods. In retaliation for their gods being insulted, the polytheists might insult Allāh in return.

To prevent harmful consequences that may arise from such actions, the verse strongly warns believers against engaging in insulting the idols. This verse provides evidence for the Sharī'a principle in Islamic jurisprudence, which states that means are judged by the outcomes they lead to, and if a permissible means leads to evil, it becomes impermissible.

In his commentary on the verse, Imam Ibn Kathir explains that Allāh and His Messenger prohibit believers from insulting the gods of the idolaters, even if there may be some truth in their claims. This is because such insults could lead to greater harm, as the polytheists would retaliate by insulting the God of Muslims, while Allāh is the Lord, where there is no other god besides Him.[81]

However, scholars have affirmed that this ruling remains valid for the Muslim ummah in all circumstances. When the disbelievers are in a position of strength, and there is a fear that they may insult Islam, the Prophet, or Allāh, it is not permissible for a Muslim

---

81 Tafsir Ibn Kathir, vol. 3, page 272.

to insult their crosses, their religion, or their churches, and they should not engage in any actions that may lead to such insults. This is considered provoking others to sin. [82]

Ibn al-Qayyim summarizes the concept of respecting Allāh by stating that "the essence and spirit of worship are to love and venerate Allāh."[83]

2.3.1.2. INSULTING THE PROPHET ﷺ

As Muslims, we should hold the Prophet Muḥammad in the highest esteem and love him more than anything else in this world. He is a role model for all Muslims and is considered the best of all creation. Making caricatures or any disrespectful or insulting depiction of the Prophet Muḥammad (ﷺ) is viewed as highly offensive and disrespectful.

The act of making caricatures or any other form of derogatory depiction of the Prophet Muḥammad is seen as a direct insult to his person and character. Muslims view such actions as a violation of the dignity of the Prophet and as an attack on their faith and beliefs.

It is important to note that Islam strongly condemns any disrespectful act concerning the prophet ﷺ. Islam emphasizes the importance of respecting and honoring the Prophet Muḥammad, as he is the final Prophet of God, and his teachings and actions serve as guidance for Muslims. Sharī'a affirms that insulting the Prophet is equivalent to insulting God, and it is a grave sin with severe consequences.

---

82 Tafsīr al-Qurtubi, 7/61.

83 Madarij al-Salikeen, 2/464.

However, Muslim scholars have expressed their stances regarding the act of insulting Allāh (ﷻ) or His Prophet (ﷺ). Ibn Taymiyah, a renowned scholar, authored a comprehensive treatise titled "The Unsheathed Sword against the One who Insults the Messenger" (الصارم المسلول على شاتم الرسول). This work delves into the concept of blasphemy, particularly regarding insults directed at the Prophet Muḥammad (ﷺ), and provides detailed information on Sharia's stance on this matter.

To support his arguments, Ibn Taymiyah drew upon various sources, most notably events documented in the literature on the biography of the Prophet (ﷺ), where he sternly dealt with those who insulted him. In his treatise, he contended that anyone who insulted the Prophet (ﷺ) had committed a hadd crime, which refers to offenses that have prescribed punishments in Islamic law. According to Ibn Taymiyah, such offenders could not escape the death penalty through repentance or conversion. He supplemented his arguments by citing statements from early scholars of the Ḥanbali, Mālikī, and Shāfi'i schools, with Qadi Iyad's "Shifa'" being an essential reference in the discourse.[84]

One of the most substantial pieces of evidence supporting the death penalty for blasphemy is the report attributed to Ibn Abbas, a companion of the Prophet. This narration is often cited as a reference to justify the death penalty as a punishment for blasphemy. Ibn 'Abbas (ﷺ) narrated :

---

84   Ibnu Taymiyah, Al-Sarim Al-Maslool Alaa Shaatim Al-Rasool, 2/13-16

«أَنَّ أَعْمَى كَانَتْ لَهُ أُمُّ وَلَدٍ تَشْتُمُ النَّبِيَّ ﷺ وَتَقَعُ فِيهِ، فَيَنْهَاهَا فَلَا تَنْتَهِي، وَيَزْجُرُهَا فَلَا تَنْزَجِرُ، فَلَمَّا كَانَ ذَاتَ لَيْلَةٍ جَعَلَتْ تَقَعُ فِي النَّبِيِّ ﷺ وَتَشْتُمُهُ، فَأَخَذَ الْمِعْوَلَ فَجَعَلَهُ وَاتَّكَأَ عَلَيْهَا فَقَتَلَهَا، فَلَمَّا أَصْبَحَ ذُكِرَ ذَلِكَ لِلنَّبِيِّ ﷺ، فَجَمَعَ النَّاسَ، فَقَالَ: أَنْشُدُ اللهَ رَجُلًا فَعَلَ مَا فَعَلَ، لِي عَلَيْهِ حَقٌّ إِلَّا قَامَ، فَقَامَ الْأَعْمَى يَتَخَطَّى النَّاسَ، وَهُوَ يَتَدَلْدَلُ حَتَّى قَعَدَ بَيْنَ يَدَيِ النَّبِيِّ ﷺ، فَقَالَ: يَا رَسُولَ اللهِ ﷺ، أَنَا صَاحِبُهَا، كَانَتْ تَشْتُمُكَ وَتَقَعُ فِيكَ، فَأَنْهَاهَا فَلَا تَنْتَهِي، وَأَزْجُرُهَا فَلَا تَنْزَجِرُ، وَلِي مِنْهَا ابْنَانِ مِثْلُ اللُّؤْلُؤَتَيْنِ، وَكَانَتْ بِي رَفِيقَةً، فَلَمَّا كَانَ الْبَارِحَةَ جَعَلَتْ تَشْتُمُكَ وَتَقَعُ فِيكَ، فَأَخَذْتُ الْمِعْوَلَ فَوَضَعْتُهُ وَاتَّكَأْتُ عَلَيْهِ حَتَّى قَتَلْتُهَا، فَقَالَ النَّبِيُّ ﷺ: أَلَا اشْهَدُوا أَنَّ دَمَهَا هَدَرٌ»

"A blind man had a pregnant slave who used to abuse the Messenger of Allāh ﷺ and defame him. The blind man forbade her, but she did not stop. One night she began to slander the Prophet ﷺ, so he took an axe, placed it on her belly, pressed it, and killed her. The Messenger of Allāh ﷺ was told about it, and thereupon he said, "Oh, people! Be witnesses that no Diya is to be paid for her blood."[85]

In his book Al-Shifa, Al-Qadi Iyad states, "Certainly, a blasphemer against Allāh, Exalted be He, from among Muslims shall be deemed a disbeliever, and killing him shall be declared lawful."[86]

In his book Al-Kafi, Ibn Qudama mentions, "Apostasy occurs by either rejecting the testimony or by insulting Allāh or the Messenger."[87]

Ibn Taymiyah, after quoting various scholars of the past, stated, "Blasphemy against Allāh or His Messenger ﷺ is an act that nullifies faith, both outwardly and inwardly, whether the blasphemer knows that this is ḥarām (forbidden), deems it ḥalāl (permissible), or is not aware of the ruling at all."[88]

Ishaq bin Rahawyh is quoted as saying, "Muslims have consensus that whoever insults Allāh or insults His Messenger or anything from what Allāh has revealed or kills a prophet, then such a person is a disbeliever, even if he affirms everything that Allāh revealed" (The Unsheathed Sword against the One who Insults the Messenger)[89]

---

85 Related by Abū Dawud with a trustworthy chain of narrators. Abū Dawud, 4361

86 Al-Shifa 2/582.

87 Al-Kafi 4/60.

88 Ibid: 512.

89 ibid

SECTION FOUR

ETIQUETTE AND BEHAVIOUR OF THE BELIEVER TOWARDS THE PROPHET'S COMPANIONS ﷺ

2.4.1. THE STATUS OF THE COMPANIONS IN ISLAM

One way to demonstrate our love for Allāh and His Prophet ﷺ is by showing respect and love towards the companions of the Prophet ﷺ. These men and women embraced the message of Islam in its earliest days, endured many hardships, and lived with and around the Prophet ﷺ.

We should be grateful to these pioneers of Islam who supported and sacrificed for the cause of the religion's flourishing and survival.

May Allāh be pleased with the companions who were the pioneers of Islam and stood by the Messenger ﷺ since Islam's inception and sacrificed their lives to confront all its hardships and challenging circumstances dominant at that same period. They have relentlessly fought for the cause of Islam to flourish and survive on this planet. Through that tireless struggle, they have dared to successfully record and transmit that golden legacy to the generations after them. Their dedication has ensured that the Quran and Sunnah remain untainted from the first day of revelation; therefore, we should hold the companions in high regard and show them our love, respect, and appreciation for being the cause that the Quran and Sunnah are still impeccable to this day.

To do this, we should refrain from expressing ill feelings towards them and avoid insulting or speaking poorly of them. Instead, we should pray for them, speak of them in the best possible manner, and think of them with the utmost admiration and gratitude. Our attitude towards them should reflect our deep appreciation for their unwavering commitment to the Prophet ﷺ and his message.

Ultimately, by honoring the companions of the Prophet ﷺ, we honor the legacy of the Prophet ﷺ himself and reinforce our love and devotion to Allāh.

In this regard Allāh says:

وَٱلَّذِينَ جَآءُو مِنۢ بَعْدِهِمْ يَقُولُونَ رَبَّنَا ٱغْفِرْ لَنَا وَلِإِخْوَٰنِنَا ٱلَّذِينَ سَبَقُونَا بِٱلْإِيمَٰنِ وَلَا تَجْعَلْ فِي قُلُوبِنَا غِلًّا لِّلَّذِينَ ءَامَنُوا۟ رَبَّنَآ إِنَّكَ رَءُوفٌ رَّحِيمٌ ﴿١٠﴾

"AND [THERE IS A SHARE FOR] THOSE WHO CAME AFTER THEM, SAYING, "OUR LORD, FORGIVE US AND OUR BROTHERS WHO PRECEDED US IN FAITH AND PUT NOT IN OUR HEARTS [ANY] RESENTMENT TOWARD THOSE WHO HAVE BELIEVED. OUR LORD, INDEED, YOU ARE KIND AND MERCIFUL." [AL-ḤASHR : 10]

Moreover, in Hadith books, we find that the Prophet ﷺ set loving companions as a criterion to measure the depth of one's faith instead of hating them, which is a sign of hypocrisy. Therefore, our love and respect for the companions are crucial in strengthening and assuring our faith. He said in an authentic narration on the authority of Anas:

«آيَةُ الْإِيمَانِ حُبُّ الْأَنْصَارِ، وَآيَةُ النِّفَاقِ بُغْضُ الْأَنْصَارِ»

"The sign of faith is the love of the Ansar, and the sign of hypocrisy is the hatred of Ansar." [Al-Bukhari 3499, Muslim 108]

We should therefore focus on their merits and virtues and remain silent about the mistakes they made and about any other quarrel and conflict that occurred between them. In this sense, the Prophet ﷺ said in a narration reported by Abū Sa'i Al-Khudari:

«لَا تَسُبُّوا أَحَدًا مِن أَصْحَابِي، فَإِنَّ أَحَدَكُمْ لَو أَنْفَقَ مِثْلَ أُحُدٍ ذَهَبًا، مَا أَدْرَكَ مُدَّ أَحَدِهِمْ، وَلَا نَصِيفَهُ»

"Do not abuse my Companions, for if any of you were to spend gold equal to (mountain of) Uhud in charity, it would not equal a handful of one of them or even half of that." **[Al-Bukhari vol:4,195].]**

2.4.2. VIRTUES OF THE COMPANIONS IN ISLAM

The virtues of the companions cannot be counted and are also unmatchable in such a way that the entire Ummah cannot weigh them in deeds, let alone their status in Islam and the heart of the prophet ﷺ.

The coming seven verses praise their extraordinary sacrifice, struggle, and migration for the sake of Allāh and His Prophet ﷺ, leaving behind their properties and families to attain Allāh's pleasure of them. Allāh said:

A-

وَإِذْ يَعِدُكُمُ اللَّهُ إِحْدَى الطَّآئِفَتَيْنِ أَنَّهَا لَكُمْ وَتَوَدُّونَ أَنَّ غَيْرَ ذَاتِ الشَّوْكَةِ تَكُونُ لَكُمْ وَيُرِيدُ اللَّهُ أَن يُحِقَّ الْحَقَّ بِكَلِمَٰتِهِۦ وَيَقْطَعَ دَابِرَ الْكَٰفِرِينَ ۝

"BUT THOSE WHO HAVE BELIEVED AND EMIGRATED AND FOUGHT IN THE CAUSE OF ALLĀH AND THOSE WHO GAVE SHELTER AND AIDED - IT IS THEY WHO ARE THE BELIEVERS, TRULY. FOR THEM IS FORGIVENESS AND NOBLE PROVISION". **[AL-ANFAL : 7]**

B-

لَٰكِنِ الرَّسُولُ وَالَّذِينَ ءَامَنُوا مَعَهُ جَٰهَدُوا بِأَمْوَٰلِهِمْ وَأَنفُسِهِمْ وَأُوْلَٰئِكَ لَهُمُ الْخَيْرَٰتُ وَأُوْلَٰئِكَ هُمُ الْمُفْلِحُونَ ۝

أَعَدَّ ٱللَّهُ لَهُمْ جَنَّٰتٍ تَجْرِى مِن تَحْتِهَا ٱلْأَنْهَٰرُ خَٰلِدِينَ فِيهَا ۚ ذَٰلِكَ ٱلْفَوْزُ ٱلْعَظِيمُ ﴿٨٩﴾

"BUT THE MESSENGER AND THOSE WHO BELIEVED WITH HIM FOUGHT WITH THEIR WEALTH AND THEIR LIVES. THOSE WILL HAVE [ALL THAT IS] GOOD, AND IT IS THOSE WHO ARE THE SUCCESSFUL. ALLĀH HAS PREPARED FOR THEM GARDENS BENEATH WHICH RIVERS FLOW, WHEREIN THEY WILL ABIDE ETERNALLY. THAT IS THE GREAT ATTAINMENT".

[AT-TAWBAH : 88-89]

C-

وَٱلسَّٰبِقُونَ ٱلْأَوَّلُونَ مِنَ ٱلْمُهَٰجِرِينَ وَٱلْأَنصَارِ وَٱلَّذِينَ ٱتَّبَعُوهُم بِإِحْسَٰنٍ رَّضِىَ ٱللَّهُ عَنْهُمْ وَرَضُوا۟ عَنْهُ وَأَعَدَّ لَهُمْ جَنَّٰتٍ تَجْرِى تَحْتَهَا ٱلْأَنْهَٰرُ خَٰلِدِينَ فِيهَآ أَبَدًا ۚ ذَٰلِكَ ٱلْفَوْزُ ٱلْعَظِيمُ ﴿١٠٠﴾

"AND THE FIRST FORERUNNERS [IN THE FAITH] AMONG THE MUHAJIREEN AND THE ANSAR AND THOSE WHO FOLLOWED THEM WITH GOOD CONDUCT - ALLĀH IS PLEASED WITH THEM AND THEY ARE PLEASED WITH HIM, AND HE HAS PREPARED FOR THEM GARDENS BENEATH WHICH RIVERS FLOW, WHEREIN THEY WILL ABIDE FOREVER. THAT IS THE GREAT ATTAINMENT". **[AT-TAWBAH : 100]**

D-

مِّنَ ٱلْمُؤْمِنِينَ رِجَالٌ صَدَقُوا۟ مَا عَٰهَدُوا۟ ٱللَّهَ عَلَيْهِ ۖ فَمِنْهُم مَّن قَضَىٰ نَحْبَهُۥ وَمِنْهُم مَّن يَنتَظِرُ ۖ وَمَا بَدَّلُوا۟ تَبْدِيلًا ﴿٢٣﴾

"AMONG THE BELIEVERS ARE MEN TRUE TO WHAT THEY PROMISED ALLĀH. AMONG THEM IS HE WHO HAS FULFILLED HIS VOW [TO THE DEATH], AND AMONG THEM IS HE WHO AWAITS [HIS CHANCE]. AND THEY DID NOT ALTER [THE TERMS OF THEIR COMMITMENT] BY ANY ALTERATION" **[AL-AHZAB : 23]**

E-

لِلْفُقَرَآءِ ٱلْمُهَٰجِرِينَ ٱلَّذِينَ أُخْرِجُوا۟ مِن دِيَٰرِهِمْ وَأَمْوَٰلِهِمْ يَبْتَغُونَ فَضْلًا مِّنَ ٱللَّهِ وَرِضْوَٰنًا وَيَنصُرُونَ ٱللَّهَ وَرَسُولَهُۥٓ ۚ أُو۟لَٰٓئِكَ هُمُ ٱلصَّٰدِقُونَ ﴿٨﴾

"FOR THE POOR EMIGRANTS WHO WERE EXPELLED FROM THEIR HOMES AND THEIR PROPERTIES, SEEKING BOUNTY FROM ALLĀH AND [HIS] APPROVAL AND SUPPORTING ALLĀH AND HIS MESSENGER, [THERE IS ALSO A SHARE]. THOSE ARE THE TRUTHFUL".

[AL-HASHR : 8]

F-

لَا يَسْتَوِى مِنكُم مَّنْ أَنفَقَ مِن قَبْلِ ٱلْفَتْحِ وَقَٰتَلَ أُوْلَٰٓئِكَ أَعْظَمُ دَرَجَةً مِّنَ ٱلَّذِينَ أَنفَقُواْ مِنۢ بَعْدُ وَقَٰتَلُواْ وَكُلًّا وَعَدَ ٱللَّهُ ٱلْحُسْنَىٰ وَٱللَّهُ بِمَا تَعْمَلُونَ خَبِيرٌ ﴿١٠﴾

"NOT EQUAL AMONG YOU ARE THOSE WHO SPENT BEFORE THE CONQUEST [OF MAKKAH] AND FOUGHT [AND THOSE WHO DID SO AFTER IT]. THOSE ARE GREATER IN DEGREE THAN THEY WHO SPENT AFTERWARDS AND FOUGHT. BUT TO ALL ALLĀH HAS PROMISED THE BEST [REWARD]. AND ALLĀH, WITH WHAT YOU DO, IS ACQUAINTED". [AL-ḤADID : 10]

G-

۞ لَّقَدْ رَضِىَ ٱللَّهُ عَنِ ٱلْمُؤْمِنِينَ إِذْ يُبَايِعُونَكَ تَحْتَ ٱلشَّجَرَةِ فَعَلِمَ مَا فِى قُلُوبِهِمْ فَأَنزَلَ ٱلسَّكِينَةَ عَلَيْهِمْ وَأَثَٰبَهُمْ فَتْحًا قَرِيبًا ﴿١٨﴾

"CERTAINLY, WAS ALLĀH PLEASED WITH THE BELIEVERS WHEN THEY PLEDGED ALLEGIANCE TO YOU, [O MUḤAMMAD], UNDER THE TREE, AND HE KNEW WHAT WAS IN THEIR HEARTS, SO HE SENT DOWN TRANQUILITY UPON THEM AND REWARDED THEM WITH AN IMMINENT CONQUEST" [AL-FATḤ : 18]

The above verses and numerous prophetic traditions bear witness to Allāh's everlasting honor and respect for the noble companions. The Quranic verses and Hadiths highlight their virtues and how Allāh exclusively gave them His endless forgiveness, pleasure, and special praise. These unchangeable divine verses, which Allāh commands us to recite, refute the beliefs of any extremist who claims that the companions became apostates after the Prophet's death ﷺ. They also reject the opinions of those who deny their righteousness and piety. We recite these verses repeatedly, day in and day out, in all situations, to acknowledge their elevated rank and status with Allāh. We study them to derive lessons that inspire us to emulate their examples, hoping we will reunite them in paradise on the Day of Judgement.

2.4.3. SHIA'S VIEW OF THE COMPANIONS.

Honoring and respecting the companions of the Prophet ﷺ is significant due to the presence of incorrect and slanderous beliefs about them among some Shi'a communities. These individuals believe that spreading false information and cursing the companions will lead to rewards and proximity to Allāh, which is contradictory to the values upheld by the larger Islamic community. It is perplexing that some Shi'a elevate their Imams to the status of deities while showing little to no respect for the companions, who were among the most righteous people on earth. This belief among certain Shi'a groups is not a fabrication but rather a reality that can be found in their own reliable references.

As Muḥammad Malala pointed out in his book, "The primary and authentic references of the Shi'a are filled with accusations and disparagements against the companions. This demonstrates the hatred and malice that the Shi'a harbor towards our beloved companions. Their blind attacks on the transmitters of Islam aim to destroy Islam because it reaches us through companions. To slander them is to slander the Sunnah of our beloved Prophet. Thus, slandering the narrators is equivalent to slandering the narration itself, as these people conveyed the Sunnah of the Prophet, the second source of guidance after the noble Qur'an. [90]

A few quotations from their sources -al-Kafi by al-kuleini- support the above-said fact.

On the authority of Ali ibn Jaafar as reported in al-Kafi, Shi'as claim that "the companions were deprived of the bounty of Īmān and its sweetness."[91]

---

90 Muḥammad Malala, "Shi'a and the Interpolation of Quran" by Pp:56-59
91 *al Kafi* (vol. 2 pg. 400)

'Abd al-Raḥmān Ibn Kathīr narrates that Abū 'Abdallah (al Sadiq) mentioned, regarding the verse:

$$\text{إِنَّ الَّذِينَ ءَامَنُوا ثُمَّ كَفَرُوا ثُمَّ ءَامَنُوا ثُمَّ كَفَرُوا ثُمَّ ازْدَادُوا كُفْرًا لَّمْ يَكُنِ اللَّهُ لِيَغْفِرَ لَهُمْ وَلَا لِيَهْدِيَهُمْ سَبِيلًا ﴿١٣٧﴾}$$

"INDEED, THOSE WHO HAVE BELIEVED THEN DISBELIEVED, THEN BELIEVED, THEN DISBELIEVED, AND THEN INCREASED IN DISBELIEF — NEVER WILL ALLĀH FORGIVE THEM."

[AN NISA : 137]

He said: "This verse was revealed concerning so (Abū Bakr), and so ('Umar) and so ('Uthman), they believed in the prophet ﷺ initially, then disbelieved when the wilayah was presented to them when the prophet ﷺ said: 'whoever's mawla I am then 'Ali is his mawla,' then they believed by taking the pledge with Amir al Mu'minin then disbelieved when the prophet (ﷺ) passed away. So, they did not adhere to the pledge, and they increased in disbelief by attacking those who took his pledge, so nothing of belief was left in them".[92]

From Abū 'Abdallah (al Sadiq) under the commentary of the verse:

$$\text{إِنَّ الَّذِينَ ارْتَدُّوا عَلَىٰ أَدْبَارِهِم مِّن بَعْدِ مَا تَبَيَّنَ لَهُمُ الْهُدَى}$$

"INDEED, THOSE WHO REVERTED BACK (TO DISBELIEF) AFTER GUIDANCE HAD BECOME CLEAR TO THEM." [MUHAMMAD : 25]

He said: This refers to so (Abū Bakr) and so ('Umar) and so ('Uthman). They reverted back to disbelief by leaving the wilayah of 'Ali Amir al Mu'minin.[93] It is also reported on the second page from Abū 'Abdallah (al Sadiq) under the commentary of the verse:

---

92 Ibid, Vol: 2, pg. 387. '

93 ibid, p,388

وَهُدُوٓاْ إِلَى ٱلطَّيِّبِ مِنَ ٱلْقَوْلِ وَهُدُوٓاْ إِلَىٰ صِرَٰطِ ٱلْحَمِيدِ

"And they had been guided (in worldly life) to good speech, and they were guided to the path of the praiseworthy.» [AL-HAJJ : 24][94]

He said: "This refers to Hamzah, Jaafar, 'Ubaidah, Salman, Abū Dhar, al Miqdad ibn al Aswad and 'Ammar, they were guided to Amir al Mu'minin 'alayh al Salam. And when Allāh said:

وَلَٰكِنَّ ٱللَّهَ حَبَّبَ إِلَيْكُمُ ٱلْإِيمَٰنَ وَزَيَّنَهُۥ فِى قُلُوبِكُمْ وَكَرَّهَ إِلَيْكُمُ ٱلْكُفْرَ وَٱلْفُسُوقَ وَٱلْعِصْيَانَ

"Allāh has endeared to you the faith and has made it pleasing in your hearts (meaning Amir al Mu'minin) and has made hateful to you disbelief, defiance, and disobedience." He said: "The first one is (Abū Bakr), the second one is ('Umar), and the third one is ('Uthman)." [AL-HUJURAT : 7][95]

The above quotations merely scratch the surface of the numerous verses and prophetic traditions that highlight the significance of honoring the companions. While we hold them in high regard, we do not consider them infallible or elevate them to the level of prophets or angels. Rather, they are an exemplary generation, unmatched in their piety and devotion to Islam. However, it is important to note that not all Shi'a sects hold the same views towards the companions. There are three distinct groups, each with its own perspective:

The first group rejects the fundamental principles of Islam and, as such, is considered non-Muslim regardless of any claims they make to the contrary.

The second group also rejects certain Islamic principles, but they hold the view that Ali ﷺ is the most superior among all the companions. Such Shi'a are not deemed non-Muslims but rather fasiqs (those who openly transgress the laws of Islam).

---

94 Ibid, volume:2 p. 399.

95 ibid

The beliefs of the third group are unclear due to the ambiguity surrounding them. According to scholars, this group cannot be classified as either Muslims or non-Muslims[96]

It is crucial to avoid painting all Shi'a sects with the same brush when it comes to their stance on the companions. It is important to approach the matter objectively and acknowledge the diversity of opinions within the Shi'a community.

---

96 Mufti Muḥammad al-Shafi, Jawaahirul Fiqh Vol:1 Pg:59-63 (Maktabah Darul Uloom Karachi) and Ibn Taymiyyah, Majmoo'ul fatawa, vol: 356.

SOCIAL MORALITY IN THE QURAN

SECTION ONE

MARRIAGE AND MORALS IN ISLAM

3.1.1. PART 1- IMPORTANCE OF MARRIAGE:

Marriage plays a profound role in shaping the morality of a society. It is not simply one of many social institutions but rather the most important and foundational moral institution in any society. The moral impact of marriage is so pervasive and essential that it often goes unnoticed, much like the beating of one's own heart. From an Islamic perspective:

A- Islam acknowledges the religious virtue, social necessity, and moral advantages of marriage. This is why marriage is considered a sacred duty, a moral safeguard, and a social commitment in Islam. As such, Islam encourages and invites those who are capable to enter into marriage, with a particular emphasis on the youth who are in dire need of it, even more so than other segments of society. Accordingly, the renowned companion, Ibnu Mas'ud, may Allāh be pleased with him, related from the prophet ﷺ and said:

«يَا مَعْشَرَ الشَّبَابِ، مَنِ اسْتَطَاعَ مِنْكُمُ البَاءَةَ فَلْيَتَزَوَّجْ، فَإِنَّهُ أَغَضُّ لِلْبَصَرِ، وَأَحْصَنُ لِلْفَرْجِ، وَمَن لَمْ يَسْتَطِعْ فَعليه بالصَّوْمِ، فإِنَّه له وِجَاءٌ»

"We were with the Prophet ﷺ, young men who had nothing of wealth. So, the Messenger of Allāh ﷺ said to us: "O young men, whoever among you can afford it, let him get married, for it is more effective in lowering the gaze and guarding one's chastity. And whoever cannot afford it should fast, for it will be a shield for him."[97]

B- Marriage attains true bliss and success when it is built upon religiosity, which serves as the foundation of morality, surpassing worldly gains and considerations. Islam regards marriage as a means of reducing crime within the community and addressing youth issues, provided that it adheres to Islam's criteria and moral standards. The Sunnah emphasizes the significance of marriage through two sayings, offering instructions and recommendations in this regard: Abū Huraira reported that the Prophet ﷺ said:

$$\text{«إِذَا جَاءكم مَنْ تَرْضَوْنَ دِينَهُ وَخُلُقَهُ فَزَوِّجُوهُ إِلاَّ تَفْعَلُوا تَكُنْ فِتْنَةٌ فِي الأَرْضِ وَفَسَادٌ كبير»}$$

"If one whose character and religion pleases you comes to you (with a proposal), you should marry him (to your single woman). If you do not do so, there will be tribulations in the land and great corruption"[98].

Abū Huraira also narrated that the Prophet ﷺ said:

$$\text{«تُنْكَحُ الْمَرْأَةُ لأَرْبَعٍ لِمَالِهَا وَلِحَسَبِهَا وَجَمَالِهَا وَلِدِينِهَا، فَاظْفَرْ بِذَاتِ الدِّينِ تَرِبَتْ يَدَاكَ»}$$

"A woman is married for four things, i.e., her wealth, family status, beauty, and religion. So you should marry the religious woman, may your hand be besmeared with dust (otherwise) you will be a loser"[99].

C- Islam considers marriage a strong bond known as Mithaqun Ghaleez, a challenging obligation. It is a commitment to the dignified survival of the human race, fulfilling one's pleasure,

---

97 The ḥadīth was narrated by al-Bukhaari (5066) and Muslims (1400).

98 At-Tirmithi 1080

99 Bukhari 5099 and Muslim 1466

and preserving one's dīn. The believers' religious adherence and their commitment to Islamic teachings are demonstrated through marriage.

وَكَيْفَ تَأْخُذُونَهُ وَقَدْ أَفْضَى بَعْضُكُمْ إِلَى بَعْضٍ وَأَخَذْنَ مِنكُم مِّيثَٰقًا غَلِيظًا ﴿٢١﴾

"AND HOW COULD YOU TAKE IT WHILE YOU HAVE GONE IN UNTO EACH OTHER AND THEY HAVE TAKEN FROM YOU A SOLEMN COVENANT?" [AN-NISA' : 21]

The Quran states that guarding one's private parts and avoiding unlawful sexual contact with the opposite sex can only be afforded by a true believer and a fully devoted religious person. As stated in the Quran:

وَالَّذِينَ هُمْ لِفُرُوجِهِمْ حَٰفِظُونَ ﴿٥﴾

إِلَّا عَلَىٰ أَزْوَٰجِهِمْ أَوْ مَا مَلَكَتْ أَيْمَٰنُهُمْ فَإِنَّهُمْ غَيْرُ مَلُومِينَ ﴿٦﴾

فَمَنِ ابْتَغَىٰ وَرَاءَ ذَٰلِكَ فَأُولَٰئِكَ هُمُ الْعَادُونَ ﴿٧﴾

"AND THEY WHO GUARD THEIR PRIVATE PARTS". "EXCEPT FROM THEIR WIVES OR THOSE THEIR RIGHT HANDS POSSESS, FOR INDEED, THEY WILL NOT BE BLAMED -BUT WHOEVER SEEKS BEYOND THAT, THEN THOSE ARE THE TRANSGRESSORS." [AL-MU'MINŪN : 5 – 7]

Marriage also fulfills the purposes for which Allāh created natural sexual desires in human beings. Imam Ibn Al-Qayyem, in his book At-Tibb An-Nabawi, highlighted the purposes of sex by stating that it was created to preserve and propagate the human race, expelling semen, fulfilling physical desires, and enjoying sexual pleasure. The Prophet (ﷺ) used to enjoy normal intimate relations with his wives, and he considered women and perfume dear to him in this world, as stated in a narration by Anas Bin Malik:

«حُبِّبَ إِلَيَّ مِنْ دُنْيَاكُمْ ثَلاثٌ: الطِّيبُ، وَالنِّسَاءُ، وَجُعِلَتْ قُرَّةُ عَيْنِي فِي الصَّلاةِ»

"In your world, women and perfume have been made dear to me."[100]

---

100   Narrated by Aḥmad 3/128 and An-Nasa'I 7/61.

Moreover, Ibnu Al-Qayyem added by saying: Sex is a means of maintaining good health, lowering the gaze, enabling self-control, and keeping away from prohibited things, and all of these benefits are achieved for both men and women.[101]

In Islam, the purpose of marriage goes beyond worldly gains. The guidelines and teachings of Islam emphasize that marriage is a religious duty that should be fulfilled to attain maximum righteousness. Islam encourages believers to prioritize religiosity and spirituality over material aspects when considering marriage.

Procreation of offspring in Islam is viewed as a means of increasing the number of Allāh's servants on earth rather than solely seeking worldly advantages. Through marriage, a Muslim can draw closer to their Creator by fulfilling the responsibilities and obligations associated with marriage, such as demonstrating tolerance, patience, and other virtues. Marriage in Islam provides a means for emotional and sexual satisfaction, acts as a mechanism for reducing tension, facilitates legitimate procreation, promotes social placement, and fosters inter-family alliances and group solidarity. Most importantly, it offers opportunities for acts of worship ('Ibādah) and the practice of piety.

In his article "The Morality of Marriage and the Transformative Power of Inclusion," Lynn D. Wardle argues that marriage plays a vital role in numerous ways in establishing the moral core, baseline, and standards for society. He cites several reasons he believes marriage is the most potent and crucial institution for generating morality in any society. Firstly, marriage is a ubiquitous social institution that forms the cultural infrastructure of any society. It is a foundation upon which all surviving societies are built. Secondly, marriage is the institution where most children are

---

101   At-Tibb An-Nabawi (Medicine of the Prophet) page: 249.

born and experience their earliest socialization, including forming moral ideals. Thirdly, marriage is usually the family's foundation, the social unit where the earliest human socialization occurs, and the family's most successful and stable foundation. Fourthly, in marriage and family, the individual acquires his core kinship identity, essential for not feeling like an outsider. Fifthly, marriage and family are where most people learn about relationships and the morality of living in them. Sixthly, marriage is the hub of the most connective experiences and the most transformative personal experiences for most people, making kin of strangers and bridging between generations and genders. Seventhly, marriage is the site of some of the most critical and challenging steps in most individuals' moral development. Eighthly, marriage is the institution with the most special connection with one of the most powerful and heavily stimulated human passions - sexual relations. Finally, ninthly, religion and marriage are closely linked conceptually, symbolically, practically, and often legally, with morality due to religion's direct or indirect influence.[102]

3.1.2. PART 2: MORAL CODES AND GUIDELINES ON MARITAL HARMONY IN QURAN AND SUNNAH.

The Quranic verses and prophetic narrations presented below explicitly and implicitly illustrate the moral objectives and wisdom behind marriage. These sacred texts provide guidelines that revolve around various moral themes, encapsulating Islam's perspective on marriage as an institution that contributes to the ethical fabric of societies.

MORAL SIGNIFICANCE OF VERSE 223 OF SURAT Al-Baqarah: (Emphasizing Procreation, Chastity, and God-consciousness in Marriage)

---

102 Wardle, Lynn D. "The Morality of Marriage and the Transformative Power of Inclusion" (September 1, 2008).

نِسَآؤُكُمْ حَرْثٌ لَّكُمْ فَأْتُوا۟ حَرْثَكُمْ أَنَّىٰ شِئْتُمْ وَقَدِّمُوا۟ لِأَنفُسِكُمْ وَٱتَّقُوا۟ ٱللَّهَ وَٱعْلَمُوٓا۟ أَنَّكُم مُّلَٰقُوهُ وَبَشِّرِ ٱلْمُؤْمِنِينَ ٢٢٣

"YOUR WIVES ARE A PLACE OF SOWING OF SEED FOR YOU, SO COME TO YOUR PLACE OF CULTIVATION HOWEVER YOU WISH AND PUT FORTH [RIGHTEOUSNESS] FOR YOURSELVES. AND FEAR ALLĀH AND KNOW THAT YOU WILL MEET HIM. AND GIVE GOOD TIDINGS TO THE BELIEVERS". **[AL-BAQARAH : 223]**

In this verse, the importance of procreation is highlighted as a fundamental aspect of marriage, as it allows for the continuation of the human race. The fulfillment of natural sexual desires within the confines of marriage is considered essential in maintaining chastity and preserving moral standards, according to Islam.

The latter part of the verse, "And fear Allāh and know that you will meet Him," reminds spouses to remain conscious of Allāh and their accountability to Him. It underscores the need to maintain righteousness and spiritual connection while fulfilling their physical needs. This awareness helps believers adhere to the moral guidelines mentioned in the verse.

Islam acknowledges the significance of natural sexual desires and promotes a secure and harmonious environment within marriage to satisfy those needs. However, it emphasizes that the enjoyment of sexual satisfaction should be in accordance with Islamic teachings and principles.

"This verse not only addresses the physical aspects of the marital relationship but presents a comprehensive framework that sanctifies and contextualizes it within a moral, faith-based, and eschatological perspective. It elevates the marital relationship from a purely physical act to an embodiment of faith, harmoniously combining the moral and sensual dimensions."[103]

In order to cultivate a spiritual atmosphere within marital relationships, Islam emphasizes the elevation of feelings from mere animalistic desires to a higher level of human connection. Islamic teachings highlight that the pursuit of pleasure in sexual relations should not be driven solely by carnal instincts. However, they should instead express love and affection between husband and wife. Islam introduces certain spiritual acts to be performed during sexual relations, such as making supplications (du'ā) and observing ritual purification (ghusl) afterward. It is important to note that other practices or customs surrounding sexual relations may vary based on cultural, traditional, or personal views.

Drawing from the verse mentioned above and the traditions of the Prophet, some etiquettes and manners can be derived, including:

D- Believers should have a sincere intention to engage in sexual relations solely for the sake of Allāh so that they can be rewarded. And their intention should be the following:

- Protecting oneself and one's wife from doing forbidden things. On the authority of Abū Dharr, the Messenger of Allāh (ﷺ) said:

«وَفِي بُضْعِ أَحَدِكُمْ صَدَقَةٌ»، قَالُوا: يا رَسُولَ اللهِ، أَيَأْتِي أَحَدُنَا شَهْوَتَهُ وَيَكُونُ له فِيهَا أَجْرٌ؟ قَالَ: «أَرَأَيْتُمْ لو وَضَعَهَا فِي حَرَامٍ، أَكَانَ عليه فِيهَا وِزْرٌ؟ فَكَذلكَ إذَا وَضَعَهَا فِي الحَلَالِ كَانَ له أَجْرٌ»

____

103   (The Moral Space of Marriage in The Holy Quran: "Relation between Spouses" from the Qura'nic Perspective and the Juristic Reading, Hend Mustafa, May 2018

"When any of you engages in sexual intercourse, there is a reward" (meaning, when he has intercourse with his wife). They said, "O Messenger of Allāh, when any of us fulfills his desire, will he be rewarded? He (ﷺ) said: "Do you not see that if he were to do it unlawfully, he would be punished for that? So if he does it lawfully, he will be rewarded."[104]

- Aiming to increase the number of the Muslim ummah to raise its status above other nations, our prophet (ﷺ) will take pride and honor in his people, outnumbering other prophets' people. He said on the authority of Anas Bin Malik:

«تَزَوَّجوا الودودَ الوَلُودَ فإنِّي مُكاثِرٌ بِكُمُ الأُمَمَ»

"Marry women who are loving and very prolific, for I shall outnumber the people by you."

- They should show total reliance on Him and seek His protection from satan as they start the action. On the authority of Ibnu Abbas the prophet (ﷺ) said:

«أَمَا لو أَنَّ أَحَدَهُمْ يَقولُ حِينَ يَأْتي أَهْلَهُ: باسْمِ اللهِ، اللَّهُمَّ جَنِّبْني الشَّيْطانَ، وجَنِّبِ الشَّيْطانَ ما رَزَقْتَنا، ثُمَّ قُدِّرَ بينَهُما في ذلكَ، أَوْ قُضِيَ ولَدٌ؛ لَمْ يَضُرَّهُ شيطانٌ أَبَدًا»

"If anyone of you, when having sexual intercourse with his wife, says: "In the name of Allāh. O Allāh! Keep us away from Satan and keep Satan away from what You bestow on us (our children)." The Prophet (ﷺ) also added by saying:

«فإنْ قَضَى اللهُ بينَهما في ذلك ولدًا، لم يضُرَّه الشيطانُ أبدًا»

"If Allāh decrees that they should have a child, Satan will never harm him."[105]

The Hadith guides believers to be rewarded for their actions, even when seeking immediate pleasure and enjoyment. It emphasizes the importance of starting the action by mentioning Allāh and

---

104   Muslim 1672

105   Al-Bukhari 9/187.

seeking His protection from the influence of Satan. The Prophet (ﷺ) taught us to recite the following supplication (Du'ā) before engaging in sexual relations:

This supplication serves as a means of seeking Allāh's protection and blessing, acknowledging His authority over the act of procreation. It reinforces the spiritual dimension of sexual relations and highlights the belief that Allāh's decree and protection are integral to the outcome of procreation. By reciting this supplication, believers express their reliance on Allāh and their desire to involve Him in their intimate moments.

- Kind words, playfulness, and affectionate gestures, including kisses, as a prelude to intercourse. Almighty Allāh states in the Quran (interpretation of the meaning): "Your wives are a place of sowing of seed for you, so come to your place of cultivation however you wish and put forth [righteousness] for yourselves."[106]

Interpretations of this verse by most scholars, in light of sound narrations from the Prophet Muḥammad (ﷺ), suggest that the phrase "وَقَدِّمُوا لِأَنفُسِكُمْ" can be translated as "but do some good act for your souls beforehand." This highlights the importance of engaging in foreplay and affectionate behavior that increases interest and creates a comfortable atmosphere.

It is important to note that the verse emphasizes that sexual relations should occur within the wife's vagina, as it is the natural place of procreation. This indicates that the act of intercourse should be performed respectfully and appropriately while adhering to the prescribed boundaries.

---

106   Quran, Al-Baqarah 2:223

Islam recognizes the significance of emotional and physical intimacy within the marital relationship by promoting kind words, playfulness, and affectionate gestures. These actions contribute to the overall well-being of both spouses, fostering a deeper connection and enhancing the enjoyment of sexual intimacy.

Jabir ibn 'Abdallah (ﷺ) said:

«إذَا أَتَى الرَّجُلُ امْرَأَتَهُ مِنْ دُبُرِهَا فِي قُبُلِهَا، كَانَ الوَلَدُ أَحْوَلَ، فَنَزَلَتْ: ﴿نِسَاؤُكُمْ حَرْثٌ لَكُمْ فَأْتُوا حَرْثَكُمْ أَنَّى شِئْتُمْ﴾ فقال رسول الله ﷺ: «مُقْبِلَةً ومُدبِرةً، إذا كان ذلك في الفرْجِ»

"The Jews used to say that if a man had intercourse with his wife in her vagina from behind, the child would have a squint." Then this verse was revealed: Your wives are a place of sowing of seed for you, so come to your place of cultivation however you wish and put forth [righteousness] for yourselves".[107] So The Messenger of Allāh ﷺ said: "From the front or the back, as long as it is in the vagina."[108]

Under any circumstances, it is important to clarify that in Islam, it is not permissible for a husband to engage in sexual intercourse with his wife in her back passage. The verse in question (Al-Baqarah 2:223) refers to the wife's vagina as the designated place for marital relations, as it is the natural and intended means of procreation. The term "place of 'tilth'" signifies the reproductive organ from which the hope of conceiving a child arises. This emphasizes the importance of preserving the sanctity and purpose of sexual intimacy within the marital bond while adhering to Islam's moral and ethical teachings. Furthermore, this evil act has been strictly prohibited also in the sunnah, "It is narrated from Khuzaymah bin Thābit that he said that the Prophet (ﷺ) said three times that:

«إِنَّ اللَّهَ لَا يَسْتَحْيِي مِنَ الْحَقِّ ثَلَاثَ مَرَّاتٍ لَا تَأْتُوا النِّسَاءَ فِي أَدْبَارِهِنَّ»

---

107   Al-Baqarah: 223

108   Al-Bukhari 8/154 and Muslim 4/156 .

'Indeed, Allāh (Most High) does not hesitate to mention the truth – do not have intercourse with women in their back passages.'"[109]

The Prophet (ﷺ) tells us in another Hadith that this action will cause the doer to be deprived of Allāh's mercy, the meaning of the curse mentioned in the Hadith.

«مَلعُونٌ مَن يأتِي النِّساءَ في محاشِّهِنَّ. يعني: أدبارَهنَّ»

"He is cursed who has intercourse with women in their back passages."[110]

Some prophetic narrations not only warn against engaging in forbidden actions but also emphasize the severity of the consequences. These narrations caution that the act of engaging in such forbidden actions, including specific sinful behaviors, may result in a state of being deprived of divine mercy and even lead to a weakening or loss of faith in the Holy Revelation. This serves as a strong admonition, emphasizing the gravity of these actions and their potentially detrimental effects on one's spiritual well-being. It underscores the importance of adhering to the teachings and guidance of the Holy Revelation to safeguard one's faith and maintain a righteous path. In this regard, the prophet (ﷺ) said:

«مَنْ أَتَى حَائِضًا أَوِ امْرَأَةً فِي دُبُرِهَا أَوْ كَاهِنًا، فَقَدْ كَفَرَ بِمَا أُنْزِلَ عَلَى مُحَمَّدٍ ﷺ»

"On the authority of Abū Hurayrah, the Prophet of Allāh ﷺ said, 'The one who has intercourse with the menstruating woman, or has intercourse through her back passage or goes to a soothsayer, has disbelieved in what was revealed to the Prophet ﷺ.'"[111]

---

109   Sunan ibn Mājah, Hadīth 1924, vol 2, pg 450

110   Ibnu Adiy 1/211. Sh. Albani graded it as an authentic narration in his book of Ādab al-Ziff.

111   Sunan al-Tirmidhī, vol 1, pg 185, Hadīth 135

Islam forbids sexual intercourse with a woman while she is menstruating, considering it both unlawful and a major sin. This narration further highlights another prohibition related to intimate relations, explicitly addressing the act of engaging in intercourse during menstruation. This prohibition emphasizes respecting the natural biological process and observing the prescribed guidelines for intimate relations. It reminds individuals to exercise restraint and refrain from engaging in such acts during this specific period. Allāh says:

وَيَسْـَٔلُونَكَ عَنِ ٱلْمَحِيضِ قُلْ هُوَ أَذًى فَٱعْتَزِلُوا۟ ٱلنِّسَآءَ فِى ٱلْمَحِيضِ وَلَا تَقْرَبُوهُنَّ حَتَّىٰ يَطْهُرْنَ فَإِذَا تَطَهَّرْنَ فَأْتُوهُنَّ مِنْ حَيْثُ أَمَرَكُمُ ٱللَّهُ إِنَّ ٱللَّهَ يُحِبُّ ٱلتَّوَّٰبِينَ وَيُحِبُّ ٱلْمُتَطَهِّرِينَ ﴿٢٢٢﴾

"AND THEY ASK YOU ABOUT MENSTRUATION. SAY, "IT IS HARM, SO KEEP AWAY FROM WIVES DURING MENSTRUATION. AND DO NOT APPROACH THEM UNTIL THEY ARE PURE. AND WHEN THEY HAVE PURIFIED THEMSELVES, THEN COME TO THEM FROM WHERE ALLĀH HAS ORDAINED FOR YOU. INDEED, ALLĀH LOVES THOSE WHO ARE CONSTANTLY REPENTANT AND LOVES THOSE WHO PURIFY THEMSELVES." [AL-BAQARAH : 222]

However, it is permissible for the husband to engage in other forms of physical intimacy and enjoy the company of his wife during her menstruation period without engaging in sexual intercourse. This allowance recognizes the importance of maintaining emotional closeness and affection between spouses, even during this time when sexual intercourse is prohibited. It encourages alternative ways of expressing love and intimacy while adhering to the guidelines set forth by Islamic teachings. By abstaining from intercourse during menstruation, couples can still nurture their bond and strengthen their relationship through acts of love, companionship, and mutual support. According to a hadith by A'ishah (رضي الله عنها), in which she said:

«كان رسول الله ﷺ يأمر إحدانا إذا كانت حائضًا أن تتَّزِر ثمَّ يُضاجعُها زوجُها»

"The Messenger of Allāh ﷺ would tell one of us, when she was menstruating, to wear a waist wrapper, then her husband would lie with her."[112]

The narration clearly emphasizes that considering prohibited acts as permissible is a grave matter, leading one to disbelief. Allowing and considering anal intercourse as ḥalāl (permissible) contradicts the clear teachings of Allāh (Most High) and is an act of kufr (disbelief). Even if a believer engages in such acts while recognizing their prohibition, it still constitutes a major sin. It is essential to understand that, as Muslims, we must adhere to the principles set by Allāh and avoid actions that go against the teachings of Islam.

In addition to the religious perspective, engaging in anal intercourse goes against human beings' fiṭrah (natural inclination) and is repulsive to those with healthy human nature. It also deprives the woman of her rightful share of pleasure. Furthermore, the back passage is a place associated with impurity and filth, and various other reasons affirm the prohibition of such actions.

Therefore, it is crucial for believers to respect and uphold the moral and ethical guidelines set by Islam, recognizing the wisdom behind these prohibitions and adhering to the teachings that promote physical and emotional well-being within the framework of righteousness and purity.

4- The intimate affairs between spouses should remain confidential and not be disclosed to others. It is impermissible for either spouse to divulge the private details of their marital life. In fact, this is considered one of the most reprehensible actions one can commit. So the Quran directs:

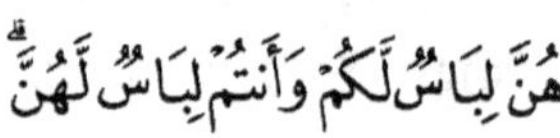

هُنَّ لِبَاسٌ لَّكُمْ وَأَنتُمْ لِبَاسٌ لَّهُنَّ

"THEY ARE CLOTHING FOR YOU AND YOU ARE CLOTHING FOR THEM." **[AL-BAQARAH : 187]**

---

112   Agreed upon; Bukhari 300 and Muslim 293

The Prophet ﷺ also stated, on the authority of Abū Sa'id, by saying:

«إنَّ من شرِّ الناسِ عندَ اللهِ منزلةً يومَ القيامةِ ، الرجلُ يُفضِي إلى امرأتِه وتُفضِي إليهِ ، ثم يَنشرُ سِرَّها»

"Among the most evil of people before Allāh on the Day of Resurrection will be a man who comes to his wife and has intercourse with her, then he spreads her secrets."113

It was also reported from Asma' bint Yazid that she said that She was with the Prophet ﷺ, and men and women were sitting with him, and the Prophet ﷺ said,

«لعلَّ رجُلًا يقولُ ما يفعَلُ بأهْلِهِ، ولعلَّ امرأةً تخبرُ بما فعلَت معَ زوجِها؟! فأمَّ القومُ،-أي سكتوا ولم يجيبوا- فقلتُ : إي واللهِ يا رسولَ اللهِ ! إنهنَّ ليفعلنَ، وإنَّهم ليفعلونَ. قالَ: «فلا تفعَلوا، فإنَّما ذلِكَ مَثَلُ الشَّيطانِ لقيَ شيطانةً في طريقٍ فغَشِيَها والنَّاسُ ينظُرونَ»

"Would any man say what he did with his wife? Would any woman tell others what she did with her husband?" The people remained silent and did not answer. I [Asma'] said: "Yes, by Allāh, O Messenger of Allāh! They (women) do that, and they (men) do that." He said, "Do not do that. It is like a male devil meeting a female devil on the road and having intercourse with her while the people watch." 114

MORAL CODES OF VERSES 2:228 OF AL-BAQARA AND 4:19 OF AL-NISA.

- The moral code emphasizes the principle of Maʿrūf (معروف) as the basis for reciprocal rights and obligations between spouses.

- Maʿrūf encompasses kindness and mercy, promoting compassion and love rather than cruelty and hatred.

---

113   Muslim 4/157.

114   Abū Dawud 1/339. Al-bani: Ādab Al-zifaf 143

For couples to establish a mutually respectful and morally upright relationship, Islam instructs them to adhere to the Quran's moral teachings in their interactions and dealings. By following these guidelines, couples can cultivate a harmonious and fulfilling marital bond that reflects Allāh's mercy in their shared life In this, the Quran says:

وَلَهُنَّ مِثْلُ الَّذِى عَلَيْهِنَّ بِالْمَعْرُوفِ وَلِلرِّجَالِ عَلَيْهِنَّ دَرَجَةٌ وَاللَّهُ عَزِيزٌ حَكِيمٌ ﴿٢٢٨﴾

"AND DUE TO THE WIVES IS SIMILAR TO WHAT IS EXPECTED OF THEM, ACCORDING TO WHAT IS REASONABLE. BUT THE MEN HAVE A DEGREE OVER THEM [IN RESPONSIBILITY AND AUTHORITY]. AND ALLĀH IS EXALTED IN MIGHT AND WISE". [AL-BAQARAH : 228]

وَعَاشِرُوهُنَّ بِالْمَعْرُوفِ فَإِن كَرِهْتُمُوهُنَّ فَعَسَىٰ أَن تَكْرَهُوا شَيْئًا وَيَجْعَلَ اللَّهُ فِيهِ خَيْرًا كَثِيرًا ﴿١٩﴾

"AND LIVE WITH THEM IN KINDNESS. FOR IF YOU DISLIKE THEM - PERHAPS YOU DISLIKE A THING AND ALLĀH MAKES THEREIN MUCH GOOD". [AN-NISA' : 19.]

The foundation of a husband-wife relationship should be built upon the exchange of rights, mutual assistance, and a circle of love, affection, respect, and honor, encapsulated by the term "Ma'rūf." the Quranic verses emphasize that the rights and obligations between spouses should be rooted in reciprocity rather than strict equality. These verses recognize and highlight each spouse's distinct roles and functions, which are separate yet complementary.

"Ma'rūf" encompasses the entire concept of ethical behavior in the context of marriage. It represents the fundamental principles Islam sets forth for a shared life. The Quran repeatedly mentions this term, signifying its significance and importance in various scenarios and situations. "Ma'rūf" appears in different grammatical cases as a definite and indefinite noun, adjective, adverb, and noun, appearing 39 times in 36 verses. Often paired with "iḥsān" (kindness), it serves as both an instruction on how something should be done and what should be done.[115]

It is worth noting that the term "Maʿrūf," in its various usages, primarily addresses men. It highlights the importance of men considering their wives' cultural norms and expectations when it comes to setting standards and making requests. Men are advised not to expect anything unusual or contrary to the accepted lifestyle of their wives or the community they belong to. This guidance makes family life more manageable and joyful.

While the phrase pertains to the general relationship between men and women, it explicitly emphasizes men's behavior, interactions, and overall conduct toward women rather than the other way around.

To gain a deeper understanding of the term "Maʿrūf" with the help of the Holy Quran, A. Kevin Reinhart cites a quote from Marshall G.S. Hodgson's book "The Venture of Islam: Conscience and History in a World Civilization." The quote highlights that the Quran does not need to outline every detail and method of action explicitly. It assumes that some aspects of goodness and righteousness are already known without specific revelation. The Quran acknowledges that individuals possess ordinary moral knowledge and urges them to act accordingly. It emphasizes performing actions with kindness and sincerity, adhering to the spirit of the law rather than merely its literal interpretation. In essence, the Quran not only imparts unique knowledge through

---

115 "What We Know about Maʿrūf" by A. Kevin Reinhart in the Journal of Islamic Ethics

revelation but also acknowledges the moral knowledge held by the Meccans, Medinans, and all Arabs who heard the Quran during the period from 612 to 632 CE.[116]

The moral space of marriage in the Holy Quran explores the interconnection between spouses from a Quranic perspective and a juristic interpretation. Therefore, " Al-Ma'rūf " defines every action recognized as good through intellectual understanding or legislative guidance. It signifies the concept of performing good deeds. Combined with these two meanings, "Al-Ma'rūf" is the foundational framework for marital relationships and broader family connections. It extends to the realm of relationships within the entire community of believers.[117]

The term "Ma'rūf" represents a lifestyle that aligns entirely with Allāh's creation and desires. It encompasses a natural way of life that should be universally recognized and acknowledged, even by those who may not have knowledge of a holy book. It implies that Ma'rūf is a customary law established by Allāh, meaning that every community has its own understanding of Ma'rūf. However, it is essential to note that every Ma'rūf should be in accordance with the laws of Allāh.

In this context, the Quran recognizes that communal laws, customs, and habits that are not in contradiction with divine laws are considered Ma'rūf. This implies that practices and norms within a community are considered Ma'rūf as long as they are in harmony with the teachings and principles outlined by Allāh.

---

116   "The Venture of Islam: Conscience and History in a World Civilization" by Marshall G.S. Hodgson, quoted by A. Kevin Reinhart.

117   "The Moral Space of Marriage in The Holy Quran: 'Relation between Spouses' from the Qura'nic Perspective and the Juristic Reading" by Hend Mustafa.

In general, Maʿrūf represents a standard of righteousness and goodness that transcends cultural and temporal boundaries, rooted in the laws and guidance of Allāh.

It is equally remarkable when the verse "ولهن مثل الذي عليهن بالمعروف" (And due to them [women] is similar to what is expected of them, according to what is reasonable) addresses the responsibility of women in such a manner. It establishes a balanced approach that considers both their obligations and rights. While the reciprocity of duties and rights is equal, the Quran introduces the condition of Maʿrūf, which encompasses the most comprehensive and inclusive term in Arabic, defining our treatment and interactions as spouses.

It is important to note that the term "Maʿrūf" is robust and inclusive, encompassing all the reciprocal rights and obligations within a marital relationship. The Quran does not elaborate on these rights, as they fall under the "Maʿrūf" umbrella, which is evident and known to everyone.

When examining the Quranic verses concerning the relationship between husbands and wives, one may notice a significant absence of a detailed list of specific "Do's and Don'ts" regarding their rights and interactions in their shared life. Unlike the extensive explanations Muslim scholars and jurists provided in their writings, the Quran does not explicitly lay out these rights and obligations comprehensively. This distinction in approach is because the Quran and Sunnah aim to convey their content and context lucidly and understandably, allowing readers to comprehend the principles and values underlying the marital relationship.

The concluding part of verse 19 of Al-Nisa states, "For if you dislike them - perhaps you dislike a thing, and Allāh makes therein much good," highlights, in the context of "Al-Maʿrūf" and its implications, that marriage is founded upon affection and compassion. Therefore, it should be entered into through voluntary choice, creating an environment where mutual love, understanding, and compassion can flourish. In this regard, Islam advises husbands that even if they have moments of disliking their wives, those very wives may bring much goodness to their lives. Hence, the marriage bond should be cherished and not severed based on passing whims or fleeting emotions. Since marriage is a significant human institution, it should be approached with seriousness, and its longevity should not be subject to impulsive outbursts or superficial changes in sentiment.[118] The prophet (ﷺ) summarizes the whole concept of "Ma'rūf" in three narrations: On the authority of Abūhurayra, the messenger ﷺ, said:

1- Messenger of Allāh (ﷺ) said:

«لا يَفرَكْ مؤمن مؤمنة، إن كره منها خُلقًا رضي منها آخر أو قال غيره»

"A believer must not hate (his wife) believing woman; if he dislikes one of her characteristics, he will be pleased with another."119

2- Abū Huraura also reported that the prophet ﷺ said:

«استوصوا بالنساء، فإن المرأة خلقت من ضلع، وإن أعوج شيء في الضلع أعلاه، فإن ذهبت تقيمه كسرته، وإن تركته لم يزل أعوج، فاستوصوا بالنساء»

"And I advise you to treat women kindly, for they are created from a rib, and the most crooked portion of the rib is its upper part; if you try to straighten it, it will break, and if you leave it, it will remain crooked, so I urge you to treat women kindly."120

3- Amr Bin Al-Ahwas Al-Jushamy said that the Messenger of Allāh said:

---

118   Fizilal-Al-Quran, pages 19-20.

119   Muslim 1468.

120   [Bukhari,114

«الاَ وَاسْتَوْصُوا بِالنِّسَاءِ خَيْرًا، فَإِنَّمَا هُنَّ عَوَانٌ عِنْدَكُمْ. أَلاَ وَإِنَّ لَكُمْ عَلَى
نِسَائِكُمْ حَقًّا، وَلِنِسَائِكُمْ عَلَيْكُمْ حَقًّا، فَأَمَّا حَقُّكُمْ عَلَى نِسَائِكُمْ فَلاَ يُوطِئْنَ
فُرُشَكُمْ مِن تَكْرَهُونَ، وَلا يَأْذَنَّ فِي بُيُوتِكُمْ لِمَنْ تَكْرَهُونَ»

"O People, treat your women well and be kind to them; they are your partners
and committed helpers. You indeed have certain rights concerning your
women, but they also have right over you. And it is your right that they do not
make friends with any one of whom you do not approve, as well as never to
commit adultery".[121]

MORAL CODES OF VERSES: 4:1 OF SURAT AN-NISA, 7:189 OF Al-A'raf, 16:72 OF AL-NAHL, AND 30:21 OF AL-RUM.

- These verses emphasize that familial relationships, integral to our human identity and the continuation of society, must be approached with morality and reverence, recognizing them as sacred bonds.

Surat Al-Nisa's introduction emphasizes key topics crucial for constructing a robust Islamic community and establishing a stable family structure, which serves as the core of a strong ummah. Additionally, the surah offers guidance to believers on how to unite their ranks and maintain their collective strength. The surah consistently underscores the significance of possessing a virtuous moral character in developing a resilient community. Moreover, it provides instructions on the rights and responsibilities of both spouses, enabling them to resolve their family disputes and cultivate a harmonious and well-regulated family life.

The surah, beginning with its sacred guidelines and directives, instructs us on how to establish a strong connection with Allāh, the Creator, as well as our fellow human beings, Allāh says:

---

121 Tirmidi 116

يَـٰٓأَيُّهَا ٱلنَّاسُ ٱتَّقُواْ رَبَّكُمُ ٱلَّذِى خَلَقَكُم مِّن نَّفْسٍ وَٰحِدَةٍ وَخَلَقَ مِنْهَا زَوْجَهَا وَبَثَّ مِنْهُمَا رِجَالًا كَثِيرًا وَنِسَآءً وَٱتَّقُواْ ٱللَّهَ ٱلَّذِى تَسَآءَلُونَ بِهِۦ وَٱلْأَرْحَامَ إِنَّ ٱللَّهَ كَانَ عَلَيْكُمْ رَقِيبًا ۝

"O MANKIND, FEAR YOUR LORD, WHO CREATED YOU FROM ONE SOUL AND CREATED
FROM IT ITS MATE AND DISPERSED FROM BOTH OF THEM MANY MEN AND WOMEN. AND
FEAR ALLĀH, THROUGH WHOM YOU ASK ONE ANOTHER, AND THE WOMBS. INDEED ALLĀH
IS EVER, OVER YOU, AN OBSERVER. [AN-NISA" : 1.]

After commanding us to have Taqwa (consciousness and fear of Allāh), Allāh reveals His divine plan that human existence on Earth begins with a single family, highlighting the family unit as the foundation of human life. Allāh states, "and dispersed from both of them many men and women," signifying that from Adam and Hawwa (Eve), numerous men and women were created and distributed throughout the world in diverse forms, traits, colors, and languages. Ultimately, all of humanity will be gathered and returned to Allāh.

Allāh further instructs, "And fear Allāh, through whom you ask one another, and the wombs," reminding us to be mindful of Allāh in our interactions and transactions with others. According to some interpretations, this phrase implies that when seeking rights or making demands, we should invoke the name of Allāh and acknowledge the ties of kinship. It is mentioned by scholars such as Ibrahim, Mujahid, and Al-Ḥasan.[122]

According to Ad-Dahhak, "Fear Allāh Whom you invoke when you conduct transactions and contracts."[123] This highlights the importance of conducting our dealings with others in a manner that is mindful of Allāh's presence.

---

122   At-Tabari 7:519
123   At-Tabari 7:518

Additionally, we are reminded to honor and maintain kinship ties, symbolized by the womb. Ibn Abbas, Ikrimah, Mujahid, Al-Ḥasan, Ad-Dahhak, Ar-Rabi, and others have emphasized the significance of not severing family ties but preserving and respecting them.[124]

In the prologue of Surah Al-Nisa in his book "Fi Zilal Al-Quran," Sayyid Qutb engages in a comprehensive discussion. Initially, he highlights the historical mistreatment and deprivation of women's rights in pre-Islamic societies. This sets the backdrop for understanding the societal context in which women existed during that era.

Qutb observes that the low status attributed to women in those societies had a detrimental impact on the foundational structure of families. The rules governing adoption and alliances often clashed with the bonds of kinship, leading to confusion and instability. Furthermore, chaotic relationships between men and women and within families were prevalent due to the prevalence of illicit relationships and societal norms at the time.

These factors contributed to an environment marked by disarray and disharmony. Qutb's analysis sheds light on the societal challenges faced during that period, providing insight into the importance of the Quranic guidance in rectifying these issues.[125]

In response to the prevailing oppressive treatment of women during that time, Islam emerged as a transformative force, elevating their status and granting them their rightful rights. This significant shift, which took place 1400 years ago, can be considered a revolutionary step in recognizing and valuing women's contributions and roles. Islam emphasizes the

---

124   At-Tabari 7:521,522

125   Sayyid Qutb, "Fi Zilal Al-Quran," Surah Al-Nisa, Page 6

celebration of the inherent differences between men and women, acknowledging the diverse abilities and responsibilities that arise from their distinct genders. This acknowledgment is rooted in the understanding that Allāh's creation encompasses a remarkable range of variations. No two individuals are identical, as evidenced by the multitude of variations in physical attributes, personalities, behaviors, skills, concerns, and functions. This diversity serves as a testament to the boundless power of Allāh, the Creator, who designed humankind with such incredible variation.[126]

However, it is essential to note that the differences between males and females, particularly in their roles and capabilities, should not be used as a means to exclude or deny rights to either gender. In the context of marital life, these differences exist within the boundaries of human ethics. Although they represent a form of distinction, they ultimately reflect a unity of nature and origin. Both males and females have been created from the same soul, and the Qur'an refers to them using the same term: "a mate" or "a spouse."[127]

As mentioned in the noble verse, the initial distinction between males and females serves the purpose of attraction, convergence, procreation, and the concept of "acquaintance" as described in the Qur'an. Through this concept, all things are created from the integration of two different spouses, ensuring the continuation of life's cycle and the ongoing movement of the cosmic wheel until it reaches its predetermined conclusion.[128]

The Qur'an's remarkable perfection becomes evident once again as we delve into the verses that constitute the moral code section of this discourse. Upon reflection, these verses eloquently convey

---

126   Ibid Page 20

127   "The Moral Space of Marriage in The Holy Quran: 'Relation between Spouses' from the Qura'nic Perspective and the Juristic Reading" by Hend Mustafa

128   ibid

the profound truth within Islam about the creation of Eve/ Hawwa from Adam, emphasizing the interconnectedness and complementary nature of men and women. The Qur'an implicitly, rationally, and convincingly portrays the relationship between man and woman as that of a root and a branch. Just as a branch relies on its root for sustenance, and the root relies on the branch for growth and expression, so too do men and women depend on each other.

The Qur'an highlights how Allāh has instilled within the couple a profound sense of mutual need and how, through their union, they complete one another's imperfections and fulfill each other's needs. This divine design signifies the essential role of both genders in perpetuating human existence and the eternal cycle of procreation.

These verses resonate with the deeper truths of human existence, affirming the importance of unity, harmony, and interdependence between men and women. The Qur'an beautifully captures the intricacies of this relationship, underscoring the divine wisdom behind the creation of Eve as a partner and companion for Adam. Through this profound understanding, Islam acknowledges the inherent value and significance of both men and women in the grand tapestry of creation. Allāh said:

۞ هُوَ ٱلَّذِى خَلَقَكُم مِّن نَّفْسٍ وَٰحِدَةٍ وَجَعَلَ مِنْهَا زَوْجَهَا لِيَسْكُنَ إِلَيْهَا ۖ فَلَمَّا تَغَشَّىٰهَا حَمَلَتْ حَمْلًا خَفِيفًا فَمَرَّتْ بِهِۦ ۖ فَلَمَّآ أَثْقَلَت دَّعَوَا ٱللَّهَ رَبَّهُمَا لَئِنْ ءَاتَيْتَنَا صَٰلِحًا لَّنَكُونَنَّ مِنَ ٱلشَّٰكِرِينَ ﴿١٨٩﴾

"IT IS HE WHO CREATED YOU FROM ONE SOUL AND CREATED FROM IT ITS MATE THAT HE MIGHT DWELL IN SECURITY WITH HER. AND WHEN HE COVERS HER, SHE CARRIES A LIGHT BURDEN AND CONTINUES THEREIN. AND WHEN IT BECOMES HEAVY, THEY BOTH INVOKE ALLĀH, THEIR LORD, "IF YOU SHOULD GIVE US A GOOD [CHILD], WE WILL SURELY BE AMONG THE GRATEFUL." [AL-A'RAF : 189]

وَٱللَّهُ جَعَلَ لَكُم مِّنْ أَنفُسِكُمْ أَزْوَٰجًا وَجَعَلَ لَكُم مِّنْ أَزْوَٰجِكُم بَنِينَ وَحَفَدَةً وَرَزَقَكُم مِّنَ ٱلطَّيِّبَٰتِ أَفَبِٱلْبَٰطِلِ يُؤْمِنُونَ وَبِنِعْمَتِ ٱللَّهِ هُمْ يَكْفُرُونَ ﴿٧٢﴾

"AND ALLĀH HAS MADE FOR YOU FROM YOURSELVES MATES AND HAS MADE FOR YOU FROM YOUR MATES SONS AND GRANDCHILDREN AND HAS PROVIDED FOR YOU FROM THE GOOD THINGS. THEN IN FALSEHOOD DO THEY BELIEVE AND IN THE FAVOR OF ALLĀH THEY DISBELIEVE" [AN-NAHL : 72.]

Verse 21 of Al-rum and 74 of Al-furqan " The moral ingredients of marriage; love, mercy, tranquility, and caring"

وَمِنْ ءَايَٰتِهِ أَنْ خَلَقَ لَكُم مِّنْ أَنفُسِكُمْ أَزْوَٰجًا لِّتَسْكُنُوٓا۟ إِلَيْهَا وَجَعَلَ بَيْنَكُم مَّوَدَّةً وَرَحْمَةً إِنَّ فِى ذَٰلِكَ لَءَايَٰتٍ لِّقَوْمٍ يَتَفَكَّرُونَ ﴿٢١﴾

"AND OF HIS SIGNS IS THAT HE CREATED FOR YOU FROM YOURSELVES MATES THAT YOU MAY FIND TRANQUILLITY IN THEM; AND HE PLACED BETWEEN YOU AFFECTION AND MERCY. INDEED, IN THAT ARE SIGNS FOR A PEOPLE WHO GIVE THOUGHT." [AL-RUM : 21]

Verse 21 of Al-Rum clearly and confidently outlines the purposes and objectives of marriage. It acknowledges the deep emotional and instinctual bonds between a husband and wife as divine signs of Allāh's greatness and countless blessings. While marriage serves as a means to fulfill one's physical needs in a dignified manner, it emphasizes that this is not its sole purpose or justification.

These verses, categorized under the moral code section, shed light on additional aims and fundamental principles that form the solid foundation of marital relationships. They highlight the importance of tranquility, love, and mercy as essential pillars that sustain the existence and flourishing of a marriage. These pillars epitomize the essence of care and compassion within the marital bond.

These three pillars serve as a moral equilibrium, guiding spouses through the various stages of their marital journey. From the inception of their union, symbolized by the planting of the first seed, to the later stages of their lives as they age together, each word—tranquility, love, and mercy—holds significance, offering guidance and support that aligns with the unique demands and circumstances of each phase of married life.

The first moral pillar of marriage is "Tranquility." It is a state that arises when a man and a woman, driven by needs more urgent than hunger and thirst, long for each other. In this situation, both individuals feel a distinct emptiness that can only be filled through their union, as prescribed by divine laws, namely marriage. Through marriage, loneliness gives way to companionship, confusion gives way to stability, and longing and anxiety are replaced by tranquility and reassurance.

The term "لتسكنوا إليها" (translated as "finding tranquility") encapsulates the essence of marriage, representing the fundamental reason why Allāh created man and woman as spouses for one another. The root of the first Arabic word in the verse, "sakan," signifies a state of rest, quiet, calmness, and being unruffled, appeased, allayed, or motionless. This term highlights the motive behind marriage, emphasizing the deep need for tranquility that can only be fulfilled through the union of husband and wife.[129]

The second moral pillar of marriage is "Love," represented by the Arabic term "mawaddah." In the Qur'an and al-Hadith, this term is synonymous with "wud" and "hub." Commentators and linguists have differing opinions regarding the nuances between "al-wudd" and "al-ḥubb." Some suggest that "al-mawaddah" signifies the pinnacle of "al-maḥabbah." In contrast, others argue that "al-maḥabbah" is the more general term and "al-mawaddah" is more specific, indicating a natural inclination accompanied by

---

129 Sadaf Faruq: An article titled "Two Important Rules for a Blissful Marriage" (22/8/2018),

affection. However, there are also views stating that "al-maḥabbah" is more specific and "al-mawaddah" is more general, encompassing love or a sense of longing. Some even consider them complete synonyms.

Al-'Askarī supports the distinction between the two words, stating that "al-ḥubb" applies when love is dictated by wisdom and the natural disposition of the soul, while "al-wudd" is used solely when the soul is naturally inclined towards love. This can be observed when one says, "I love so-and-so and have affection for them" or "I love prayer," without using "al-wudd" to express the same sentiment.[130]

The terms "Hub" and "mawaddah" carry similar meanings to "love," but they are often used in different contexts based on the strength or degree of love involved. However, it is important to note that both terms refer to love, and the difference between them is rather subtle. "Hub" is often associated with the emotional aspect of love, particularly in the initial stages of attraction when one may not yet profoundly know the person. On the other hand, "mawaddah" is more connected to the practical side of one's behavior and attitude toward others. It represents a rational love that extends beyond emotions, especially in how one deals and interacts with everyone.

In discussing the different kinds of love within a person, it is mentioned that there are two aspects: the basic emotion of the concupiscible appetite, which is self-love driven by what benefits oneself, and the higher form of love rooted in the will, which is benevolence or willing the good of another for their own sake. These two kinds of love align with the concepts of "Hub" and

---

130   Alfuruuq Alluquwiyya, p. 121

"mawaddah." The first kind of love corresponds to the emotional feeling of love, while the second kind pertains to the rational aspect of love.

Since a marital relationship is intended to be eternal and unbreakable, it is essential to undertake whatever sustains and preserves it, ensuring its success. This is where "mawaddah" comes into play, fitting perfectly in this second relationship stage. The verse mentioned describes how the marital relationship evolves over time, gradually transforming from embodying "mawaddah" (affection, love) to becoming a paradigm of "rahmah" (mercy). [131]

Lastly, the third moral pillar is Mercy, characterized by kindness, compassion, and care. It involves a willingness to forgive, overlook mistakes, and demonstrate understanding and tolerance. In the context of marriage, mercy plays a crucial role in maintaining harmony and preventing conflicts. It fosters forgiveness and contributes to establishing a strong and resilient relationship.

The balance between "mawaddah" (love) and mercy is vital in a marital relationship, fostering mutual understanding, love, and compassion. It serves as the foundation for a solid and healthy marriage and is considered one of the essential virtues in Islam.

Al-Rahmah, or "Mercy," represents the final stage of the spouses' long marriage journey. It encompasses the phase when they may no longer be able to fully care for or fulfill each other's needs. Despite the challenges posed by time and life circumstances, they continue to treat one another with love, respect, and mercy. Rahma becomes the harvest season for what they have planted and nurtured throughout their relationship.

---

131   Sadaf Faruq, ibid.

By upholding these moral pillars and cultivating qualities of love and mercy, along with cooperation and consultation, couples can create an environment that fosters tranquility, comfort, and peace of mind within their home.

The particular order in which these words appear in the Quranic verse holds special significance as it emphasizes the gradual transformation that occurs in the spousal relationship over time, influenced by the dynamics of age and experience.[132]

Interestingly, while exploring the explanation of this verse, one might draw an analogy between the structure of the marital relationship and the construction of a building. In building construction, four pillars are necessary to provide the structure with firmness and distribute the weight from the ceiling. Without these pillars, the building cannot stand on its own. It leads to a question as to why the Quran only mentions three pillars in the marriage structure, excluding the fourth pillar, which could have been the "pillar of rights" if it were explicitly referenced. The best answer lies with Allāh, as He knows best, and it could be attributed to one or both of the following reasons:

A- A. The pillar of "rights" may not be absent but rather intertwined and coupled with the main pillars of "Al-mawaddah" and "Al-Rahma." Love acts as a constant reminder of these rights. Where there is love and affection between the spouses, they naturally recognize and fulfill each other's reciprocal rights.

B- B. As mentioned earlier, the concept of "Maʿrūf" encompasses all the reciprocal rights that arise in a marital relationship. Due to its inclusive nature, it carries a connotation of conferring

---

132 Ibid

and magnanimity. Where there is goodness and kindness (Ma'rūf), there is always a sense of caring, responsibility, and God-consciousness (Taqwa), ensuring rights are fulfilled.

These explanations highlight the comprehensive nature of the moral pillars in marriage, where love, mercy, and the concept of Ma'rūf encompass and inherently address the rights and responsibilities within the relationship.

The mutual family caring is what appears in the following verse of surat al-furqan:

$$ \text{وَالَّذِينَ يَقُولُونَ رَبَّنَا هَبْ لَنَا مِنْ أَزْوَاجِنَا وَذُرِّيَّاتِنَا قُرَّةَ أَعْيُنٍ وَاجْعَلْنَا لِلْمُتَّقِينَ إِمَامًا} ﴿٧٤﴾ $$

"AND THOSE WHO SAY, "OUR LORD, GRANT US FROM AMONG OUR WIVES AND OFFSPRING COMFORT TO OUR EYES AND MAKE US AN EXAMPLE FOR THE RIGHTEOUS."
[AL-FURQAN : 74]

The verse tells us how caring the spouse is for one another and their offspring and that they are concerned about attaining comfort within the household. Moreover, the verse indicates how tranquility constitutes the foundation of stabled and blissful life; only when tranquility and comfort are granted can people prosper and progress in their world. Enjoying tranquility paves the way to worshiping Allāh and performing one's duty in this world for the success of the hereafter. Becoming genuinely righteous is how one can qualify to be a role model for other believers; the wisdom behind them asking Allāh to elevate them to be an example for the other believer.

The verse tells us how caring the spouse is for one another and their offspring and that they are concerned about attaining comfort within the household. Moreover, the verse indicates how tranquility constitutes the foundation of stabled and blissful life; only when tranquility and comfort are granted can people prosper and progress in their world. Enjoying tranquility paves the way to worshiping Allāh and performing one's duty in this world for the success of the hereafter. Becoming genuinely righteous is how one can qualify to be a role model for other believers; the wisdom behind them asking Allāh to elevate them to be an example for the other believer.

3.1.3. PART 3- MARITAL CONFLICT RESOLUTION: MORAL GUIDELINES

Exploring Marital Harmony: Islamic Perspectives:

In previous discussions, we delved into the topic of marital harmony, examining Quranic passages, prophetic traditions, commentaries, and scholarly interpretations to shed light on its juristic dimensions. Islam greatly emphasizes fostering a tranquil and blissful marital life, recognizing the family's pivotal role in building a strong and harmonious society. The teachings of Islam emphasize the values of love, affection, mercy, and tranquility as essential components of a well-established and harmonious family relationship.

Islam's concern for marital harmony and conflict resolution is evident through the significant number of Quranic verses and authentic narrations dedicated to this subject. This demonstrates that these teachings go beyond mere directives to marry but also seek to promote sustainable and solid marital bonds characterized by harmony and minimal conflict.

Conflicts inevitably arise in any relationship, given the unpredictable nature of life and the challenges it presents. Spouses, being intimately connected, are particularly susceptible to conflicts and disagreements stemming from various sources and reasons. Islam acknowledges this reality and provides guidance and strategies to create a nurturing environment that mitigates discord and disharmony within marital relationships.

Islam offers a comprehensive approach to addressing conflicts, encompassing techniques to prevent conflicts from escalating and strategies for effectively resolving them when they do occur. These teachings encompass not only marital relationships but also general interpersonal interactions.

In Islam, we are encouraged to adopt techniques that promote harmonious relationships and prevent conflicts. These include effective communication, patience, forgiveness, empathy, and understanding. By adhering to these principles, individuals can cultivate a peaceful atmosphere within their relationships and avoid unnecessary conflicts.

Islam emphasizes the importance of upholding justice and fairness in resolving conflicts, ensuring that the rights and concerns of all parties involved are acknowledged and addressed. Moreover, Islam provides specific strategies for conflict resolution when disagreements do arise. These strategies encourage open dialogue, active listening, seeking mediation, and embracing compromise.

By adhering to these Islamic teachings, individuals can navigate conflicts within their marital relationships and maintain a healthy and harmonious bond. The guidance provided by Islam serves as a roadmap for creating and sustaining lasting peace and tranquility within families and society as a whole.

MORAL GUIDELINES OF VERSES 34,35 and128 OF SURAT AL-NISA:

- MARITAL AUTHORITY

- FINANCIAL OBLIGATION
- INTERNAL CONFLICT RESOLUTION
- (*MUTUAL RECONCILIATION*)
- EXTERNAL CONFLICT RESOLUTION (*ARBITRATION PROCEDURES*)

As mentioned earlier, the Quranic components for marital stability offer believers essential factors for maintaining a long-lasting and harmonious marriage, promoting longevity and unity between couples while preventing unnecessary family breakdowns and divorces. By examining verse 34 of Surah An-Nisa, we can observe its focused ethical approach in addressing the root causes of conflict and providing strategies for resolution through recognizing each spouse's role and responsibilities.

From the context of the verse, it becomes apparent that marital power dynamics, financial obligations, and trust issues are often the primary sources of marital conflict.

Quran says:

ٱلرِّجَالُ قَوَّٰمُونَ عَلَى ٱلنِّسَآءِ بِمَا فَضَّلَ ٱللَّهُ بَعْضَهُمْ عَلَىٰ بَعْضٍ وَبِمَآ أَنفَقُوا۟ مِنْ أَمْوَٰلِهِمْ ۚ فَٱلصَّٰلِحَٰتُ قَٰنِتَٰتٌ حَٰفِظَٰتٌ لِّلْغَيْبِ بِمَا حَفِظَ ٱللَّهُ ۚ وَٱلَّٰتِى تَخَافُونَ نُشُوزَهُنَّ فَعِظُوهُنَّ وَٱهْجُرُوهُنَّ فِى ٱلْمَضَاجِعِ وَٱضْرِبُوهُنَّ ۖ فَإِنْ أَطَعْنَكُمْ فَلَا تَبْغُوا۟ عَلَيْهِنَّ سَبِيلًا ۗ إِنَّ ٱللَّهَ كَانَ عَلِيًّا كَبِيرًا ﴿٣٤﴾

وَإِنْ خِفْتُمْ شِقَاقَ بَيْنِهِمَا فَٱبْعَثُوا۟ حَكَمًا مِّنْ أَهْلِهِۦ وَحَكَمًا مِّنْ أَهْلِهَآ إِن يُرِيدَآ إِصْلَٰحًا يُوَفِّقِ ٱللَّهُ بَيْنَهُمَآ ۗ إِنَّ ٱللَّهَ كَانَ عَلِيمًا خَبِيرًا ﴿٣٥﴾

"MEN ARE IN CHARGE OF WOMEN BY [RIGHT OF] WHAT ALLĀH HAS GIVEN ONE OVER THE OTHER AND WHAT THEY SPEND [FOR MAINTENANCE] FROM THEIR WEALTH. SO RIGHTEOUS WOMEN ARE DEVOUTLY OBEDIENT, GUARDING IN [THE HUSBAND'S] ABSENCE WHAT ALLĀH WOULD HAVE THEM GUARD. BUT THOSE [WIVES] FROM WHOM YOU FEAR ARROGANCE

- [FIRST] ADVISE THEM; [THEN IF THEY PERSIST], FORSAKE THEM IN BED; AND [FINALLY], STRIKE THEM. BUT IF THEY OBEY YOU [ONCE MORE], SEEK NO MEANS AGAINST THEM. INDEED, ALLĀH IS EVER EXALTED AND GRAND. [AN-NISA''' : 34]

"AND IF YOU FEAR DISSENSION BETWEEN THE TWO, SEND AN ARBITRATOR FROM HIS PEOPLE AND AN ARBITRATOR FROM HER PEOPLE. IF THEY BOTH DESIRE RECONCILIATION, ALLĀH WILL CAUSE IT BETWEEN THEM. INDEED, ALLĀH IS EVER KNOWING AND ACQUAINTED [WITH ALL THINGS]". [AN-NISA''' : 35]

The guidelines for conflict resolution continue in another section of the same chapter, Al-Nisa. Allāh says:

$$وَإِنِ ٱمْرَأَةٌ خَافَتْ مِنۢ بَعْلِهَا نُشُوزًا أَوْ إِعْرَاضًا فَلَا جُنَاحَ عَلَيْهِمَآ أَن يُصْلِحَا بَيْنَهُمَا صُلْحًا وَٱلصُّلْحُ خَيْرٌ وَأُحْضِرَتِ ٱلْأَنفُسُ ٱلشُّحَّ وَإِن تُحْسِنُوا۟ وَتَتَّقُوا۟ فَإِنَّ ٱللَّهَ كَانَ بِمَا تَعْمَلُونَ خَبِيرًا ۝١٢٨$$

"AND IF A WOMAN FEARS FROM HER HUSBAND CONTEMPT OR EVASION, THERE IS NO SIN UPON THEM IF THEY MAKE TERMS OF SETTLEMENT BETWEEN THEM - AND SETTLEMENT IS BEST. AND PRESENT IN [HUMAN] SOULS IS STINGINESS. BUT IF YOU DO GOOD AND FEAR ALLĀH - THEN INDEED ALLĀH IS EVER, WITH WHAT YOU DO, ACQUAINTED".
[AN-NISA''' : 128]

MARITAL AUTHORITY (*AL-QAWĀMAH*)

A- FINANCIAL OBLIGATIONS

Verse 34 of Surah Al-Nisa addresses a common question when discussing marital issues: Who should take on the leadership role within the marriage?

The concept of "Al-Qawāmah" in the Quran and the interpretations of Quran commentators.

The Quranic verse asserts that men are assigned leadership roles within the marital relationship, highlighting the importance of having a leader and authority figure. This assignment should not be misunderstood as endorsing patriarchal dominance or suppressing women's rights. Upon its arrival, Islam challenged and dismantled such oppressive concepts that denied women their rights based solely on their perceived weakness. However, it is essential to acknowledge that men and women are not identical in their physical and biological attributes. These inherent differences may lead to variations in roles, capacities, and abilities, which can influence their responsibilities within the marital framework. The Prophet Muḥammad (ﷺ) recognized these differences and assigned specific roles and tasks to each family member based on their capabilities. He said:

«كُلُّكُمْ رَاعٍ، وَكُلُّكُمْ مَسْئُولٌ عَنْ رَعِيَّتِهِ، وَالْأَمِيرُ رَاعٍ، وَالرَّجُلُ رَاعٍ عَلَى أَهْلِ بَيْتِهِ، وَالْمَرْأَةُ رَاعِيَةٌ عَلَى بَيْتِ زَوْجِهَا وَوَلَدِهِ، فَكُلُّكُمْ رَاعٍ وَكُلُّكُمْ مَسْئُولٌ عَنْ رَعِيَّتِهِ»

"Every one of you is a shepherd and is responsible for his flock. The leader of people is a guardian and is responsible for his subjects. A man is the guardian of his family and he is responsible for them. A woman is the guardian of her husband's home and his children and is responsible for them."[133]

The narration emphasizes that wives also have domestic responsibilities in accordance with their abilities and capacities, ensuring that both spouses share the same boat and that no one is left behind. It is important to recognize that men and women, by their very nature as human beings, are equal in their humanity. This equality is not only inherent but also genetic.

In addition to their role as guardians, men are tasked with providing financial support for their wives, even in cases where women are financially independent or wealthy. This financial responsibility is part of the concept of Al-qawāmah mentioned in verse 34 of Surah Al-Nisa. Al-qawāmah entails taking care of, protecting, supporting, and maintaining the interests of one's spouse, particularly in financial matters.

---

133   Bukhari 853 and Muslim 1829.

To gain a deeper understanding of the meaning and wisdom behind the Arabic word used in the Quranic text, let us refer to the following quotations from reliable sources of Tafsīr:

According to Ibn Kathir, men are described as the protectors and maintainers of women, which signifies their role as leaders who have authority over women and are responsible for guiding and disciplining them if necessary.[134]

Al-Bagawi states that men are in charge of women's interests and affairs and have the right to discipline them. [135]

Al-Baydawi explains that men assume the leadership role of being in charge of their wives and caring for them (Tafsir al-Baydawi, 2/184).

In light of these interpretations, the principle of Al-qawāmah primarily implies financial responsibility, which is why husbands are entrusted with the leadership of the household. Additionally, a clear statement in the prophetic tradition emphasizes that husbands are financially responsible for their wives.

The prophet ﷺ, as reported by Ai'sha, said:

دَخَلَتْ هِنْدٌ بِنْتُ عُتْبَةَ امْرَأَةَ أَبِي سُفْيَانَ عَلَى رَسُولِ اللهِ ﷺ، فَقَالَتْ: يَا رَسُولَ اللهِ، إِنَّ أَبَا سُفْيَانَ رَجُلٌ شَحِيحٌ، لَا يُعْطِينِي مِنَ النَّفَقَةِ مَا يَكْفِينِي وَيَكْفِي بَنِيَّ إِلَّا مَا أَخَذْتُ مِنْ مَالِهِ بِغَيرِ عِلْمِهِ، فَهَلْ عَلَيَّ فِي ذَلِكَ مِنْ جُنَاحٍ؟ فَقَالَ رَسُولُ اللهِ ﷺ: «خُذِي مِنْ مَالِهِ بِالْمَعْرُوفِ مَا يَكْفِيكِ وَيَكْفِي بَنِيكِ»

"Hind bint 'Utbah, the wife of Abū Sufyaan, entered upon the Messenger of Allaah ﷺ and said, 'O Messenger of Allaah, Abū Sufyaan is a stingy man who does not spend enough on me and my children, except for what I take from

---

134   Tafsir Ibn Kathir, 1/653.

135   Tafsir al-Bagawi, 2/206.

his wealth without his knowledge. Is there any sin on me for doing that?' The Messenger of Allaah ﷺ said, 'Take from his wealth on a reasonable basis, only what is sufficient for you and your children.'[136].

Islam, with its just principles, views the family unit as a collective endeavor where no individual, whether the husband, wife, children, or others, is inherently superior or entitled to unfair treatment. Islam does not condone husbands oppressing their wives or denying them their rights under the pretext of exercising Qawaamah. These rights should align with the concept of justice within the local and contemporary context. The term "Ma'rūf" signifies this understanding, emphasizing the importance of treating one another with kindness, fairness, and respect within the marital relationship.

- ## THE CONCEPT OF ALQAWAMAH IN JUDAISM (MEN'S AUTHORITY OVER WOMEN)

When issues of women, their rights, power (qawāmah), and their restrictive elements in society are discussed, some non-Muslims are always in favor of harboring the stereotyping view of labeling Islam as a patriarchal religion; because it stems from a patriarchal society in their view. Although that biased view is a dominating perception within the West but through unbiased study, one discovers that this immature view could apply to other religions and societies more than it is to Islam; the most restrictive elements towards women can be found first in Judaism in the Old Testament than in Christianity.

However, the issue of Al-qawwama, beating women, which will also be covered in pages of this chapter to come, in the discourse comparative topics with other religions, will unveil the reality that is not accessible to most people.

---

136   Narrated by al-Bukhaari, 5049; Muslim, 1714

Concerning the issue of Al-qawāmah at hand, the Hebrew Bible clearly states that men should rule women over. According to Judaism, men have authority over women in the household, so she is supposed to show complete submission to the husband in all his orders and what he dictates lest she gets punished for failing. -Comparing.[137]

In Genesis 3:16, God says to women: "I will greatly increase your pangs in childbearing; in pain, you shall bring forth children, yet your desire shall be for your husband, and he shall rule over you."[138]

- ## THE CONCEPT OF AL-QAWĀMAH IN CHRISTIANITY (MEN'S AUTHORITY OVER WOMEN)

Christianity, Like Judaism, endorses the view that men should rule over women in all areas of society. In the teachings of Christianity, only men are entitled to be religious authorities. Just as a woman cannot become a rabbi in Judaism, she cannot become a priest according to traditional Christian teaching. Male religious authority is emphasized in the New Testament.[139]

In First Corinthians 11:3, Paul states: "But I want you to understand that Christ is the head of every man, and the husband is the head of his wife, and God is the head of Christ."[140[In First Timothy 2:11 through 14, Paul states: "Let a woman learn in silence with full submission. I permit no woman to teach or

---

137 "Wife-beating" in Judaism, Christianity, Hinduism, Buddhism, and Islam: Muslim skeptic, August 7, 2022.

138 Genesis 3:16

139 Ibid

140 First Corinthians 11:3

to have authority over a man; she is to keep silent. For Adam was formed first, then Eve; 14 and Adam was not deceived, but the woman was deceived and became a transgressor."[141]

Christian scripture also affirms that husbands have authority over wives. This Christian view is based on the Hebrew Bible or the Old Testament. As noted above, the Hebrew Bible asserts that women are to be ruled over by their husbands. ibid

The New Testament affirms that husbands have authority over wives and compares the husband to God, asserting that the husband's authority is like God's.[142] In the Bible, Paul speaks directly to women: "Wives, be subject to your husbands as you are to the Lord. For the husband is the head of the wife just as Christ is the head of the church, the body of which he is the Savior. Just as the church is subject to Christ, so also wives ought to be, in everything, to their husbands."[143]

The Hebrew Bible also refers to the husband as "Ba'al," which means lord and owner. This term implies that the husband is the lord and owner of his wife.

- ### INTERNAL CONFLICT RESOLUTION (MUTUAL RECONCILIATION AND RESOLUTION

Allāh says:

وَٱلَّٰتِي تَخَافُونَ نُشُوزَهُنَّ فَعِظُوهُنَّ وَٱهْجُرُوهُنَّ فِي ٱلْمَضَاجِعِ وَٱضْرِبُوهُنَّ فَإِنْ أَطَعْنَكُمْ فَلَا تَبْغُوا عَلَيْهِنَّ سَبِيلًا إِنَّ ٱللَّهَ كَانَ عَلِيًّا كَبِيرًا ﴿٣٤﴾

---

141   First Timothy 2:11

142   ibid

143   Ephesians 5:22-24

BUT THOSE [WIVES] FROM WHOM YOU FEAR ARROGANCE - [FIRST] ADVISE THEM; [THEN IF THEY PERSIST], FORSAKE THEM IN BED; AND [FINALLY], STRIKE THEM. BUT IF THEY OBEY YOU [ONCE MORE], SEEK NO MEANS AGAINST THEM. INDEED, ALLĀH IS EVER EXALTED AND GRAND. [AN-NISA' : 34.]

The occurrence of marital conflicts and disputes is an undeniable reality, as disagreements can arise between spouses regardless of their compatibility. Just like any other human being, Muslim couples are not immune to such conflicts.

Recognizing the need to resolve conflicts is crucial for couples to address the existing problems. Ignoring conflicts in their early stages often worsens the situation, leading it to spiral out of control.

In the Quran, the verb "خوف" (fear) is used, which signifies anticipation, noticing, or a strong suspicion that something is amiss in the marital relationship. This serves as a call for believers to take immediate action to resolve the problem.[144]

Verse 35 of Surat Al-Nisa directs our attention to these situations within our families. The urgency emphasized in the Quranic verse highlights the importance of timely efforts to address and resolve disputes for the preservation of the marital relationship. Allāh commands us to promptly seek a resolution by appointing arbitrators from both sides of the family.

Furthermore, the verb "خوف" (fear) is reiterated in verse 128 of Al-Nisa, where it states that if a woman fears contempt or avoidance from her husband, there is no sin upon them if they seek settlement and reconciliation. This verse encourages wives to take proactive steps, either independently or through arbitration,

---

144   Al-Bagawi, vol:1, page:613

to prevent marital problems or address the behavior of overbearing husbands. It emphasizes the role of the wife in addressing issues before they escalate beyond control.

Therefore, the facts mentioned above illustrate the comprehensive nature of the Islamic discourse on marriage, as depicted in the Quran and its paradigm for fostering marital harmony and family stability.

However, it is important to note that the Quranic directive mentioned above addresses cases where women display blatant disobedience to their husbands or fail to cooperate to maintain a recognized and harmonious marital relationship (Ma'rūf).

The Holy Qur'an provides men with three steps to address the behavior of disobedient women. These steps are to be followed in the order the verse prescribes: "And those wives from whom you fear arrogance, advise them, forsake them in bed, and strike them."[145]

The first step in correcting their behavior is for the husband to engage in gentle and compassionate dialogue with his wife. فَعِظُوهُنَّ Through reminders of Allāh, forgiveness, and the importance of preserving their marriage, the husband aims to win his wife's heart and encourage reconciliation, thus preventing further deterioration of the situation.

If this initial step does not yield positive results and the wife remains obstinately defiant, the husband may proceed to the next step. وَٱهْجُرُوهُنَّ فِى ٱلْمَضَاجِعِ This involves abstaining from conjugal relations, sleeping separately, and refraining from a normal conversation with her in bed. It is essential to note that the phrase "in beds" is understood by Muslim jurists to mean

---

145   Quran 4:34

staying apart within the context of the bed rather than leaving the house entirely. This strategic approach allows women to reflect on their behavior and understand the displeasure of their husbands, potentially leading to remorse for their actions.

Finally, if the previous steps fail to change the wife's behavior positively, the Quran suggests resorting to discipline وَٱضْرِبُوهُنَّ. However, it should be emphasized that this discipline should never involve violence. Based on the biographical works and prophetic traditions, it is well-documented that the Prophet Muḥammad (ﷺ) never physically harmed women or servants, even lightly. The term "hitting" or "striking" should be understood in a non-violent and gentle manner.

It is crucial to explore the context and explanations scholars provide to grasp the intended meaning of this advice. Early commentators have clarified that any physical contact should be light enough not to leave a mark (ghayr mubarraḥ) and done using a small object like a tooth-stick while avoiding striking the face.

This comprehensive understanding of the verse emphasizes the importance of addressing marital issues with wisdom, compassion, and respect, promoting a harmonious and balanced relationship between spouses.

- UNDERSTANDING "BEATING" OR "STRIKING" WOMEN

1- FROM THE PERSPECTIVE OF THE QURAN AND QURANIC COMMENTATORS

In Islam, it is evident to those who possess knowledge that the interpretation of Quranic texts is made in conjunction with the Sunnah, which refers to the traditions and practices of the Prophet

Muḥammad (ﷺ). The understanding and implementation of the Quranic teachings were transmitted through the generations of early Muslims, mainly the companions of the Prophet and their immediate students who received authentic knowledge from them. Their profound insights and interpretations and the works of esteemed Muslim scholars throughout history, both classical and contemporary, contribute significantly to our understanding of the Quran and its sciences.

Considering this, exploring the perspectives and enlightenments these scholars offer regarding the disciplinary action mentioned in the Quranic verse concerning internal conflict resolution within marriage is valuable. Notably, the Prophet Muḥammad (ﷺ), being the recipient of the Quranic revelation from Allāh, provided the initial interpretation of this verse. His understanding and explanation carry significant weight in shaping our comprehension of its intended meaning.

According to a narration on the authority of Amr bin Al-ahwaz AL-jashami, the prophet, ﷺ enlightened what the verse means by saying:

«أَلَا وَاسْتَوْصُوا بِالنِّساءِ خيرًا ، فإنهن عَوَانٌ عِندَكم ، ليس تملكونَ منهن شيئًا غيرَ ذلك ؛ إلا أن يَأْتِينَ بفاحِشةٍ مُبَيِّنَةٍ ، فإنْ فَعَلْنَ فاهجُرُوهُنَّ في المَضَاجِعِ ، واضرِبُوهُنَّ ضَرْبًا غيرَ مُبَرِّحٍ ، فإنْ أطَعْنَكُمْ فلا تَبْغُوا عليهِنَّ سبيلًا»

"Fear Allāh regarding women, for they are your assistants. You have the right on them that they do not allow any person whom you dislike to step on your mat. However, if they do that, you are allowed to discipline them lightly. They have a right to you that you provide them with their provision and clothes in a reasonable manner".[146]

---

146   Al-tirmizi 1163, Al-nasa'I of Al-kubra 9169, and Ibnu Majah 1851.

Based on the narration that elucidates the meaning of "وَاضْرِبُوهُنَّ" and how the beating referred to in verse should be understood, it is unanimously agreed upon by scholars that the striking mentioned in verse is to be done "without severity" (ghayru mubarriḥ) or "without causing pain" (ghayru mu'allim). This consensus among scholars is crucial because, without the Prophet's (ﷺ) clarification, there would be a risk of husbands misusing this verse to harm women, as is unfortunately witnessed in some cases of domestic violence today, where reports of such incidents continue to rise. Here are some quotes from scholars regarding their comments on this verse, taking into account the narration mentioned earlier:

In the interpretation of this verse, various scholars have provided their insights, shedding light on the meaning of "وَاضْرِبُوهُنَّ" and how it should be understood. Here are some notable quotes from renowned scholars:

In his Tafsir, Ibn Abbas mentions that striking should be done in a "mild unexaggerated manner."[147]

Al-Zamakhshari states that scholars agree that the striking mentioned in the verse should be "without severity." It should not cause injury or break bones; the face should be avoided.[148]

Al-Qurtubi comments that the striking referred to in the verse "is a form of discipline without severity, aiming to rectify behavior rather than causing harm."[149]

---

147 Abbas, Ibn. 2008. *Tafsir Ibn Abbas.* Translated by Mokrane Guezzou. Louisville: Fons Vitae

148 Al-Kashshāf 4:34

149 Tafsīr al-Qurṭubī 4:34

Al-Razi mentions that "striking should be done with a folded handkerchief or the palm of the hand, emphasizing that whips or clubs should not be used."[150]

Ibn Kathir elaborates on the verse by stating, "If advice and ignoring her in the bed do not yield the desired results, one is allowed to discipline the wife without severe beating ."[151]

Ibn Hajar writes that "striking women is not allowed without restrictions, and there are situations where it is disliked or even prohibited."[152]

Al-Suyuti emphasizes that "among the rights of women is the importance of good living conditions and avoiding harm."[153]

These perspectives highlight scholars' understanding regarding the verse and provide guidance on the proper interpretation and application of the instruction within the context of marital relationships.

According to Sayyid Quṭub in his Tafsir Fii Zilal Al-Quran, the measures mentioned in the Quranic verse are intended to be pre-emptive actions aimed at achieving early reconciliation when there is a fear of rebellion. These measures should not be used to worsen the situation or increase animosity. It is important to note that these measures are not applicable in a healthy relationship between a husband and wife. Instead, they are preventive measures to protect the family from collapsing in an unhealthy situation.[154]

---

150   Tafsīr al-Rāzī 4:34

151   Tafsīr ibn Katheer: vol:1 page: 504.

152   Fat-hul bari vol:9 pages 302-303

153   Tafsīr al-Jalalayn 2:228.

154   Qutb, Sayyid. n.d. *In the Shade of the Quran.* Translated by Adil Salahi. Vol. 4. Kalamullah.com

Abū Al-a'la Al-Maududi also states in his work "The Meaning of the Quran" that while these measures have been permitted, they should be applied with a sense of proportion, taking into account the nature and extent of the offense. If a gentle admonition is sufficient to bring about a positive change, there is no need to resort to more severe measures. Furthermore, it is important to note that the act of beating was reluctantly allowed by the Holy Prophet and was not something that he preferred".[155]

In the translations by Yusuf Ali, Wahiduddin Khan, and Dr. Mustapha Khattab, the word "lightly" is added after the phrase "strike them," which signifies a necessary restriction for a correct understanding of the verse. Other commentators such as T.B. Irving, Syed Vickar Ahamed, and Dr. Munir Munshey include words like "finally," "lastly," or "if it is useful" in their interpretations. Including these additional words in English translations highlights their consensus and significance in comprehending even the fundamental meaning of the verse. This analysis provides insights into interpreting the so-called.[156]

While some Muslim scholars vigorously defend the practice of disciplinary measures mentioned in the Quran as a divine law that is not open to discussion, they also emphasize the importance of implementing these measures in a controlled manner that avoids violence and harm to women. It is important to understand that the concept of "striking" in this context is primarily intended as a symbolic means to convey the gravity of unwarranted behavior, with divorce being the final step thereafter. The Prophet

---

155   Maududi, Abūl A'la. 1976. *The Meaning of the Quran Vol II*. Lahore: Islamic Publications LTD.

156   "wife-beating verse" (4:34) of the Holy Quran, as discussed in an article published on TMV on January 20, 2019.

Muḥammad (ﷺ) used similar symbolic gestures with his male companions to capture their attention and convey important messages.[157]

Regarding the application of these measures, it is crucial to ensure a proportionate response to the offense committed. It is worth mentioning that these measures should not be employed all at once but rather in cases where a wife persists in obstinate defiance. Additionally, it is evident that when a gentle approach can be effective, resorting to harsher measures should be avoided.[158]

In conclusion, from an Islamic perspective, it is prohibited to cause harm or physical injury to women through acts of violence. Under no circumstances is a husband allowed to cause bruises, injuries, or any form of harm to his wife. If a woman feels that her husband is exceeding his bounds or if she experiences physical harm, she has the legal right to seek assistance from her guardian and pursue legal action, which may include divorce, khulʿ (divorce upon a settlement), or faskh (marriage annulment). [159]

The verse concludes by emphasizing that if the wives rectify themselves through the disciplinary steps mentioned, they should not be subjected to unjust treatment and should be treated with kindness and fairness (maʿrūf). This verse serves as a reminder that the ultimate solution for any dispute, including marital discord, lies in turning to Allāh. Couples should collectively seek Allāh's guidance and submit to His commands when resolving their

---

157   Abū Amina Elias, Does the Quran let men beat their wive? March 14, 2013.

158   Tafheemul Quran commentary on verse 4:35.

159   The article "Marital Harmony and Conflict Resolution: The Quranic Paradigm" by Muḥammad Ziyad Batha. It was published on August 19, 2022.

issues and finding harmony in their relationship. By returning to Allāh and following His guidance, couples can find the path to reconciliation and a peaceful resolution.

2- STRIKING OR HITTING WOMEN IN THE VIEW OF JUDAISM

In order to gain a comprehensive understanding of the topic and its broader dimensions, it is vital to consider the teachings of other scriptures, such as Judaism and Christianity, alongside Islam and its divine law. By conducting a comparative study, we can ensure fairness and a more nuanced perspective on the practice of disciplining wives when they display defiance. Exploring the teachings of different faiths will provide valuable insights and contribute to a well-rounded examination of this issue. In Judaism, it reads as follows: "A wife who refuses to perform any kind of work that she is obligated to do may be compelled to perform it, even by scourging her with a rod"[160] Also, in Deuteronomy Chapter 25 of the Bible, we read: "If two men are fighting and the wife of one of them comes to rescue her husband from his assailant, and she reaches out and seizes him by his private parts, you shall cut off her hand. Show her no pity."[161]

"What is noteworthy about this Biblical passage is that it gives the husband the authority to chop off his wife's hand. The plain reading of the verse indicates that no authorities need to get involved. The husband does not have to call the police or go before a judge. Nope, no need for any due process or any formality. He has the authority to chop up his wife himself.

---

160   Isshu 21:10
161   Deuteronomy 25:11

Furthermore, add salt to the wound. The Bible says, Do not even show her pity,"162

3- STRIKING OR HITTING WOMEN IN THE VIEW OF CHRISTIANITY

In Christianity: From the Christian perspective, a husband's authority includes that he is entitled to have the right to discipline his wife physically. For example, Gratian's twelfth-century canon law text Decretum was highly influential in forming the Christian doctrine on spousal discipline for generations: "A man may chastise his wife and beat her for her own correction; for she is of his household, and therefore the lord may chastise his own [...] so likewise the husband is bound to chastise his wife in moderation [...] unless he be a clerk, in which case he may chastise her more severely."163

The Church authority Cherubino of Siena, in 1477, wrote his famous text "Rules of Married Life." In this text, he states:

"When you see your wife commit an offense, do not rush at her with insults and violent blows...Scold her sharply, bully, and terrify her. And if this still does not work...take up a stick and beat her soundly, for it is better to punish the body and correct the soul than to damage the soul and spare the body...then readily beat her, not in rage but out of charity and concern for her soul, so that the beating will redound to your merit and her good."164

• EXTERNAL CONFLICT RESOLUTION (*ARBITRATION PROCEDURES*)

---

162   Comparing "wife-beating" in Judaism, Christianity, Hinduism, Buddhism, and Islam: Muslim skeptic, August 7, 2022

163   As cited in Coulton 1II.234

164   The Oxford Handbook of Women and Gender in Medieval Europe (New York: Oxford University Press, 2013):161-180

وَإِنْ خِفْتُمْ شِقَاقَ بَيْنِهِمَا فَابْعَثُواْ حَكَمًا مِّنْ أَهْلِهِۦ وَحَكَمًا مِّنْ أَهْلِهَآ إِن يُرِيدَآ إِصْلَٰحًا يُوَفِّقِ ٱللَّهُ بَيْنَهُمَآ إِنَّ ٱللَّهَ كَانَ عَلِيمًا خَبِيرًا ﴿٣٥﴾

"AND IF YOU FEAR DISSENSION BETWEEN THE TWO, SEND AN ARBITRATOR FROM HIS PEOPLE AND AN ARBITRATOR FROM HER PEOPLE. IF THEY BOTH DESIRE RECONCILIATION, ALLĀH WILL CAUSE IT BETWEEN THEM. INDEED, ALLĀH IS EVER KNOWING AND ACQUAINTED [WITH ALL THINGS]". [AN-NISA' : 35.]

Within the verse, the fourth directive provides ongoing instructions and guidelines for resolving marital conflicts. It addresses those critical moments when tensions escalate and there is a heightened concern about the possibility of breaching the marriage contract. In such circumstances, Islam offers guidance to believers, urging them to turn to spousal arbitration. The Quranic command highlights that arbitration should come into play only after exhausting sincere and thorough domestic efforts to resolve the conflict, thus upholding the privacy and confidentiality of the family. This approach emphasizes conciliation and presents a fruitful process aimed at preserving and nurturing the sacred bond of marriage.

Islam recognizes and emphasizes its role as a means to reconcile differences and restore harmony within families. The arbitration process holds significant importance in addressing family disputes and conflicts within the familial and communal spheres. It allows for a more expedient, wholehearted, and flexible resolution process in a less formal setting than in a courtroom environment. Similarly, family arbitration offers a swift and efficient mechanism for couples navigating through challenging circumstances to resolve their disputes.

The arbitration procedure plays a crucial function in family disputes and conflicts on the familial and communal levels. Islam recognizes and emphasizes it as a tool to reconcile disputes and reunite families. Likewise, family arbitration is a quick process that enables couples going through family breakdowns to resolve disputes more quickly, wholeheartedly, and in a more flexible and less formal setting than a courtroom.

It is well-documented that the Arabs were familiar with and utilized arbitration to settle conflicts. This practice was also common among other ancient civilizations and communities. Moreover, a historical examination of the Arabs and their judicial system prior to the emergence of Islam highlights the deep-rooted practice of arbitration as a means to resolve various disputes. It predates the establishment of formal state judiciary systems and even predates the formation of organized states themselves.

Furthermore, it is important to note that in the pre-Islamic era, the use of arbitration was discretionary and dependent on the voluntary agreement of the involved parties. It was primarily based on tribal customs and practices, with the chief of the tribe and respected individuals serving as arbitrators rather than relying on a formalized judicial system. This highlights the significance of arbitration as a longstanding tradition in the region, preceding the introduction of organized legal systems.[165]

Similarly to Islam, the practice of arbitration existed in pre-Islamic Arabia, where tribes would resolve disputes by referring them to a neutral third party who was trusted and respected. Islam recognized and affirmed this form of dispute resolution, indicating its compatibility with the Sharia. Historical evidence demonstrates that arbitration is not foreign to Sharia law but, on the contrary, is explicitly recommended by it. All four major schools of Islamic thought endorse arbitration with different approaches. For

---

165   "Finding your path: Arbitration, Sharia and Modern Middle East," An article published in August-September 2011.

instance, the Hanafi school associates arbitration closely with conciliation, considering the awarded decision less binding than a court judgment.

On the other hand, the Hanbali school, known for its conservatism, considers the arbitrator's decision as binding as a court judgment, requiring the arbitrator to possess qualifications similar to a judge. This illustrates how the interpretation and application of Sharia law can vary and evolve over time, despite the fundamental principles remaining the same. This insight is found in the same source mentioned earlier.

Regarding interpreting the verse at hand, it is essential to approach it holistically rather than relying on a superficial, verse-by-verse explanatory method of tafsir. Such an atomistic approach may fail to understand the verse's depth and content comprehensively. Therefore, it is crucial to highlight the keywords of the verse in their sequential order, as each part carries its specific meaning and is accompanied by additional rules and moral principles:

1- The Quranic enjoinment of فابعثوا

2- Nomination of the arbitrators
حكما من أهله وحكما من أهلها

3- Genuineness of the mediators
إن يريدا إصلاحا يوفق الله بينهما

1- The Quranic enjoinment of فابعثوا (send)

Concerning the Quranic word فابعثوا (fā'ba'thū), Muslim scholars and jurists hold different opinions regarding the addressee in the verse: Al-Tabari, in his Tafsīr, suggests that the addressed person is السلطان (the ruler), and the majority of scholars widely supports this view.[166]

---

166 Jami'ul bayan fii ta'weel Al-Quran vol:8 pages: 318-330

Al-imam Malik, representing the majority of scholars who believe the addressee is السلطان (the ruler), supports this opinion.[167]

Al-Qurtubi suggests that the addressees are the guardians of the couple.[168]

Al-imam Al-Shafie holds the opinion that the addressees are the couple directly involved in the issue.[169]

Despite these differences in the scholars' views regarding the addressee, these opinions can be reconciled because each party involved has a distinct role: the ruler has the authority to command the appointment of arbitrators, and the couple has the responsibility to choose and appoint their representatives in the arbitration process since it directly concerns them. The role of the guardians may be to provide consultation to the couple and offer their opinion on the couple's choice.[170]

2- Nomination of the arbitrators:

Regarding the competence and selection of arbitrators, Ibn Kathir provides the following explanation: "The jurists have stated that in cases of disagreement between spouses, a judge appoints a reliable person from the wife's family and a trustworthy person from the husband's family to mediate and examine their situation. These individuals assess the dispute and determine whether the couple should separate or remain together to prevent further wrongdoing."[171]

---

167   Bidayatul Mujtahid vol: 2 page: 97, Al-Hanbila school of thought, and others

168   Vol:5, page 178

169   Al-Muqni Al-Muhtah vol: 2 page: 207

170   Article: "ندب الحكمين في الخلع" "Empowering the arbitrators in the khula (divorce upon a settlement)" by Dr. Sami 'Abduslam, 10/6/2015, published on Aluka net.

171   Tafsir Ibn Kathir, Vol. 2, p. 447 or The Electronic copy page 1033

The Qur'an uses the term "hakam" to refer to these appointed individuals, emphasizing their necessary qualifications. They should be capable of making a fair decision regarding the dispute, typically found in knowledgeable and trustworthy individuals. Al-Qurtubi says: "If there is a fear of dispute between spouses, it is recommended to appoint an arbitrator from the man's family and an arbitrator from the woman's family. These arbitrators should possess qualities of justice and a deep understanding of Islamic jurisprudence, as they are more familiar with the situation of the couple involved. If suitable candidates cannot be found among their families, then two just and knowledgeable individuals from outside can be appointed."[172]

According to Al-Qurtubi, the qualifications of the arbitrators include being just and having a comprehensive understanding of Islamic jurisprudence. Their competence is essential for successfully resolving the dispute and the goal of reuniting and fostering peace and harmony between the married couple. The requirement for arbitrators to be "Just" ensures fair treatment of both parties and encourages the conflicting couple to reconcile their differences.

3- The genuineness of the mediators:

"If they both desire reconciliation, Allāh will cause it between them."

According to the Quran's recommendation, "Sulh agreement" or mediation is an effective method for resolving marital disputes. It serves as an act of worship and empowers both parties, particularly the wife, to determine what is in their best interest. This process is conducted under strict confidentiality, allowing the couple to prioritize finding a mutually beneficial resolution. The Quran

---

172   Al-Qurtubi, Vol. 5, page 175

emphasizes the importance of the "Sulh agreement" in the chapter of Al-Nisa, encouraging couples to prioritize reconciliation and peaceful resolution." The verse reads:

$$فَلَا جُنَاحَ عَلَيْهِمَآ أَن يُصْلِحَا بَيْنَهُمَا صُلْحًا ۚ وَٱلصُّلْحُ خَيْرٌ$$

"THERE IS NO SIN UPON THEM IF THEY MAKE TERMS OF SETTLEMENT BETWEEN THEM - AND SETTLEMENT IS BEST." [AL-NISA : 128]

• THE DIFFERENCE BETWEEN SULH AGREEMENT AND ARBITRATION

"In Islam, arbitration differs from Sulh in three ways. Firstly, Sulh allows for a voluntary settlement between the parties, with or without the involvement of others, while arbitration requires the appointment of a third party. Parties engaged in Sulh can use an arbitrator to reach an agreement. Thus, arbitration can serve as a tool within the Sulh process. Secondly, a Sulh agreement is not legally binding unless made in front of a court, whereas arbitration, according to most jurists, is enforceable without court intervention. Thirdly, Sulh is applicable only when a conflict has already occurred and cannot be used to address potential disputes. In contrast, arbitration can be employed to resolve both existing and potential disputes."[173]

However, the verse also includes a condition at the end that highlights an aspect of the mediation process and its mechanism, as the Quran explicitly states:

$$إِن يُرِيدَآ إِصْلَٰحًا يُوَفِّقِ ٱللَّهُ بَيْنَهُمَآ ۗ إِنَّ ٱللَّهَ كَانَ عَلِيمًا$$

---

173   Aseel Al-Ramahi, Sulh: A Crucial Part of Islamic Arbitration, London School of Economics and Political Science, Law Department, p.12.

It means: "If these two arbitrators (or the couple)[174] desire to set things right, Allāh Almighty will help them bring harmony between the husband and the wife."

Hence, since Al-ṣulḥ (mediation) serves as a tool for arbitration, the sincerity and genuine desire of the parties involved to resolve the issue are crucial for the effectiveness of mediation in achieving an amicable resolution.

Regarding the insights derived from the verse regarding the arbitrators, Mohamed Shafi' Al-Othman, in his tafsir book "Maariful Quran," highlights the following:

The success of the arbitration process and the restoration of mutual rapport between the disputing couple depend on both arbitrators' good intentions and sincere desire to bring about peace. Consequently, if the desired reconciliation is not achieved, it may indicate a lack of perfect sincerity on the part of one of the arbitrators in pursuing the goal of peace-making. With the genuine efforts of the arbitrators, Allāh's unseen help will facilitate the creation of love and harmony in the couple's hearts.

The appointment of the two arbitrators is specifically intended to foster peace and amity between the husband and wife without involving any other matters. However, if the parties involved in the dispute agree to appoint these arbitrators as their representatives and grant them full authority in all aspects, they would acknowledge that any decision jointly made by the arbitrators is acceptable and binding upon both of them. In such cases, the arbitrators possess absolute authority to decide the case. If they agree on divorce as the solution, it will be executed accordingly. Similarly, if they determine that the woman should be released

---

174   Al-Baqawi 8/332)

through khul', a form of dissolution of marriage, the khul' will take effect, and their decision will be binding. Ḥasan al-Basri and Imam Abū Hanifah support this viewpoint.[175]

4- AUTHORITY OF THE MEDIATORS:

Regarding the authority of mediators, there are differing opinions among Muslim jurists. The Hanafi and Shāfiʿi schools maintain that mediators typically do not possess the authority to issue a binding verdict. Their role is primarily to recommend a solution they believe is appropriate, after which the spouses have the right to accept or reject it. However, if the spouses have specifically designated the mediators to act on their behalf concerning talaq or khul' (divorce or annulment), they would be obligated to abide by the mediators' decision. This perspective is supported by the Hanafi and Shāfiʿi schools.

On the other hand, a group of jurists, including Ḥasan al-Basri and Qatadah, argue that mediators' authority is limited to facilitating reconciliation between spouses and does not extend to the annulment of the marriage.

Conversely, another group of scholars, including Ibn ʿAbbas, Saʾid b. Jubayr, Ibrahim al-Nakhaʾi, al-Shaʾbi, Muḥammad b. Sinn, and several other authorities, assert that mediators possess full authority regarding reconciliation and marriage annulment. However, Muslim jurists hold varying opinions on the extent of authority granted to mediators. While some believe mediators only provide recommendations, others argue they have the power to facilitate reconciliation and even annul marriages."[176]

---

175   Rūḥ al-Maʿānī, etc." Al-Nisa: verse 35 - Maariful Quran: Quran.com

176   Tafsīr Tafheem-ul-Quran by Syed Abū-al-Aʾla Maududi, Al-nisa, verse 35/ Al-Mawardi: Al-hawi Al-kbeer vol:9 page 1425 / Al-Mawardi: AL-Insaf vol: 8 page 379 / Iʾanatu Dalibeen vol: 3:378 / Al-Kafi fii fiq Al-hanbali vol: 3 page 139.

In contrast to the Hanafi and Shāfi'i schools, the perspective of Ibn Abbas and others emphasizes that an arbitral award holds jurisdictional significance. It is considered binding and enforceable, and the judge's role is limited to examining certain formal aspects of the arbitration process, such as a valid arbitration agreement and whether the award addresses the subject matter of the dispute. Consequently, the judge cannot refuse to enforce the arbitral decision.

It is important to note that the differences of opinion among Islamic schools of thought, as mentioned earlier, do not pertain to the authority of arbitrators to resolve the issue at hand, as they are mandated to do so by the Quran. Rather, the scholars' arguments revolve around the extent to which mediators or arbitrators can independently arrive at a final decision or issue a verdict regarding their assigned task of reconciling the couple's marital relationship or annulment.

Based on the arguments mentioned above, the prevailing juristic view asserts that arbitrators possess full authority to issue a verdict, irrespective of whether the couple accepts it. This viewpoint finds support in the following evidence:

1- The Quran titled the arbitrators as حكم, which means "judge. By this, the Quran endorses their authority to reach a final decision.[177] On the authority of Ubeidah:

ان عليا رضي الله عنه بعث رجلين فقال لهما: أتريان ما عليكما؟ عليكما إن رأيتما أن تجمعا جمعتما, وإن رأيتما أن تفرقا فرقتما, فقال الرجل أما هذا فلا, فقال: كذبت والله لا تبرح حتى ترضى بكتاب الله عز وجل لك وعليك, فقالت المرأة : رضيت بكتاب الله

---

177   Al-Shirazi, Al-Muhzab vol: 2 pages: 488

"Ali Bin Abi Talib addressed two men who appointed them as arbitrators by saying: 'Do you know your responsibility? Do you know what you must do? Hear me. If both of you agree to keep the husband and wife together and make peace between them, then do it. And if you come to the conclusion that matters cannot be set right between them or that they will not stay right later on, and both of you concur with the option that separation between them is the expedient course, then do it; the husband said: 'Separation and divorce are things I will not accept under any condition. Ali said: 'No, you are wrong. You should authorize the arbitrators; otherwise, you will depart here. When the woman heard this, she said: 'I accept the Divine law."[178]

The narration demonstrates clearly that the arbitrators have full authority and, therefore, can issue a verdict independently without referring to the judge and that the couple's acceptance is not a prerequisite in the arbitration.

Furthermore, a judge's intervention is only necessary when the two arbitrators differ in decision and opinion for a decisive outcome.

Finally, and far most significantly, it is worth mentioning that the only and final hope for the marital relationship's survival- if Allāh wills- is the mediator's endeavor and success to save the marriage from breakdown.

Therefore, since mediation is the spouse's last chance, it is wise for the couple to show mutual respect and understanding if they wish their marriage to continue; both men and women are equally responsible and will be held countable by Allāh in the hereafter should they fail to preserve the marital harmony. Hence, they are encouraged to seek help from family members or community elders, besides arbitrators, if the difficulties in their marriage seem to be developing to the worst; professional counseling might help resolve issues among couples at risk of divorcing.

MORAL GUIDELINES FROM VERSE 1 OF AL-TALAQ

---

178   Al-Istizkar Al-jam limzahib fuqaha Al-Amsar, Hadith no: 27068 page 109.

MORAL VALUES AND ETIQUETTE SURROUNDING DIVORCE

- ## FEARING ALLĀH IN THE CONTEXT OF DIVORCE

- ## AVOIDING OPPRESSION AND INJUSTICE IN DIVORCE

- ## DIVORCE GUIDELINES FROM THE QURAN AND SUNNAH

يَـٰٓأَيُّهَا ٱلنَّبِيُّ إِذَا طَلَّقْتُمُ ٱلنِّسَآءَ فَطَلِّقُوهُنَّ لِعِدَّتِهِنَّ وَأَحْصُوا ٱلْعِدَّةَ وَٱتَّقُوا ٱللَّهَ رَبَّكُمْ لَا تُخْرِجُوهُنَّ مِنۢ بُيُوتِهِنَّ وَلَا يَخْرُجْنَ إِلَّآ أَن يَأْتِينَ بِفَـٰحِشَةٍ مُّبَيِّنَةٍ وَتِلْكَ حُدُودُ ٱللَّهِ وَمَن يَتَعَدَّ حُدُودَ ٱللَّهِ فَقَدْ ظَلَمَ نَفْسَهُ لَا تَدْرِى لَعَلَّ ٱللَّهَ يُحْدِثُ بَعْدَ ذَٰلِكَ أَمْرًا ﴿١﴾

"O PROPHET, WHEN YOU [MUSLIMS] DIVORCE WOMEN, DIVORCE THEM FOR [THE COMMENCEMENT OF] THEIR WAITING PERIOD AND KEEP COUNT OF THE WAITING PERIOD, AND FEAR ALLĀH, YOUR LORD. DO NOT TURN THEM OUT OF THEIR [HUSBANDS'] HOUSES, NOR SHOULD THEY [THEMSELVES] LEAVE [DURING THAT PERIOD] UNLESS THEY ARE COMMITTING A CLEAR IMMORALITY. AND THOSE ARE THE LIMITS [SET BY] ALLĀH. AND WHOEVER TRANSGRESSES THE LIMITS OF ALLĀH HAS CERTAINLY WRONGED HIMSELF. YOU KNOW NOT; PERHAPS ALLĀH WILL BRING ABOUT AFTER THAT A [DIFFERENT] MATTER."

[AT-TALAQ: 1]

The verse above emphasizes the importance of believers ending the marriage bond and parting ways amicably in situations where the mediation procedure fails or all attempts to reconcile the couple prove unsuccessful. It highlights that divorce should be seen as a last resort, a right that can be exercised when there is harm or when the couple genuinely believes they can no longer continue their relationship together.

"Sometimes divorce is obligatory when any one of the spouses causes any harm that will not be removed except with divorce. Sometimes divorce is unlawful when any one of the spouses has caused any harm, and the divorce will not bring any benefit to overcome the harm, or both the harm and the benefit are equal".[179]

---

179   Minhaj al-Muslim vol:2 page 355.

From a juristic standpoint emphasizing "balancing advantages and disadvantages," divorce is considered a context-specific matter. Its permissibility or prohibition varies depending on the circumstances that arise, as illustrated in the following two narrations:

A- It was narrated from 'Abdallah bin 'Umar that: the Messenger of Allāh ﷺ said:

«أَبْغَضُ الْحَلَالِ إِلَى اللَّهِ الطَّلَاقُ»

"The most hated of permissible things to Allāh is divorce."[180]

B- It was narrated from Thawban that the Messenger of Allāh, ﷺ said:

«أَيُّما امرأةٍ سَأَلَتْ زَوجَها الطَّلاقَ في غيرِ ما بَأسٍ، فحَرامٌ عليها رائحةُ الجنَّةِ»

«Any woman who asks her husband for a divorce when it is not necessary, the fragrance of Paradise will be forbidden to her. »[181]

Based on the two sayings mentioned above, the first one, narrated by 'Abdallah Bin Omer, highlights that divorce is something Allāh dislikes, indicating general disapproval. On the other hand, the second Hadith, narrated by Thawban, specifies that divorce is permissible when genuine harm is present in the marriage.

• FEARING ALLĀH

All the verses in the Qur'an that address marital family issues, including marriage and divorce, highlight the moral and psychological dimensions inherent in these relationships in various forms. A noticeable aspect for the reader is the consistent emphasis on the knowledge of Allāh, specifically His all-knowing

---

180   Ibn Majah: 2018.

181   Ibid 2055

and fully encompassing of what is concealed within the depths of human beings. This notion is evident when reflecting on the concluding statements of just five verses from Surah Al-Baqara, which specifically discuss the topic of divorce. These verses (231 to 235 of Chapter Al-Baqara) are compelling examples that reinforce this observation.

1-

وَٱعْلَمُوٓا۟ أَنَّ ٱللَّهَ بِكُلِّ شَىْءٍ عَلِيمٌ ۝

" AND BE MINDFUL OF ALLĀH AND KNOW THAT HE HAS FULL KNOWLEDGE OF EVERYTHING." [AL-BAQARAH : 231]

2-

وَٱللَّهُ يَعْلَمُ وَأَنتُمْ لَا تَعْلَمُونَ ۝

"ALLĀH KNOWS, AND YOU DO NOT." [AL-BAQARAH : 232]

3-

وَٱعْلَمُوٓا۟ أَنَّ ٱللَّهَ بِمَا تَعْمَلُونَ بَصِيرٌ ۝

"AND KNOW THAT ALLĀH SEES EVERYTHING YOU DO." [AL-BAQARAH : 233]

4-

وَٱللَّهُ بِمَا تَعْمَلُونَ خَبِيرٌ ۝

"ALLĀH IS FULLY AWARE OF WHAT YOU DO" [AL-BAQARAH : 234]

5-

وَٱعْلَمُوٓا۟ أَنَّ ٱللَّهَ غَفُورٌ حَلِيمٌ ۝

"REMEMBER THAT ALLĀH IS MOST FORGIVING AND FORBEARING." [AL-BAQARAH : 235]

These verses encompass the profound psychological dimensions that greatly influence the intimate aspect of the marital relationship. They serve as a reminder and warning against any injustice within this hidden realm. These dimensions are intricately defined by the innate conscience of individuals, with their nature known only to Allāh the Almighty.

Similarly, the Quran emphasizes the paramount importance of Taqwa (God-consciousness) for believers. The term "Taqwa" itself is mentioned in over 60 locations throughout the Quran, while its derivatives are found in more than 190 locations across various chapters. The quality of Taqwa acts as a protective barrier, preventing the oppression of others. In the context of divorce, three specific verses emphasize the significance of Taqwa, cautioning Muslims against mistreating their wives during and after the emotionally challenging divorce process. The repetition of Taqwa in relation to divorce serves as a vital reminder for believers to stay connected with their Creator, remaining conscious of their actions and responsibilities, particularly during heated divorce moments. The three verses of "Taqwa" in surat al-talaq are:

وَمَن يَتَّقِ اللَّهَ يَجْعَل لَّهُۥ مَخْرَجًا ﴿٢﴾

"AND WHOEVER FEARS ALLĀH - HE WILL MAKE FOR HIM A WAY OUT" [AT-TALAQ: 2]

وَمَن يَتَّقِ اللَّهَ يَجْعَل لَّهُۥ مِنْ أَمْرِهِۦ يُسْرًا ﴿٤﴾

"AND WHOEVER FEARS ALLĀH - HE WILL MAKE FOR HIM OF HIS MATTER EASE."
[AT-TALAQ: 4]

وَمَن يَتَّقِ اللَّهَ يُكَفِّرْ عَنْهُ سَيِّئَاتِهِۦ وَيُعْظِمْ لَهُۥٓ أَجْرًا ﴿٥﴾

"AND WHOEVER FEARS ALLĀH - HE WILL REMOVE FOR HIM HIS MISDEEDS AND MAKE GREAT FOR HIM HIS REWARD." [AT-TALAQ: 5]

- ## AVOIDING OPPRESSION AND INJUSTICE

In a narration preserved by Imam Muslim, as mentioned previously, the Prophet Muḥammad (ﷺ) advised, "Fear Allāh in your treatment of women, for you have taken them as a trust from Allāh." This profound statement highlights that oppressing and treating wives unjustly goes against Allāh's trust in husbands.

Furthermore, the subsequent verses directly address the subject of divorce and clearly warn against any kind of oppression towards women. These verses emphasize that such oppression is unacceptable, regardless of the reasons or circumstances surrounding the divorce. It reinforces the importance of treating women with fairness, respect, and kindness throughout the marital relationship and during the process of divorce.

MORAL TEACHINGS FROM VERSE 231 OF SURAT Al-Baqarah

وَإِذَا طَلَّقْتُمُ ٱلنِّسَآءَ فَبَلَغْنَ أَجَلَهُنَّ فَأَمْسِكُوهُنَّ بِمَعْرُوفٍ أَوْ سَرِّحُوهُنَّ بِمَعْرُوفٍ وَلَا تُمْسِكُوهُنَّ ضِرَارًا لِّتَعْتَدُوا وَمَن يَفْعَلْ ذَٰلِكَ فَقَدْ ظَلَمَ نَفْسَهُ وَلَا تَتَّخِذُوا ءَايَٰتِ ٱللَّهِ هُزُوًا وَٱذْكُرُوا نِعْمَتَ ٱللَّهِ عَلَيْكُمْ وَمَآ أَنزَلَ عَلَيْكُم مِّنَ ٱلْكِتَٰبِ وَٱلْحِكْمَةِ يَعِظُكُم بِهِ وَٱتَّقُوا ٱللَّهَ وَٱعْلَمُوا أَنَّ ٱللَّهَ بِكُلِّ شَىْءٍ عَلِيمٌ ﴿٢٣١﴾

"AND WHEN YOU DIVORCE WOMEN AND THEY HAVE [NEARLY] FULFILLED THEIR TERM, EITHER RETAIN THEM ACCORDING TO ACCEPTABLE TERMS OR RELEASE THEM ACCORDING TO ACCEPTABLE TERMS, AND DO NOT KEEP THEM, INTENDING HARM, TO TRANSGRESS [AGAINST THEM]. AND WHOEVER DOES THAT HAS CERTAINLY WRONGED HIMSELF. AND DO NOT TAKE THE VERSES OF ALLĀH IN JEST. AND REMEMBER THE FAVOR OF ALLĀH UPON YOU AND WHAT HAS BEEN REVEALED TO YOU OF THE BOOK AND WISDOM BY WHICH HE INSTRUCTS YOU. AND FEAR ALLĀH AND KNOW THAT ALLĀH IS KNOWING OF ALL THINGS.

[AL-BAQARAH : 231]

In the mentioned verse:

- Husbands are advised against keeping their wives in a state of transgression if they no longer desire to maintain the marital relationship.

- Engaging in such oppressive behavior towards wives is regarded as a mockery of Allāh's teachings and a blatant violation of their rights.

MORAL TEACHINGS FROM VERSE 232 OF Al-Baqarah

وَإِذَا طَلَّقْتُمُ ٱلنِّسَآءَ فَبَلَغْنَ أَجَلَهُنَّ فَلَا تَعْضُلُوهُنَّ أَن يَنكِحْنَ أَزْوَٰجَهُنَّ إِذَا تَرَٰضَوْا۟ بَيْنَهُم بِٱلْمَعْرُوفِ ذَٰلِكَ يُوعَظُ بِهِۦ مَن كَانَ مِنكُمْ يُؤْمِنُ بِٱللَّهِ وَٱلْيَوْمِ ٱلْءَاخِرِ ذَٰلِكُمْ أَزْكَىٰ لَكُمْ وَأَطْهَرُ وَٱللَّهُ يَعْلَمُ وَأَنتُمْ لَا تَعْلَمُونَ ﴿٢٣٢﴾

"AND WHEN YOU DIVORCE WOMEN, AND THEY HAVE FULFILLED THEIR TERM, DO NOT PREVENT THEM FROM REMARRYING THEIR [FORMER] HUSBANDS IF THEY AGREE AMONG THEMSELVES ON AN ACCEPTABLE BASIS. THAT IS INSTRUCTED TO WHOEVER OF YOU BELIEVES IN ALLĀH AND THE LAST DAY. THAT IS BETTER FOR YOU AND PURER, AND ALLĀH KNOWS, AND YOU KNOW NOT". [AL-BAQARAH : 232]

In the verse mentioned above:

- The verse prohibits preventing wives from remarrying their former husbands, as it is considered an act of oppression and injustice against them. It is worth noting that scholars have clarified that the addressee in this verse is the guardian of the wife.

- By abstaining from oppressing their wives, believers showcase their sincere and strong faith in Allāh and the belief in the Hereafter.

MORAL TEACHINGS FROM VERSE 4 OF AL-NISA

وَءَاتُوا۟ ٱلنِّسَآءَ صَدُقَٰتِهِنَّ نِحْلَةً فَإِن طِبْنَ لَكُمْ عَن شَىْءٍ مِّنْهُ نَفْسًا فَكُلُوهُ هَنِيٓـًٔا مَّرِيٓـًٔا ﴿٤﴾

"AND GIVE THE WOMEN [UPON MARRIAGE] THEIR [BRIDAL] GIFTS GRACIOUSLY. BUT IF THEY GIVE UP WILLINGLY TO YOU ANYTHING OF IT, THEN TAKE IT IN SATISFACTION AND EASE".
[AN-NISA' : 4]

In verse above:

Another form of oppression is depriving wives of their rightful dowries and bridal gifts.

MORAL TEACHINGS FROM VERSE 19 OF AL-NISA

يَٰٓأَيُّهَا ٱلَّذِينَ ءَامَنُوا۟ لَا يَحِلُّ لَكُمْ أَن تَرِثُوا۟ ٱلنِّسَآءَ كَرْهًا ۖ وَلَا تَعْضُلُوهُنَّ لِتَذْهَبُوا۟ بِبَعْضِ مَآ ءَاتَيْتُمُوهُنَّ إِلَّآ أَن يَأْتِينَ بِفَٰحِشَةٍ مُّبَيِّنَةٍ ۚ وَعَاشِرُوهُنَّ بِٱلْمَعْرُوفِ ۚ فَإِن كَرِهْتُمُوهُنَّ فَعَسَىٰٓ أَن تَكْرَهُوا۟ شَيْـًٔا وَيَجْعَلَ ٱللَّهُ فِيهِ خَيْرًا كَثِيرًا ﴿١٩﴾

"O YOU WHO HAVE BELIEVED, IT IS NOT LAWFUL FOR YOU TO INHERIT WOMEN BY COMPULSION. AND DO NOT MAKE DIFFICULTIES FOR THEM IN ORDER TO TAKE [BACK] PART OF WHAT YOU GAVE THEM UNLESS THEY COMMIT A CLEAR IMMORALITY. AND LIVE WITH THEM IN KINDNESS. FOR IF YOU DISLIKE THEM - PERHAPS YOU DISLIKE A THING AND ALLAH MAKES THEREIN MUCH GOOD". [AN-NISA' : 19]

In the verse mentioned above:

- The verse emphasizes that women cannot be treated as inheritable property, opposing the pre-Islamic custom prevalent in the Arabian peninsula. This custom forced women to marry their deceased husband's brother or closest relative against their will.

- Husbands are encouraged to treat their wives kindly and maintain good relations with them in all situations and circumstances. This includes supporting and caring for them during difficult and happy times, as harmony between spouses is crucial for a successful marital bond.

MORAL TEACHINGS FROM VERSE 1 OF AL-TALAQ

يَٰٓأَيُّهَا ٱلنَّبِيُّ إِذَا طَلَّقْتُمُ ٱلنِّسَآءَ فَطَلِّقُوهُنَّ لِعِدَّتِهِنَّ وَأَحْصُوا۟ ٱلْعِدَّةَ ۖ وَٱتَّقُوا۟ ٱللَّهَ رَبَّكُمْ ۖ لَا تُخْرِجُوهُنَّ مِنۢ بُيُوتِهِنَّ وَلَا يَخْرُجْنَ إِلَّآ أَن يَأْتِينَ بِفَٰحِشَةٍ مُّبَيِّنَةٍ ۚ وَتِلْكَ حُدُودُ ٱللَّهِ ۚ وَمَن يَتَعَدَّ حُدُودَ ٱللَّهِ فَقَدْ ظَلَمَ نَفْسَهُ ۚ لَا تَدْرِى لَعَلَّ ٱللَّهَ يُحْدِثُ بَعْدَ ذَٰلِكَ أَمْرًا ﴿١﴾

"O PROPHET, WHEN YOU [MUSLIMS] DIVORCE WOMEN, DIVORCE THEM FOR [THE COMMENCEMENT OF] THEIR WAITING PERIOD AND KEEP COUNT OF THE WAITING PERIOD, AND FEAR ALLĀH, YOUR LORD. DO NOT TURN THEM OUT OF THEIR [HUSBANDS'] HOUSES, NOR SHOULD THEY [THEMSELVES] LEAVE [DURING THAT PERIOD] UNLESS THEY ARE COMMITTING A CLEAR IMMORALITY. AND THOSE ARE THE LIMITS [SET BY] ALLĀH. AND WHOEVER TRANSGRESSES THE LIMITS OF ALLĀH HAS CERTAINLY WRONGED HIMSELF. YOU KNOW NOT; PERHAPS ALLĀH WILL BRING ABOUT AFTER THAT A [DIFFERENT] MATTER".

[AT-TALAQ: 1]

In verse above:

- Divorce should be conducted in accordance with the teachings of the Sunnah, which will be further discussed in subsequent pages of this section.

- It is important to note that divorced women should not be forcefully expelled from their homes until the completion of their prescribed waiting period, known as 'Iddah, which serves as a time of transition and reflection before considering marriage again.

$$\text{وَتِلْكَ حُدُودُ اللَّهِ وَمَن يَتَعَدَّ حُدُودَ اللَّهِ فَقَدْ ظَلَمَ نَفْسَهُ لَا تَدْرِى لَعَلَّ اللَّهَ يُحْدِثُ بَعْدَ ذَٰلِكَ أَمْرًا ۝}$$

(..AND THOSE ARE THE LIMITS [SET BY] ALLĀH. AND WHOEVER TRANSGRESSES THE LIMITS OF ALLĀH HAS CERTAINLY WRONGED HIMSELF) **[AT-TALAQ: 1]**

"The phrase حُدُودَ اللَّهِ (the limits prescribed by Allāh) refers to the sacred laws set down by the Sharī'ah of Islam. The phrase وَمَن يَتَعَدَّ (And whoever exceeds the limits prescribed by Allāh) implies 'whoever violates the sacred laws.' The phrase فَقَدْ ظَلَمَ نَفْسَهُ (wrongs his own self) implies that he has not damaged Allāh s sacred laws or the Shari' ah. In fact, he has caused loss to himself. The loss could be religious, or it could be mundane".[182]

---

182   Ma'rūf Quran: Quran.com

A- DIVORCE GUIDELINES FROM THE QURAN AND SUNNAH

- ## GUIDELINES FOR DIVORCE PROCEDURES "'IDDAH AND ITS RULINGS"

- ## GUIDELINES FOR DIVORCE PROCEDURES

فَطَلِّقُوهُنَّ لِعِدَّتِهِنَّ وَأَحْصُوا ٱلْعِدَّةَ

"DIVORCE THEM FOR [THE COMMENCEMENT OF] THEIR WAITING PERIOD AND KEEP COUNT OF THE WAITING PERIOD. » [AL-TALAQ : 1]

In this verse, divorce categorization and guidelines according to Quran and Sunnah:

Category 1: Sunni Divorce (الطلاق السني) - This refers to a divorce pronounced during the wife's state of purity, wherein the husband has not engaged in any sexual intercourse with her. In such cases, the husband must wait until the wife's next state of purity after menstruation before proceeding with the divorce.

Category 2: Innovated Divorce (الطلاق البدعي) - This refers to a divorce pronounced by the husband in certain prohibited situations, which include:

a). During the wife's menstruation period.

b). During the wife's postnatal period.

c). During the wife's state of purity after engaging in sexual intercourse.

d). Pronouncing divorce thrice in one word or repeating it three times simultaneously, such as saying, "She is divorced, she is divorced, she is divorced."[183]

However, the above rulings and restrictions concerning divorce, its way, and time can be provable through the prophetic traditions that elaborate the meaning of the Quranic commandment (فَطَلِّقُوهُنَّ لِعِدَّتِهِن وَأَحْصُوا اَلْعِدَّةَ) together with the consensus of the scholars and their sayings which gave illustrations on the rulings involved:

- Ibn 'Umar divorced his wife while she was menstruating. When 'Umar ibnulkhatab mentioned this to the Messenger of Allāh, ﷺ heard this, he became very indignant and said:

«مره ليراجعها ثم يمسكها حتّى تطهر ثم تحيض فتطهر ، فان بدا له فليطلقها طاهرًاقبل ان يمسّها ، فتلك العدّه التّى امرها اللّه تعالىٰ ان يطلّق بها النّساء۔»

"He must take her back and keep her till she is purified, then has another menstrual cycle and is purified. If it then seems proper for him to pronounce another divorce to her, he may do so when she is pure from the menstrual discharge before having conjugal relations with her, for that is the ''iddah that Allāh has commanded for the divorce of women."[184]

Al-imam Bukhari commented on the narration by saying:

Al-Imam Al-Bukhari said: "The Sunnah Talaq is to divorce her in a state of purity with no intercourse and in the presence of two witnesses."[185]

---

183 Wahbat Zuheili, Al-fiqh Al-shafi'i Al-Muyasar, Vol. 2, pages 124-127. Abū al-Hassan, Bidayat al-Mubtadi, p. 68. Tha'labi, al-Talqīn fī al-fiqh al-Mālikī, Vol. 1, p. 124-125. Nawawi, Rawdat al-Talibeen, Vol. 8, p. 3-8. Minhajul Muslim, Vol. 2, page 358.

184 Ṣaḥīḥ Bukhari 5251 and Muslim 1471.

185 Ṣaḥīḥ Al-Bukhari 7/52.

Ibnu Rushd mentioned that there is a scholarly consensus, a binding proof, on this issue whereby he said in his book of Bidyat Al-mujtahid:

> "The jurists have unanimously agreed that Sunnah divorce concerning the consummated marriage is to pronounce the divorce on the wife in a state of purity in which he did not have intercourse with her and the one who divorces during the menses period, he did not divorce following the Sunnah." [186]

Furthermore, it is important to highlight that according to Ibn Rushd's interpretation in the quotation above, the phrase "the consummated marriage" refers to a marriage that has been physically consummated through sexual intercourse. In the case of a marriage that has not been consummated yet, the husband has the right to divorce his wife at any time, regardless of her state of purity. This is because the waiting period ('iddah) mentioned in the Quranic verse in Surat Al-Ahzab does not apply in such a situation. The ruling regarding divorce without a waiting period specifically applies to marriages that have not been consummated. The Quran says:

$$\text{يَـٰٓأَيُّهَا ٱلَّذِينَ ءَامَنُوٓا۟ إِذَا نَكَحْتُمُ ٱلْمُؤْمِنَـٰتِ ثُمَّ طَلَّقْتُمُوهُنَّ مِن قَبْلِ أَن تَمَسُّوهُنَّ فَمَا لَكُمْ عَلَيْهِنَّ مِنْ عِدَّةٍ تَعْتَدُّونَهَا ۖ فَمَتِّعُوهُنَّ وَسَرِّحُوهُنَّ سَرَاحًا جَمِيلًا ﴿٤٩﴾}$$

"O YOU WHO HAVE BELIEVED, WHEN YOU MARRY BELIEVING WOMEN AND THEN DIVORCE THEM BEFORE YOU HAVE TOUCHED THEM, THEN THERE IS NOT FOR YOU ANY WAITING PERIOD TO COUNT CONCERNING THEM. SO, PROVIDE FOR THEM AND GIVE THEM A GRACIOUS RELEASE». [AL-AHZAB : 49]

To provide further clarification on the ruling mentioned in the Quranic verse, it states that if a woman is divorced before the consummation of her marriage, meaning before any sexual intercourse takes place with her husband, she is not subject to the waiting period ('iddah) rulings mentioned earlier. Therefore, she is not required to comply with those specific rulings. On the other

---

186 Ibnu Rushd, Bidayat Al-Mujtahid, vol: 3 pages: 86.

hand, if a woman has consummated her marriage and had sexual contact with her husband, she is obligated to observe the waiting period ('iddah), during which she is expected to preserve the rights of both her husband and herself.

Furthermore, divorcing a wife by uttering the word "divorced" three times in one instance is not in accordance with the Sunnah. The Prophet expressed his disapproval when he heard that a man had divorced his wife by pronouncing three divorces in one statement without any interval between them. This incident is mentioned in the following Hadith: On the authority of Mahmud Bin Labid, he said:

اخبرني رسول الله ﷺ عن رجل طلق إمرأته ثلاث تطيقات جميعا فغضب وقال:
«أيلعب بكتاب الله وأنا بين أظهركم ؟»

"That, when the prophet was informed about a man who divorced his wife with three pronouncements in one word, the prophet ﷺ became angry and said: « Is play being made of Allāh's book while I am among you?"[187]

However, there is a difference of opinion among scholars regarding the effectiveness of "INNOVATED DIVORCE" in breaking the marriage bond, despite it being disliked in the Sharia. The majority of scholars hold the view that innovative divorce does indeed have an impact and ultimately leads to the dissolution of the marital bond.

- THE WISDOM BEHIND FOLLOWING THE SUNNAH IN DIVORCE; HOW AND WHEN

The Divine legislation surrounding the strict guidelines, stipulations, and restrictions on divorce carries within it valuable wisdom and primary goals, including the following:

---

187   Al-Nasaa'i, vol: 6, pages: 143-144.

The preservation of the spousal relationship is one of the main objectives of the Sharia, emphasizing the importance of maintaining strong family bonds through all available means.

Removing obstacles and barriers that may separate a husband and wife is a key consideration. Therefore, divorce should only be pronounced during the wife's state of purity, signifying the husband's willingness to reconsider his decision and thoughts of divorce.

The verse "You know not; perhaps Allāh will bring about after that a [different] matter" (At-Talaq, verse 1) indicates the potential for change during the waiting period ('Iddah). It suggests that the couple may reconcile and experience a better relationship. These profound words from the Quran highlight the psychological transformation that can occur during this period, where the husband may reflect on the comforts and services provided by his wife in managing the household and caring for their children. This reflection may lead to remorse, prompting him to retract the divorce and reconcile with his wife.

The 'Iddah (waiting period) should not be unnecessarily prolonged. If divorce occurs during menstruation, the 'Iddah may start from the next menstrual cycle. Conversely, if divorce happens during purity, the 'Iddah may start from her immediate menstruation period. This approach ensures that the wife's waiting period is efficiently managed, saving her time.

Intercourse during the non-menstruating period, known as "tuhr," should be avoided to prevent the possibility of pregnancy. In such cases, the 'Iddah period will only conclude once the wife gives birth to the child. This situation may result in a more extended waiting period, similar to divorce during the menstrual period.

In summary, the Divine legislation surrounding divorce serves several significant purposes, including preserving marital bonds, the potential for reconciliation, efficient management of the 'Iddah period, and considerations related to pregnancy.

- **'IDDAH AND ITS RULINGS**

فَطَلِّقُوهُنَّ لِعِدَّتِهِنَّ وَأَحْصُوا الْعِدَّةَ

"DIVORCE THEM FOR [THE COMMENCEMENT OF] THEIR WAITING PERIOD AND KEEP COUNT OF THE WAITING PERIOD. » [AL-TALAQ: 1]

And the previous narriation of Bukhari[188] and Muslim[189] on the authority of Ibn Umar:

«فتلك العدّه الّتى امرها الله تعالىٰ ان يطلّق بها النّساء»

"..for that is the '' iddah that Allāh has commanded for the divorce of women.»

As previously discussed, the verse mentioned above serves as the foundation for the concept of 'Iddah and its associated rulings. Muslim jurists and Quran commentators have further elaborated on these matters, drawing insights from explanatory prophetic traditions, including the narration of Ibn Umar mentioned earlier. These elaborations shed light on the various rulings and rights pertaining to 'Iddah and its procedures. The following are some of the key rulings and rights concerning 'Iddah:

- **'IDDAH AND ITS PRESCRIBED PERIOD:**
- **DEFINITIONS AND OBJECTIVES OF 'IDDAH (MAQASID AL-'IDDAH)-**

---

188   5251

189   1471

Definition of 'Iddah: 'Iddah is an Islamic concept pertaining to divorce and a husband's death. Derived from Arabic, it signifies a legally prescribed waiting period during which a woman is not permitted to remarry after being widowed or divorced.

The observance of 'Iddah serves several primary purposes:

- Establishing pregnancy and determining the legitimate paternity of a child before allowing remarriage in cases of divorce or death.

- Allowing a period for potential reconciliation, as divorce is considered a last resort in resolving family problems according to prescribed measures.

- Providing a mourning period for the deceased husband, whose companionship is terminated by death.

- Granting a waiting period in case a husband has disappeared, allowing the woman time before considering remarriage.

- Ensuring that a woman receives the necessary care and support during pregnancy, particularly following the death of her husband.[190]

- ## THE PRESCRIBED PERIOD OF 'IDDAH

There are four categories of women with specific durations of 'Iddah prescribed for each, as determined by Islamic teachings and supported by references from the Quran.

- The first category pertains to pregnant women, whether widowed or divorced, whose 'Iddah period concludes upon delivery of the child.

---

190   Dr. Busari Mshood, "Iddatul-talaq and iddatul wafat: A re-interpretation of the phrase 'Hatta yada'na hamlahuna'" (2017).

Allāh says:

$$\text{وَأُوْلَٰتُ ٱلْأَحْمَالِ أَجَلُهُنَّ أَن يَضَعْنَ حَمْلَهُنَّ}$$

"...AND FOR THOSE WHO ARE PREGNANT, THEIR TERM IS UNTIL THEY GIVE BIRTH"

[AT-TALAQ: 4]

The second category pertains to non-pregnant widows, for whom the prescribed duration of 'Iddah is four months and ten days following the death of their husband. The Quran states:

$$\text{وَٱلَّذِينَ يُتَوَفَّوْنَ مِنكُمْ وَيَذَرُونَ أَزْوَٰجًا يَتَرَبَّصْنَ بِأَنفُسِهِنَّ أَرْبَعَةَ أَشْهُرٍ وَعَشْرًا}$$

"AND THOSE WHO ARE TAKEN IN DEATH AMONG YOU AND LEAVE WIVES BEHIND - THEY, [THE WIVES, SHALL] WAIT FOUR MONTHS AND TEN [DAYS]." [AL-BAQARAH : 234]

The third category pertains to menstruating women, for whom the prescribed duration of 'Iddah is three menstrual cycles. Verse in Surat Al-Baqarah mentions:

$$\text{وَٱلْمُطَلَّقَٰتُ يَتَرَبَّصْنَ بِأَنفُسِهِنَّ ثَلَٰثَةَ قُرُوٓءٍ}$$

"DIVORCED WOMEN REMAIN IN WAITING FOR THREE PERIODS» [AL-BAQARAH : 228]

- The fourth category pertains to women who do not menstruate due to being either too young or too old. For such women, the prescribed duration of 'Iddah is typically a period of three lunar months. Allāh says:

$$\text{وَٱلَّٰٓـِٔى يَئِسْنَ مِنَ ٱلْمَحِيضِ مِن نِّسَآئِكُمْ إِنِ ٱرْتَبْتُمْ فَعِدَّتُهُنَّ ثَلَٰثَةُ أَشْهُرٍ وَٱلَّٰٓـِٔى لَمْ يَحِضْنَ}$$

"..AND THOSE WHO NO LONGER EXPECT MENSTRUATION AMONG YOUR WOMEN - IF YOU DOUBT, THEN THEIR PERIOD IS THREE MONTHS, AND [ALSO FOR] THOSE WHO HAVE NOT MENSTRUATED». [AT-TALAQ: 4]

- ## RIGHTS AND OBLIGATIONS DURING 'IDDAH

The divorced wife, under revocable divorce (طلاق رجعة), cannot enter into a marriage contract with another man, as the divorce is still revocable, indicating that the previous marriage is not entirely terminated.

During the revocable period of 'Iddah, the husband has the right to reconcile and resume the marital relationship without requiring the wife's acceptance or permission. However, in cases of irrevocable divorce, the divorcing man no longer possesses this right. Once an irrevocable divorce takes effect, he is treated like any other man seeking to marry her. She can accept him for a new marriage with a new contract and dowry if desired. Alternatively, she can reject and refuse him. Irrevocable divorce may occur when:

a). The prescribed period of 'Iddah concludes.

b). Divorce is initiated through Khul' (mutual separation) or arbitration.

c). Divorce occurs before the consummation of marriage (prior to sexual relations), as mentioned earlier.

d). Divorce is pronounced for the third time after completing two previous divorces.)[191]

As the wifely-related rulings continue during the 'Iddah period, the divorced wife has the right to receive full financial support, housing accommodation, and other necessary provisions until her prescribed period is completed.

In the event of pregnancy, she is obligated to inform her husband as it affects the extension of the 'Iddah period and relates to the child he will father.

---

191 (Minhajul Muslim vol: 2 pages:359-360

SECTION TWO

ETIQUETTE AND MORALITY TOWARD PARENTS

3.2.1. THE SIGNIFICANCE OF ETIQUETTE AND MORALITY TOWARDS PARENTS IN ISLAMIC TEACHINGS

This topic holds a unique and significant scope, focusing on the parent-child code of behavior. It encompasses various dimensions, including qualities such as forgiveness, patience, and respect toward parents. Islam, unlike any other religion, emphasizes the utmost respect and care towards parents, with no comparable level of importance given to any other relationship except that of the Prophet (). What sets this code apart is its foundation in the divine law of Allāh, which exemplifies its perfection and completeness.

Searching for "kindness to parents" on Google shows that six out of the first ten results are Islamic articles highlighting the importance of being dutiful and kind to parents. This prominence is due to

Islam being a religion that emphasizes qualities such as mercy, tolerance, and respect. God has commanded the good treatment of parents and warned against treating them with disrespect.[192]

Moreover, the methodology of sublime morality regarding parent-child relations adopted by Islam surpasses that of other religions and culturally-based morals and etiquettes. The Quran's commandments and the Prophet Muḥammad's teachings (ﷺ) contain balanced imperatives that cultivate healthy and positive relationships, encompassing mutual obligations and reciprocal arrangements on both sides.

A study of various Quranic verses concerning parents reveals the elevated status that Allāh has bestowed upon them. Islam decrees respect for parents immediately after believing in Allāh and worshiping Him alone, emphasizing the tremendous value of this obligation. The Holy Qur'an underscores this obligation by mentioning it more than fifteen times, emphasizing our indebtedness to our parents and the extensive rights we owe them.

As we delve into the Quranic commandments and the sayings of the Prophet Muḥammad (ﷺ), it becomes evident that compassion, reverence, and respect towards parents hold exceptional importance in the Islamic way of life. The revelations regarding this theme are abundant and highlight the qualities mentioned thus far, along with others that further emphasize how deeply these moral values are embedded in the teachings of Islam.

• THE HOLY QURAN:

Allāh says in the Holy Quran the following:

192　Aisha Stacey, "Kindness to Parents: Duty and Devotion." Published on July 21, 2008, on IslamReligion.com.

وَإِذْ أَخَذْنَا مِيثَقَ بَنِى إِسْرَٰءِيلَ لَا تَعْبُدُونَ إِلَّا ٱللَّهَ وَبِٱلْوَٰلِدَيْنِ إِحْسَانًا وَذِى ٱلْقُرْبَىٰ وَٱلْيَتَٰمَىٰ وَٱلْمَسَٰكِينِ وَقُولُوا۟ لِلنَّاسِ حُسْنًا وَأَقِيمُوا۟ ٱلصَّلَوٰةَ وَءَاتُوا۟ ٱلزَّكَوٰةَ ثُمَّ تَوَلَّيْتُمْ إِلَّا قَلِيلًا مِّنكُمْ وَأَنتُم مُّعْرِضُونَ ﴿٨٣﴾

"AND [RECALL] WHEN WE TOOK THE COVENANT FROM THE CHILDREN OF ISRAEL, [ENJOINING UPON THEM], "DO NOT WORSHIP EXCEPT ALLĀH; AND TO PARENTS DO GOOD AND TO RELATIVES, ORPHANS, AND THE NEEDY. AND SPEAK TO PEOPLE GOOD [WORDS] AND ESTABLISH PRAYER AND GIVE ZAKAH." THEN YOU TURNED AWAY, EXCEPT A FEW OF YOU, AND YOU WERE REFUSING." **[AL-BAQARAH" : 83]**

In the Quran, Allāh consistently emphasizes the duty of being kind and compassionate to our parents in close proximity to the command to worship Him alone. This parallel placement of Allāh's rights and parents' rights signifies their simultaneous importance and serves as a reminder of their intertwined significance within one verse.

- He also says:

۞ وَٱعْبُدُوا۟ ٱللَّهَ وَلَا تُشْرِكُوا۟ بِهِۦ شَيْـًٔا وَبِٱلْوَٰلِدَيْنِ إِحْسَانًا وَبِذِى ٱلْقُرْبَىٰ وَٱلْيَتَٰمَىٰ وَٱلْمَسَٰكِينِ وَٱلْجَارِ ذِى ٱلْقُرْبَىٰ وَٱلْجَارِ ٱلْجُنُبِ وَٱلصَّاحِبِ بِٱلْجَنۢبِ وَٱبْنِ ٱلسَّبِيلِ وَمَا مَلَكَتْ أَيْمَٰنُكُمْ إِنَّ ٱللَّهَ لَا يُحِبُّ مَن كَانَ مُخْتَالًا فَخُورًا ﴿٣٦﴾

"WORSHIP ALLĀH AND ASSOCIATE NOTHING WITH HIM, AND TO PARENTS DO GOOD, AND TO RELATIVES, ORPHANS, THE NEEDY, THE NEAR NEIGHBOR, THE NEIGHBOR FARTHER AWAY, THE COMPANION AT YOUR SIDE, THE TRAVELER, AND THOSE WHOM YOUR RIGHT HANDS POSSESS. INDEED, ALLĀH DOES NOT LIKE THOSE WHO ARE SELF-DELUDING AND BOASTFUL". **[AN-NISA' : 36]**

- Repeating the same injunction, Allāh says:

۞ قُلْ تَعَالَوْا۟ أَتْلُ مَا حَرَّمَ رَبُّكُمْ عَلَيْكُمْ أَلَّا تُشْرِكُوا۟ بِهِۦ شَيْـًٔا وَبِٱلْوَٰلِدَيْنِ إِحْسَانًا وَلَا تَقْتُلُوٓا۟ أَوْلَٰدَكُم مِّنْ إِمْلَٰقٍ نَّحْنُ نَرْزُقُكُمْ وَإِيَّاهُمْ وَلَا تَقْرَبُوا۟ ٱلْفَوَٰحِشَ مَا ظَهَرَ مِنْهَا وَمَا بَطَنَ وَلَا تَقْتُلُوا۟ ٱلنَّفْسَ ٱلَّتِى حَرَّمَ ٱللَّهُ إِلَّا بِٱلْحَقِّ ذَٰلِكُمْ وَصَّىٰكُم بِهِۦ لَعَلَّكُمْ تَعْقِلُونَ ﴿١٥١﴾

"SAY, "COME, I WILL RECITE WHAT YOUR LORD HAS PROHIBITED TO YOU. [HE COMMANDS] THAT YOU NOT ASSOCIATE ANYTHING WITH HIM, AND TO PARENTS, GOOD TREATMENT, AND DO NOT KILL YOUR CHILDREN OUT OF POVERTY; WE WILL PROVIDE FOR YOU AND THEM. AND DO NOT APPROACH IMMORALITIES - WHAT IS APPARENT OF THEM AND WHAT IS CONCEALED. AND DO NOT KILL THE SOUL WHICH ALLĀH HAS FORBIDDEN [TO BE KILLED] EXCEPT BY [LEGAL] RIGHT. THIS HAS HE INSTRUCTED YOU THAT YOU MAY USE REASON". [AL-AN'AM : 151.]

Once again, in the preceding two verses, the focus on Tawḥīd, the belief in the oneness of Allāh and worshiping Him alone, is evident. This emphasis is then followed by a command to display compassion towards parents and relatives, as highlighted in verse 36 of Al-Nisa, and to refrain from committing various grave sins, as mentioned in Al-An'am verse 152. These divine instructions from our Merciful Creator address the needs and obligations of both parents and children, ensuring that neither is neglected.

However, it is vital to acknowledge the psychological aspect of this matter. The younger generation naturally tends to look forward rather than backward, focusing on their own aspirations and the well-being of their own offspring. Yet, it is crucial to recognize that parents hold a significant place in our lives. They are the ones who brought us into this world and played a pivotal role in our upbringing, which significantly contributes to our eventual success and development.

By emphasizing the obligation of compassion and kindness towards parents, the verses aim to remind children of the profound debt of gratitude they owe to their parents above anyone else. It is a reminder of the immense sacrifice and effort parents have invested in raising their children. Recognizing and fulfilling this duty of compassion becomes essential for maintaining a harmonious and balanced society.

However, the verses emphasize the importance of Tawḥīd, worshiping Allāh alone, while also highlighting the significance of displaying kindness and compassion towards parents and avoiding sinful actions. They address the innate tendency of younger individuals to focus on their own future, urging them to reflect upon the vital role parents play in their lives. Parents deserve our utmost compassion and respect as the source of our existence and instrumental figures in our upbringing.[193]

۞ وَقَضَىٰ رَبُّكَ أَلَّا تَعْبُدُوٓا۟ إِلَّآ إِيَّاهُ وَبِٱلْوَٰلِدَيْنِ إِحْسَـٰنًا ۚ إِمَّا يَبْلُغَنَّ عِندَكَ ٱلْكِبَرَ أَحَدُهُمَآ أَوْ كِلَاهُمَا فَلَا تَقُل لَّهُمَآ أُفٍّ وَلَا تَنْهَرْهُمَا وَقُل لَّهُمَا قَوْلًا كَرِيمًا ۝

وَٱخْفِضْ لَهُمَا جَنَاحَ ٱلذُّلِّ مِنَ ٱلرَّحْمَةِ وَقُل رَّبِّ ٱرْحَمْهُمَا كَمَا رَبَّيَانِى صَغِيرًا ۝

"AND YOUR LORD HAS DECREED THAT YOU NOT WORSHIP EXCEPT HIM, AND TO PARENTS, GOOD TREATMENT. WHETHER ONE OR BOTH OF THEM REACH OLD AGE [WHILE] WITH YOU, SAY NOT TO THEM [SO MUCH AS], "UFF," AND DO NOT REPEL THEM BUT SPEAK TO THEM A NOBLE WORD. AND LOWER TO THEM THE WING OF HUMILITY OUT OF MERCY AND SAY, "MY LORD, HAVE MERCY UPON THEM AS THEY BROUGHT ME UP [WHEN I WAS] SMALL."

[AL-ISRA' : 23- 24]

This passage, encompassing two verses and a famous verse from the Quran regarding parent-child relations, effectively delves into the subject matter's profound depth and various dimensions. If there were no other verses addressing the moral behavior between parents and children, these two verses would still be sufficient to convey the comprehensive message encompassing all aspects of the discourse.

However, the articles within these Quranic directives explicitly proclaim the rights of parents alongside the rights of Allāh, establishing the primacy of parental rights as the greatest among all human rights. Thus, these verses extend beyond mere moral recommendations; they form the foundation of parental rights

---

193   Fizilal Al-Quran p.123

and authority, with further details elucidated in the Books of Hadith and Fiqh, as eloquently expressed by Abū A'la in his book "Al-Tafheem." Furthermore, demonstrating respectful behavior, obedience, and honoring the rights of parents constitutes an indispensable element of both practical education and moral training within Islamic society and civilization, as emphasized in verses 23-27 of "Al-Tafheem."[194]

Additionally, the passage imparts a valuable practical lesson, teaching us the significance of prioritizing love, affection, kindness, and mercy towards our parents, particularly as they age and become dependent on our care. Thus, the duty to prioritize and prioritize our parents' needs and well-being over other obligations is firmly emphasized. This concept was also emphasized by the Prophet Muḥammad (ﷺ) in one of his sayings. On a specific occasion, when directing one of his companions, he emphasized the need to prioritize serving one's parents over engaging in Al-jihad (striving for the cause of Islam) and Al-hijrah (migrating for the sake of Islam). This profound teaching, narrated by ʿAbdallah ibn Umar, serves as a powerful reminder of the paramount importance of filial piety and caring for our parents throughout their lives, especially during their elder years.

أقبل رجل إلى نبي الله ﷺ فقال: أبايعك على الهجرة والجهاد، أبتغي الأجر من الله، قال: «فهل من والديك أحد حي؟» قال: نعم، بل كلاهما، قال: «فتبتغي الأجر من الله؟» قال: نعم، قال: «فارجع إلى والديك فأحسن صحبتهما»

"A MAN CAME TO THE PROPHET OF ALLĀH ﷺ AND SAID: I PLEDGE ALLEGIANCE TO YOU ON IMMIGRATION AND JIHAD, SEEKING REWARD FROM GOD. HE SAID: ARE ANY OF YOUR PARENTS ALIVE? HE SAID: YES, BUT BOTH OF THEM. SO HE SAID: DO YOU SEEK REWARD FROM GOD? HE SAID: YES, HE SAID: GO BACK TO YOUR PARENTS AND BE GOOD TO THEM".[195]

---

194   verses 23-27 "Al-Tafheem.

195   Bukhari 3004

The core purpose of Islamic teachings regarding the treatment of parents is to express and bestow upon them our profound mercy. Mercy is the foundational moral behavior our parents deserve, and it is the central theme emphasized in this passage. Mercy, in essence, is the compassionate sentiment that fosters a deep emotional bond between parents and their children, encompassing both material and spiritual aspects.

Furthermore, the verses within the Quran acknowledge that there may be instances when one or both parents exhibit exceedingly challenging or offensive behavior. Even in such circumstances, it is strictly forbidden to neglect or show annoyance towards our parents. Neglect and annoyance demonstrate a lack of respect and gratitude toward those who have raised and supported us throughout our lives. If it becomes necessary to address their behavior, it should be done with patience, open communication, and a sincere effort to peacefully resolve the issue. Regardless of the situation, one should refrain from expressing mild disgust or disapproval. Instead, from a young age, children should be taught to respect and honor the elderly. They should exhibit tolerance towards their parents, even during tense moments, showing restraint and refraining from speaking ill of them, especially considering any capricious behavior as a sign of old age. It is equally important to extend respect to the parents of one's spouse ﷺ, as these actions further nurture love and harmony within the marital relationship.

The emphasis placed on honoring parents in Islam is so significant that Muslims consider it an exceptional opportunity to attain paradise through serving one's parents. Sadly, many individuals fail to seize this immense blessing bestowed upon them. Regrettably, only those fortunate enough to grasp this rare and precious chance can truly benefit from it. The Prophet Muḥammad (ﷺ) warns against neglecting this reward, as it serves as a means to ultimately achieve our goal of entering paradise.

The teachings of Islam stress the significance of showing mercy to parents, which forms the bedrock of their treatment. The passage emphasizes the importance of compassionately caring for our parents and addresses navigating challenging situations with patience and respect. It also underscores the immense reward associated with fulfilling the rights of parents, highlighting the opportunity it provides to attain paradise.

On the authority of Abūhuraira, the prophet ﷺ said:

رغم أنف ثم رغم أنف ثم رغم أنف قيل من يا رسول الله قال من أدرك أبويه عند الكبر أحدهما أو كليهما فلم يدخل الجنة

"May a man whose parents reached old age in his presence, and they were not a cause for his entrance to Paradise (by being dutiful to them), be humiliated."[196]

Hence, one of the most significant acts that pave the way to paradise is Birrul Walideen, which encompasses both obedience and treating parents with kindness and respect. This concept of Birrul Walideen holds tremendous importance in Islam, as it is regarded as one of the best and most beloved deeds in the sight of Allāh, second only to prayer.

In a report by Ibnu mas'ud, the messenger ﷺ said:

سألت رسول الله ﷺ: «أي العمل أحب إلى الله قال: الصلاة على وقتها. قال ثم أي؟ قال: ثم بر الوالدين. قال: ثم أي؟ قال: الجهاد في سبيل الله» قال حدثني بهن ولو استزدته لزادني..

---

196   Tirmidhi 3545.

"The best of the deeds or deed is the (observance of) prayer at its proper time and kindness to the parents."[197]

Conversely, disobeying and mistreating parents can lead to the consequences of hellfire. Abū al-Faraj Ibn Al-Jawzi eloquently expands on the ethical concept of "al-birr" and how it should be manifested in our behavior and manners towards our parents. He emphasizes that being kind to our parents entails obeying their commands unless they ask us to do something forbidden by Allāh, prioritizing their instructions over voluntary acts of worship, refraining from what they forbid us to do, providing for their needs, serving them, approaching them with humility and mercy, refraining from raising our voice or fixing our gaze on them, and avoiding calling them by their names. Patience in dealing with them is also essential. [198]

It is crucial to exercise caution and refrain from using insulting interjections when communicating with our parents.[199] In the Quran, Allāh commands us not to even utter the smallest disrespectful comment towards our parents. Even saying "uff" to our parents is considered inappropriate.

The word "uff" is an interjection that expresses displeasure and should not be used when conversing with our parents.

Furthermore, the verses in the Quran guide us not to scold or reprimand our parents due to their old age. Instead, we should treat them with kindness and supplicate to Allāh, asking Him to shower them with His mercy, just as they have shown us

---

197   Ṣaḥīḥ Muslim 85

198   Ibn al-Jawzi, Birr al-Wālidayn, page 5, Pdf.

199   Abū Mahdi, an article: parents in the Quran, September 22, 2020

mercy during our childhood. Since Allāh's blessings and favors are bestowed through His mercy, seeking Allāh's mercy for our parents encompasses seeking all other divine blessings.

According to Al-Ghazali, the happiness of children in this world and the hereafter depends on the prayers of their parents. The prayers of parents are accepted and hold immense weight. Neglecting or upsetting our parents carries a tremendous sin, equivalent to the weight of mountains. Failing to respond to our parents' calls burdens our souls significantly (Ibid). Al-Ghazali emphasizes that those with a conscience should not bring distress to their parents, as the consequences are severe.

The Prophet Muḥammad (ﷺ) highlighted the correlation between parental satisfaction and attaining the pleasure of Allāh. If parents are pleased with their children, it is an indication that they have also attained Allāh's pleasure. Conversely, if parents are displeased with their children, it signifies a lack of Allāh's pleasure ﷻ. This emphasizes the immense importance of maintaining a strong and respectful bond with our parents (Ibid). On the authority of 'Abdallah ibn Umar the Prophet ﷺ said: :

(رضى الرب في رضى الوالد , وسخط الرب في سخط الوالد)

"The Lord's pleasure is in the parent's pleasure, and the Lord's anger is in the parent's anger,"[200]

Allāh says in the following chapters of Al-ankabut, Luqman, and Al-ahqaf:

---

200   Tirmidhi 1899

A-

وَوَصَّيْنَا الْإِنسَانَ بِوَالِدَيْهِ حُسْنًا وَإِن جَاهَدَاكَ لِتُشْرِكَ بِي مَا لَيْسَ لَكَ بِهِ عِلْمٌ فَلَا تُطِعْهُمَا إِلَيَّ مَرْجِعُكُمْ فَأُنَبِّئُكُم بِمَا كُنتُمْ تَعْمَلُونَ ﴿٨﴾

"AND WE HAVE ENJOINED UPON MAN GOODNESS TO PARENTS. BUT IF THEY ENDEAVOR TO MAKE YOU ASSOCIATE WITH ME THAT OF WHICH YOU HAVE NO KNOWLEDGE, DO NOT OBEY THEM. TO ME IS YOUR RETURN, AND I WILL INFORM YOU ABOUT WHAT YOU USED TO DO". [AL-ANKABUT : 8]

B-

وَوَصَّيْنَا الْإِنسَانَ بِوَالِدَيْهِ حَمَلَتْهُ أُمُّهُ وَهْنًا عَلَىٰ وَهْنٍ وَفِصَالُهُ فِي عَامَيْنِ أَنِ اشْكُرْ لِي وَلِوَالِدَيْكَ إِلَيَّ الْمَصِيرُ ﴿١٤﴾

"AND WE HAVE ENJOINED UPON MAN [CARE] FOR HIS PARENTS. HIS MOTHER CARRIED HIM, [INCREASING HER] IN WEAKNESS UPON WEAKNESS, AND HIS WEANING IS IN TWO YEARS. BE GRATEFUL TO ME AND TO YOUR PARENTS; TO ME IS THE [FINAL] DESTINATION".
[LUQMAN : 14]

C-

وَوَصَّيْنَا الْإِنسَانَ بِوَالِدَيْهِ إِحْسَانًا حَمَلَتْهُ أُمُّهُ كُرْهًا وَوَضَعَتْهُ كُرْهًا وَحَمْلُهُ وَفِصَالُهُ ثَلَاثُونَ شَهْرًا حَتَّىٰ إِذَا بَلَغَ أَشُدَّهُ وَبَلَغَ أَرْبَعِينَ سَنَةً قَالَ رَبِّ أَوْزِعْنِي أَنْ أَشْكُرَ نِعْمَتَكَ الَّتِي أَنْعَمْتَ عَلَيَّ وَعَلَىٰ وَالِدَيَّ وَأَنْ أَعْمَلَ صَالِحًا تَرْضَاهُ وَأَصْلِحْ لِي فِي ذُرِّيَّتِي إِنِّي تُبْتُ إِلَيْكَ وَإِنِّي مِنَ الْمُسْلِمِينَ ﴿١٥﴾

"AND WE HAVE ENJOINED UPON MAN, TO HIS PARENTS, GOOD TREATMENT. HIS MOTHER CARRIED HIM WITH HARDSHIP AND GAVE BIRTH TO HIM WITH HARDSHIP, AND HIS GESTATION AND WEANING [PERIOD] IS THIRTY MONTHS. [HE GROWS] UNTIL, WHEN HE REACHES MATURITY AND REACHES [THE AGE OF] FORTY YEARS, HE SAYS, "MY LORD, ENABLE ME TO BE GRATEFUL FOR YOUR FAVOR WHICH YOU HAVE BESTOWED UPON ME AND UPON MY PARENTS AND TO WORK RIGHTEOUSNESS OF WHICH YOU WILL APPROVE AND MAKE RIGHTEOUS FOR ME MY OFFSPRING. INDEED, I HAVE REPENTED TO YOU, AND INDEED, I AM OF THE MUSLIMS." [AL-AHQAF : 15.]

The Quranic commandments further unfold through three additional verses, each commencing with the verb "وصى" (which can be translated as enjoin, command, or order). In its various forms and connotations, these verbs emphasize the vital significance of relaying the message of the Creator to humanity. Consequently, the information contained within these verses holds great value and should be implemented in our behavior and attitude toward our parents, with a particular emphasis on providing special care and consideration to mothers who often endure more hardships than fathers.

These verses illuminate mothers' profound and unconditional love for their children, their selfless and unrecompensed sacrifices, and the numerous trials and tribulations they endure. From the difficulties faced during pregnancy to the pains and illnesses experienced during childbirth, mothers bear the brunt of physical, psychological, and emotional challenges. These trials elevate their status to a level higher than that of fathers, as emphasized by the Prophet Muḥammad (ﷺ) in an authentic narration recorded by Imam Muslim.

Abū Huraira reported that a person said:

جاء رجل إلى رسول الله ﷺ فقال: يا رسول الله من أحق الناس بحسن صحابتي؟ "قال: أمك، قال: ثم من؟ قال: ثم أمك، قال ثم من؟ قال: ثم أمك، قال: ثم من؟ قال: ثم أبوك».

"Allāh's Messenger, who amongst the people is most deserving of my good treatment? He said: Your mother, again your mother, again your mother, then your father, then your nearest relatives according to the order (of nearness)."[201]

Unsurprisingly, in the Books of Hadith, 'Abdallah Ibn Abbas has highlighted treating one's mother as the most virtuous deed in strengthening one's relationship with Allāh. He profoundly expressed: He said:

قال ابن عباس: لا أعلم عملاً أقرب إلى الله عز وجل من بر الوالدة

---

201   Muslim 2548.

"I know of no other deed that brings people closer to Allāh than kind treatment and respect towards one's mother."[202]

The preceding evidence clearly demonstrates how Islam elevates the status of mothers to the highest level. The honor bestowed upon parents and, specifically, mothers in Islam surpasses that found in any other religion, ideology, or culture.

---

202   Al-Ādab al-Mufrad Bukhârî 1/45.

SECTION THREE

PARENTAL MORAL OBLIGATIONS TOWARD CHILDREN

3.3.1. PART 1: ISLAMIC PERSPECTIVE ON PARENT-CHILD RELATIONSHIPS

A- Procreation as a Fulfillment of Shariah's Fundamental Objectives:

In Islam, one of Shariah's grand objectives is preserving life. This objective is actualized through the institution of marriage and the act of procreation, which serve as vital means for the continuation of human existence and survival. Recognizing children's lofty status in Islam, the religion encourages believers to embrace parenthood. The Messenger of Allāh, ﷺ, urged men to seek out spouses who possess qualities of love and fertility, emphasizing the importance of having children as a means to fulfill this noble goal. On the authority of Anas Bin Malik, may Allāh be pleased with him:

"جاء رجل إلى النبي ﷺ, فقال: إني أصبت امرأة ذات حسب وجمال, وأنها لا تلد, أفأتزوجها قال: لا ثم أتاه الثانية فنهاه, ثم أتاه الثالثة , فقال: تزوجوا الولود الودود فإني مكاثر بكم الأمم"

A man came to the Prophet (ﷺ) and said: I have found a woman of rank and beauty, but she does not give birth to children. Should I marry her? He said: No. He came again to him, but he prohibited him. He came to him the third time, and he (the Prophet) said: "Marry the one who is loving and fertile, for I shall outnumber the peoples by you."[203]

In contrast to the Western perception of children as burdensome, Islam holds a distinct perspective. Across Europe, modern birth control methods and population control measures have significantly declined fertility rates. According to the United Nations, the projected population of the EU block is expected to decrease from 446 million today to 365 million by 2100. While birth control has been practiced throughout history, some extreme measures, such as infanticide, have been employed as forms of population control. However, it is crucial to emphasize that Islam rejects such practices and upholds the value and protection of children. Poverty and the inability to provide for children should never be used as justifications for committing evil acts. [204]

B- Children are a blessing:

The Quranic teachings highlight the significance of acknowledging and cherishing the gift of children to foster gratitude towards the Creator. Children are among the countless and immeasurable blessings bestowed upon humanity by Allāh. As servants of Allāh, it is our duty to express gratitude for these blessings, knowing that by doing so, we can experience their increase and continuity, as promised by Allāh in the Quran. Through our gratitude and responsible nurturing, we can ensure the perpetuation of this divine blessing in our lives and the lives of future generations.

---

203   Abū Daud 2050

204   'Abdul Malik Sheikh explores the Islamic perspective on childhood and child protection in his work "Darul Īmān Birmingham."Al-nasa'I 3227. Al-bani graded it as ḥasan ṣaḥīḥ.

وَإِذْ تَأَذَّنَ رَبُّكُمْ لَئِن شَكَرْتُمْ لَأَزِيدَنَّكُمْ وَلَئِن كَفَرْتُمْ إِنَّ عَذَابِى لَشَدِيدٌ ۝

"AND [REMEMBER] WHEN YOUR LORD PROCLAIMED, 'IF YOU ARE GRATEFUL, I WILL SURELY INCREASE YOU [IN FAVOR]; BUT IF YOU DENY, INDEED, MY PUNISHMENT IS SEVERE."

[SURAT IBRAHIM : 7]

In addition, it is mentioned in the Quran across various chapters that every blessing carries its own responsibility. The magnitude of a blessing directly correlates with the extent of responsibility placed upon us. We are held accountable by Allāh for each and every type of blessing bestowed upon us, irrespective of its scale or nature. Allāh states:

ثُمَّ لَتُسْأَلُنَّ يَوْمَئِذٍ عَنِ ٱلنَّعِيمِ ۝

"THEN YOU WILL SURELY BE ASKED THAT DAY ABOUT PLEASURE [SURAT AL-TAKATHUR, 8]

However, the Quran provides numerous instances where prophets and righteous individuals sought blessings from Allāh through their supplications and expressed profound gratitude upon receiving them. These verses exemplify different manifestations of seeking and appreciating blessings from Allāh. Allāh says:

دَعَوَا ٱللَّهَ رَبَّهُمَا لَئِنْ ءَاتَيْتَنَا صَٰلِحًا لَّنَكُونَنَّ مِنَ ٱلشَّٰكِرِينَ ۝

"THEY BOTH INVOKE ALLĀH, THEIR LORD, "IF YOU SHOULD GIVE US A GOOD [] [CHILD], WE WILL SURELY BE AMONG THE GRATEFUL" [AL-A'RAF : 189]

The previous verse is linked to the context of Adam and Eve's story, highlighting their sincere supplications and vows to Allāh. They fervently requested a pious child and promised to express gratitude to Allāh if He granted their request. This narrative emphasizes that children are indeed a blessing that warrants deep appreciation and thankfulness towards Allāh.

It also reads in Quran:

وَٱلَّذِينَ يَقُولُونَ رَبَّنَا هَبْ لَنَا مِنْ أَزْوَٰجِنَا وَذُرِّيَّٰتِنَا قُرَّةَ أَعْيُنٍ وَٱجْعَلْنَا لِلْمُتَّقِينَ إِمَامًا ۝

"AND THOSE WHO SAY, "OUR LORD, GRANT US FROM AMONG OUR WIVES AND OFFSPRING COMFORT TO OUR EYES AND MAKE US AN EXAMPLE FOR THE RIGHTEOUS."

[AL-FURQAN : 74]

Prophet Abraham praising Allāh for the blessing, Quranic states:

ٱلْحَمْدُ لِلَّهِ ٱلَّذِى وَهَبَ لِى عَلَى ٱلْكِبَرِ إِسْمَٰعِيلَ وَإِسْحَٰقَ إِنَّ رَبِّى لَسَمِيعُ ٱلدُّعَآءِ ۝

رَبِّ ٱجْعَلْنِى مُقِيمَ ٱلصَّلَوٰةِ وَمِن ذُرِّيَّتِى رَبَّنَا وَتَقَبَّلْ دُعَآءِ ۝

"PRAISE TO ALLĀH, WHO HAS GRANTED TO ME IN OLD AGE ISHMAEL AND ISAAC. INDEED, MY LORD IS THE HEARER OF SUPPLICATION. MY LORD, MAKE ME AN ESTABLISHER OF PRAYER, AND [MANY] FROM MY DESCENDANTS. OUR LORD, AND ACCEPT MY SUPPLICATION"

[IBRAHIM : 39 – 40]

Upon close examination of the verses above, the Quran portrays children as a source of comfort to the eyes and a gift that Allāh can only bestow in response to sincere supplication offered by His servants. This is exemplified in verse 74 of Al-Furqan, where the pious servants of Allāh express their desire to be granted righteous offspring as solace in their eyes. Additionally, we see the case of Prophet Abraham, who fervently prayed to Allāh despite his old age and expressed gratitude when he was blessed with his beloved sons, Ishmael and Isaac.

Furthermore, the Quran provides clarification regarding the gender of a child. It affirms that while Allāh holds the authority to determine and select the gender, His servants are granted the freedom to express their desires through supplication. However, it is essential to recognize that the ultimate decision rests with Allāh alone. The Quran states:

لِلَّهِ مُلْكُ ٱلسَّمَٰوَٰتِ وَٱلْأَرْضِ يَخْلُقُ مَا يَشَاءُ يَهَبُ لِمَن يَشَاءُ إِنَٰثًا وَيَهَبُ لِمَن يَشَاءُ ٱلذُّكُورَ ﴿٤٩﴾

أَوْ يُزَوِّجُهُمْ ذُكْرَانًا وَإِنَٰثًا وَيَجْعَلُ مَن يَشَاءُ عَقِيمًا إِنَّهُ عَلِيمٌ قَدِيرٌ ﴿٥٠﴾

"TO ALLĀH BELONGS THE DOMINION OF THE HEAVENS AND THE EARTH; HE CREATES WHAT HE WILLS. HE GIVES TO WHOM HE WILLS FEMALE [CHILDREN], AND HE GIVES TO WHOM HE WILLS MALES" "OR HE MAKES THEM [BOTH] MALES AND FEMALES, AND HE RENDERS WHOM HE WILLS BARREN. INDEED, HE IS KNOWING AND COMPETENT". [AL-SHURA 49-50]

The verse above highlights that the selection of a child's gender is solely in the hands of Allāh. It is He who determines whether the child will be male or female, and He alone has the power to bestow fertility or infertility upon individuals.

As believers, we should joyfully embrace the gift bestowed by Allāh, irrespective of the child's gender, recognizing that the ultimate decision rests with Allāh's wisdom and choice. However, the act of despising daughters and engaging in discriminatory behavior towards them is a repugnant practice rooted in the Days of Ignorance. It reflects a lack of understanding of religious teachings and indicates a weakness in one's faith.

The Quran draws attention to this regressive custom in two verses from separate chapters, highlighting the disturbing practice of devaluing and even burying newborn daughters alive during the era of ignorance.

The first verse in surat Al-Nahl:

وَإِذَا بُشِّرَ أَحَدُهُم بِٱلْأُنثَىٰ ظَلَّ وَجْهُهُ مُسْوَدًّا وَهُوَ كَظِيمٌ ﴿٥٨﴾

يَتَوَٰرَىٰ مِنَ ٱلْقَوْمِ مِن سُوءِ مَا بُشِّرَ بِهِ أَيُمْسِكُهُ عَلَىٰ هُونٍ أَمْ يَدُسُّهُ فِي ٱلتُّرَابِ أَلَا سَاءَ مَا يَحْكُمُونَ ﴿٥٩﴾

"..AND WHEN ONE OF THEM IS INFORMED OF [THE BIRTH OF] A FEMALE, HIS FACE BECOMES DARK, AND HE SUPPRESSES GRIEF. HE HIDES HIMSELF FROM THE PEOPLE BECAUSE OF THE ILL OF WHICH HE HAS BEEN INFORMED. SHOULD HE KEEP IT IN HUMILIATION OR BURY IT IN THE GROUND? UNQUESTIONABLY, EVIL IS WHAT THEY DECIDE". [AN-NAHL : 58 -59]

And again, in surat Al-Zukhruh:

وَإِذَا بُشِّرَ أَحَدُهُم بِمَا ضَرَبَ لِلرَّحْمَٰنِ مَثَلًا ظَلَّ وَجْهُهُ مُسْوَدًّا وَهُوَ كَظِيمٌ ۝

"..AND WHEN ONE OF THEM IS GIVEN GOOD TIDINGS OF THAT WHICH HE ATTRIBUTES TO THE MOST MERCIFUL IN COMPARISON, HIS FACE BECOMES DARK, AND HE SUPPRESSES GRIEF".
[AZ-ZUKHRUF : 17]

In order to reject the habit that Islam strongly condemns, it is imperative that we practice fairness and equality in our treatment of both sons and daughters. Taking care of our daughters and giving them proper attention fulfills our duties and holds a special reward, as promised by the Prophet Muḥammad (ﷺ). He assured us that those who raise their daughters with love and compassion will be granted the companionship of the Prophet in Paradise in the hereafter. This serves as a profound encouragement to value and nurture our daughters with utmost care. Anas ﷺ reported: The Prophet ﷺ said:

"من أعال جاريتين (بنتين) حتى تبلغا جاء يوم القيامة أنا وهو وضم أصابعه"

"Whoever supports two girls till they attain maturity, he and I will come on the Day of Resurrection (close to each other) like this –The Messenger of Allāh joined his fingers to illustrate closeness."[205]

C- Children are adornment.

Children are indeed a source of beauty and happiness in this world. They bring immense joy and delight to our lives. Allāh, the Exalted, affirms this in the Quran, saying:

---

205   Muslim 2631

ٱلۡمَالُ وَٱلۡبَنُونَ زِينَةُ ٱلۡحَيَوٰةِ ٱلدُّنۡيَاۖ وَٱلۡبَٰقِيَٰتُ ٱلصَّٰلِحَٰتُ خَيۡرٌ عِندَ رَبِّكَ ثَوَابًا وَخَيۡرٌ أَمَلًا ﴿٤٦﴾

"WEALTH AND CHILDREN ARE [BUT] ADORNMENT OF THE WORLDLY LIFE" [AL-KAHF : 46]

زُيِّنَ لِلنَّاسِ حُبُّ ٱلشَّهَوَٰتِ مِنَ ٱلنِّسَآءِ وَٱلۡبَنِينَ وَٱلۡقَنَٰطِيرِ ٱلۡمُقَنطَرَةِ مِنَ ٱلذَّهَبِ وَٱلۡفِضَّةِ وَٱلۡخَيۡلِ ٱلۡمُسَوَّمَةِ وَٱلۡأَنۡعَٰمِ وَٱلۡحَرۡثِۗ ذَٰلِكَ مَتَٰعُ ٱلۡحَيَوٰةِ ٱلدُّنۡيَاۖ وَٱللَّهُ عِندَهُۥ حُسۡنُ ٱلۡمَـَٔابِ ﴿١٤﴾

"BEAUTIFIED FOR PEOPLE IS THE LOVE OF THAT WHICH THEY DESIRE - OF WOMEN AND SONS, HEAPED-UP SUMS OF GOLD AND SILVER, FINE BRANDED HORSES, AND CATTLE AND TILLED LAND. THAT IS THE ENJOYMENT OF WORLDLY LIFE, BUT ALLĀH HAS WITH HIM THE BEST RETURN". [AL-E-IMRAN : 14]

The love for offspring is undeniably one of the most cherished pleasures of this worldly life. It is intertwined with other enjoyable aspects such as wealth, luxurious possessions like horses, fertile lands, and livestock, collectively encompassing the sum of worldly delights. Nevertheless, parents' love for children is an innate and natural inclination to care for them, show kindness, and display compassion. It is a beautiful adornment of the world. Without this inherent love and motivation, humanity could have faced extinction.

Essentially, these verses offer advice to prioritize the rewards and blessings of the Hereafter over those of the worldly life. Furthermore, these verses compare the temporary pleasures of this world that entice people and the everlasting pleasure of the Hereafter. They caution believers against becoming captivated by worldly comforts and desires.

"All these desires and similar ones are the fleeting comforts of this life. It is worth noting that the term 'this life' or 'dunyā' in the Arabic text signifies 'the lower life.' Therefore, these comforts do not pertain to the sublime and higher realm. They are merely the easy delights of the worldly life. What surpasses all these pleasures, both in nobility and in safeguarding the human soul from being consumed by worldly desires, is that which is eternal and remains with God."206

D- Children are فتنة trail:

Besides being an adornment and a blessing, children can also be a test or trial, as mentioned in the Quran. Allāh addresses this aspect, saying:

وَٱعْلَمُوٓا۟ أَنَّمَآ أَمْوَٰلُكُمْ وَأَوْلَٰدُكُمْ فِتْنَةٌ وَأَنَّ ٱللَّهَ عِندَهُۥٓ أَجْرٌ عَظِيمٌ ﴿٢٨﴾

"AND KNOW THAT YOUR PROPERTIES AND YOUR CHILDREN ARE BUT A TRIAL AND THAT ALLĀH HAS WITH HIM A GREAT REWARD." [AL-ANFAL:28]

The mentioned verse emphasizes that when Allāh blesses us with children, it serves as a test to assess how parents will fulfill their responsibilities in raising them. It examines the sincerity with which parents adhere to Islamic principles of nurturing (Tarbīyah), such as displaying kindness, love, and respect towards their children. It also evaluates parents' readiness to establish a faith-centered and morally grounded environment that connects their children to their Creator, thereby equipping them for the challenges of the Hereafter and ensuring their preparedness for Paradise.

E- CHILDREN ARE A TRUST

يَٰٓأَيُّهَا ٱلَّذِينَ ءَامَنُوا۟ لَا تَخُونُوا۟ ٱللَّهَ وَٱلرَّسُولَ وَتَخُونُوٓا۟ أَمَٰنَٰتِكُمْ وَأَنتُمْ تَعْلَمُونَ ﴿٢٧﴾

O YOU WHO HAVE BELIEVED, DO NOT BETRAY ALLĀH AND THE MESSENGER OR BETRAY YOUR TRUSTS WHILE YOU KNOW [THE CONSEQUENCE]. [AL-ANFAL : 27]

Allāh, in His honor, has blessed us with sons and daughters as a means of testing and trial. This trial examines whether we will fulfill our responsibilities towards them, which include caring for them, providing guidance, imparting knowledge, and nurturing

---

206   Zilal Al-Quran, Surat Al-Imran, Verse 14

their character. It measures whether we will diligently fulfill this trust or neglect it, wasting the opportunity and obligation given to us.

The Quran extensively praises the qualities of the believers whose faith and salvation are affirmed by fulfilling this sacred trust. These believers are recognized for their commitment to upholding the Amānah (the trust) bestowed upon them. This is evident at the beginning of Surah al-Mu'minūn, where Allāh highlights the attributes of those whose faith is genuine and steadfast. Allāh said:

"CERTAINLY, WILL THE BELIEVERS HAVE SUCCEEDED" [SURAT AL-MU'MINŪN 1.]

Furthermore, in subsequent verses, those who attained success are described as individuals who possess the quality of trustworthiness:

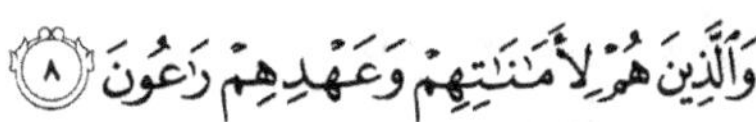

"AND THEY WHO ARE TO THEIR TRUSTS AND THEIR PROMISES ATTENTIVE." [SURAT AL-MU'MINŪN 8]

According to Al-Imam Ghazali, the child is regarded as a trust from Allāh bestowed upon parents. He beautifully describes the purity and malleability of a child's heart, comparing it to an uncut jewel that can be shaped and influenced in various ways. The child's heart is likened to a simple mirror that can absorb and reflect the impressions and influences it receives.

Al-Ghazali further emphasizes the crucial role of parents and caregivers in guiding and instructing the child. They are responsible for nurturing the child towards true success in both this world and the hereafter. The upbringing and instruction provided by parents greatly influence the child's future actions and choices. Whether the child ultimately succeeds or fails, the parents and all those who contribute to the child's guidance and education will share in the outcome.

Conversely, neglecting their moral development and allowing them to be influenced by negative influences can lead to misery and ruin. In such cases, the guardians and supervisors of the child bear the responsibility for the negative outcome.[207]

F-   Children are a responsibility:

Islam places significant emphasis on nurturing children in a manner that is pleasing to Allāh and beneficial to society. The home serves as the primary educational institution for children, where parents assume the central role in shaping their character and establishing the initial foundation of their personalities. Parents are responsible for instilling moral values and teaching etiquettes that enable children to discern between right and wrong, good and evil, and what is lawful (Ḥalāl) and unlawful (Ḥarām).

Due to their vital role in children's upbringing, parents are held accountable for their crucial duty of tarbīyah (nurturing and upbringing). Allāh addresses this responsibility in the Quran, emphasizing the significance of the parent's role.

يَٰٓأَيُّهَا ٱلَّذِينَ ءَامَنُوا۟ قُوٓا۟ أَنفُسَكُمْ وَأَهْلِيكُمْ نَارًا وَقُودُهَا ٱلنَّاسُ وَٱلْحِجَارَةُ عَلَيْهَا مَلَٰٓئِكَةٌ غِلَاظٌ شِدَادٌ لَّا يَعْصُونَ ٱللَّهَ مَآ أَمَرَهُمْ وَيَفْعَلُونَ مَا يُؤْمَرُونَ ﴿٦﴾

"O YOU WHO HAVE BELIEVED, PROTECT YOURSELVES AND YOUR FAMILIES FROM A FIRE WHOSE FUEL IS PEOPLE AND STONES, OVER WHICH ARE [APPOINTED] ANGELS, HARSH AND SEVERE; THEY DO NOT DISOBEY ALLĀH IN WHAT HE COMMANDS THEM BUT DO WHAT THEY ARE COMMANDED." [AT-TAHRIM : 6]

وَأْمُرْ أَهْلَكَ بِٱلصَّلَوٰةِ وَٱصْطَبِرْ عَلَيْهَا لَا نَسْـَٔلُكَ رِزْقًا نَّحْنُ نَرْزُقُكَ وَٱلْعَٰقِبَةُ لِلتَّقْوَىٰ ﴿١٣٢﴾

---

207   Al-Ghazali, Ihya Ulumudeen vol:2 page: 70

"AND ENJOIN PRAYER UPON YOUR FAMILY [AND PEOPLE] AND BE STEADFAST THEREIN. WE ASK YOU NOT FOR PROVISION; WE PROVIDE FOR YOU, AND THE [BEST] OUTCOME IS FOR [THOSE OF] RIGHTEOUSNESS". [TA-HA : 132]

وَكَانَ يَأْمُرُ أَهْلَهُ بِالصَّلَوٰةِ وَالزَّكَوٰةِ وَكَانَ عِندَ رَبِّهِۦ مَرْضِيًّا ﴿٥٥﴾

"AND HE USED TO ENJOIN ON HIS PEOPLE PRAYER AND ZAKAH AND WAS TO HIS LORD PLEASING." [MARYAM : 55]

The aforementioned Quranic verses highlight that a crucial aspect of raising children, which is a profound responsibility and noble task for parents, is establishing a strong connection between the children and their Creator, Allāh. A comprehensive approach must be adopted to nurture children in the spirit of religion, particularly focusing on their ʿAqīdah (belief system), as beliefs guide actions. It involves fostering Īmān (faith) and Taqwa (God-consciousness) within their hearts. Only when children are taught to wholeheartedly submit to Allāh in their thoughts, words, and actions can they be expected to exert their utmost efforts to please Him.

It is essential for children to develop a love for Allāh that surpasses their love for any other person or worldly possession. By nurturing children with good morals, parents lay the foundation for their spiritual and ethical growth.

Authentic narrations Throughout Islamic teachings emphasize the significance of cultivating children with virtuous morals. Some of these narrations serve as guidance in this noble endeavor.

On the authority of Amr Bin Al-As, in which the prophet ﷺ said:

"مَا نَحَلَ وَالِدٌ وَلَدَّه مِن نُحْلٍ أَفْضَلَ مِن أَدَبٍ حَسَنٍ"

"No father can give his child anything better than good manners."[208]

• In a narration Ibnu Umar, prophet ﷺ said:

(كلكم راع وكلكم مسؤول عن رعيته: الإمام راع ومسئول عن رعيته، والرجل راع في أهله ومسئول عن رعيته، والمرأة راعية في بيت زوجها ومسئولة عن رعيتها) وقال - ﷺ -: (إن الله سائل كل راع عما استرعاه أحفظ، أم ضيع؟ حتى يسأل الرجل عن أهل بيته) .

"All of you are shepherds, and each is responsible for his flock; The man is the guardian of the family of his household and is responsible for his subjects, and the woman is the guardian of her husband's home and his children and is responsible for them."[209] In another version by the same companion, may Allāh be pleased with him, the prophet said: "Allāh will ask everyone about what he had entrusted with so much so that the man will be asked about his household."[210]

As stated earlier, the narrations underscore the critical and paramount responsibility of parenting. It highlights that parents should prioritize not only the immediate nurturing and protection of their children in this worldly life but also focus on preparing them for the future. This broader perspective encourages parents to consider their children's long-term development and growth beyond the present moment.

• Ibnu Umar also said:

(أدب ابنك فإنك مسئول عنه ، ماذا أدبته وماذا علمته ؟ وهو مسئول عن برك وطواعيته لك)

"Discipline your child, for verily; you are responsible for him on the Day of Judgement: with what did you discipline him and what did you teach him?"[211]

---

208   Tirmidi 1952 and Aḥmad 4/77-78

209   Ṣaḥīḥ al-Bukhari 5188

210   Al-Nasa'I 292 and Al-tirmidi 4/180, and Sh Al-Bani approved its conformity to the ṣaḥīḥ standards

211   al-Bayḥaqī, Sunan al-Kubrā: 5301

'Abdallah Ibn 'Umar, the narrator of the hadiths mentioned above, further expounded on the significance of the meaning he conveyed and how the responsibility of nurturing children should be fulfilled. He emphasized that on the Day of Judgment, we will be held accountable before Allāh for how we have discharged this responsibility, including whether we have disciplined and guided our children appropriately.

Indeed, parenting holds immense importance in Islam, to the extent that on the Day of Judgment, Allāh will first inquire from the child about the effectiveness of the parent before questioning the parent regarding the child's obedience. This highlights the weightiness and magnitude of the parental role in shaping the lives and character of their children.

G- Children are innately born with fitrah (natural inclination towards righteousness)

On the authority of Abū Huraira, the prophet ﷺ, said:

«مَا مِنْ مَوْلُودٍ إِلاَّ يُولَدُ عَلَى الْفِطْرَةِ فَأَبَوَاهُ يُهَوِّدَانِهِ وَيُنَصِّرَانِهِ وَيُمَجِّسَانِهِ كَمَا تُنْتَجُ الْبَهِيمَةُ بَهِيمَةً جَمْعَاءَ هَلْ تُحِسُّونَ فِيهَا مِنْ جَدْعَاءَ » ثُمَّ يَقُولُ أَبُو هُرَيْرَةَ : وَاقْرَءُوا إِنْ شِئْتُمْ فطرة الله التي فطر الناس عليها لا تبديل لخلق الله. الروم ٣٠

"There is none born but is created to his true nature (Islam). It is his parents who make him a Jew or a Christian or a Magian quite as beasts produce their young with their limbs perfect. Do you see anything deficient in them? Then he quoted the Qur'an., The nature made by Allāh in which He has created men, there is no altering of Allāh's creation; that is the right religion."[212]

Al-Imam Al-Nawawi elaborating on the breadth and depth of the meaning of this narration, said: The majority of Muslim scholars have reached a consensus that when children from the Muslims pass away, they are considered among the inhabitants of Jannah

---

212   Ar-Rum:30, Muslim 2658

(Paradise) as they are not held accountable due to their young age and lack of legal responsibility. Some who did not hold this position refrained from taking such a definitive stance due to the hadith of Aaishah, to which the scholars respond that perhaps he ﷺ wanted to prevent her from rushing to a definitive conclusion without having had definitive evidence to support it, just as he corrected Sa'd ibn Abi Waqqaas when he said, "Verily I see him be a mu'min," so he ﷺ said, "or a Muslim." And perhaps he ﷺ said this before he knew that the children of Muslims are in Jannah, for it is known that he ﷺ said, "Any Muslim who loses three children before they reach the age of maturity will be granted Jannah by Allāh, the Exalted, out of His Mercy for them" and elsewhere in other hadith narrations. And Allāh knows best".[213]

In this narration, the Prophet (ﷺ) affirms that children are born with an innate belief in Allāh, the Almighty, and an inclination towards the pure monotheistic 'Aqīdah (belief system). What a child absorbs, whether good or evil, plays a significant role in shaping their character as they grow older. It is their surroundings and environmental factors that can potentially influence them negatively. Hence, the role of guardians, especially parents, becomes vital in raising children free from moral corruption and deviation from the path of the Dīn (religion).

Parents are profoundly responsible for safeguarding and nurturing their children's Fiṭrah (natural disposition) and preventing its decline and degradation. They are also tasked with being exemplary role models, as failing to do so can have a detrimental impact on their children's morality.

---

213   Al-Nawawi, Sharḥ Ṣaḥīḥ Muslim vol:16 page 261. The translated by Tulayha word press 8/9/2013

Regrettably, what Ibn al-Qayim highlighted is observable in our world today, as too many parents fail this test. Muslim parents, in particular, are missing out on the exceptional opportunity for eternal and spiritual rewards by neglecting their children and falling short in this duty.

Ibnul Qayim stressing the significance of the stage of upbringing, said: "How many people had caused misery to their own children, the apple of their eyes, in this world-life and the Afterlife, by neglecting them, not disciplining them, encouraging them to follow their whims and desires, thinking that they were honoring them when they were humiliating them, that they were being merciful to them when in fact they were wronging them They have not benefited from having a child, and they have made the child lose his share in this worldly life and the Afterlife. If you think about children's corruption, you will see that in most cases, it is because of the parents."[214]

It is disheartening to observe that Ibn al-Qayim's observation holds true in our present world, as many parents fail in their responsibility. This failure is particularly significant among Muslim parents who miss out on the excellent opportunity for eternal and spiritual rewards by neglecting their children and falling short in this test.

The prophet Muḥammad ﷺ clearly demonstrated the critical role of parents in shaping their offspring's moral character and overall personality and emphasized it by Himself. An authentic hadith highlights the profound significance of parental care and attitudes in transforming a child, regardless of their innate nature, attributes, and disposition at birth. No child is born as an armed robber, a drug addict, or a prostitute, just as no one is born

---

214 Al-Imam ibn al-Qayyim Tuhfat al-Mawdūd bi-Ahkām il-Mawlūd, Page 146

trustworthy, law-abiding, or a peacemaker. These traits develop and evolve throughout life, greatly influenced by the environment in which one grows up. It is through the permission and guidance of the Almighty that the environment molds and shapes us into whom we become[215]

H- Children are a source of reward for parents.

Believers have a profound obligation to strive for good deeds in order to attain Allāh's pleasure. However, considering the brevity of life, it becomes challenging to achieve a significant amount of good in the limited time allotted to individuals. In His wisdom, Allāh has provided believers with alternative opportunities through their offspring, enabling the continuation of rewards both during the parents' lifetime and after their departure from this world. This is especially significant as parents considerably require these rewards for salvation from hellfire and elevation to higher ranks in heaven.

The Prophet Muḥammad (ﷺ) has conveyed three beautiful narrations that affirm the reality mentioned above, and these narrations hold true according to the standards of authenticity set by the scholars of Hadith. These narrations bring great glad tidings to the believers, serving as a source of encouragement and motivation in their journey towards righteousness and the pursuit of eternal rewards.

He said :

- Abū Hurairah reported that the Messenger of Allāh ﷺ said:

---

215   Dr. ʿAbdul-Razzaq ʿAbdul-Majeed Alaro, "Children Moral Upbringing: The Shariah Recipe," Allawh Journal of Arabic and Islamic Studies, University of Maiduguri, Maiduguri, Nigeria, 1st June 2017.

إذا مات ابن آدم انقطع عمله إلا من ثلاث صدقة جارية أو علم ينتفع به أو ولد صالح يدعو له.

"When a man dies, his deeds come to an end, except for three: A continuous charity, knowledge by which people derive benefit, a pious son who prays for him." [216]

- Allāh's Messenger said, as reported by Abū Huraira:

» الْقِنْطَارُ اثْنَا عَشَرَ أَلْفَ أُوقِيَّةٍ كُلُّ أُوقِيَّةٍ خَيْرٌ مِمَّا بَيْنَ السَّمَاءِ وَالأَرْضِ « . وَقَالَ رَسُولُ اللَّهِ ـ ﷺ ـ » إِنَّ الرَّجُلَ لَتُرْفَعُ دَرَجَتُهُ فِي الْجَنَّةِ فَيَقُولُ أَنَّى هَذَا فَيُقَالُ بِاسْتِغْفَارِ وَلَدِكَ لَكَ «

"Qintar is twelve thousand 'Uqiyah, each 'Uqiyah of which is better than what is between heaven and earth." And the Messenger of Allāh(ﷺ) said: "A man will be raised in status in Paradise and will say: 'Where did this come from?' And it will be said:'From your son's praying for forgiveness for you.'"[217]

Both narrations highlight the profound significance of obedient children in providing lasting good deeds for their parents through supplication.

On the authority of Abū Musa Al-Asha'ri, the Messenger of Allāh (ﷺ) said:

»إذا مات ولد العبد قال الله تعالى لملائكته: قبضتم ولد عبدي؟ فيقولون : نَعَمْ ، فيقول : قَبَضْتُمْ ثَمَرَةَ فُؤَادِهِ ؟ فيقولون : نَعَمْ ، فيقول : فماذا قال عبدي؟ فيقولون: حمدك واسترجع، فيقول الله تعالى: ابنوا لعبدي بيتًا في الجنة، وسموه بيت الحمد«. رواه الترمذي وقال حديث حسن.

"When a slave's child dies, Allāh, the Most High, asks His angels, 'Have you taken out the life of the child of My slave?" They reply in the affirmative. He then asks, 'Have you taken the fruit of his heart?' They reply in the affirmative. Thereupon he asks, 'What has My slave said?' They say: 'He has praised You and

---

216   Muslim Book 7, Hadith 94

217   Ibnu Majah 3660, Book 33 Hadith 4

said: Inna lillahi wa inna ilaihi raji'un (We belong to Allāh and to Him we shall be returned). Allāh says: 'Build a house for My slave in Jannah and name it as Bait-ul-Hamd' (the House of Praise)[218]

The previous narrations provide us with valuable insights, from which we can infer the following points:

- Serve as a reminder that obedient and righteous children can contribute to their parents' record of good deeds. Through their sincere supplications and prayers, children can continue to benefit their parents even after passing. This is a source of immense comfort and hope for parents as their children become a means of endless blessings and rewards in this world and the Hereafter.

- Emphasize the importance of nurturing and raising children in a way that instills obedience to Allāh and righteousness. By doing so, parents fulfill their responsibility towards their children's upbringing and create a lasting legacy of good deeds that can benefit them in the realm of the unseen.

- The narrations are also a powerful reminder of the potential impact of a child's piety and prayers on their parents' spiritual journey, encouraging believers to strive for the upbringing and guidance of their children in the best possible manner.

Moreover, The third Hadith narrated by Abū Musa illustrates that if a child passes away during the lifetime of their parents, the child will intercede for their parents, granting them entry into Paradise. Similarly, the Hadith is uniquely a profound reminder of the mercy and intercession that can come from the loss of a child. It highlights the special status and intercessory role a departed child can have on behalf of their parents. The child's innocence, purity, and righteous state serve as a means of attaining Paradise for the grieving parents. On the other hand, it offers solace to

---

218   Al-bani, Silsialtu Al-Aḥadīth Al-Saheehah vol 3 page: 482

parents who have experienced the loss of a child, assuring them that their departed child holds a unique position in the sight of Allāh. It serves as a source of hope and comfort, reassuring that their beloved child will advocate on their behalf on the Day of Judgment.

Understanding these narrations encourages parents to cherish their children and nurture them in accordance with Islamic teachings. It emphasizes the importance of fostering a loving and righteous environment that promotes their spiritual growth and well-being.

3.3.2. PART 2: MORAL PARENTING COMPASS IN THE QURAN (MORAL CODES)

THE ROLE OF PARENTS IN CHILD MORAL UPBRINGING IN ISLAM

A- The Story of Luqman and His Son

The Moral Upbringing Code in Verses 13-19 of Surah Luqman

Regarding the well-known story of Luqman and his guidance on child-raising in the Quran, Allāh states:

وَإِذْ قَالَ لُقْمَانُ لِابْنِهِۦ وَهُوَ يَعِظُهُۥ يَٰبُنَىَّ لَا تُشْرِكْ بِٱللَّهِ إِنَّ ٱلشِّرْكَ لَظُلْمٌ عَظِيمٌ ﴿١٣﴾

وَوَصَّيْنَا ٱلْإِنسَٰنَ بِوَٰلِدَيْهِ حَمَلَتْهُ أُمُّهُۥ وَهْنًا عَلَىٰ وَهْنٍ وَفِصَٰلُهُۥ فِي عَامَيْنِ أَنِ ٱشْكُرْ لِي وَلِوَٰلِدَيْكَ إِلَىَّ ٱلْمَصِيرُ ﴿١٤﴾

وَإِن جَٰهَدَاكَ عَلَىٰٓ أَن تُشْرِكَ بِي مَا لَيْسَ لَكَ بِهِۦ عِلْمٌ فَلَا تُطِعْهُمَا وَصَاحِبْهُمَا فِي ٱلدُّنْيَا مَعْرُوفًا وَٱتَّبِعْ سَبِيلَ مَنْ أَنَابَ إِلَىَّ ثُمَّ إِلَىَّ مَرْجِعُكُمْ فَأُنَبِّئُكُم بِمَا كُنتُمْ تَعْمَلُونَ ﴿١٥﴾

يَبُنَيَّ إِنَّهَآ إِن تَكُ مِثْقَالَ حَبَّةٍ مِّنْ خَرْدَلٍ فَتَكُن فِي صَخْرَةٍ أَوْ فِي ٱلسَّمَٰوَٰتِ أَوْ فِي ٱلْأَرْضِ يَأْتِ بِهَا ٱللَّهُ إِنَّ ٱللَّهَ لَطِيفٌ خَبِيرٌ ﴿١٦﴾

يَبُنَيَّ أَقِمِ ٱلصَّلَوٰةَ وَأْمُرْ بِٱلْمَعْرُوفِ وَٱنْهَ عَنِ ٱلْمُنكَرِ وَٱصْبِرْ عَلَىٰ مَآ أَصَابَكَ إِنَّ ذَٰلِكَ مِنْ عَزْمِ ٱلْأُمُورِ ﴿١٧﴾

وَلَا تُصَعِّرْ خَدَّكَ لِلنَّاسِ وَلَا تَمْشِ فِي ٱلْأَرْضِ مَرَحًا إِنَّ ٱللَّهَ لَا يُحِبُّ كُلَّ مُخْتَالٍ فَخُورٍ ﴿١٨﴾

وَٱقْصِدْ فِي مَشْيِكَ وَٱغْضُضْ مِن صَوْتِكَ إِنَّ أَنكَرَ ٱلْأَصْوَٰتِ لَصَوْتُ ٱلْحَمِيرِ ﴿١٩﴾

"AND [MENTION, O MUHAMMAD], WHEN LUQMAN SAID TO HIS SON WHILE HE WAS INSTRUCTING HIM, "O MY SON, DO NOT ASSOCIATE [ANYTHING] WITH ALLĀH. INDEED, ASSOCIATION [WITH HIM] IS GREAT INJUSTICE. AND WE HAVE ENJOINED UPON MAN [CARE] FOR HIS PARENTS. HIS MOTHER CARRIED HIM, [INCREASING HER] IN WEAKNESS UPON WEAKNESS, AND HIS WEANING IS IN TWO YEARS. BE GRATEFUL TO ME AND TO YOUR PARENTS; TO ME IS THE [FINAL] DESTINATION. BUT IF THEY ENDEAVOR TO MAKE YOU ASSOCIATE WITH ME THAT OF WHICH YOU HAVE NO KNOWLEDGE, DO NOT OBEY THEM BUT ACCOMPANY THEM IN [THIS] WORLD WITH APPROPRIATE KINDNESS AND FOLLOW THE WAY OF THOSE WHO TURN BACK TO ME [IN REPENTANCE]. THEN TO ME WILL BE YOUR RETURN, AND I WILL INFORM YOU ABOUT WHAT YOU USED TO DO. [AND LUQMAN SAID], "O MY SON, INDEED IF WRONG SHOULD BE THE WEIGHT OF A MUSTARD SEED AND SHOULD BE WITHIN A ROCK OR [ANYWHERE] IN THE HEAVENS OR IN THE EARTH, ALLĀH WILL BRING IT FORTH. INDEED, ALLĀH IS SUBTLE AND ACQUAINTED. "O MY SON, ESTABLISH PRAYER, ENJOIN WHAT IS RIGHT, FORBID WHAT IS WRONG, AND BE PATIENT OVER WHAT BEFALLS YOU. INDEED, [ALL] THAT IS OF THE MATTERS [REQUIRING] DETERMINATION. AND DO NOT TURN YOUR CHEEK [IN CONTEMPT] TOWARD PEOPLE AND DO NOT WALK THROUGH THE EARTH EXULTANTLY. INDEED, ALLĀH DOES NOT LIKE EVERYONE SELF-DELUDED AND BOASTFUL. AND BE MODERATE IN YOUR PACE AND LOWER YOUR VOICE; INDEED, THE MOST DISAGREEABLE OF SOUNDS IS THE VOICE OF DONKEYS." [LUQMAN : 13 -19]

By contemplating this long Quranic passage that contains the fundamental principles of the Islamic method of upbringing children, we learn that Luqman, in his preaching and speech with his son, left no vital tarbiyyah item unexplained. His wise and beautiful words, which to this day echo in the ears of millions of people, covered all the significant foundations of Tarbīyah, ranging from monotheism down to a detailed and practical-individual and social-based-moral code of Islamic Tarbīyah.

Accordingly, his walk-talk speech can be summarized in seven main categories, which are as follows:

- (VERSE 13) The prohibition of Shirk as a "great injustice."

Tawḥīd is the basis of all that is in Islam. It should be introduced to children at an early age. Neglecting this essential principle of Islam can cause children to have doubts and unanswered questions that preoccupy their minds. Teaching them tawḥīd means maintaining the fitrah with which the children were born. In his advice to his son, Luqman warned him against shirk, the worst and the greatest sin ever committed by human beings on earth. Every prophet or messenger warned his nation against shirk or associating with Allāh others, which is injustice concerning the rights of Allāh upon His servants.

If parents skip this critical part of the dīn, Tawḥīd, and concentrate on the other practical aspects of Islam, the fruits we reap from our long struggle with upbringing them Islamicly will end up in vain.

- (VERSE 14) Good treatment towards parents; the weaknesses a mother bears when she carries her child and breastfeeding him for two years; being grateful to Allāh and parents.

Luqman alerted his son on obedience to the parents with a particular focus on the mother since she has more rights than the father, as discussed earlier in this book in the chapter on moralities with the parents.

- (VERSE 15) Not to follow one's parents if they call towards shirk; to dwell with them well in this world; and to follow the path of the one who turns towards Allāh (whomever it might be), because the final return is to Allāh, Who will then inform us of all that we did.

Parents deserve to be respected and must always be obeyed at all times except when their obedience leads to the disobedience of Allāh and His prophet, ﷺ; when they call to shirk or associate with Allāh others, then they are not to be obeyed in the such matter though the good treatment remains as it is.

- (VERSE 16) Allāh knows every little thing, where ever it might be in the Heavens and the earth, and He will bring it forth. Luqman tries to inculcate in the heart of his son the surveillance of Allāh, The Almighty, and his watchfulness over His creatures where Allāh observers the inns and the outs of every creature in every space and time, a potential and a meaningful item of Tarbīyah that teaches the child the integrity and being God-conscious in all his actions and sayings, and intentions and thinking.

- (VERSE 17) Among the pieces of Luqman's wisdom to his son was the Establishment of prayer, commanding what is good, prohibiting what is evil, and remaining patient in facing what happens while doing these three things, which requires determination. This part of Luqman's golden advice is more practical than the pieces of wisdom mentioned earlier as it touches on the most important pillar of Islam after Tawḥīd, prayer. Similarly, it lays down another essential principle of guidance for the Muslims to invite others to keep to the true faith and good deeds as necessary as their submission to the Holy Qur'an and Sunnah. Without sincere efforts, to the best of one's ability, to invite others to the right path, one's good deeds are not enough for one's salvation. Especially if a person does not take care of the spiritual and moral welfare of his wife, children, and family and turns a blind eye to their unrighteous deeds, he is blocking his way to salvation - no matter how pious he might be. Therefore, the Qur'an and the Sunnah make it obligatory for every Muslim to do his best to invite others to the good deeds and warn them against evil acts.

Furthermore, being patient in the cause of implementing the principles of da'wa is a primary requirement while serving Islam. See Ma'rif-ul-Quran, Surat Al-Asr.

- (VERSES 18) Not turning one's cheek towards people (in contempt), not strutting about on earth (arrogantly) because Allāh does not love the vainglorious boaster. "In verse 18, it was said: (وَلَا تُصَعِّرْ خَدَّكَ لِلنَّاسِ) And do not turn your cheek away from people). The expression: (لَا تُصَعِّرْ la tusa'ir) is a derivation from (صَعَرَ sa' ara), which is a disease among camels that causes a tilt in the neck similar to the stroke among human beings that makes a face crooked. It carries the sense of turning one's face away (in disdain). Thus, the verse means: 'Do not turn your face away from people when you meet them and talk to them for it is a sign of avoidance and arrogance and very much against the norms of gentle manners". Ibid

In addition, he warned his son against being arrogant while walking, a bad habit that Allāh hates.

(VERSE 19)Being moderate in one's gait and keeping one's voice low, as the most disliked of all voices, is the braying of the ass. In lowering one's voice, one shows good manners with people and Allāh. "Had there been any merit in the loud, harsh, shrill voice, the donkey would not be singled out with such a voice; the donkey's baseness and stupidity are well-known. Furthermore, it is disrespectful to others when they are spoken in that manner of harshness."[219]

---

219   Fuad Ibn 'Abdul- Azeez Asha-Shaulboob, the book of Manners, page:180, translated by FaisalAl-Shafiq, Darrusalam, 2003

B- NUH AND HIS SON

The Moral Upbringing Code in Verses 41-47 of SURAT HUD. (NUH AND HIS SON)

Allāh narrates the story of Nuh (Noah) and his son in Surah Hud, the only chapter in the Quran explicitly mentioning this particular historical incident not found in any other part of the Quran.

VERSES 41-44

Allāh says:

وَقَالَ ٱرْكَبُوا۟ فِيهَا بِٱسْمِ ٱللَّهِ مَجْرٜىٰهَا وَمُرْسَىٰهَآ إِنَّ رَبِّى لَغَفُورٌ رَّحِيمٌ ۝

وَهِىَ تَجْرِى بِهِمْ فِى مَوْجٍ كَٱلْجِبَالِ وَنَادَىٰ نُوحٌ ٱبْنَهُۥ وَكَانَ فِى مَعْزِلٍ يَٰبُنَىَّ ٱرْكَب مَّعَنَا وَلَا تَكُن مَّعَ ٱلْكَٰفِرِينَ ۝

قَالَ سَـَٔاوِىٓ إِلَىٰ جَبَلٍ يَعْصِمُنِى مِنَ ٱلْمَآءِ قَالَ لَا عَاصِمَ ٱلْيَوْمَ مِنْ أَمْرِ ٱللَّهِ إِلَّا مَن رَّحِمَ وَحَالَ بَيْنَهُمَا ٱلْمَوْجُ فَكَانَ مِنَ ٱلْمُغْرَقِينَ ۝

وَقِيلَ يَٰٓأَرْضُ ٱبْلَعِى مَآءَكِ وَيَٰسَمَآءُ أَقْلِعِى وَغِيضَ ٱلْمَآءُ وَقُضِىَ ٱلْأَمْرُ وَٱسْتَوَتْ عَلَى ٱلْجُودِىِّ وَقِيلَ بُعْدًا لِّلْقَوْمِ ٱلظَّٰلِمِينَ ۝

AND [NOAH] SAID, "EMBARK THEREIN; IN THE NAME OF ALLĀH IS ITS COURSE AND ITS ANCHORAGE. INDEED, MY LORD IS FORGIVING AND MERCIFUL." 41 AND IT SAILED WITH THEM THROUGH WAVES LIKE MOUNTAINS, AND NOAH CALLED TO HIS SON WHO WAS APART [FROM THEM], "O MY SON, COME ABOARD WITH US AND BE NOT WITH THE DISBELIEVERS." 42 [BUT] HE SAID, "I WILL TAKE REFUGE ON A MOUNTAIN TO PROTECT ME FROM THE WATER." [NOAH] SAID, "THERE IS NO PROTECTOR TODAY FROM THE DECREE OF ALLĀH, EXCEPT FOR WHOM HE GIVES MERCY." AND THE WAVES CAME BETWEEN THEM, AND HE WAS AMONG THE DROWNED. 43 AND IT WAS SAID, "O EARTH, SWALLOW YOUR WATER, AND O SKY, WITHHOLD [YOUR RAIN]." AND THE WATER SUBSIDED, AND THE MATTER WAS ACCOMPLISHED, AND THE SHIP CAME TO REST ON THE [MOUNTAIN OF] JUDIYY. AND IT WAS SAID, "AWAY WITH THE WRONGDOING PEOPLE." **[SURAT HUD : 41- 44]**

VERSE 45-47

وَنَادَىٰ نُوحٌ رَّبَّهُۥ فَقَالَ رَبِّ إِنَّ ٱبْنِى مِنْ أَهْلِى وَإِنَّ وَعْدَكَ ٱلْحَقُّ وَأَنتَ أَحْكَمُ ٱلْحَٰكِمِينَ ﴿٤٥﴾

AND NOAH CALLED TO HIS LORD AND SAID, "MY LORD, INDEED MY SON IS OF MY FAMILY; AND INDEED, YOUR PROMISE IS TRUE; AND YOU ARE THE MOST JUST OF JUDGES!" **[HUD : 45]**

قَالَ يَٰنُوحُ إِنَّهُۥ لَيْسَ مِنْ أَهْلِكَ إِنَّهُۥ عَمَلٌ غَيْرُ صَٰلِحٍ فَلَا تَسْـَٔلْنِ مَا لَيْسَ لَكَ بِهِۦ عِلْمٌ إِنِّىٓ أَعِظُكَ أَن تَكُونَ مِنَ ٱلْجَٰهِلِينَ ﴿٤٦﴾

قَالَ رَبِّ إِنِّىٓ أَعُوذُ بِكَ أَنْ أَسْـَٔلَكَ مَا لَيْسَ لِى بِهِۦ عِلْمٌ وَإِلَّا تَغْفِرْ لِى وَتَرْحَمْنِىٓ أَكُن مِّنَ ٱلْخَٰسِرِينَ ﴿٤٧﴾

HE SAID, "O NOAH, INDEED HE IS NOT OF YOUR FAMILY; INDEED, HE IS [ONE WHOSE] WORK WAS OTHER THAN RIGHTEOUS, SO ASK ME NOT FOR THAT ABOUT WHICH YOU HAVE NO KNOWLEDGE. INDEED, I ADVISE YOU, LEST YOU BE AMONG THE IGNORANT." **[HUD : 46]**

[NOAH] SAID, "MY LORD, I SEEK REFUGE IN YOU FROM ASKING THAT OF WHICH I HAVE NO KNOWLEDGE. AND UNLESS YOU FORGIVE ME AND HAVE MERCY UPON ME, I WILL BE AMONG THE LOSERS." **[HUD : 47]**

This Quranic passage, depicting the story of Nuh (Noah) and his son, highlights a crucial aspect of Islamic tarbīyah and its implementation. The story emphasizes that faith and morality form the foundation of Islamic upbringing, distinguishing it with unique characteristics and an effective and practical approach.

Key insights regarding the upbringing of a child's faith can be derived from this story:

- Nuh exerted his utmost effort to win his son's heart, despite the eventual rejection of the invitation to Tawḥīd (monotheism).

- Parents or guardians should not be overly concerned about the outcome, as it ultimately lies in the hands of Allāh, the Almighty.

- Nuh's son was among those whom Nuh tirelessly and wholeheartedly invited to believe in Allāh for a remarkable period of 950 years. This is a profound example of the boundless nature of time and the commitment required in tarbīyah and dawa (invitation to Islam).

- Patience plays a crucial role in the moral upbringing of children. Allāh commands us to remain patient and steadfast when calling our children to prayer. As the Quran states:

وَأْمُرْ أَهْلَكَ بِالصَّلَوٰةِ وَاصْطَبِرْ عَلَيْهَا ۖ لَا نَسْـَٔلُكَ رِزْقًا ۖ نَّحْنُ نَرْزُقُكَ ۗ وَالْعَٰقِبَةُ لِلتَّقْوَىٰ ۝

"AND ENJOIN PRAYER UPON YOUR FAMILY [AND PEOPLE] AND BE STEADFAST THEREIN. WE ASK YOU NOT FOR PROVISION; WE PROVIDE FOR YOU, AND THE [BEST] OUTCOME IS FOR [THOSE OF] RIGHTEOUSNESS". [TA-HA : 132]

From the story, we understand the distinctive principle that sets apart the Islamic perspective on relationships and connections. In Islam, what truly binds people together is not based on blood relations, family, land, country, tribe, nation, color, language, race, profession, or social class. Rather, it is faith in Allāh and belief in His oneness that serves as the defining factor.

When Prophet Nuh appealed to Allāh to save his son Kan'an, assuming that their biological bond would be a sufficient reason, Allāh responded by emphasizing that Kan'an could no longer be considered part of Nuh's family due to his unrighteous conduct and lack of faith. The tie of faith truly unites individuals within the Islamic framework.

The unique bond of the Islamic faith is rooted in specific objectives and aspirations outlined by divine guidance. It surpasses otherworldly connections, as they can be severed despite the existence of various ties.

"The tie which binds people together in the Islamic faith is unique. It relates to certain objectives and aspirations which are peculiar to this divine constitution. This tie of Islamic society has nothing to do with family or blood relations, land or country, tribe or nation, color or language, race or sex, profession or class. All such ties may exist between two individuals, yet their relations may, nevertheless, still be severed."[220]

Islam emphasizes that the strongest bond between individuals lies in their shared faith and commitment to Allāh, transcending any other worldly affiliations.

C- IBRAHIM AND HIS SONS

The Moral Upbringing Code in Verses 37 OF SURAT IBRAHIM, VERSES 131-133 OF SURAT Al-Baqarah, AND VERSES 100-106 OF SURAT AL-SAFAT: (IBRAHIM AND HIS SONS)

VERSE 37

Allāh says in surat Ibrahim:

رَّبَّنَا إِنِّي أَسْكَنتُ مِن ذُرِّيَّتِي بِوَادٍ غَيْرِ ذِى زَرْعٍ عِندَ بَيْتِكَ ٱلْمُحَرَّمِ رَبَّنَا لِيُقِيمُوا۟ ٱلصَّلَوٰةَ فَٱجْعَلْ أَفْئِدَةً مِّنَ ٱلنَّاسِ تَهْوِىٓ إِلَيْهِمْ وَٱرْزُقْهُم مِّنَ ٱلثَّمَرَٰتِ لَعَلَّهُمْ يَشْكُرُونَ ﴿٣٧﴾

"OUR LORD, I HAVE SETTLED SOME OF MY DESCENDANTS IN AN UNCULTIVATED VALLEY NEAR YOUR SACRED HOUSE, OUR LORD, THAT THEY MAY ESTABLISH PRAYER. SO MAKE HEARTS AMONG THE PEOPLE INCLINE TOWARD THEM AND PROVIDE FOR THEM FROM THE FRUITS THAT THEY MIGHT BE GRATEFUL". **[IBRAHIM : 37]**

VERSES 131-133

In surat Al-Baqarah, Allāh says:

---

220   Zilal al-Qur'ān, an online Tafsīr (interpretation), on page 192 of Surat Hud

إِذْ قَالَ لَهُۥ رَبُّهُۥٓ أَسْلِمْ قَالَ أَسْلَمْتُ لِرَبِّ ٱلْعَٰلَمِينَ ﴿١٣١﴾

وَوَصَّىٰ بِهَآ إِبْرَٰهِـۧمُ بَنِيهِ وَيَعْقُوبُ يَٰبَنِىَّ إِنَّ ٱللَّهَ ٱصْطَفَىٰ لَكُمُ ٱلدِّينَ فَلَا تَمُوتُنَّ إِلَّا وَأَنتُم مُّسْلِمُونَ ﴿١٣٢﴾

أَمْ كُنتُمْ شُهَدَآءَ إِذْ حَضَرَ يَعْقُوبَ ٱلْمَوْتُ إِذْ قَالَ لِبَنِيهِ مَا تَعْبُدُونَ مِنۢ بَعْدِى قَالُوا۟ نَعْبُدُ إِلَٰهَكَ وَإِلَٰهَ ءَابَآئِكَ إِبْرَٰهِـۧمَ وَإِسْمَٰعِيلَ وَإِسْحَٰقَ إِلَٰهًا وَٰحِدًا وَنَحْنُ لَهُۥ مُسْلِمُونَ ﴿١٣٣﴾

WHEN HIS LORD SAID TO HIM, "SUBMIT", HE SAID "I HAVE SUBMITTED [IN ISLAM] TO THE LORD OF THE WORLDS."
AND ABRAHAM INSTRUCTED HIS SONS [TO DO THE SAME] AND [SO DID] JACOB, [SAYING], "O MY SONS, INDEED ALLĀH HAS CHOSEN FOR YOU THIS RELIGION, SO DO NOT DIE EXCEPT WHILE YOU ARE MUSLIMS."
"OR WERE YOU WITNESSES WHEN DEATH APPROACHED JACOB, WHEN HE SAID TO HIS SONS, "WHAT WILL YOU WORSHIP AFTER ME?" THEY SAID, "WE WILL WORSHIP YOUR GOD AND THE GOD OF YOUR FATHERS, ABRAHAM AND ISHMAEL AND ISAAC - ONE GOD. AND WE ARE MUSLIMS [IN SUBMISSION] TO HIM." [AL-BAQARAH 131-133]

VERSES 100-106

رَبِّ هَبْ لِى مِنَ ٱلصَّٰلِحِينَ ﴿١٠٠﴾ فَبَشَّرْنَٰهُ بِغُلَٰمٍ حَلِيمٍ ﴿١٠١﴾ فَلَمَّآ أَسْلَمَا وَتَلَّهُۥ لِلْجَبِينِ ﴿١٠٣﴾

وَنَٰدَيْنَٰهُ أَن يَٰٓإِبْرَٰهِيمُ ﴿١٠٤﴾ قَدْ صَدَّقْتَ ٱلرُّءْيَآ إِنَّا كَذَٰلِكَ نَجْزِى ٱلْمُحْسِنِينَ ﴿١٠٥﴾

فَلَمَّا بَلَغَ مَعَهُ ٱلسَّعْىَ قَالَ يَٰبُنَىَّ إِنِّىٓ أَرَىٰ فِى ٱلْمَنَامِ أَنِّىٓ أَذْبَحُكَ فَٱنظُرْ مَاذَا تَرَىٰ قَالَ يَٰٓأَبَتِ ٱفْعَلْ مَا تُؤْمَرُ سَتَجِدُنِىٓ إِن شَآءَ ٱللَّهُ مِنَ ٱلصَّٰبِرِينَ ﴿١٠٢﴾

إِنَّ هَٰذَا لَهُوَ ٱلْبَلَٰٓؤُا۟ ٱلْمُبِينُ ﴿١٠٦﴾

"MY LORD, GRANT ME [A CHILD] FROM AMONG THE RIGHTEOUS." SO WE GAVE HIM GOOD TIDINGS OF A FORBEARING BOY. AND WHEN HE REACHED WITH HIM [THE AGE OF] EXERTION, HE SAID, "O MY SON, INDEED I HAVE SEEN IN A DREAM THAT I [MUST] SACRIFICE YOU, SO SEE WHAT YOU THINK." HE SAID, "O MY FATHER, DO AS YOU ARE COMMANDED. YOU WILL FIND ME, IF ALLĀH WILLS, OF THE STEADFAST." AND WHEN THEY HAD BOTH SUBMITTED AND HE PUT HIM DOWN UPON HIS FOREHEAD, WE CALLED TO HIM, "O ABRAHAM, YOU HAVE FULFILLED THE VISION." INDEED, WE THUS REWARD THE DOERS OF GOOD. INDEED, THIS WAS THE CLEAR TRIAL». [AS-SAAFFAT : 103-106]

Verse 37 of Surat Ibrahim provides valuable lessons about successful parenting and the devotion required when raising children with strong moral values. From the story of Prophet Ibrahim and his family, we can learn the following essential principles of tarbīyah:

- The utmost fairness is required. Children's obedience to their parents is closely tied to the parents' obedience to Allāh. When Allāh tested Prophet Ibrahim by instructing him to leave his wife Hajirah and son Ismael in the open desert, Ibrahim obeyed without complaint. His wife asked if it was his decision or a command from Allāh, to which she responded that Allāh would take care of them and never neglect them. This teaches parents that relying on Allāh is crucial in raising their children. When parents obey Allāh, they set an example for their children.

- Prophet Ibrahim's primary concern was the faith and religiosity of his family. He prioritized their devotion to Allāh and the establishment of prayers in the house of Allāh. This highlights an important lesson for parents who seek to raise their children with a strong religious foundation. Creating a conducive environment where children can worship Allāh and maintain their Islamic identity is essential for their upbringing.

- Hajirah, the wife of Ibrahim, provides a particular lesson for mothers on how to raise a child alone without the support of a husband or family. Despite enduring all the hardships alone, she raised a dutiful child to Allāh, who obeyed his father. She nurtured Ismael with utmost care and manners. This is a powerful and practical lesson of tarbīyah for single parents, whether fathers or mothers, who are raising their children alone.

Verse 37 of Surat Ibrahim offers valuable insights into successful parenting. It emphasizes the importance of parents' obedience to Allāh, the priority of nurturing a child's faith and religiosity, and the ability to raise children alone with dedication and care. These lessons serve as guidance for parents striving to raise their children in accordance with Islamic values.

Furthermore, in verses 131-133 of Surat Al-Baqarah, we gain important insights:

- The journey of Tarbīyah, or nurturing and upbringing, extends throughout one's entire life. This serves as a lesson for parents to remain committed to the Tarbīyah curriculum they instill in their children, recognizing that the process continues until their own death.

- Following the teachings of his father Ibrahim, Prophet Yakub conveyed the message of Tawḥīd (the belief in the oneness of Allāh) to his children on his deathbed. This is a practical lesson for Muslim parents, highlighting the significance of raising their children with a strong foundation in Tawḥīd. Tawḥīd should be at the core of their Tarbīyah efforts.

- Like his father before him, Prophet Yakub was deeply concerned about his children's worship of Allāh alone and their adherence to the path of monotheism. This highlights the goal that every Muslim parent should strive for to ensure their children die as pure Muslims, firmly grounded in the belief in the oneness of Allāh. Parents should prioritize this objective before they depart from this world.

- It is incumbent upon parents to pass on the legacy of Tawḥīd to their children, ensuring that the belief in the oneness of Allāh resonates in future generations. This emphasizes the importance of transmitting the teachings of Tawḥīd to succeeding generations, ensuring its continuity and impact.

In conclusion, verses 131-133 of Surat Al-Baqarah provide valuable lessons for parents. They underscore the lifelong nature of the Tarbīyah journey, the importance of raising children on the foundation of Tawḥīd, the significance of parents' concern for their children's faith, and the duty of passing on the legacy of Tawḥīd to future generations. By internalizing these lessons, parents can strive to raise their children upon the principles of Tawḥīd, ensuring a strong and lasting connection with Allāh throughout their lives.

Regarding verses 103-106 of Surat Al-Saffat, we can derive several significant lessons from Prophet Ismail's readiness to obey the command of Allāh as conveyed by his father, Prophet Ibrahim:

- Prophet Ismail's remarkable maturity is evident despite his young age. His immediate acceptance and obedience to Allāh's command showcase his deep understanding and devotion.

- This obedience and maturity could not have been achieved without his parents' guidance and successful upbringing. It emphasizes parents' crucial role in raising obedient and morally nurtured children who have a strong connection with Allāh and their parents. Ismail's beautiful response, "O my father, do as you are commanded. You will find me if Allāh wills, of the steadfast," exemplifies the essence of true obedience.

- Prophet Ibrahim's effective and successful guidance of his son was rooted in divine revelation. This highlights the importance of effective communication between parents and children in fostering a positive upbringing.

- Prophet Ibrahim's approach to addressing his son as "Ya Bunayya," which conveys affection and endearment, reflects his loving and gentle manner of dealing with his son. Instead of relying on authority and power, Ibrahim approached his son with good manners, love, and affection.

- In the previous verse (102), Prophet Ibrahim's consultative approach with his son, saying, "So see what you think," emphasizes the importance of avoiding authoritarianism and empowering children to make decisions about their own lives. This approach helps build their personality, cultivate confidence, and foster independence.

The Quran acknowledges that the incident served as a test of faith for both Prophet Ibrahim and Ismail, examining their obedience to Allāh despite their hardships and challenges. This highlights the concept that tests and evaluations, not limited to formal education, can be used by parents as tools for character-building and developing their children's potential. Challenging tasks and assessments can be employed methodologically to uplift and elevate children's character and test their resilience.

In conclusion, verses 103-106 of Surat Al-Saffat offer valuable lessons for parents. They highlight the importance of nurturing obedience and moral values in children, emphasizing the role of parents in providing guidance and instilling a strong connection with Allāh. These verses also underscore the significance of effective communication, love, and affection in parent-child relationships and the value of empowering children and utilizing tests and assessments as tools for character development. By incorporating these lessons into their parenting approach, parents can raise obedient, morally upright, and resilient children in their faith.[221]

D- YAKUB AND HIS SONS

The Moral Upbringing Code in Verses 3-4, 13, 67, AND 97-98 OF SURAT YUSUF.

(YAKUB AND HIS SONS)

Verses 3-4

نَحْنُ نَقُصُّ عَلَيْكَ أَحْسَنَ ٱلْقَصَصِ بِمَآ أَوْحَيْنَآ إِلَيْكَ هَٰذَا ٱلْقُرْءَانَ وَإِن كُنتَ مِن قَبْلِهِۦ لَمِنَ ٱلْغَٰفِلِينَ ﴿٣﴾

إِذْ قَالَ يُوسُفُ لِأَبِيهِ يَٰٓأَبَتِ إِنِّى رَأَيْتُ أَحَدَ عَشَرَ كَوْكَبًا وَٱلشَّمْسَ وَٱلْقَمَرَ رَأَيْتُهُمْ لِى سَٰجِدِينَ ﴿٤﴾

[OF THESE STORIES MENTION] WHEN JOSEPH SAID TO HIS FATHER, "O MY FATHER, INDEED I HAVE SEEN [IN A DREAM] ELEVEN STARS AND THE SUN AND THE MOON; I SAW THEM PROSTRATING TO ME." HE SAID, "O MY SON, DO NOT RELATE YOUR VISION TO YOUR BROTHERS OR THEY WILL CONTRIVE AGAINST YOU A PLAN. INDEED SATAN, TO MAN, IS A MANIFEST ENEMY". [YUSUF : 4- 5]

VERSE 12- 13

أَرْسِلْهُ مَعَنَا غَدًا يَرْتَعْ وَيَلْعَبْ وَإِنَّا لَهُۥ لَحَٰفِظُونَ ﴿١٢﴾

قَالَ إِنِّى لَيَحْزُنُنِىٓ أَن تَذْهَبُوا۟ بِهِۦ وَأَخَافُ أَن يَأْكُلَهُ ٱلذِّئْبُ وَأَنتُمْ عَنْهُ غَٰفِلُونَ ﴿١٣﴾

"SEND HIM WITH US TOMORROW THAT HE MAY EAT WELL AND PLAY. AND INDEED, WE WILL BE HIS GUARDIANS.
[JACOB] SAID, "INDEED, IT SADDENS ME THAT YOU SHOULD TAKE HIM, AND I FEAR THAT A WOLF WOULD EAT HIM WHILE YOU ARE OF HIM UNAWARE." [YUSUF : 12- 13]

VERSE 67

---

221   Dr. Muḥammad Hanif Hassan. Powerful conversations between a father and a son: lessons from Ibrahim and Prophet Ismail As. 19/7/2021

وَقَالَ يَٰبَنِيَّ لَا تَدْخُلُوا مِنۢ بَابٍ وَٰحِدٍ وَٱدْخُلُوا مِنْ أَبْوَٰبٍ مُّتَفَرِّقَةٍ ۖ وَمَآ أُغْنِي عَنكُم مِّنَ ٱللَّهِ مِن شَيْءٍ ۖ إِنِ ٱلْحُكْمُ إِلَّا لِلَّهِ ۖ عَلَيْهِ تَوَكَّلْتُ ۖ وَعَلَيْهِ فَلْيَتَوَكَّلِ ٱلْمُتَوَكِّلُونَ ﴿٦٧﴾

"And he said, "O my sons, do not enter from one gate but enter from different gates; and I cannot avail you against [the decree of] Allāh at all. The decision is only for Allāh ; upon Him I have relied, and upon Him let those who would rely [indeed] rely." [YUSUF : 67]

VERSES 97-98

قَالُوا يَٰأَبَانَا ٱسْتَغْفِرْ لَنَا ذُنُوبَنَآ إِنَّا كُنَّا خَٰطِئِينَ ﴿٩٧﴾

قَالَ سَوْفَ أَسْتَغْفِرُ لَكُمْ رَبِّيٓ ۖ إِنَّهُۥ هُوَ ٱلْغَفُورُ ٱلرَّحِيمُ ﴿٩٨﴾

"They said, "O our father, ask for us forgiveness of our sins; indeed, we have been sinners." He said, "I will ask forgiveness for you from my Lord. Indeed, it is He who is the Forgiving, the Merciful." [YUSUF : 97 - 98]

Surat Yusuf contains many historical episodes, but this writing focuses on the parent-child relations depicted in the surah. The following aspects can be learned from the surah:

Verses 3-4 highlight the strong bond between Yusuf and his father, Yakub. This close relationship was cultivated through Yakub's nurturing of his son, fostering an environment of trust and friendship where Yusuf felt comfortable sharing his secrets and dreams with his father. Such a friendship between parent and child leaves a lasting impact on their character and facilitates the parent's ability to closely attend to their child's moral well-being.

Verse 12, mentioning the word "play," emphasizes the importance of allowing children to experience and enjoy their childhood. Play is a crucial source of learning basic social morals and skills necessary for life, and it should be valued as an essential aspect of a child's character-building and personality development. Allowing children to play is integral to their upbringing, contributing to their physical and emotional development.

Verses 13 and 67 highlight the caring and protective nature parents should have towards their children's security, well-being, and safety. Yakub expresses his sadness and concern when his child is exposed to potentially dangerous situations, such as being vulnerable to wolves, in verse 13. Similarly, in verse 67, Yakub advises his sons to enter the town through separate gates to protect them from the evil eye, envy, suspicion, or any other potential harm. This demonstrates the parental responsibility to ensure the safety and protection of their children.

Verses 97-98 teach parents the importance of forgiveness and praying for their children. Despite Yusuf's siblings' grave mistakes of mistreating him out of jealousy, neither Yusuf nor their father reminds them of their past failures. Constantly reminding a child of their past mistakes can have negative effects and potentially encourage them to repeat those mistakes. Opening a new chapter for a child after they make mistakes, without dwelling on the past, can foster self-confidence and motivate them to make better choices in the future.

In conclusion, Surat Yusuf provides valuable insights into parent-child relationships. It emphasizes the importance of building a strong bond of friendship, allowing children to enjoy their childhood through play, prioritizing the safety and protection of children, and practicing forgiveness while guiding them toward personal growth. By reflecting on these lessons, parents can strive to create a nurturing and supportive environment for their children's holistic development.

3.3.3. RIGHTEOUSNESS OF PARENTS

The Moral Upbringing Code in Verses 9 OF SURAT AL-NISA, 82 OF SURAT AL-KAHF, AND 21 OF SURAT AL-TUR. (RIGHTEOUSNESS OF PARENTS AND ITS INFLUENCE ON THEIR OFFSPRING)

The purpose of nurturing children with good morals and etiquette is to guide them and foster a strong connection with their Creator, the Almighty, to seek His pleasure and attain success and prosperity in their lives. Upon reflecting on various Quranic verses, one can infer that through the parents' righteousness, Allāh bestows upon their offspring care, blessings, success, protection, and salvation from the torment of hell in the hereafter. Three verses in the Quran, found in different chapters, implicitly and explicitly demonstrate how the piety and righteousness of parents can benefit their children and lead them to success in all aspects of their lives. The following are the three verses, along with their explanations:

In Surat Al-Nisa, Allāh says:

وَلْيَخْشَ ٱلَّذِينَ لَوْ تَرَكُوا مِنْ خَلْفِهِمْ ذُرِّيَّةً ضِعَٰفًا خَافُوا عَلَيْهِمْ فَلْيَتَّقُوا ٱللَّهَ وَلْيَقُولُوا قَوْلًا سَدِيدًا ﴿٩﴾

"AND LET THOSE [EXECUTORS AND GUARDIANS] FEAR [INJUSTICE] AS IF THEY [THEMSELVES] HAD LEFT WEAK OFFSPRING BEHIND AND FEARED FOR THEM. SO LET THEM FEAR ALLĀH AND SPEAK WORDS OF APPROPRIATE JUSTICE". [AL-NISA : 9]

In surat Al-Kahf, the verse reads as follows:

وَكَانَ أَبُوهُمَا صَٰلِحًا

"AND THEIR FATHER HAD BEEN RIGHTEOUS" [AL-KAHF : 82]

Allāh said in surat Al-Tur:

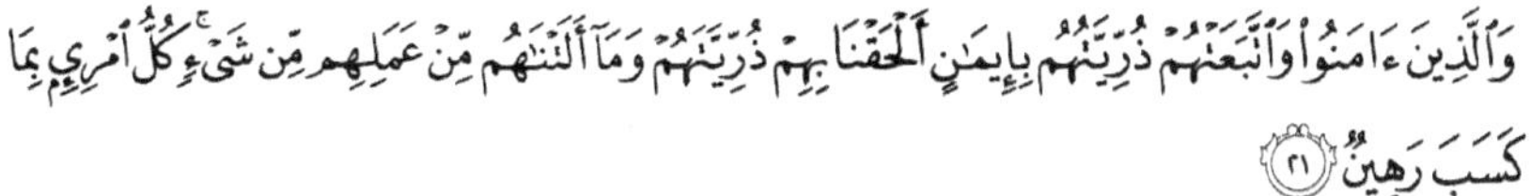

وَٱلَّذِينَ ءَامَنُوا۟ وَٱتَّبَعَتْهُمْ ذُرِّيَّتُهُم بِإِيمَٰنٍ أَلْحَقْنَا بِهِمْ ذُرِّيَّتَهُمْ وَمَآ أَلَتْنَٰهُم مِّنْ عَمَلِهِم مِّن شَىْءٍ ۚ كُلُّ ٱمْرِئٍ بِمَا كَسَبَ رَهِينٌ ۝

"AND THOSE WHO BELIEVED AND WHOSE DESCENDANTS FOLLOWED THEM IN FAITH - WE WILL JOIN WITH THEM THEIR DESCENDANTS, AND WE WILL NOT DEPRIVE THEM OF ANYTHING OF THEIR DEEDS. EVERY PERSON, FOR WHAT HE EARNED, IS RETAINED".

[AT-TUR : 21]

In his comments on VERSE 9 OF AL-NISA Al-Qusheiry says: "It is proven in this verse that what a Muslim should save for his children is piety and righteousness, not money. Because Allāh did ask the parents to collect money, build many houses, or leave them a piece of furniture. All that Allāh asked them for was to fear Him, and He will take care of them by being righteous". [222]

At the end of the verse, it states, "So let them fear Allāh and speak words of appropriate justice," which demonstrates that the parent's adherence to the teachings of Islam in terms of his/her word "being just and truthteller" and action " being God-conscious" can be helpful to the offspring and secure their life and well-being during and after the parent's life. Al-Qusheyr's comment on the verse is well-said that the best legacy of a parent to his/her offspring is righteousness instead of money, Real-states, or any other worldly material which people take pride in its possession.

Ibnu Katheer elaborating on VERSE 82 OF AL-KAHF, said:

وكان أبوهما صالحا:

"Their father was a righteous man) indicates that a righteous person's offspring will be taken care of and that the blessing of his worship will extend to them in this world and the Hereafter. This will occur through his intercession for them and their status being raised to the highest levels of Paradise so that he may find

---

222   Al-Kusheiry, Lata'If Al-Isharat vol: page: 316.

joy in them. This was stated in the Qur'an and reported in the Sunnah. Sa`id bin Jubayr narrated from Ibn `Abbas: "They were taken care of because their father was a righteous man, although it is not stated that they were righteous."[223]

It also reads in Maarif ul-Quran that:

"Muḥammad ibn al-Munkadir says: 'It is because of the piety and righteousness of a servant of His that Allāh Ta' ala protects his children, and the children of his children, and his family, even the homes built around his own.'"[224]

Added to the illustrations in verse is that of Al-Qurtubi, where he said in his Tafsīr: "The verse indicates that Allāh, the Almighty, preserves the righteous in himself, his children, and his grandchildren. It was narrated that Allāh, the Almighty, preserves the righteous in seven of his offspring, And this is evidenced by His saying- the Almighty: Indeed my protector is Allāh, who has sent down the book; and He is an ally to the righteous (protects him)."[225]

Allāh promises to care for the offspring of His servants and provide them protection when the servant demonstrates commitment and wholeheartedly follows the teachings of Allāh in their words and actions. By being devout and dedicated to their faith, individuals can ensure the well-being and safeguarding of their children.

Regarding Verse 21 of Al-Tur, as explained by renowned Quran commentators like Ibnu Katheer and others, it emphasizes that if righteous parents serve as role models for their children in matters

____

223   Tafsīr ibn katheer vol: 6 page 185

224   (Mazhari) Al-A'raf 196. Maarif ul-Quran and Tafsīr Al-Qurtubi vol: 10 page: 407

225   Al-A'raf 196. Tafsīr Al-Qurtubi vol: 10 pages: 407

of faith and piety, Allāh, in the hereafter, rewards the parents by elevating their children to the same rank as them. Consequently, they will all be united in Paradise. Ibnu Katheer provides the following quotation to support this interpretation:

"In this Āyāh, Allāh the Exalted affirms His favor, generosity, graciousness, compassion, and beneficence towards His creation. When the offspring of the righteous believers imitate their parents regarding faith, Allāh will elevate the latter to the ranks of the former, even though the latter did not perform deeds as goodly as their parents. Allāh will comfort the eyes of the parents by seeing their offspring elevated in their grades. Indeed, Allāh will gather them together in the best manner, and He will not decrease the reward or the grades of those higher in rank for joining them together, hence His statement, "To them shall We join their offspring, and We shall not decrease the reward of their deeds in anything.) Ath-Thawri reported that Amr ibn Murah said that Said bin Jubeir said that Ibn ʿAbbas said, "Verily, Allāh elevates the ranks of the believers' offspring to the rank of their parents, even though the latter has not performed as well as the former so that the eyes of the parents are comforted." Ibn ʿAbbas then recited this Āyāh (And those who believe and whose offspring follow them in faith, -- to them shall We join their offspring.) saying, "They are the offspring of the believers who died on the faith. If their parents' ranks are higher than theirs, they will be joined with their parents. No part of the reward their parents received for their good deeds will be reduced for them.' 226

3.3.4. CHILD DISCIPLINING

The Moral Upbringing Code in Verse 58 of Al-Nur

"The Optimal Time to Begin Disciplining a Child"

---

226   Ibn Katheer vol: 13 pages: 232

Allāh says:

يَـٰٓأَيُّهَا ٱلَّذِينَ ءَامَنُوا۟ لِيَسْتَـْٔذِنكُمُ ٱلَّذِينَ مَلَكَتْ أَيْمَـٰنُكُمْ وَٱلَّذِينَ لَمْ يَبْلُغُوا۟ ٱلْحُلُمَ مِنكُمْ ثَلَـٰثَ مَرَّٰتٍ مِّن قَبْلِ صَلَوٰةِ ٱلْفَجْرِ وَحِينَ تَضَعُونَ ثِيَابَكُم مِّنَ ٱلظَّهِيرَةِ وَمِنۢ بَعْدِ صَلَوٰةِ ٱلْعِشَآءِ ثَلَـٰثُ عَوْرَٰتٍ لَّكُمْ لَيْسَ عَلَيْكُمْ وَلَا عَلَيْهِمْ جُنَاحٌۢ بَعْدَهُنَّ طَوَّٰفُونَ عَلَيْكُم بَعْضُكُمْ عَلَىٰ بَعْضٍ كَذَٰلِكَ يُبَيِّنُ ٱللَّهُ لَكُمُ ٱلْـَٔايَـٰتِ وَٱللَّهُ عَلِيمٌ حَكِيمٌ ۝

"O YOU WHO HAVE BELIEVED, LET THOSE WHOM YOUR RIGHT HANDS POSSESS AND THOSE WHO HAVE NOT [YET] REACHED PUBERTY AMONG YOU ASK PERMISSION OF YOU [BEFORE ENTERING] AT THREE TIMES: BEFORE THE DAWN PRAYER AND WHEN YOU PUT ASIDE YOUR CLOTHING [FOR REST] AT NOON AND AFTER THE NIGHT PRAYER. [THESE ARE] THREE TIMES OF PRIVACY FOR YOU. THERE IS NO BLAME UPON YOU NOR UPON THEM BEYOND THESE [PERIODS], FOR THEY CONTINUALLY CIRCULATE AMONG YOU - SOME OF YOU, AMONG OTHERS. THUS DOES ALLĀH MAKE CLEAR TO YOU THE VERSES; AND ALLĀH IS KNOWING AND WISE". [AN-NUR : 58]

In verse above, "Let those who have not [yet] reached puberty among you ask permission of you [before entering]," it instructs the parents on the right time when they should start teaching their children the basic etiquette of Islam, such as asking permission before entering the house because of privacy.

At this early stage (middle childhood), and the age when the child has the conscience to perceive and distinguish between right and wrong and simultaneously understand the instructions given to him by the parent is when it is highly recommended to raise the child on morals, manners, and etiquettes of Islam.

It is, undoubtedly, the proper and the most fitting stage to morally prepare them. That is why sharī'a encourages the parents to consider starting nurturing the child at this very stage because of the easiness of molding and shaping the children in this period.

Accordingly, the prophet, peace upon him, commands the believers to order their children to pray at the age of seven so that the prayer becomes the first step of the child's connection with Allāh;

Amr bin Shu'aib reported on his father's authority that his grandfather ﷺ said that the

messenger of Allāh ﷺ said:

$$\text{(مروا أولادكم بالصلاة وهم أبناء سبع سنين ..)}$$

"Command your children to perform Ṣalāt (prayer) when they are seven years old."[227]

The childhood period, from birth to age eight, is crucial for instilling discipline and cultivating desirable qualities in children. This is a period when children are like sponges, eagerly absorbing everything their parents show, teach, and tell them. During this time, parents have significant influence over their children's development. It is essential for parents to nurture their children, shaping them into individuals that align with their aspirations.

According to Shahid Athar's article "Influencing the Behavior of Muslim Youth and their Parents," parents strongly influence their children, especially during the early years (0-8 years), accounting for up to 80% of their influence. However, as children grow, they begin to explore new friendships and encounter diverse ideas, which gradually make them independent from the sole influence of their parents.

Likewise, around the age of seven, children start displaying a natural inclination towards logical reasoning and developing an understanding of Islamic ethics. Their constant and inquisitive

____

227   Abū Daud Al-Sunan, Hadith, No: 496, Aḥmad, Al-Musnad 6689.

questioning about their surroundings, whether it be what they see, hear, think, or even imagine, indicates their readiness to receive instruction and guidance.

Children possess a remarkable receptivity to various influences. As described by Athar, "They are like molten cement, easily molded by anything that falls upon them, leaving lasting impressions." Their minds resemble untouched soil, eager to accept any seed planted within. As they mature, their ability to absorb new ideas and influences expands. We must filter the experiential factors that shape a child's development, ensuring they embrace positive ideas and behaviors while rejecting negative influences.[228]

Furthermore, Ibnul Qayim emphasized the paramount importance of nurturing children and instilling them with good moral conduct during their formative years. He stated:

> "One of the most urgent needs of a child is close attention to their moral well-being. They grow up influenced by the habits and behaviors they are accustomed to in their early years. If they are exposed to resentment, anger, arguments, impatience, succumbing to whims and desires, foolishness, a quick temper, and greed, it will be challenging for them to change these traits as they grow older. Consequently, we find that many people have deviant characters due to their upbringing." [229]

In conclusion, the Islamic perspective highlights several essential principles that are crucial to parent-child relationships. The extensive discussion and analysis of Quranic verses in this context clearly demonstrate that parents play a vital role in shaping their children's mindset, attitudes, moral standards, and overall strength and positivity.

---

228   ibid.

229   Ibnul Qayim, Tuhfatul Mowluud 240

Hence, if parents strive to their utmost ability, serving as role models for their children's moral conduct and raising them with righteousness to safeguard them from the perils of hellfire, as commanded by Allāh in verse 6 of Surat Al-Tahreem, they will ultimately succeed in nurturing a morally upright generation capable of making significant and positive contributions to Islam and humanity as a whole. However, to realize this vision, parents must approach this task with seriousness, sincerity, and a genuine commitment to displaying impeccable virtues and moral conduct that will shape their children's character and overall personality.

SECTION FOUR

MORAL ETTEQUITES OF THE BELIEVER WITH RELATIVES

In Islam, the concept of family extends beyond just one's parents and siblings to encompass grandparents, aunts, uncles, cousins, and even in-laws. This bond is referred to as "Raḥīm," and the relationship maintained with them is known as "Silat Al-Raḥīm.

However, for more linguistic illustration: "The word أَرْحَام 'arḥam' is the plural of رَحَم 'Raḥīm' (womb). This is a receptacle or repository in the mother where the young humans are conceived, held, protected, and developed before birth. Because that is the source of all relationships and kinship, it is idiomatically used in the sense of human relationship and kinship".[230]

The Quran and Sunnah stress the importance of maintaining good relations with one's relatives in Islam. Family ties are considered significant in the religion, and Muslims are encouraged to treat their relatives with kindness, respect, and compassion, regardless of their faith or background. Through forgiveness and reconciliation, we are encouraged to maintain these ties with

---

230   Ma'riful Quran, Tafsīr Surat Al-Nisa verse 1

relatives who may have wronged or mistreated us solely to please Allāh, who has commanded us to do so. Allāh emphasizes the need to foster these relationships at all times, stating:

وَٱلَّذِينَ يَصِلُونَ مَآ أَمَرَ ٱللَّهُ بِهِۦٓ أَن يُوصَلَ وَيَخْشَوْنَ رَبَّهُمْ وَيَخَافُونَ سُوٓءَ ٱلْحِسَابِ ﴿٢١﴾

"AND THOSE WHO JOIN THAT WHICH ALLĀH HAS ORDERED TO BE JOINED AND FEAR THEIR LORD AND ARE AFRAID OF THE EVIL OF [THEIR] ACCOUNT" [AR-RA'D : 21]

Al-Sa'di commenting on this verse, said: "This is general and applies to every bond that Allāh has commanded people to uphold, which includes believing in Him and His Messenger, loving Him and His Messenger submitting in full servitude to Him alone, with no partner or associate, obeying His Messenger upholding ties with their fathers and mothers, honoring them in word and deed and not disobeying them, upholding ties with relatives and kin by treating them kindly in word and deed, and paying attention to spouses, friends, and servants by giving them their rights in full, whether religious or worldly."[231] To show how significant the blood relation is, Allāh says:

وَأُوْلُواْ ٱلْأَرْحَامِ بَعْضُهُمْ أَوْلَىٰ بِبَعْضٍ

"AND THOSE OF [BLOOD] RELATIONSHIP ARE MORE ENTITLED [TO INHERITANCE]."
[AL-AHZAB : 6]

The verse highlights the value and superiority of blood relations, which bring two individuals together as they recognize that they share the same blood. The genes they inherit come from the same origin, and despite the importance of brotherhood based on Islam, which Islam has emphasized, there can be nothing more precious than blood ties. The verse refers to an existing situation where inheritance was based on brotherhood in Islam. This verse abrogates that ruling, from the time of its revelation, the inheritance will be based only on blood relations.

---

231   Al-Sa'di, Tafsīr (sunniconnet), juz 13, page 91

One of the Quranic injunctions that explicitly emphasizes the significance of relatives in Islam and the good treatment that we owe to them is found in Surat Al-Nisa. The verse states:

۞ وَٱعْبُدُوا۟ ٱللَّهَ وَلَا تُشْرِكُوا۟ بِهِۦ شَيْـًٔا ۖ وَبِٱلْوَٰلِدَيْنِ إِحْسَٰنًا وَبِذِى ٱلْقُرْبَىٰ وَٱلْيَتَٰمَىٰ وَٱلْمَسَٰكِينِ وَٱلْجَارِ ذِى ٱلْقُرْبَىٰ وَٱلْجَارِ ٱلْجُنُبِ وَٱلصَّاحِبِ بِٱلْجَنۢبِ وَٱبْنِ ٱلسَّبِيلِ وَمَا مَلَكَتْ أَيْمَٰنُكُمْ ۗ إِنَّ ٱللَّهَ لَا يُحِبُّ مَن كَانَ مُخْتَالًا فَخُورًا ﴿٣٦﴾

"WORSHIP ALLĀH AND ASSOCIATE NOTHING WITH ḤIM, AND TO PARENTS DO GOOD, AND TO RELATIVES, ORPHANS, THE NEEDY, THE NEAR NEIGHBOR, THE NEIGHBOR FARTHER AWAY, THE COMPANION AT YOUR SIDE, THE TRAVELER, AND THOSE WHOM YOUR RIGHT HANDS POSSESS. ĪNDEED, ĀLLĀH DOES NOT LIKE THOSE WHO ARE SELF-DELUDING AND BOASTFUL".

[AN-NISA' : 36]

This verse places relatives in the third position of importance, right after the obligation to worship Allāh alone and the obligation to honor one's parents. Among all the categories mentioned in the verse, no other category holds more rights than relatives.

فَهَلْ عَسَيْتُمْ إِن تَوَلَّيْتُمْ أَن تُفْسِدُوا۟ فِى ٱلْأَرْضِ وَتُقَطِّعُوٓا۟ أَرْحَامَكُمْ ﴿٢٢﴾

"SO WOULD YOU PERHAPS, IF YOU TURNED AWAY, CAUSE CORRUPTION ON EARTH AND SEVER YOUR [TIES OF] RELATIONSHIP?" [MUḤAMMAD : 22]

Concerning the meaning of the verse and the context, it referred to, "In the Pre-Islamic Days, according to the practices of jahiliyyah, corruption and severed ties of kinship. For example, they practiced injustice; they cut each other's throat; one tribe attacked another tribe; they committed carnage and massacre; and they buried alive their daughters with their own hands. Islam abolished and wiped out all these and other heinous practices of the Days of ignorance. In these heinous crimes of those days".[232]

And the comment continued by saying:

---

232 Ma'riful Quran, Tafsīr surat Muḥammad, verse 22

"This involves a general prohibition of spreading corruption on earth and a specific prohibition of severing the ties of kinship. In fact, Allāh has commanded the people to establish righteousness on earth, as well as to join the ties of kinship by treating the relatives well in speech, actions, and spending wealth in charity".[233]

In many of his teachings, Prophet Muḥammad (ﷺ) emphasized the importance of maintaining good relations with family members. Doing so is considered a crucial aspect of faith and a means of earning Allāh's pleasure, becoming beloved to Allāh and one's relatives, and experiencing blessings in family and wealth. Furthermore, the Prophet taught that strengthening ties with relatives is a cause of:

1- Expansion of provision and a longer life, according to a narration by Abū Hurayra who reported that he heard the Messenger of Allāh say,

مَنْ سَرَّهُ أَنْ يُبْسَطَ لَهُ فِي رِزْقِهِ، وَأَنْ يُنْسَأَ لَهُ فِي أَثَرِهِ، فَلْيَصِلْ رَحِمَهُ.

"Anyone who wants to have his provision expanded and his term of life lengthened should maintain ties of kinship."[234]

Becoming a wealthy and a beloved person by the relatives. Ibn 'Umar said:

مَنِ اتَّقَى رَبَّهُ، وَوَصَلَ رَحِمَهُ، نُسِّئَ فِي أَجَلِهِ، وَثَرَى مَالُهُ، وَأَحَبَّهُ أَهْلُهُ.

"If someone fears his Lord and maintains ties of kinship, his term of life will be prolonged, he will have abundant wealth, and his people will love him."[235]

Attaining salvation and entrance to paradise. Abū Ayyub al-Ansari told him that:

---

233   Ibnu Katheer, Tafsīr surat Muḥammad, verse 22
234   Al-Ādab Al-Mufrad 57
235   Al-Ādab Al-Mufrad 58

أَنَّ أَعْرَابِيًّا عَرَضَ عَلَى النَّبِيِّ ﷺ فِي مَسِيرِهِ، فَقَالَ: أَخْبِرْنِي مَا يُقَرِّبُنِي مِنَ الْجَنَّةِ، وَيُبَاعِدُنِي مِنَ النَّارِ؟ قَالَ: تَعْبُدُ اللَّهَ وَلَا تُشْرِكُ بِهِ شَيْئًا، وَتُقِيمُ الصَّلَاةَ، وَتُؤْتِي الزَّكَاةَ، وَتَصِلُ الرَّحِمَ.

"A bedouin came to the Prophet while he was travelling. He asked, "Tell me what will bring me near to the Garden and keep me far from the Fire." He replied, "Worship Allāh and do not associate anything with Him, perform the prayer, pay zakat, and maintain ties of kinship." [236]

On the contrary, severing ties with one's kinship brings swift punishment from Allāh in this world before the hereafter. It is considered a grave sin. Abū Bakra reported that the Messenger of Allāh, may Allāh bless him and grant him peace, said:

مَا مِنْ ذَنْبٍ أَحْرَى أَنْ يُعَجِّلَ اللَّهُ لِصَاحِبِهِ الْعُقُوبَةَ فِي الدُّنْيَا، مَعَ مَا يَدَّخِرُ لَهُ فِي الْآخِرَةِ، مِنْ قَطِيعَةِ الرَّحِمِ وَالْبَغْيِ.

"There is no wrong action which Allāh is swifter to punish in this world - in addition to the punishment which He has stored up for the wrongdoer in the Next World - than cutting off ties of kinship and injustice." [237]

Finally, resolving conflicts or misunderstandings promptly is essential to avoid severing ties with our relatives. We should be quick to forgive, seek forgiveness, and aim to reconcile with one another with mutual respect and understanding. By doing so, we fulfill our religious obligations and strengthen our families' bonds of love and support.

---

236   Al-Ādab Al-Mufrad 49, Classed as ṣaḥīḥ by Al-Bāni

237   Al-Ādab Al-Mufrad 67

SECTION FIVE

MORAL ETTEQUITES OF THE BELIEVER WITH THE NEIGHBORS

Islam places significant emphasis on neighbors' moral and ethical treatment, with several religious teachings outlining the proper etiquette and behavior towards them. These teachings stress the importance of demonstrating kindness, respect, and consideration towards neighbors, regardless of their faith, ethnicity, or background.

One Quranic verse in Surat Al-Nisa serves as the foundation for these moral behaviors towards neighbors, and several authentic narrations further elaborate on these morals and rights. The verse explicitly references the rights of nine categories of people, apart from Allāh, with neighbors ranked sixth and seventh. This ranking highlights the high regard in which Islam holds neighbors.

Allāh says:

﴿ وَٱعْبُدُوا۟ ٱللَّهَ وَلَا تُشْرِكُوا۟ بِهِۦ شَيْـًٔا ۖ وَبِٱلْوَٰلِدَيْنِ إِحْسَٰنًا وَبِذِى ٱلْقُرْبَىٰ وَٱلْيَتَٰمَىٰ وَٱلْمَسَٰكِينِ وَٱلْجَارِ ذِى ٱلْقُرْبَىٰ وَٱلْجَارِ ٱلْجُنُبِ وَٱلصَّاحِبِ بِٱلْجَنۢبِ وَٱبْنِ ٱلسَّبِيلِ وَمَا مَلَكَتْ أَيْمَٰنُكُمْ ۗ إِنَّ ٱللَّهَ لَا يُحِبُّ مَن كَانَ مُخْتَالًا فَخُورًا ﴾ ﴿٣٦﴾

"WORSHIP ALLĀH AND ASSOCIATE NOTHING WITH HIM, AND TO PARENTS DO GOOD, AND TO RELATIVES, ORPHANS, THE NEEDY, THE NEAR NEIGHBOR, THE NEIGHBOR FARTHER AWAY, THE COMPANION AT YOUR SIDE, THE TRAVELER, AND THOSE WHOM YOUR RIGHT HANDS POSSESS. INDEED, ALLĀH DOES NOT LIKE THOSE WHO ARE SELF-DELUDING AND BOASTFUL".

[AN-NISA' : 36]

The verse instructs us to treat our neighbors with the same level of kindness and respect that we would desire for ourselves. This entails being generous and showing consideration toward them.

In a narration reported by Abū Huraira, it is stated that treating one's neighbor is a primary requirement and condition of our faith. The Messenger of Allāh, peace and blessings be upon him, emphasized the importance of treating neighbors with kindness and respect, underlining the significance of this behavior in Islam. He said:

مَنْ كَانَ يُؤْمِنُ بِاللَّهِ وَالْيَوْمِ الْآخِرِ فَلْيَقُلْ خَيْرًا أَوْ لِيَصْمُتْ وَمَنْ كَانَ يُؤْمِنُ بِاللَّه وَالْيَوْمِ الْآخِرِ فَلْيُكْرِمْ جَارَهُ وَمَنْ كَانَ يُؤْمِنُ بِاللَّهِ وَالْيَوْمِ الْآخِرِ فَلْيُكْرِمْ ضَيْفَهُ

"Whoever believes in Allāh and the Last Day, let him speak goodness or remain silent. Whoever believes in Allāh and the Last Day, let him honor his neighbor. Whoever believes in Allāh and the Last Day, let him honor his guest".[238]

Likewise, in another narration by Aisha, the Prophet, ﷺ, recommends maintaining good relations with our neighbors without any differentiation based on faith or culture. This includes greeting them warmly, assisting them when needed, and celebrating their happy occasions with them. He said:

مَا زَالَ جِبْرِيلُ ﷺ يُوصِينِي بِالْجَارِ حَتَّى ظَنَنْتُ أَنَّهُ سَيُوَرِّثُهُ.

"Jibril, may Allāh bless him and grant him peace, kept on recommending that I treat neighbors well until I thought that he would order me to treat them as my heirs."[239]

---

238   Ṣaḥīḥ Al-Bukhari 5672

239   Al-Adad Al-Mufrad 102, classed as ṣaḥīḥ by Al-Albani

Expanding on Jibril's recommendation in light of Islam's general guidelines regarding good behavior with the neighbor, it includes a wide range of actions that promote kindness, respect, and consideration towards them. Muslims are encouraged to help their neighbors when they seek help, whether it be with household chores or other matters. They are also encouraged to visit them when they fall ill, offering words of comfort and support.

When neighbors experience something positive, such as a new baby or a wedding, Muslims are encouraged to congratulate them and share in their joy. Likewise, when neighbors face hardships, such as losing a loved one or financial difficulties, Muslims are encouraged to offer condolences and assistance in any way possible.

Being kind in speech to neighbors, including their children, is also emphasized in Islam. Muslims are encouraged to speak gently and politely to their neighbors, showing respect and consideration for their feelings. They are also encouraged to guide their neighbors towards what is best for their religion and worldly life, sharing knowledge and advice to help them improve their lives.

At the same time, it is important not to intrude into their private matters, respect their privacy and boundaries, and not constrain them due to one's building or renovations. Muslims should be careful not to cause their neighbors to harm, whether by letting trash onto their property or in front of their household or engaging in any other behavior that may cause discomfort or annoyance.

Overall, these actions form part of the goodness that Muslims are ordered to perform toward their neighbors in Islam. By following these teachings, Muslims can strengthen their relationships with their neighbors and fulfill their religious obligations towards them.

Moreover, harming one's neighbor could nullify one's good deeds. The Prophet received a report about two righteous women who both maintained a good relationship with Allāh in terms of their devotion and commitment to worshiping the Creator. However, one of the two women was rude and harmful to her neighbor, while the other treated her neighbor with kindness and respect. When asked about their fates, the Prophet said that the one who was harmful to her neighbor belonged in Hellfire, while the other woman who did not harm her neighbor would go to Paradise. The narration reads as follows: Abū Hurayra said,

قِيلَ لِلنَّبِيِّ ﷺ: يَا رَسُولَ اللهِ، إِنَّ فُلَانَةَ تَقُومُ اللَّيْلَ وَتَصُومُ النَّهَارَ، وَتَفْعَلُ، وَتَصَّدَّقُ، وَتُؤْذِي جِيرَانَهَا بِلِسَانِهَا؟ فَقَالَ رَسُولُ اللهِ ﷺ: لاَ خَيْرَ فِيهَا، هِيَ مِنْ أَهْلِ النَّارِ، قَالُوا: وَفُلَانَةٌ تُصَلِّي الْمَكْتُوبَةَ، وَتَصَّدَّقُ بِأَثْوَارٍ، وَلاَ تُؤْذِي أَحَدًا؟ فَقَالَ رَسُولُ اللهِ ﷺ: هِيَ مِنْ أَهْلِ الْجَنَّةِ.

"The Prophet, may Allāh bless him and grant him peace, was asked, 'Messenger of Allāh! A certain woman prays in the night, fasts in the day, acts and gives sadaqah, but injures her neighbors with her tongue.' The Messenger of Allāh, may Allāh bless him and grant him peace, said, 'There is no good in her. She is one of the people of the Fire.' They said, 'Another woman prays the prescribed prayers and gives bits of curd as sadaqah and does not injure anyone.' The Messenger of Allāh, may Allāh bless him and grant him peace, said, 'She is one of the people of the Garden".'[240]

The affirming that the neighbors should not be harmed said:

فَلَا يُؤْذِي جَارَهُ

"Let him not harm his neighbor."[241]

In conclusion, the above teachings and many others place great emphasis on the moral and ethical treatment of neighbors; kindness, respect, and consideration towards their neighbors,

---

240   Al-Ādab Al-Mufrad 109, Al-Albani classed it as ṣaḥīḥ.

241   Ṣaḥīḥ Muslim 47,

regardless of their faith or background. Following these teachings, Muslims can create harmonious and peaceful communities where everyone is treated with dignity and respect.

INDIVIDUAL MORALITY IN THE QURAN

SECTION ONE

IMPORTANCE OF GOOD MANNERS WITH PEOPLE

4.1.1. THE ROLE OF A MUSLIM'S MORALITY IN ACHIEVING SALVATION IN THE HEREAFTER

The importance of individual morality is exemplified in the Hadith of Bankruptcy, a prophetic narration in which the Prophet (ﷺ) urged his companions to treat all people with good manners, regardless of their religious affiliation or physical appearance. Al-Imam Muslim recorded a Hadith narrated by Abū Hurayra in which the Messenger of Allāh (ﷺ) said:

عَنْ أَبِي هُرَيْرَةَ أَنَّ رَسُولَ اللَّهِ صَلَّى اللَّهُ عَلَيْهِ وَسَلَّمَ قَالَ أَتَدْرُونَ مَا الْمُفْلِسُ قَالُوا الْمُفْلِسُ فِينَا مَنْ لاَ دِرْهَمَ لَهُ وَلاَ مَتَاعَ فَقَالَ إِنَّ الْمُفْلِسَ مِنْ أُمَّتِي يَأْتِي يَوْمَ الْقِيَامَةِ بِصَلاَةٍ وَصِيَامٍ وَزَكَاةٍ وَيَأْتِي قَدْ شَتَمَ هَذَا وَقَذَفَ هَذَا وَأَكَلَ مَالَ هَذَا وَسَفَكَ دَمَ هَذَا وَضَرَبَ هَذَا فَيُعْطَى هَذَا مِنْ حَسَنَاتِهِ وَهَذَا مِنْ حَسَنَاتِهِ فَإِنْ فَنِيَتْ حَسَنَاتُهُ قَبْلَ أَنْ يُقْضَى مَا عَلَيْهِ أُخِذَ مِنْ خَطَايَاهُمْ فَطُرِحَتْ عَلَيْهِ ثُمَّ طُرِحَ فِي النَّارِ

'Do you know who the muflis (bankrupt) is?' They said: 'The muflis among us is the one without a dirham (or money).' He ﷺ said: 'The muflis in my Ummah is the one who comes on the Day of Judgement with prayer, fasting, and zakat. He comes but has insulted so and so, falsely accused so and so, eaten someone's wealth, spilt someone's blood, and struck someone. His good deeds are given to them. If his good deeds finish before that which is upon him, is not paid off, the sins of those whom he hurt are transferred into his account. Then he is thrown into the Fire."[242]

The Hadith of Bankruptcy teaches us important lessons about individual morality and behavior. It emphasizes that performing acts of worship alone is not enough; good manners and dealings with others are equally essential. Transactions test a Muslim's faith, and acts of worship can give them the energy to remain steadfast and succeed in this test. Thus, religion is not limited to one's relationship with the Creator; good behavior towards fellow human beings is an indispensable part of Islam.

Good deeds must result in good behavior towards others or at least restrain our evil impulses. Performing religious devotions while being rude, repulsive, or engaging in cheating and deception toward others contradicts one's faith and Islam. Those who transgress the rights of others and engage in wrongdoing are the true bankrupt, as their good deeds are canceled out by their sins.

The Hadith shows that the "Muflis" to whom the Prophet referred had a strong connection with the Creator but failed in his/her relationships and dealings with others. Mistreating others ultimately leads to his/her downfall and entry into hellfire. Islam not only requires individuals to be virtuous and preoccupied with themselves but also to enjoin virtue and contribute to the moral health of society as a whole. Therefore, while self-accountability is of utmost importance, actively engaging in promoting good morals and eschewing moral corruption in society is equally essential.

By disseminating good morals and values, everyone can contribute to society's collective success, progress, and moral preparedness.

---

242 Ṣaḥīḥ Muslim 2581

Muḥammad Al-Gazali points out that the progress and survival of the nations, the nourishment and development of their civilization and culture, and the consolidation of their power and strength depend on morality. If the people have good and excellent moral character, all these good qualities will be found in them, but if their moral character is at a lower level, then kingdom and rule will soon end:

Aḥmad Shawqi,

فإن هم ذهبت أخلاقهم ذهبوا إنما الأمم الأخلاق ما بقيت

Nations live till their morality lives. When their moral character declines, they also decline".[243]

4.1.2. THE SIGNIFICANCE OF INDIVIDUAL MORALITY FOR THE SOCIETY

وَٱتَّقُوا۟ فِتْنَةً لَّا تُصِيبَنَّ ٱلَّذِينَ ظَلَمُوا۟ مِنكُمْ خَآصَّةً وَٱعْلَمُوٓا۟ أَنَّ ٱللَّهَ شَدِيدُ ٱلْعِقَابِ ﴿٢٥﴾

"AND FEAR A TRIAL WHICH WILL NOT STRIKE THOSE WHO HAVE WRONGED AMONG YOU EXCLUSIVELY AND KNOW THAT ALLĀH IS SEVERE IN PENALTY." [AL-ANFAL : 25]

The verse indicates that individual morality can be taken care of through social responsibility whereby the community stands up to the wrongdoers to stop their moral corruption within the society lest there might be a collective punishment from Allāh on society. Therefore, the overall moral concern of society is an essential requirement to keep good morals prevail. And that can be realized by preventing evil practices from becoming widespread and public and their harmful effects remain limited. But when the collective conscience of the society is weakened to a point whereby

---

243   The poem is by Aḥmad Al-Shawky: Muḥammad Al-Gazali, Muslim's Character, 6.

immoral practices are not suppressed, Such a society becomes the victim of a scourge that does not distinguish between the grain and the chaff. Abū A'la Al-moududi illustrates the verse with a beautiful example, saying:

"This refers to those widespread social evils whose baneful effects are not confined only to those addicted to them but which affect even those who, although they might not be addicted to those sins, are a part of that society. For example, if filth is found in just a few places in a locality, it will possibly affect only those who have not kept themselves or their houses clean. However, if it becomes widespread and no one is concerned with removing uncleanliness and maintaining sanitary conditions, everything, including water and soil, will become contaminated. As a result, if epidemics break out, they will not only afflict those responsible for spreading filth and living in unsanitary conditions, but virtually all the residents of that locality".[244]

Concerning the significance of society's overall moral concern and conscience to stop the wrongdoers' immorality, the Prophet, ﷺ, sets a lucid parable that explains it in Narration that Al-Numan ibn Bashir reported that the Prophet ﷺ said:

(مَثَلُ الْقَائِمِ عَلَى حُدُودِ اللَّهِ وَالْوَاقِعِ فِيهَا كَمَثَلِ قَوْمٍ اسْتَهَمُوا عَلَى سَفِينَةٍ فَأَصَابَ بَعْضُهُمْ أَعْلَاهَا وَبَعْضُهُمْ أَسْفَلَهَا فَكَانَ الَّذِينَ فِي أَسْفَلِهَا إِذَا اسْتَقَوْا مِنْ الْمَاءِ مَرُّوا عَلَى مَنْ فَوْقَهُمْ فَقَالُوا لَوْ أَنَّا خَرَقْنَا فِي نَصِيبِنَا خَرْقًا وَلَمْ نُؤْذِ مَنْ فَوْقَنَا فَإِنْ يَتْرُكُوهُمْ وَمَا أَرَادُوا هَلَكُوا جَمِيعًا وَإِنْ أَخَذُوا عَلَى أَيْدِيهِمْ نَجَوْا وَنَجَوْا جَمِيعًا)

"The parable of those who respect the limits of Allāh and those who violate them is that of people who board a ship after casting lots, some of them residing in its upper deck and others in its lower deck. When those on the lower deck want water, they pass by the upper deck and say: If we tear a hole in the bottom of the ship, we will not harm those above us. If those in the upper deck let them do what they want, they will all be destroyed together. If they restrain them, they will all be saved together."[245]

---

244   Tafheemul Quran, Tafsīr Surat Al-Anfal page 262

245   Saheh al-Bukhārī 2493

"The description of the Messenger of Allāh ﷺ of the Muslim society as being like a community of people on a ship, whose actions each can affect the other, explains that the Islamic view that society must be maintained by its members, each of whom is responsible for maintaining the public good, thereby explaining the true relationship between the individual and the society. This is in contrast to the individualistic outlook which dominates in contemporary times and the philosophy that society is solely made up of individuals, so each is free to act as they please, where each person's concern is for themselves without any or little regard for others. This is reflected in the endemic corruption, crime rates, and neglect of the younger and elder generations.

Imam al-'Ayni mentioned that when the action of preventing the infringements is carried out, all people are saved, not just those on the upper deck. And therefore, the implementation of Islam and the enjoining of the good and forbidding of the evil is how society is protected and served".[246]

We learn from this Ḥadīth that the consequences of committing acts forbidden in Islam are not confined only to those who commit them, but the whole society has to suffer the consequences. Therefore, the people who commit sinful acts and violate Divine injunctions should be checked to save the whole society from destruction. If this is not done, society must face Divine punishment.[247]

However, it is crucial to recognize that individuals' actions and behaviors directly impact the well-being of society as a whole. Therefore, every member of society should strive to cultivate

---

246   Abū Luqman Fathullah, the sixty Sultaniyya: A collection of narrations relating to ruling with brief notes and selected commentary page: 75

247   Riyadusalliheen Hadith No: 187

good morals and uphold their social responsibilities to contribute to the betterment of their community. Indeed, the teachings of Islam emphasize the importance of individual morality and social responsibility in creating a just and balanced society.

Islam emphasizes the importance of accountability for one's actions, whether towards Allāh or other individuals in society. Therefore, one must be mindful of his/her actions and strive to live a life guided by good morals and values. By doing so, individuals can create a just and balanced society where everyone can live in peace and prosperity.

4.1.3. INDIVIDUAL MORAL QUALITIES IN THE QURAN

As the divine guidance revealed to humanity, the Quran offers guidance to Muslims in all aspects of life, including shaping their moral behavior. Its directives, found in its chapters and verses, encourage Muslims to cultivate multiple character traits, both individually and socially. These character traits serve as essential components of morality. When developed genuinely, it can form the foundation of good moral behavior that benefits Muslims and every nation striving to exist and thrive.

SECTION TWO

THE MOST SIGNIFICANT MORAL QUALITIES IN ISLAM

This section will attempt to discuss, from the Quranic perspective, the most significant moral values crucial for every Muslim individual to excel in his/her personal life.

4.2.1. TRUST (AMAANAH)

In this discourse, "trust" refers to an individual's morality in Islam. And that is due to its close relevance to people's dealings and interactions with one another in various levels and situations involving agreements, contracts, and financial rights, a widely discussed theme by Muslim scholars and jurists in their books. Trust is a vital aspect of a Muslim's life, as they are expected to show loyalty, trustworthiness, reliability, and faithfulness in fulfilling and upholding the trust that has been placed upon them. The Prophet, ﷺ, emphasized the importance of trust and urged Muslims to take care of it as it will be the first thing to be neglected in Islam. Accordingly, the prophet, ﷺ, said- on the authority of Anas- :

أَوَّلُ مَا تَفْقِدُونَ مِنْ دِينِكُمُ الْأَمَانَةُ وَآخِرُ مَا تَفْقِدُونَ الصَّلَاةُ

"The first thing you will lose in your religion is trust, and the final thing you will lose is prayer."[248]

However, the Quran explicitly discusses this moral quality in five main verses:

Verse 283 of Surat Al-Baqarah:

۞ وَإِن كُنتُمْ عَلَىٰ سَفَرٍ وَلَمْ تَجِدُوا۟ كَاتِبًا فَرِهَٰنٌ مَّقْبُوضَةٌ ۖ فَإِنْ أَمِنَ بَعْضُكُم بَعْضًا فَلْيُؤَدِّ ٱلَّذِى ٱؤْتُمِنَ أَمَٰنَتَهُۥ وَلْيَتَّقِ ٱللَّهَ رَبَّهُۥ ۗ وَلَا تَكْتُمُوا۟ ٱلشَّهَٰدَةَ ۚ وَمَن يَكْتُمْهَا فَإِنَّهُۥٓ ءَاثِمٌ قَلْبُهُۥ ۗ وَٱللَّهُ بِمَا تَعْمَلُونَ عَلِيمٌ ﴿٢٨٣﴾

"AND IF YOU ARE ON A JOURNEY AND CANNOT FIND A SCRIBE, THEN A SECURITY DEPOSIT [SHOULD BE] TAKEN. AND IF ONE OF YOU ENTRUSTS ANOTHER, THEN LET HIM WHO IS ENTRUSTED DISCHARGE HIS TRUST [FAITHFULLY] AND LET HIM FEAR ALLĀH, HIS LORD. AND DO NOT CONCEAL TESTIMONY, FOR WHOEVER CONCEALS IT - HIS HEART IS INDEED SINFUL, AND ALLĀH IS KNOWING OF WHAT YOU DO". [AL-BAQARAH : 283]

In this verse, Allāh commands the believers to be conscious of fulfilling their trust and being honest in all their dealings, which includes:

Firstly- Explicitly agreed-upon items in contracts such as renting, borrowing, profit sharing, appointing someone as an agent, partnerships, and collateral for loans, as well as any items considered a trust for the benefit of others, like deposits kept with someone else, such as money, watches, gold, or other valuable items.

Secondly- Cases where no contract is involved, such as picking up lost property or returning items that the wind has blown into a neighbor's house. Such cases are known as "shar'i trust."[249]

Verse 58 of AL-Nisa

---

248 Musnad al-Shihāb 216, Grade: Ṣaḥīḥ li ghayrihi (authentic due to external evidence) according to Al-Albani

249 Al-Mawsoo'ah al-Fiqhiyyah al-Kuwaitiyyah (6/236):

۞ إِنَّ ٱللَّهَ يَأْمُرُكُمْ أَن تُؤَدُّوا۟ ٱلْأَمَٰنَٰتِ إِلَىٰٓ أَهْلِهَا وَإِذَا حَكَمْتُم بَيْنَ ٱلنَّاسِ أَن تَحْكُمُوا۟ بِٱلْعَدْلِ ۚ إِنَّ ٱللَّهَ

نِعِمَّا يَعِظُكُم بِهِۦٓ ۗ إِنَّ ٱللَّهَ كَانَ سَمِيعًۢا بَصِيرًا ﴿٥٨﴾

"INDEED, ALLĀH COMMANDS YOU TO RENDER TRUSTS TO WHOM THEY ARE DUE AND WHEN YOU JUDGE BETWEEN PEOPLE TO JUDGE WITH JUSTICE. EXCELLENT IS THAT WHICH ALLĀH INSTRUCTS YOU. INDEED, ALLĀH IS EVER HEARING AND SEEING". [AN-NISA': 58]

This verse summarizes the moral code for Muslim believers: the fulfillment of trust and maintaining justice. Scholars have identified two kinds of trusts that this verse refers to:

A- The first kind of trust is referred to as (المجاهدة), «striving hard within oneself," which involves showing full commitment and total submission to Islam so that one's life, feelings, actions, and behavior become a practical translation of faith. When people observe a believer's behavior, values, manners, and moral standards, they recognize that it is due to their belief in Islam that they are able to attain such high standards.

B- The second kind of trust implied in the verse involves dealing with people and delivering to them whatever they have entrusted us with. This includes honesty in daily transactions, giving honest counsel to rulers and ruled, taking good care of young children, protecting the community's interests, defending it against hostile forces, and observing all duties and obligations outlined by the Divine code. All of these are trusts that must be fulfilled.[250]

Verse 28 of Al-Anfal

يَٰٓأَيُّهَا ٱلَّذِينَ ءَامَنُوا۟ لَا تَخُونُوا۟ ٱللَّهَ وَٱلرَّسُولَ وَتَخُونُوٓا۟ أَمَٰنَٰتِكُمْ وَأَنتُمْ تَعْلَمُونَ ﴿٢٧﴾

"O YOU WHO HAVE BELIEVED, DO NOT BETRAY ALLĀH AND THE MESSENGER OR BETRAY YOUR TRUSTS WHILE YOU KNOW [THE CONSEQUENCE]." [AL-ANFAL : 27]

---

250 Ibid

This verse highlights the importance of honesty and condemns all forms of betrayal, whether related to fulfilling Allāh's rights upon His servants or to the dealings and rights among individuals. The honesty expected of a believer is comprehensive and includes all acts in which a person is involved, such as:

- Honesty in worship: A Muslim should fulfill the obligations imposed by Allāh and perform them to the best of their ability according to Islamic teachings.

- Honesty in protecting the human body: A Muslim must preserve their limbs and organs and not use them in ways that displease Allāh.

- Honesty in handling deposits: A Muslim must return entrusted items to their rightful owner.

- Honesty at work: A Muslim must exhibit good performance, commitment, punctuality, and integrity.

- Honesty in speech: A Muslim should be truthful and avoid lying.

- Honesty in keeping secrets: A Muslim should not reveal or leak confidential information to others.[251]

The Prophet, ﷺ, strictly prohibiting betrayal and treachery said on the authority of Abū Huraira:

قَالَ النَّبِيُّ صَلَّى اللَّهُ عَلَيْهِ وَسَلَّمَ أَدِّ الْأَمَانَةَ إِلَى مَنْ ائْتَمَنَكَ وَلَا تَخُنْ مَنْ خَانَكَ

"Fulfill the trust of those to whom they are due, and do not be treacherous to the one who betrays you."[252]

Verse 8 of Al-Mu'minūn

---

251 Muslim's character, ibid

252 Sunan al-Tirmidhī 1264 Grade: Ṣaḥīḥ (authentic) according to Al-Albani

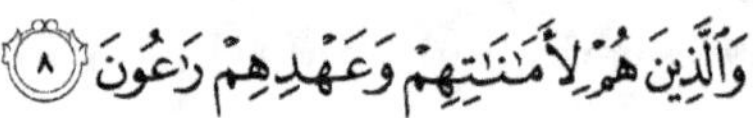

وَٱلَّذِينَ هُمْ لِأَمَٰنَٰتِهِمْ وَعَهْدِهِمْ رَٰعُونَ ۝

"AND THEY WHO ARE TO THEIR TRUSTS AND THEIR PROMISES ATTENTIVE"
[AL-MU'MINŪN : 8]

Ibnu Katheer commented on the verse by saying:

"Those who are faithfully true to their Amanat and to their covenants) When they are entrusted with something, they do not betray that trust, but they fulfill it, and when they make a promise or make a pledge, they are true to their word. This is not like the hypocrites about whom the Messenger of Allāh said, as reported by Abū Huraira:

(أية المنافق ثلاثة: إذا حدذث كذب وإذا وعد أخلف وإذا اؤتمن خان)

(The signs of the hypocrite are three: when he speaks he lies, when he makes a promise he breaks it, and when he is entrusted with something he betrays that trust.) »

Trustworthiness is a fundamental and essential characteristic of Muslims, and they must embody it daily. A person can become deceptive, treacherous, deviant, and corrupt without trustworthiness. Therefore, it is considered one of the successful believers' key attributes and distinguishing features.

Verse 72 of Al-Ahzab

إِنَّا عَرَضْنَا ٱلْأَمَانَةَ عَلَى ٱلسَّمَٰوَٰتِ وَٱلْأَرْضِ وَٱلْجِبَالِ فَأَبَيْنَ أَن يَحْمِلْنَهَا وَأَشْفَقْنَ مِنْهَا وَحَمَلَهَا ٱلْإِنسَٰنُ إِنَّهُۥ كَانَ ظَلُومًا جَهُولًا ۝

"INDEED, WE OFFERED THE TRUST TO THE HEAVENS AND THE EARTH AND THE MOUNTAINS, AND THEY DECLINED TO BEAR IT AND FEARED IT; BUT MAN [UNDERTOOK TO] BEAR IT. INDEED, HE WAS UNJUST AND IGNORANT". [AL-AHZAB : 72]

In this verse, Allāh describes humankind as ignorant and unjust and reproaches them for underestimating the command of Allāh. Scholars have offered various interpretations and opinions regarding the meaning of "Amānah" in this verse. Ibn Katheer quoted the following views:

(Mujahid, Sa'id bin Jubayr, Ad-Dahhak, Al-Ḥasan Al-Basri, and others said Al-Amānah means Al-Fara'id.

• Others said that it meant obedience.

Al-A'mash narrated from Abū Ad-Duha from Masruq that Ubayy bin Ka'b said: "Part of Al-Amānah means that woman was entrusted with her own chastity."

Qatadah said: "Al-Amānah means religion, obligatory duties, and prescribed punishments."

Malik narrated that Zayd bin Aslam said: "Al-Amānah means three things: prayer, fasting, and performing Ghusl to cleanse oneself from sexual impurity.")

Ibn Katheer, after these quotations, commented by saying:

"There is no contradiction between all of these views; they are all in agreement, and all refer to responsibility and the acceptance of commands and prohibitions with their attendant conditions, which is that the one who fulfills this responsibility will be rewarded, while the one who neglects it, will be punished.»253

As described in this verse, Allāh highlights that humankind is ignorant and unjust and reproaches them for underestimating the command of Allāh. The concept of Amānah is a significant responsibility and trust that humans are not fully qualified to bear. Their negligence in fulfilling this responsibility affirms

---

253   Tafsīr Ibn Katheer (6/489).

the Prophet's forewarning. In a lengthy narration reported by Hudeifah Bin Al-Yaman, a companion in whom the Prophet confided, the Prophet, ﷺ, spoke about this matter and said:

حدثنا رسول الله ﷺ، حديثين قد رأيت أحدهما، وأنا أنتظر الآخر: حدثنا أن الأمانة نزلت في جذر قلوب الرجال، ثم نزل القرآن فعلموا من القرآن، وعلموا من السنة، ثم حدثنا عن رفع الأمانة فقال: «ينام الرجل النومة فتقبض الأمانة من قلبه، فيظل أثرها مثل الوكت، ثم ينام النومة فتبض الأمانة من قلبه، فيظل أثرها مثل أثر المجل، كجمر دحرجته على رجلك، فنفط فتراه منتبرًا وليس فيه شيء » ثم أخذ حصاة فدحرجه على رجله »فيصبح الناس يتبايعون، فلا يكاد أحد يؤدي الأمانة حتى يقال:'' إن في بني فلان رجلاً أمينًا، حتى يقال للرجل، ما أجلده ما أظرفه، ما أعقله! وما في قلبه مثقال حبة من خردل من إيمان . ولقد أتى علي زمان وما أبالي أيكم بايعت؛ لئن كان مسلمًا ليردنه علي دينه، ولئن كان نصرانيا أو يهودياً ليردنه علي ساعيه، وأما اليوم فما كنت أبايع منكم إلا فلانًا و فلانًا»

"Messenger of Allāh ﷺ foretold to us two Ahadith. I have seen one (being fulfilled), and I am waiting for the other. He ﷺ told us, "Amānah (the trust) descended in the innermost (root) of the hearts of men (that is, it was in their heart innately, by Fitrah, or pure human nature). Then the Qur'an was revealed, and they learned from the Quran, and they learned from the Sunnah." Then the (Prophet ﷺ told us about the removal of Amānah. He said, "The man would have some sleep, and Amānah would be taken away from his heart leaving the impression of a faint mark. He would again sleep, and Amānah would be taken away from his heart, leaving an impression of a blister, as if you rolled down an ember on your foot and it was vesicled. He would see a swelling having nothing in it." He (the Prophet ﷺ then took up a pebble and rolled it over his foot and said, "The people would enter into transactions with one another and hardly a person would be left who would return (things) entrusted to him (and there would look like an honest person) till it would be said: 'In such and such tribe there is a trustworthy man.' And they would also say about a person: 'How prudent he is! How handsome he is and how intelligent he is!' whereas in his heart there would be no grain of Faith." Hudhaifah bin Al-Yaman ﷺ added: I had a time when I did not care with whom amongst you I did business; I entered into a transaction, for if he were a Muslim, his Faith would compel him to discharge his obligation to me; and if he were a Christian or a Jew, his guardian (surety) would compel him to discharge his obligation to me. But today, I would not enter into a transaction except with so-and-so".[254]

---

254   Al-Bukhari 3606 and Muslim 1847.

According to this Hadith, several key points are demonstrated:

- Amānah (the trust) was ingrained initially in people's hearts through their innate pure human nature (fitrah).

- People were not left without guidance but were given access to learning about Amānah from the Quran and the Prophet's teachings.

- The true sense of Amānah will gradually decline as moral values deteriorate. Eventually, it will be lost entirely except for a superficial appearance.

- A reduction in trustworthy people will be seen, which is a sign of the end of the world.

Unfortunately, we can see that what the Prophet foretold is now coming true in our contemporary world. Trustworthy individuals are becoming increasingly rare, to the point where only a few people in certain areas are deemed trustworthy. This is a clear sign of the nearness of the Hour. The phenomenon of negligent and unqualified individuals assuming leadership positions manifests the loss of Amānah in our world today. The following Narration of Abū Huraira is indicative of that:

«عليكم بالصدق، فإن الصدق يهدي إلى البِرِّ، وإن البر يهدي إلى الجنة، وما يزال الرجل يصدق وَيَتَحَرَّى الصدق حتى يكتب عند الله صِدِّيقًا، وإياكم والكذب، فإن الكذب يهدي إلى الفجور، وإن الفجور يهدي إلى النار، وما يزال الرجل يكذب وَيَتَحَرَّى الكذب حتى يكتب عند الله كَذَّابا»

Abū Hurairah ﷺ reported: Once the Prophet was speaking to us when, a bedouin came and asked him: "When will the Last Day be?" The Messenger of Allāh ﷺ continued his talk. Some of those present thought that he had heard him but disliked the interruption, and the other said that he had not hear him. When the Messenger of Allāh ﷺ concluded his speech he asked, "Where is the one who inquired about the Last Day?" The man replied: "Here I am." The Messenger of Allāh ﷺ replied, "When the practice of honoring a trust is lost, expect the Last Day." He asked: "How could it be lost?" He replied, "When the matter/ government is entrusted to the undeserving people, then wait for the Last Day."[255]

4.2.2. TRUTH

One of the essential requirements for a functional human society, especially in today's world, is the practice of truthfulness in both words and actions. Such truthfulness can only arise from a sense of God-consciousness and self-accountability. It is an essential aspect of our faith and a vital component of our complete practice of Islam. Unfortunately, many societies are plagued by a lack of truthfulness in their dealings, transactions, and promises, a pervasive bad habit that manifests in other negative behaviors. Muḥammad Sakura defines this problem as follows: "The conformity of the outer with the inner, the action with the intention, the speech with belief, and the practice with the preaching. Truthfulness is the cornerstone of the upright Muslim's character and the springboard for his virtuous deeds."[256]

Similarly, Ibnu al-Qayyim phrased it nicely, describing truthfulness as:

"Truthfulness is the greatest of stations, from it sprouts all the various stations of those traversing the path to God; and from it sprouts the upright path which, if not trodden, perdition is that person's fate. Through it is the hypocrite distinguished from the believer and the inhabitant of Paradise from the denizen of Hell. It is the sword of God in His earth: it is not placed on anything except that it cuts it; it does not face falsehood expect that it hunts it and vanquishes it; whoever fights with it will not be defeated; and whoever speaks it, his word will be made supreme over his

---

255   Al-Bukhari 3606 and Muslim 1847.

256   Muḥammad Sakura: The virtue of truthfulness in Islam. 1st edition. December 11, 2016.

opponent. It is the very essence of deeds and the well spring of spiritual states, it allows the person to embark boldly into dangerous situations, and it is the door through which one enters the presence of the One possessing Majesty. It is the foundation of the building of Islam, the central pillar of the edifice of certainty, and the next level in ranking after the level of prophethood."[257]

Following are Quranic verses and prophetic narrations on the virtues of truthfulness:

VERSE 69 OF SURAT AL-NISA:

وَمَن يُطِعِ ٱللَّهَ وَٱلرَّسُولَ فَأُوْلَٰٓئِكَ مَعَ ٱلَّذِينَ أَنْعَمَ ٱللَّهُ عَلَيْهِم مِّنَ ٱلنَّبِيِّـۧنَ وَٱلصِّدِّيقِينَ وَٱلشُّهَدَآءِ وَٱلصَّٰلِحِينَ وَحَسُنَ أُوْلَٰٓئِكَ رَفِيقًا ﴿٦٩﴾

"AND WHOEVER OBEYS ALLĀH AND THE MESSENGER - THOSE WILL BE WITH THE ONES UPON WHOM ALLĀH HAS BESTOWED FAVOR OF THE PROPHETS, THE STEADFAST AFFIRMERS OF TRUTH, THE MARTYRS AND THE RIGHTEOUS. AND EXCELLENT ARE THOSE AS COMPANIONS".

[AN-NISA : 69]

In this verse, Allāh mentions the elevated status of truthful individuals in paradise, placing them in the best companionship between the prophets and martyrs. They are ranked next to the prophets, ahead of the martyrs and the righteous people. This indicates the high regard and honor that awaits them in the hereafter. Notably, the Quran uses the attribute "Siddiq" instead of "Sadiq," highlighting the linguistic difference in their denotation in the Arabic language. According to Al-Mawardy's Tafsīr, "Siddiq" holds greater significance and is of a higher level than "Sadiq." Therefore, being truthful is not only a moral virtue but also a means to attain a lofty status in the eyes of Allāh. Al-Mawardy said:

---

257   Madaraj Al-Salikeen vol: 2 page : 269

"The distinction between "Sadiq" and "Siddiq" lies in the fact that "Sadiq" refers to someone who speaks the truth with their tongue, while "Siddiq" is someone who upholds truthfulness in their inward and outward actions, in both public and private matters. Every "Siddiq" is also a "Sadiq," but not every "Sadiq" can be considered a "Siddiq."258

Therefore, "Siddiq denotes someone who is utterly honest, someone whose devotion to truth has reached a very high point. Such a person is always upright and straightforward in his dealings. He supports nothing but right and justice and does so with sincerity. He opposes whatever is contrary to truth and does not waver in his opposition to falsehood. His life is so unblemished and selfless that even enemies, let alone friends, expect of him unadulterated probity and justice".259

According to Al-Imam Al-Gazali, in his renowned and voluminous book known as "Ihya Ulum al-Din," the attribute of being "Siddiq" is described as the highest and most elevated level of all six ranks of "truthfulness." He said:

Rank 1: Truthful in speech, refraining from lying or deceiving others in communication.

Rank 2: Truthful and sincere intentions, harboring no ulterior motives or hidden agendas.

Rank 3: Truthful in determination and decision-making, adhering to what one believes to be accurate and just.

Rank 4: Truthful in fulfilling promises, following through on commitments made with sincere intention.

Rank 5: Truthful in deeds, aligning one's actions with their inner convictions and verbal statements.

---

258   Al-Mawardy, Al-Tafsīr, vol:3 page: 43

259   ibid

Rank 6: The highest rank is "Al-Siddiq," embodying all the preceding stations and reaching the pinnacle of truthfulness. However, one's rank will ultimately depend on the degree to which they have attained and internalized these stations.[260]

However, in contrast to the "Siddiq," there is the "Kaddab" who repeatedly lies and hardly ever tells the truth. The Prophet, ﷺ, described both the "Siddiq" and the "Kaddab" in a narration on the authority of 'Abdallah ibn Mas'ud. He pointed out that truthfulness is the foundation of righteousness, the road to Paradise. If a person is keen on being truthful, they will be labeled among the truthful in the sight of Allāh, which predicts a good and safe ending for them. On the other hand, lying is the foundation of wickedness. If a person lies continuously and repeatedly, they will be labeled, in the sight of Allāh, among the mendacious or perjurer ones, which also predicts an awful ending. The narration, as reported by Ibn Mas'ud, reads as follows:

عليكم بالصدق، فإن الصدق يهدي إلى البرِّ، وإن البر يهدي إلى الجنة، وما يزال الرجل يصدق وَيَتَحَرَّى الصدق حتى يكتب عند الله صِدِّيقًا، وإياكم والكذب، فإن الكذب يهدي إلى الفجور، وإن الفجور يهدي إلى النارِ، وما يزال الرجل يكذب وَيَتَحَرَّى الكذب حتى يكتب عند الله كَذَّابا

"Adhere to truthfulness, for truthfulness leads to righteousness, and righteousness leads to Paradise. A man will keep speaking the truth and striving to speak the truth until he will be recorded with Allāh as the most truthful. Beware of lying, for lying leads to wickedness, and wickedness leads to Hellfire. A man will keep telling lies and striving to tell lies until he is recorded with Allāh as the most liar."[261]

---

260   Al-Imam Al-Gazali, Ihya Ulumudeen, vol:4 page 387. Darul-Ma'rifa, Beirut.

261   Al-Bukhaari, 6094 and Muslim, 2607.

One of the significant harms of lying is that it erodes the trust and confidence that others have in us. Mutual trust and general confidence are crucial assets in any society, and lying, treachery, and fraud can undermine and destroy them. This is one of the key reasons why telling the truth and avoiding lies hold great importance in Islamic teachings. Therefore, the Prophet (ﷺ) warned us about the harms of lying and described it as a sign of hypocrisy, as reported by Abū Hurairah:

«آية المنافق ثلاث: إذا حدث كذب، وإذا وعد أخلف، وإذا اؤتمن خان» زاد في ((رواية لمسلم)): «وإن صام وصلى وزعم أنه مسلم»

Abū Hurairah ﷺ reported: Messenger of Allāh (ﷺ) said, "Three are the signs of a hypocrite: When he speaks, he lies; when he makes a promise, he breaks it; and when he is trusted, he betrays his trust."[262] Another narration adds the words: "Even if he observes Ṣawm (fasts), performs Ṣalāt (prayer) and claims to be a Muslim."[263]

Al-Imam Al-Nawawi, commenting on the Ḥadīth, said: "According to most scholars and commentators, these characteristics are indicative of hypocrisy, and the person who exhibits them shares similarities with hypocrites."[264]

The Prophet's- ﷺ - statement, 'He is a pure hypocrite,' implies a strong resemblance to hypocrites due to these traits. Some scholars suggest that this applies to those in whom these characteristics are dominant, and those who exhibit them infrequently are exempt. This is the most widely accepted interpretation of this hadith. Imam Abū 'Eesa al-Tirmidhi conveyed this interpretation from scholars and stated that it refers to hypocrisy in one's actions.[265]

---

262   Al-Bukhari 34 and Muslim 58

263   Muslim 119

264   Sharḥ Muslim, 2/46-47

265   ibid

VERSE 119 OF AL-MA'IDA

It reads:

قَالَ ٱللَّهُ هَٰذَا يَوْمُ يَنفَعُ ٱلصَّٰدِقِينَ صِدْقُهُمْ لَهُمْ جَنَّٰتٌ تَجْرِى مِن تَحْتِهَا ٱلْأَنْهَٰرُ خَٰلِدِينَ فِيهَآ أَبَدًا رَّضِىَ ٱللَّهُ عَنْهُمْ وَرَضُواْ عَنْهُ ذَٰلِكَ ٱلْفَوْزُ ٱلْعَظِيمُ ﴿١١٩﴾

"ALLĀH WILL SAY, "THIS IS THE DAY WHEN THE TRUTHFUL WILL BENEFIT FROM THEIR TRUTHFULNESS." FOR THEM ARE GARDENS [IN PARADISE] BENEATH WHICH RIVERS FLOW, WHEREIN THEY WILL ABIDE FOREVER, ALLĀH BEING PLEASED WITH THEM, AND THEY WITH HIM. THAT IS THE GREAT ATTAINMENT". [AL-MA'IDAH : 119]

The verse brings glad tidings to the believers, as it shows that truthfulness is a noble trait that leads to Allāh's pleasure and, as a result, brings success and contentment in both this life and the hereafter. On the Day of Judgment, the truthful will receive special rewards: they will be saved from calamity and granted salvation by their Creator, and their final and eternal abode will be the paradise that has been prepared for them.

The paradise that is prepared for the truthful ones is the one described by the Prophet, ﷺ, in a narration reported by Ubadah ibn al-Samit. The Messenger of Allāh, peace and blessings be upon him, said:

«اضْمَنُوا لِي سِتًّا مِنْ أَنْفُسِكُمْ أَضْمَنْ لَكُمُ الْجَنَّةَ اصْدُقُوا إِذَا حَدَّثْتُمْ وَأَوْفُوا إِذَا وَعَدْتُمْ وَأَدُّوا إِذَا اؤْتُمِنْتُمْ وَاحْفَظُوا فُرُوجَكُمْ وَغُضُّوا أَبْصَارَكُمْ وَكُفُّوا أَيْدِيَكُمْ»

"Guarantee for me six deeds, and I will guarantee for you Paradise: Be truthful when you speak, keep your promises when you make them, fulfill the trust when you are trusted, guard your chastity, lower your gaze, and restrain your hands from harming others).[266]

VERSE 119 OF SURAT AL-TAWBAH

---

266 Musnad Aḥmad 22251. According to Al-Albani, grade: Ṣaḥīḥ li ghayri (authentic due to external evidence

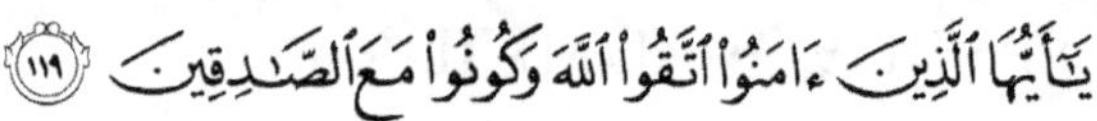

"O YOU WHO HAVE BELIEVED, FEAR ALLĀH AND BE WITH THOSE WHO ARE TRUE." [AT-TAWBAH : 119]

Ibn Katheer said this verse means: "Adhere to and always say the truth so that you become among its people and be saved from destruction. Allāh will make way for you out of your concerns and a refuge".[267]

The verse serves as an invitation from Allāh to His servants to fear Him and to keep the company of truthful people. This companionship is a testament to the depth of their faith and the strength of their Islam. Being among truthful means being among those who live their words by worshiping Allāh with pure and sincere hearts, speaking the truth, keeping their promises, and engaging in honest dealings free from deceit and fraud. When we are true to ourselves, behave sincerely and authentically in all aspects of life, and avoid pretense and hypocrisy, we become true believers as Allāh commands.

> "it was hinted that the only way to achieve Taqwa was to frequent the company of those who are good in their deeds and true in their words and to approximate one's own conduct to theirs."[268]

VERSES 23-24 OF SURAT AL-AHZAB

Allāh says:

---

267   Tafsīr Ibn Katheer Vol:2 page: 414

268   Muḥammad Shafi Al-Uthmani, Ma'ariful Quran, surat Al-Tawbah verse 119 Quran.com.

مِنَ ٱلْمُؤْمِنِينَ رِجَالٌ صَدَقُوا۟ مَا عَٰهَدُوا۟ ٱللَّهَ عَلَيْهِ ۖ فَمِنْهُم مَّن قَضَىٰ نَحْبَهُۥ وَمِنْهُم مَّن يَنتَظِرُ ۖ وَمَا بَدَّلُوا۟ تَبْدِيلًا ﴿٢٣﴾

لِّيَجْزِىَ ٱللَّهُ ٱلصَّٰدِقِينَ بِصِدْقِهِمْ وَيُعَذِّبَ ٱلْمُنَٰفِقِينَ إِن شَآءَ أَوْ يَتُوبَ عَلَيْهِمْ ۚ إِنَّ ٱللَّهَ كَانَ غَفُورًا رَّحِيمًا ﴿٢٤﴾

"AMONG THE BELIEVERS ARE MEN TRUE TO WHAT THEY PROMISED ALLĀH. AMONG THEM IS HE WHO HAS FULFILLED HIS VOW [TO THE DEATH], AND AMONG THEM IS HE WHO AWAITS [HIS CHANCE]. AND THEY DID NOT ALTER [THE TERMS OF THEIR COMMITMENT] BY ANY ALTERATION" -THAT ALLĀH MAY REWARD THE TRUTHFUL FOR THEIR TRUTH AND PUNISH THE HYPOCRITES IF HE WILLS OR ACCEPT THEIR REPENTANCE. 'INDEED, ALLĀH IS EVER FORGIVING AND MERCIFUL". [AL-AHZAB : 23 - 24]

In Islam, fulfilling one's promises to Allāh is the pinnacle of truthfulness and a fundamental belief. The verses above highlight how Allāh praises the believers who adhere to this principle. The groups mentioned in the verses deserve this praise because they upheld the truthfulness of their promises, vows, and pledges to Allāh. As a result, Allāh rewards them with forgiveness and a great reward.

VERSE 35 OF AL-AHZAB

This verse contains a list of ten characteristics that distinguish true believers, both men, and women, as those who are loyal to their Creator. Allāh says:

إِنَّ ٱلْمُسْلِمِينَ وَٱلْمُسْلِمَٰتِ وَٱلْمُؤْمِنِينَ وَٱلْمُؤْمِنَٰتِ وَٱلْقَٰنِتِينَ وَٱلْقَٰنِتَٰتِ وَٱلصَّٰدِقِينَ وَٱلصَّٰدِقَٰتِ وَٱلصَّٰبِرِينَ وَٱلصَّٰبِرَٰتِ وَٱلْخَٰشِعِينَ وَٱلْخَٰشِعَٰتِ وَٱلْمُتَصَدِّقِينَ وَٱلْمُتَصَدِّقَٰتِ وَٱلصَّٰٓئِمِينَ وَٱلصَّٰٓئِمَٰتِ وَٱلْحَٰفِظِينَ فُرُوجَهُمْ وَٱلْحَٰفِظَٰتِ وَٱلذَّٰكِرِينَ ٱللَّهَ كَثِيرًا وَٱلذَّٰكِرَٰتِ أَعَدَّ ٱللَّهُ لَهُم مَّغْفِرَةً وَأَجْرًا عَظِيمًا ﴿٣٥﴾

"INDEED, THE MUSLIM MEN AND MUSLIM WOMEN, THE BELIEVING MEN AND BELIEVING WOMEN, THE OBEDIENT MEN AND OBEDIENT WOMEN, THE TRUTHFUL MEN AND TRUTHFUL WOMEN, THE PATIENT MEN AND PATIENT WOMEN, THE HUMBLE MEN AND HUMBLE WOMEN, THE CHARITABLE MEN AND CHARITABLE WOMEN, THE FASTING MEN AND FASTING

WOMEN, THE MEN WHO GUARD THEIR PRIVATE PARTS AND THE WOMEN WHO DO SO, AND THE MEN WHO REMEMBER ALLĀH OFTEN AND THE WOMEN WHO DO SO - FOR THEM ALLĀH HAS PREPARED FORGIVENESS AND A GREAT REWARD." [AL-AHZAB : 35.]

Allāh highlights ten characteristics that greatly reward men and women in this verse. Among these characteristics, truthfulness holds the fourth position. Those who possess these qualities will have their sins forgiven and their souls purified. Additionally, they will receive an immense reward that no one can fathom its greatness, except for the Creator Himself. Paradise holds unimaginable treasures beyond what any human eye has seen, any ear has heard, or any mind has ever conceived.

VERSES 70-71 OF AL-AHZAB

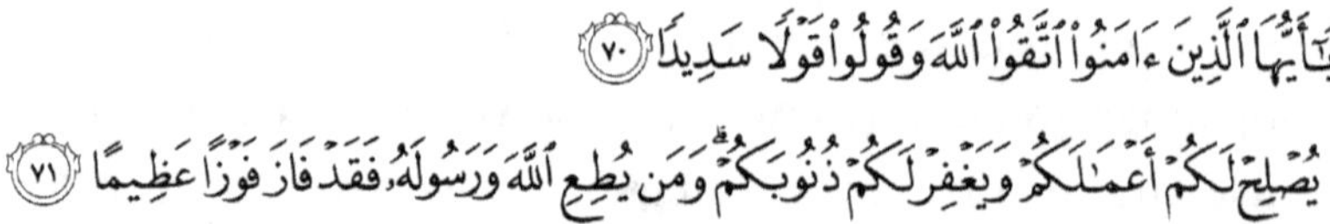

"O YOU WHO HAVE BELIEVED, FEAR ALLĀH AND SPEAK WORDS OF APPROPRIATE JUSTICE. HE WILL [THEN] AMEND FOR YOU YOUR DEEDS AND FORGIVE YOU YOUR SINS. AND WHOEVER OBEYS ALLĀH AND HIS MESSENGER HAS CERTAINLY ATTAINED A GREAT ATTAINMENT". [AL-AHZAB : 70 - 71]

The verse above emphasizes the importance of fearing Allāh and how our internal righteousness is reflected in our external behavior. Our words and actions reflect what we hold in our hearts. When we have greater righteousness, we feel a greater sense of responsibility in our interactions with others, and we are less likely to deceive, lie, or harm them. Taqwa, or God-consciousness, is not limited to piety; it encompasses character development, attitudes, behaviors, beliefs, and morality and should reflect in all our interactions with God, ourselves, and others.

The verse comprises three interconnected parts: fearing Allāh, speaking truthfully and justly, and amending our actions. Fearing Allāh leads to speaking truthfully and justly, resulting in the amendment of our actions. Our good actions reflect our internal righteousness, a product of our God-consciousness. Therefore, it is crucial to cultivate Taqwa in our lives and allow it to influence all aspects of our relationships and interactions with others.

Therefore, holistically describing it, "Taqwa is a composite, multi-relational concept, yet many believers wrongly reduce it to a relationship between you and God only. This reductive view of Taqwa ignores that your relationship with God should be reflected in your relationships with yourself and others: Taqwa is not limited to dealing with God by obeying His commands and avoiding what He forbids. It is also to consider God when you deal with yourself and with others".[269]

Through Taqwa (piety) and truthfulness, we can receive blessings from Allāh in our earnings when engaging in business and commercial transactions. However, if we resort to deceit, lies, concealing defects in goods, and denying the rights of others, we risk being deprived of these blessings. Hakim bin Hizam Narrated that the Prophet ﷺ said:

«الْبَيِّعَانِ بِالْخِيَارِ مَا لَمْ يَتَفَرَّقَا، فَإِنْ صَدَقَا وَبَيَّنَا بُورِكَ لَهُمَا فِي بَيْعِهِمَا، وَإِنْ كَذَبَا وَكَتَمَا مُحِقَتْ بَرَكَةُ بَيْعِهِمَا»

"The buyer and the seller have the option of canceling or confirming the bargain unless they separate, and if they spoke the truth and made clear the defects of the goods, then they would be blessed in their bargain, and if they told lies and hid some facts, their bargain would be deprived of Allāh's blessings."[270]

---

269 Ayman Refaat, pleasing Allāh through Taqwa. June 27, 202, AlJumuah Magazine

270 Ṣaḥīḥ Al Bukhari 2110.

To sum up, truthfulness is the foundation of human relationships in all aspects of life. Trust is built on the reliability of one's word, where we believe in each other without any doubt. If truth is absent from our daily interactions, trust cannot be established among us.

4.2.3. MODESTY (HAYA)

Modesty is a sense of shame or shyness in human beings that arises from a deep inner consciousness of one's morality and virtue. It is a quality that prevents one from engaging in foul conduct or encouraging others to misbehave. In Islamic ethics, modesty encompasses more than just how a person dresses or behaves in public; it also extends to one's speech, conduct, and even private behavior toward Allāh. It is integral to a Muslim's spirituality, centered around worship and obedience to Allāh alone.

Furthermore, the significance of modesty is conveyed through the concept of haya, which encompasses both shyness and a more profound sense of modesty rooted in faith. A Muslim's sense of haya should influence their behavior in the presence of others and when they are alone and in their relationship with Allāh, the Creator.

However, given the vastness of the theme of modesty, we will focus on two particularly relevant aspects: modesty in terms of dressing and modesty of the eyes by lowering the gaze. These two aspects are essential in helping Muslims maintain their chastity and resist their lusts, passions, and whims.

MORAL CODES OF DRESSING IN THE QURAN: VERSES 26-27 OF SURAT AL-A'RAF AND VERSE 59 OF AL-AHZAB.

Dressing is a crucial aspect in Islam, and it should be in accordance with decencey and modesty that reflect one's faith and values. However, the Quran emphasizes modesty and encourages both men and women to dress in a manner that covers their bodies appropriately

يَٰبَنِىٓ ءَادَمَ قَدْ أَنزَلْنَا عَلَيْكُمْ لِبَاسًا يُوَٰرِى سَوْءَٰتِكُمْ وَرِيشًا وَلِبَاسُ ٱلتَّقْوَىٰ ذَٰلِكَ خَيْرٌ ذَٰلِكَ مِنْ ءَايَٰتِ ٱللَّهِ لَعَلَّهُمْ يَذَّكَّرُونَ ﴿٢٦﴾

يَٰبَنِىٓ ءَادَمَ لَا يَفْتِنَنَّكُمُ ٱلشَّيْطَٰنُ كَمَآ أَخْرَجَ أَبَوَيْكُم مِّنَ ٱلْجَنَّةِ يَنزِعُ عَنْهُمَا لِبَاسَهُمَا لِيُرِيَهُمَا سَوْءَٰتِهِمَآ إِنَّهُۥ يَرَىٰكُمْ هُوَ وَقَبِيلُهُۥ مِنْ حَيْثُ لَا تَرَوْنَهُمْ إِنَّا جَعَلْنَا ٱلشَّيَٰطِينَ أَوْلِيَآءَ لِلَّذِينَ لَا يُؤْمِنُونَ ﴿٢٧﴾

"O CHILDREN OF ADAM, WE HAVE BESTOWED UPON YOU CLOTHING TO CONCEAL YOUR PRIVATE PARTS AND AS ADORNMENT. BUT THE CLOTHING OF RIGHTEOUSNESS - THAT IS BEST. THAT IS FROM THE SIGNS OF ALLĀH THAT PERHAPS THEY WILL REMEMBER". "O CHILDREN OF ADAM, LET NOT SATAN TEMPT YOU AS HE REMOVED YOUR PARENTS FROM PARADISE, STRIPPING THEM OF THEIR CLOTHING TO SHOW THEM THEIR PRIVATE PARTS. INDEED, HE SEES YOU, HE AND HIS TRIBE, FROM WHERE YOU DO NOT SEE THEM. INDEED, WE HAVE MADE THE DEVILS ALLIES TO THOSE WHO DO NOT BELIEVE". [AL-A'RAF : 26-27]

Concerning verse 26 above, Sayed, in his Tafsīr, comments by saying: "He also made it a law for them to wear clothing to cover their nakedness, replacing the ugliness of nakedness with the beauty of dressing up. The term used in the Arabic text for "clothing" is often used to denote revelation, giving the Qur'anic statement added connotations to mean that God has legislated clothing in the revelations He has sent down."[271]

Modesty is a heart-centered trait that influences a Muslim's behavior, attitude, and character and physically affects the rest of the body. The statement in verse, "But the clothing of righteousness - that is best," serves as a metaphorical gesture that

---

271   Fi Zilal Al-Quran, Surat Al-a'arf, page 57

emphasizes the importance of the heart in modesty. It suggests that while appearance is significant, what truly matters is the heart, which is the source of modesty.

Verse 27 warns us of the dangers of Awra, which refers to the act of showing one's private parts. It describes this behavior as a plot by Satan and his followers to lure Muslims into disobeying Allāh. Unfortunately, in our contemporary world, we witness constant and diligent efforts to promote moral corruption within our conservative Muslim communities, both within and outside the Muslim world. Hence, "Revealing much of the body, which is characteristic of all ignorant societies, past and present, is the direct result of listening to Satan's whisperings. He is a most persistent enemy who utilizes nudity to achieve his goal of seducing Adam and his offspring."[272]

Clearly, the adversaries of modesty employ various tactics daily to hinder Muslims' devotion to their faith and loyalty to their Creator. They use various slogans, organize conferences, and spend millions of dollars on projects aimed at promoting nudity. Their ultimate goal is to eradicate modesty and reduce humanity to the level of animals, devoid of rationality, intellect, morals, and ethics. The enemy of Islam often stirs confusion in the minds of Muslims, particularly teenagers, by promoting the idea that modesty in terms of dressing is solely related to the traditions and cultures of societies and has nothing to do with any divine revelation. This is a blatant attack on chastity and decency. "Being modest and covering one's body are not matters of social tradition, as claimed by those who try to destroy the humanity of people by attacking their sense of shame and chastity."[273]

---

272   Ibid

273   ibid

Allāh says, regarding women particularly:

يَـٰٓأَيُّهَا ٱلنَّبِىُّ قُل لِّأَزْوَٰجِكَ وَبَنَاتِكَ وَنِسَاءِ ٱلْمُؤْمِنِينَ يُدْنِينَ عَلَيْهِنَّ مِن جَلَـٰبِيبِهِنَّ ذَٰلِكَ أَدْنَىٰٓ أَن يُعْرَفْنَ فَلَا يُؤْذَيْنَ وَكَانَ ٱللَّهُ غَفُورًا رَّحِيمًا ۞ ٩٥ ۞

"O Prophet, tell your wives and your daughters and the women of the believers to bring down over themselves [part] of their outer garments. That is more suitable that they will be known and not be abused. And ever is Allāh Forgiving and Merciful."[274]

Scholars have emphasized that Muslim females who have reached the age of puberty are commanded to dress as the verse above dictates. Some scholars have provided elaboration on the verse and its commandment, which includes:

Al-Jassas al-Hanafi said: "The verse indicates that young women are commanded to cover their faces in front of non-mahram men and to observe modesty when they go out to prevent people with impure thoughts from being attracted to them."[275]

Al-Suyuti confirmed that "this is the verse of hijab, which applies to all women and mandates them to cover their heads and faces."[276]

Shaykh al-Islam ibn Taymiyah affirmed: "that it is not permissible for women to expose their faces in front of non-mahrams, and the authorities should enforce this law and punish those who disobey it to deter them from repeating it."[277]

---

274 Al'A Ahkam al-Qur'ān, 5/245'raf, verse 59.

275 Ah-kam Al-Quran 3/410

276 Awn al-Ma'bud, 11/106

277 Majmu' al-Fatawa, 24/382

According to Ibn Jazi al-Kalbi al-Mālikī, "the Arab women used to uncover their faces, which was an invitation for men to gaze at them, so Allāh commanded them to cover their faces with their jilbabs."[278]

In order to preserve the modesty of women and prevent them from drawing unwanted attention, scholars have derived the conditions for hijab, or covering, for Muslim women from evidence found in verse 59 of Surah Al-Ahzab and other sources in the Sunnah. If a woman adheres to these conditions, her attire in public and elsewhere can be whatever she chooses, and her hijab will be considered Islamic. The conditions are as follows:

- The hijab must cover the entire body.
- It should be thick enough to conceal what is underneath it.

It should be loose-fitting, not tight.

- It should not be so attractive to draw men's attention to it.
- It should not be perfumed.
- It should not be a garment of fame and vanity (i.e., it should not be extravagant or excessively opulent).
- It should not resemble men's clothing.

It should not resemble the clothing of non-Muslim women.

- It should not be adorned with crosses or pictures of animate beings.[279]

THE ROLE OF LOWERING THE GAZE IN MAINTAINING MODESTY IN VERSES 27 AND 30, AND 31 OF AL-NUR.

---

278   Al-Tas-hil li 'Uloom al-Tanzil, 3/144

279   Al- Albani, Jilbab Al-Mar'ah Al-Muslimah p: 37

Since modesty is a heart-centered trait, it is essential to note that there is a strong connection between the eyes and the heart. This means that the state of one can affect the other, and if one becomes good, the other will follow suit. Conversely, if one becomes corrupt, the other will also become corrupt. When the heart is corrupt, it can corrupt the gaze, and a corrupt gaze can lead to a corrupt heart. Therefore, the Quran and Sunnah emphasize the importance of controlling and lowering the gaze to prevent it from becoming a conduit for sin and corruption that can lead to moral decay and a negative character.

Accordingly, Allāh commands in the following verses to lower our gazes:

يَٰٓأَيُّهَا ٱلَّذِينَ ءَامَنُوا۟ لَا تَدْخُلُوا۟ بُيُوتًا غَيْرَ بُيُوتِكُمْ حَتَّىٰ تَسْتَأْنِسُوا۟ وَتُسَلِّمُوا۟ عَلَىٰٓ أَهْلِهَآ ذَٰلِكُمْ خَيْرٌ لَّكُمْ لَعَلَّكُمْ تَذَكَّرُونَ ﴿٢٧﴾

"O YOU WHO HAVE BELIEVED, DO NOT ENTER HOUSES OTHER THAN YOUR OWN HOUSES UNTIL YOU ASCERTAIN WELCOME AND GREET THEIR INHABITANTS. THAT IS BEST FOR YOU; PERHAPS YOU WILL BE REMINDED". [AN-NUR : 27.]

In this verse, Allāh provides us with a general guideline on how to control our gaze with respect to people's private areas. It advises us not to enter their homes without their prior permission and knowledge, in order to avoid inadvertently seeing someone's private parts. Ibn Taymiyah has explained that lowering the gaze not only means refraining from looking at the 'awrahs of others and other ḥarām things but also includes refraining from looking into people's houses. A person's home conceals their body just like their clothes do. Allāh has mentioned lowering the gaze and guarding one's private parts after the verse about seeking permission to enter because a person's home covers them just as their clothing does.[280]

---

280 (Majmoo' al-Fataawa, vol. 15, p. 379)

Similarly, Ibn al-Qayyim (﷽) has stated that ḥarām forms of looking include looking at 'awrahs, which can occur in two ways: through clothing and behind closed doors.[281]

Additionally, the 26th and 27th verses of Surat Al-Nur concern controlling our gaze in public places.

Allāh said:

وَلَا يُبْدِينَ زِينَتَهُنَّ إِلَّا مَا ظَهَرَ مِنْهَا وَلْيَضْرِبْنَ بِخُمُرِهِنَّ عَلَى جُيُوبِهِنَّ وَلَا يُبْدِينَ زِينَتَهُنَّ

"NOT EXPOSE THEIR ADORNMENT EXCEPT THAT WHICH [NECESSARILY] APPEARS THEREOF AND TO WRAP [A PORTION OF] THEIR HEADCOVERS OVER THEIR CHESTS AND NOT EXPOSE THEIR ADORNMENT." [AL-NUR : 31]

قُل لِّلْمُؤْمِنِينَ يَغُضُّوا مِنْ أَبْصَٰرِهِمْ وَيَحْفَظُوا فُرُوجَهُمْ ذَٰلِكَ أَزْكَىٰ لَهُمْ إِنَّ ٱللَّهَ خَبِيرٌ بِمَا يَصْنَعُونَ ۝

وَقُل لِّلْمُؤْمِنَٰتِ يَغْضُضْنَ مِنْ أَبْصَٰرِهِنَّ وَيَحْفَظْنَ

"TELL THE BELIEVING MEN TO REDUCE [SOME] OF THEIR VISION AND GUARD THEIR PRIVATE PARTS. THAT IS PURER FOR THEM. INDEED, ALLĀH IS ACQUAINTED WITH WHAT THEY DO". "AND TELL THE BELIEVING WOMEN TO REDUCE [SOME] OF THEIR VISION AND GUARD THEIR PRIVATE PARTS". [AN-NUR : 30 - 31]

The two verses in Surat Al-Nur forbid Muslim men and women from gazing at each other with lustful intentions, except for their spouses. They command them to avoid prolonged eye contact with members of the opposite gender, whether in private or public spaces such as the streets and marketplace. Interestingly, Allāh addresses His prophet to convey the command to "Al-Mu'minūn" (the believers) instead of "Al-Muslimūn" (the Muslims). Allāh says, "Say to the believing men and women to lower their gazes." This choice of words indicates the wisdom in using the former term, as "Īmān" (faith) denotes a higher level of commitment than

---

281   (Madaarij al-Saalikeen, vol. 1, p. 117)

"Islam." Following these commandments requires a strong and unwavering faith, and thus Allāh prefers the use of "Īmān" over "Islam.

As we explore the teachings of Islam, we consistently encounter a significant correlation between modesty and faith (Īmān). The two are frequently mentioned together to illustrate that they are intertwined, and where there is a lack of modesty, there is also a deficiency in faith, and vice versa. The Prophet Muḥammad (ﷺ) affirmed this connection in various narrations, where he described modesty as an essential aspect and the twin of Īmān.

Ḥadīth no: 1- He said:

«الْإِيمَانُ بِضْعٌ وَسَبْعُونَ أَوْ بِضْعٌ وَسِتُّونَ شُعْبَةً فَأَفْضَلُهَا قَوْلُ لَا إِلَهَ إِلَّا اللَّهُ وَأَدْنَاهَا إِمَاطَةُ الْأَذَى عَنْ الطَّرِيقِ وَالْحَيَاءُ شُعْبَةٌ مِنْ الْإِيمَانِ»

"Faith consists of seventy or sixty branches, the best of which is to declare there is no God but Allāh and the least of which is to remove something harmful from the road, and modesty is a branch of faith."282

• Ḥadīth no:2 He said on the authority of Ibnu Umar:

«إِنَّ الْحَيَاءَ وَالإِيمَانَ قُرِنَا جَمِيعًا، فَإِذَا رُفِعَ أَحَدُهُمَا رُفِعَ الْآخَرُ»

Ibn 'Umar said, "Modesty and belief are together. If one of them is removed, the other is removed."

• Ḥadīth no: 3

Ibn Umar reported: The Prophet passed by a man from the helpers who was admonishing his brother about modesty. The Messenger of Allāh, peace and blessings be upon him, said:

«دَعْهُ فَإِنَّ الْحَيَاءَ مِنَ الإِيمَانِ»

---

282 Ṣaḥīḥ Bukhari 9

"Let him be, for modesty is part of faith."283

- Ḥadīth no 4:

«الْحَيَاءُ مِنَ الإِيمَانِ وَالإِيمَانُ فِي الْجَنَّةِ وَالْبَذَاءُ مِنَ الْجَفَاءِ وَالْجَفَاءُ فِي النَّارِ»

It was narrated from Abū Bakrah that the Messenger of Allāh ﷺ said: "Modesty is part of faith, and faith will be in Paradise. Obscenity in speech is part of harshness, and harshness will be in Hell.'284

The authentic narrations above demonstrate that modesty and faith are interconnected in such a way that one reflects the other. Without faith, people can easily engage in shameful and audacious behavior since they have detached themselves from the moral boundaries that faith provides. Unsurprisingly, in one of his narrations by Abū Mas'ud 'Uqba, the Prophet (ﷺ) said, "If you have no sense of shame, then do as you please," emphasizing the importance of modesty as a fundamental aspect of faith.

قَالَ النَّبِيُّ ﷺ: «إِنَّ مِمَّا أَدْرَكَ النَّاسَ مِنْ كَلَامِ النُّبُوَّةِ: إِذَا لَمْ تَسْتَحِ فَاصْنَعْ مَا شِئْتَ»

"Part of what people have learned from the words of prophethood is the statement 'If you do not feel ashamed, do whatever you like."285

Modesty is a virtue that enhances both the character and actions of an individual. It elevates their status and improves their standing both in this world and in the hereafter. Imran ibn Hussein narrated that the Messenger of Allāh ﷺ said:

«الْحَيَاءُ لَا يَأْتِي إِلَّا بِخَيْرٍ»

"Modesty does not bring anything but goodness."286

---

283   Bukhari 24,

284   Sunnan Ibn Majah 4184 Book 37 Chapter 17 Hadith.

285   Al-Ādab Al-Mufrad 597. Al-bani authenticated it and graded it as ṣaḥīḥ.

286   Bukhari 5766,

In another narration, the Prophet said:

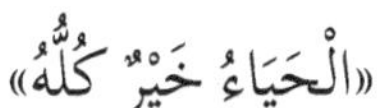

"Modesty is all that is good."[287]

4.2.4. ḤILM (FORBEARANCE)

Ḥilm is a term that refers to the quality of being patient and tolerant towards others, even when they have hurt or wronged us. It is a trait that is highly regarded and beloved by Allāh. Ḥilm is the opposite of wrath, harshness, and austerity, which can cause people to fear, hate, and turn away. This gentle and clement nature is considered one of the prophets' essential characteristics. Without this quality, a person cannot fulfill the vital duty of prophethood.

Different people have varying reactions to situations that bring about feelings of sorrow and pain. Some individuals tend to overreact to minor things, causing them to act impulsively and unwisely. On the other hand, some encounter numerous challenges and hardships but still manage to handle the situations with maturity, wisdom, tolerance, and good manners.

While a person's natural temperament and inherent disposition play a significant role in their behavior, there is a deep connection between self-confidence and how an individual interacts with others and forgives their mistakes.

A person with good manners and a perfect character possesses a generous heart, and their capacity for tolerance and forbearance is extensive. They tend to find reasons to excuse others' mistakes

---

287   Sunan Abū Daud 4796

and accept their apologies when offered. In situations where someone may try to harm them, they remain calm and composed, disregarding the offender's actions.[288]

However, this essential trait of ḥilm or clemency and gentleness of nature is highly encouraged in Islam due to its importance when dealing with others. People we interact with have different behaviors, characters, moods, and situations to which they are subjected. Therefore, understanding the nature of people and forgiving their faults and mistakes is a highly recommended virtuous trait that contributes tremendously to fostering harmony between individuals and societies. This, in turn, fosters love, respect, and appreciation in their hearts.

Therefore, while discussing the trait of Ḥilm, we will refer to two verses that can provide a deeper understanding of its moral nature and how it can be cultivated in our behavior and applied in our daily lives.

VERSES 133-136 OF SURAT AL-IMRAN ABOUT ḤILM (FORBEARANCE)

Allāh says:

---

288   Al-Gazali, Muslim character, chapter 14, tolerance, and pardon.

وَسَارِعُوٓاْ إِلَىٰ مَغْفِرَةٍ مِّن رَّبِّكُمْ وَجَنَّةٍ عَرْضُهَا ٱلسَّمَٰوَٰتُ وَٱلْأَرْضُ أُعِدَّتْ لِلْمُتَّقِينَ ﴿١٣٣﴾

ٱلَّذِينَ يُنفِقُونَ فِى ٱلسَّرَّآءِ وَٱلضَّرَّآءِ وَٱلْكَٰظِمِينَ ٱلْغَيْظَ وَٱلْعَافِينَ عَنِ ٱلنَّاسِ وَٱللَّهُ يُحِبُّ ٱلْمُحْسِنِينَ ﴿١٣٤﴾

وَٱلَّذِينَ إِذَا فَعَلُواْ فَٰحِشَةً أَوْ ظَلَمُوٓاْ أَنفُسَهُمْ ذَكَرُواْ ٱللَّهَ فَٱسْتَغْفَرُواْ لِذُنُوبِهِمْ وَمَن يَغْفِرُ ٱلذُّنُوبَ إِلَّا ٱللَّهُ وَلَمْ يُصِرُّواْ عَلَىٰ مَا فَعَلُواْ وَهُمْ يَعْلَمُونَ ﴿١٣٥﴾

أُوْلَٰٓئِكَ جَزَآؤُهُم مَّغْفِرَةٌ مِّن رَّبِّهِمْ وَجَنَّٰتٌ تَجْرِى مِن تَحْتِهَا ٱلْأَنْهَٰرُ خَٰلِدِينَ فِيهَا وَنِعْمَ أَجْرُ ٱلْعَٰمِلِينَ ﴿١٣٦﴾

"AND HASTEN TO FORGIVENESS FROM YOUR LORD AND A GARDEN AS WIDE AS THE HEAVENS AND EARTH, PREPARED FOR THE RIGHTEOUS. WHO SPEND [IN THE CAUSE OF ALLĀH] DURING EASE AND HARDSHIP AND WHO RESTRAIN ANGER AND WHO PARDON THE PEOPLE - AND ALLĀH LOVES THE DOERS OF GOOD; AND THOSE WHO, WHEN THEY COMMIT AN IMMORALITY OR WRONG THEMSELVES [BY TRANSGRESSION], REMEMBER ALLĀH AND SEEK FORGIVENESS FOR THEIR SINS - AND WHO CAN FORGIVE SINS EXCEPT ALLĀH? - AND [WHO] DO NOT PERSIST IN WHAT THEY HAVE DONE WHILE THEY KNOW. THOSE - THEIR REWARD IS FORGIVENESS FROM THEIR LORD AND GARDENS BENEATH WHICH RIVERS FLOW [IN PARADISE], WHEREIN THEY WILL ABIDE ETERNALLY; AND EXCELLENT IS THE REWARD OF THE [RIGHTEOUS] WORKERS". [AL-E-IMRAN : 133 - 136]

Concerning verse 134 of Al-Imran, Ibnu Katheer commented by saying:

﴿وَالْكَاظِمِينَ الْغَيْظَ وَالْعَافِينَ عَنِ النَّاسِ﴾

"who repress anger, and who pardon men"

For when they are angry, they control their anger and do act upon it. Rather, they even forgive those who hurt them. Imam Aḥmad recorded that Abū Hurayrah said that the Prophet said,

«لَيْسَ الشَّدِيدُ بِالصُّرَعَةِ، وَلَكِنَّ الشَّدِيدَ الَّذِي يَمْلِكُ نَفْسَهُ عِنْدَ الْغَضَبِ»

The strong person is not he who is able to physically overcome people. The strong person is he who overcomes his rage when he is angry.

﴿وَالْعَافِينَ عَنِ النَّاسِ﴾

(and who pardon men;)

They forgive those who treat them with injustice. Therefore, they do not hold any ill feelings about anyone in their hearts, and this is the most excellent conduct in this regard."[289]

VERSES 34-35 OF AL-FUSSILAT ABOUT ḤILM (FORBEARANCE)

وَلَا تَسْتَوِي الْحَسَنَةُ وَلَا السَّيِّئَةُ ادْفَعْ بِالَّتِي هِيَ أَحْسَنُ فَإِذَا الَّذِي بَيْنَكَ وَبَيْنَهُ عَدَاوَةٌ كَأَنَّهُ وَلِيٌّ حَمِيمٌ ﴿٣٤﴾

وَمَا يُلَقَّاهَا إِلَّا الَّذِينَ صَبَرُوا وَمَا يُلَقَّاهَا إِلَّا ذُو حَظٍّ عَظِيمٍ ﴿٣٥﴾

"AND NOT EQUAL ARE THE GOOD DEED AND THE BAD. REPEL [EVIL] BY THAT [DEED] WHICH IS BETTER; AND THEREUPON THE ONE WHOM BETWEEN YOU AND HIM IS ENMITY [WILL BECOME] AS THOUGH HE WAS A DEVOTED FRIEND. BUT NONE IS GRANTED IT EXCEPT THOSE WHO ARE PATIENT, AND NONE IS GRANTED IT EXCEPT ONE HAVING A GREAT PORTION [OF GOOD]". [FUSSILAT : 34 - 35]

Quoting from Ibnu Katheer, He says: "means, if you treat well those who treat you badly, this good deed will lead to reconciliation, love, and empathy, and it will be as if he is a close friend to you and he will feel pity for you and be kind to you.'

Then Allāh says:

﴿وَمَا يُلَقَّاهَا إِلَّا الَّذِينَ صَبَرُوا﴾

(But none is granted it except those who are patient) meaning no one accepts this advice and works according to it, except for those who can be patient in doing so, for it is difficult for people to do.

﴿وَمَا يُلَقَّاهَا إِلَّا ذُو حَظٍّ عَظِيمٍ﴾

---

289   Ibu Katheer, surat Al-Imran

(and none is granted it except the owner of the great portion) means the one who has a great portion of happiness in this world and in the Hereafter. `Ali bin Abi Talhah reported that Ibn `Abbas explained this Āyah: "Allāh commands the believers to be patient when they feel angry, to be forbearing when confronted with ignorance, and to forgive when they are mistreated. If they do this, Allāh will save them from the Shaytan and subdue their enemies to them until they become like close friends."[290]

In the prophetic tradition, the Messenger of Allāh emphasized the importance of Ḥilm ﷺ through his sayings and actions. He praised those with this trait, encouraging Muslims to adopt it in their behavior and conduct. One such example can be found in a hadith reported by Abū Sa'eed Al-Khudri, where the Prophet (ﷺ) praised a companion for his prudence and deliberation, highlighting the importance of Ḥilm in a believer's character:

The narration says:

«أَتَتْكُمْ وُفُودُ عَبْدِ الْقَيْسِ» وَمَا يَرَى أَحَدٌ فَبَيْنَا نَحْنُ كَذَلِكَ إِذْ جَاءُوا فَنَزَلُوا فَأَتَوْا رَسُولَ اللَّهِ ﷺ وَبَقِيَ الْأَشَجُّ الْعَصَرِيُّ فَجَاءَ بَعْدُ فَنَزَلَ مَنْزِلاً فَأَنَاخَ رَاحِلَتَهُ وَوَضَعَ ثِيَابَهُ جَانِبًا ثُمَّ جَاءَ إِلَى رَسُولِ اللَّهِ ﷺ فَقَالَ لَهُ رَسُولُ اللَّهِ ﷺ: «يَا أَشَجُّ إِنَّ فِيكَ لَخَصْلَتَيْنِ يُحِبُّهُمَا اللَّهُ الْحِلْمَ وَالتُّؤَدَةَ» قَالَ يَا رَسُولَ اللَّهِ ﷺ «أَشَيْءٌ جُبِلْتُ عَلَيْهِ أَمْ شَيْءٌ حَدَثَ لِي قَالَ رَسُولُ اللَّهِ ﷺ «بَلْ شَيْءٌ جُبِلْتَ عَلَيْهِ»

"We were sitting with the Messenger of Allahﷺ, and he said: 'The delegations of '' Abdul-Qais have come to you,' and no one had seen anyone. While we were like that, they came and alighted. They came to the Messenger of Allāh ﷺ, and Ashajj 'Ansari was left behind. He came afterward and halted at the halting-place, made his she-camel kneel down, and changed of his traveling clothes, then he came to the Messenger of Allāh ﷺ. The Messenger of Allahﷺ

---

290 Ibid.

said to him: 'O Ashajj, you have two characteristics that Allāh likes: Forbearance and deliberation.' He said: 'O Messenger of Allāh, was I born with them, or are they acquired?' He said: 'No, rather it is something that you were born with.'"[291]

A narration reported by Abū Huraira provides a tangible example of what the trait of ḥilm means and how it can be employed when we find ourselves losing control of our temper. This narration embodies the essence of Ḥilm and its practical application in real-life situations. The prophet, ﷺ, said:

ليس الشديد بالصرعة, إنما الشديد الذي يملك نفسه عند الغضب

"The strong is not the one who overcomes the people by his strength, but the strong is the one who controls himself while in anger."[292]

This hadith highlights the importance of self-control and good manners and how these traits make a person strong and truly righteous. The Prophet Muḥammad (ﷺ) praised the companion who displayed Ḥilm and deliberation because he recognized the importance of these traits in a believer's character.

Scholars have provided detailed explanations and insights into the depth of meaning contained in the hadith. Through their analysis, they have shed light on the nuances and implications of the Prophet's words, helping to deepen our understanding of the importance of Ḥilm in our daily lives.

According to Ibnu Battal, "Allāh has praised those who forgive others when they are angry, emphasizing that the rewards in the Hereafter are greater than the temporary pleasures of this world. Additionally, he mentioned that Allāh highly regards those who control their anger and forgive others".[293]

---

291   Muslim 18, Sunan Ibn Majah 4187

292   Bukhari 6114 and Muslim 2609

293   Sharḥ Ṣaḥīḥ Al-Bukhari, volume 9, page 296.

Ibn 'Abdul Bar said: "The Hadith highlights the virtue of Ḥilm (forbearance) and implies that true forbearance involves suppressing one's anger, and those who exhibit prudence are those who have self-control over their anger."[294]

"In the Hadith, the beloved Prophet (ﷺ) points out that strength is not attributed to a person who uses his muscles to overcome others, rather strength is attributed to someone who can control his anger. This is right conduct."[295]

The Prophet's exemplary character was marked by his possession of this quality, which was apparent to all those who lived with him and interacted with him. In fact, Ḥilm was such an integral part of his character that Allāh praised him for it in Surat Al-Imran.

$$\text{فَبِمَا رَحْمَةٍ مِّنَ ٱللَّهِ لِنتَ لَهُمْ ۖ وَلَوْ كُنتَ فَظًّا غَلِيظَ ٱلْقَلْبِ لَٱنفَضُّوا۟ مِنْ حَوْلِكَ ۖ فَٱعْفُ عَنْهُمْ وَٱسْتَغْفِرْ لَهُمْ وَشَاوِرْهُمْ فِى ٱلْأَمْرِ ۖ فَإِذَا عَزَمْتَ فَتَوَكَّلْ عَلَى ٱللَّهِ ۚ إِنَّ ٱللَّهَ يُحِبُّ ٱلْمُتَوَكِّلِينَ ﴿١٥٩﴾}$$

"SO BY MERCY FROM ALLĀH, [O MUḤAMMAD], YOU WERE LENIENT WITH THEM. AND IF YOU HAD BEEN RUDE [IN SPEECH] AND HARSH IN HEART, THEY WOULD HAVE DISBANDED FROM ABOUT YOU. SO PARDON THEM AND ASK FORGIVENESS FOR THEM AND CONSULT THEM IN THE MATTER. AND WHEN YOU HAVE DECIDED, THEN RELY UPON ALLĀH. INDEED, ALLĀH LOVES THOSE WHO RELY [UPON HIM]". [AL-E-IMRAN : 159.]

Thus, the way the Prophet dealt with people with Ḥilm became a cause for many to embrace Islam, including Zaid bin Sana, a Jewish scholar of the Torah who carefully analyzed the claim of prophethood by the Prophet Muḥammad (ﷺ) and confirmed all the signs of prophethood with the help of the Torah, except for a few. However, one day, Zaid lent the Prophet some gold with an agreement to repay it on an agreed-upon date. However, a few days before the due date, Zaid publicly accused the Prophet of not paying what was due and insulted him in front of his companions.

---

294   Al-Tamheed, volume 6, page 322.

295   Riyad Al-saliheen

Umar got up to respond, but the Prophet stopped him and instead instructed him to pay Zaid's loan and give him twenty extra sâ' of dates as compensation.

Zaid was so moved by the Prophet's extreme tolerance, humility, and Ḥilm in response to his insulting behavior that he embraced Islam on the spot. He explained to Umar that he had confirmed all the signs of prophethood except for Ḥilm, and the Prophet's behavior had convinced him that he was indeed the Prophet mentioned in their books.

This incident highlights the power of Ḥilm in bringing people closer to Islam and shows how the Prophet's possession of this quality played a pivotal role in the spread of Islam.[296]

In conclusion, Ḥilm is not only taught through the words of the Prophet but also demonstrated practically by him as a role model for Muslims. Another example of this is his forgiveness of the Makkans, who had tortured him and his family, and even plotted to kill him. His actions of mercy, compassion, and forgiveness serve as an inspiration for Muslims to strive towards this level of Ḥilm in their own lives, and to follow the example of the Prophet in their interactions with others.

Mu'adh bin Anas ﷺ reported:

«من كظم غيظاً ، وهو قادر على أن ينفذه، دعاه الله سبحانه وتعالى على رؤوس الخلائق يوم القيامة حتى يخيره من الحور العين ما شاء»

---

296   Dr. 'Abdurahman Ra'fat Al-Basha, Suwar Min Hayat Al-Sahabah, Vol: 2 pages: 229-231

The Prophet (ﷺ) said, "The one who suppresses anger and has the power to give effect to it, will be called out by Allāh, the Exalted, to the forefront of the creatures on the Day of Resurrection, and he will be asked to choose any of the virgins (Hur) of his liking."[297]

4.2.5. IHSAN

Ihsan is a fundamental concept in Islam that refers to the highest level of faith and worship. It derives from the Arabic word "ahsana," which means "to do something in the best possible way." Ihsan encompasses excellence, perfection, and doing good beyond the minimum requirements. In Islamic tradition, Ihsan is the third level of faith, following īmān (faith) and Islam (submission to God). It is often described as the "spiritual excellence" of a believer, representing the highest level of personal devotion to Allāh. Generally, Ihsan has three meanings in Islam: worshiping God with the awareness that He sees us, treating people with kindness and generosity, and striving for excellence in all actions.

These three meanings give us an ideal description of the relations between the servant and his Lord, the servant and people, and the servant and things in general. However, to attain Ihsan in his relationship with his Lord, a believer must constantly remember Him, maintaining awareness and awe of Him, and engaging in intimate conversation, supplication, and hope for Him. Through this, Ihsan, in the worship of his Lord, his heart becomes sound, his character is beautified, and his intentions and actions are rectified. Accordingly, a person who attains Ihsan becomes a mercy to creation, benefiting society and all people through good intentions, kind purpose, and hastening to action. However, his experience, skill, and ability to perfect the tasks entrusted to him are also essential components of this benefit.[298]

---

297   Al-Bani, Ṣaḥīḥ Al-Targeeb 2753, Abū Da'd, Al-suan, 4777

298   'Abdessalam Yassine, The three meanings of Al-Ihsan. November 22, 2016

However, in this discourse, we will focus on the importance of interacting with society and benefiting all people based on good intentions and kind purposes. Showing kindness to people indiscriminately is one of the deeds that can tip the balance in our favor in the afterlife, and it is also one of the most beloved deeds by our Creator.

Deeds can be categorized into two types: intransitive and transitive. Intransitive deeds benefit only ourselves, such as prayer and fasting, while transitive deeds benefit both ourselves and others. The latter type of deed is known as Ihsan, which encompasses various aspects of religion. If we closely examine the teachings of Islam, we will find that Ihsan is present in every aspect of the religion, with only a few exceptions that solely benefit ourselves. Knowledge, da'wa (spreading the message of Islam), charity, and other deeds can benefit people of all races, colors, and religions. All that is required is that we make an effort to help others whenever the need arises. It is no wonder that the Quran contains glad tidings for those whose character is to help others. Allāh mentions their great rewards in many verses of the Quran. He said:

$$
\text{فَـَٔاتَىٰهُمُ ٱللَّهُ ثَوَابَ ٱلدُّنۡيَا وَحُسۡنَ ثَوَابِ ٱلۡءَاخِرَةِۗ وَٱللَّهُ يُحِبُّ ٱلۡمُحۡسِنِينَ ﴿١٤٨﴾}
$$

"AND ALLĀH LOVES THE DOERS OF GOOD." [AL-E-IMRAN : 148]

$$
\text{وَٱلصُّلۡحُ خَيۡرٌۗ وَأُحۡضِرَتِ ٱلۡأَنفُسُ ٱلشُّحَّۚ وَإِن تُحۡسِنُواْ وَتَتَّقُواْ فَإِنَّ ٱللَّهَ كَانَ بِمَا تَعۡمَلُونَ خَبِيرًا ﴿١٢٨﴾}
$$

"BUT IF YOU DO GOOD AND FEAR ALLĀH - THEN INDEED ALLĀH IS EVER, WITH WHAT YOU DO, ACQUAINTED." **[AN-NISA' : 128]**

$$
\text{إِنَّ ٱلَّذِينَ ءَامَنُواْ وَعَمِلُواْ ٱلصَّـٰلِحَـٰتِ إِنَّا لَا نُضِيعُ أَجۡرَ مَنۡ أَحۡسَنَ عَمَلًا ﴿٣٠﴾}
$$

"INDEED, THOSE WHO HAVE BELIEVED AND DONE RIGHTEOUS DEEDS - INDEED, WE WILL NOT ALLOW TO BE LOST THE REWARD OF ANY WHO DID WELL IN DEEDS". **[AL-KAHF : 30]**

وَٱصۡبِرۡ فَإِنَّ ٱللَّهَ لَا يُضِيعُ أَجۡرَ ٱلۡمُحۡسِنِينَ ﴿١١٥﴾

"AND BE PATIENT, FOR INDEED, ALLĀH DOES NOT ALLOW TO BE LOST THE REWARD OF THOSE WHO DO GOOD". [HUD : 115]

۞ إِنَّ ٱللَّهَ يَأۡمُرُ بِٱلۡعَدۡلِ وَٱلۡإِحۡسَٰنِ وَإِيتَآيِٕ ذِي ٱلۡقُرۡبَىٰ وَيَنۡهَىٰ عَنِ ٱلۡفَحۡشَآءِ وَٱلۡمُنكَرِ وَٱلۡبَغۡيِ يَعِظُكُمۡ لَعَلَّكُمۡ تَذَكَّرُونَ ﴿٩٠﴾

"INDEED, ALLĀH ORDERS JUSTICE AND GOOD CONDUCT AND GIVING TO RELATIVES AND FORBIDS IMMORALITY AND BAD CONDUCT AND OPPRESSION. HE ADMONISHES YOU THAT PERHAPS YOU WILL BE REMINDED". [AN-NAHL : 90]

هَلۡ جَزَآءُ ٱلۡإِحۡسَٰنِ إِلَّا ٱلۡإِحۡسَٰنُ ﴿٦٠﴾

"IS THE REWARD FOR GOOD [ANYTHING] BUT GOOD"? [AR-RAHMAN : 60]

«أحب الناس إلى الله أنفعهم للناس ، وأحب الأعمال إلى الله عز وجل سرور تدخله على مسلم ، أو تكشف عنه كربة ، أو تقضي عنه دينا ، أو تطرد عنه جوعا ، ولأن أمشي مع أخي المسلم في حاجة أحبُّ إليّ من أن اعتكف في هذا المسجديعني مسجد المدينة – شهرا ... ومن مشى مع أخيه المسلم في حاجة حتى يثبتها له أثبت الله تعالى قدمه يوم تزول الأقدام»

Ibn Abi'l-Dunya narrated from Ibn 'Umar that the Prophet ﷺ said: "The most beloved of people to Allaah is the one who brings the most benefit to people, and the most beloved of deeds to Allaah is making a Muslim happy, or relieving him of hardship, or paying off his debt, or warding off hunger from him. For me to go with my Muslim brother to meet his need is dearer to me than observing i'tikāf in this mosque – meaning the mosque of Madeenah – for a month. Whoever goes with his Muslim brother to meet his need, Allaah will make him stand firm on the Day when all feet will slip." [299]

In conclusion, the concept of Ihsan appears to encapsulate the essence of this humble book, "Quran: The Moral Compass of the Believer - Nurturing Islamic Ethics in Western-Born Generations." The book revolves around our etiquettes with Allāh and His Prophet (ﷺ), as well as our etiquettes with other creatures. The moral quality of Ihsan is the most comprehensive moral trait that

---

299   Classed as ḥasan by al-Albaani in Ṣaḥīḥ al-Targheeb wa'l-Tarheeb, 2623.

we should cultivate in ourselves. We need to employ the quality of Ihsan to be generous and help the needy, to be just with others, and to cultivate integrity in fearing Allāh so that we do not oppress others.

Sincerity, genuineness, selflessness, kindness (to people and animals), forgiveness, honesty, and patience are all integral traits of Ihsan. The last three traits are particularly crucial for anyone who wants to be a Muhsin or help others because one has to forgive, be honest, and be patient to assist and relieve people of their suffering.

INDEX OF QURANIC VERSES

Index of Quranic Verses

Page	Index of Quranic Verses
11	وَنَفْسٍ وَمَا سَوَّىٰهَا ۞ فَأَلْهَمَهَا فُجُورَهَا وَتَقْوَىٰهَا ۞ قَدْ أَفْلَحَ مَن زَكَّىٰهَا ۞ وَقَدْ خَابَ مَن دَسَّىٰهَا
12	أَلَا يَعْلَمُ مَنْ خَلَقَ وَهُوَ ٱللَّطِيفُ ٱلْخَبِيرُ ﴿ ٤١ ﴾
13	أَمْ تَأْمُرُهُمْ أَحْلَٰمُهُم بِهَٰذَآ أَمْ هُمْ قَوْمٌ طَاغُونَ ﴿ ٣٢ ﴾
14	۞ لَّيْسَ ٱلْبِرَّ أَن تُوَلُّوا۟ وُجُوهَكُمْ قِبَلَ ٱلْمَشْرِقِ وَٱلْمَغْرِبِ وَلَٰكِنَّ ٱلْبِرَّ مَنْ ءَامَنَ بِٱللَّهِ وَٱلْيَوْمِ ٱلْءَاخِرِ وَٱلْمَلَٰئِكَةِ وَٱلْكِتَٰبِ وَٱلنَّبِيِّـۧنَ وَءَاتَى ٱلْمَالَ عَلَىٰ حُبِّهِۦ ذَوِى ٱلْقُرْبَىٰ وَٱلْيَتَٰمَىٰ وَٱلْمَسَٰكِينَ وَٱبْنَ ٱلسَّبِيلِ وَٱلسَّآئِلِينَ وَفِى ٱلرِّقَابِ وَأَقَامَ ٱلصَّلَوٰةَ وَءَاتَى ٱلزَّكَوٰةَ وَٱلْمُوفُونَ بِعَهْدِهِمْ إِذَا عَٰهَدُوا۟ ۖ وَٱلصَّٰبِرِينَ فِى ٱلْبَأْسَآءِ وَٱلضَّرَّآءِ وَحِينَ ٱلْبَأْسِ ۗ أُو۟لَٰئِكَ ٱلَّذِينَ صَدَقُوا۟ وَأُو۟لَٰئِكَ هُمُ ٱلْمُتَّقُونَ ﴿ ١٧٧ ﴾
15	۞ وَٱعْبُدُوا۟ ٱللَّهَ وَلَا تُشْرِكُوا۟ بِهِۦ شَيْـًٔا ۖ وَبِٱلْوَٰلِدَيْنِ إِحْسَٰنًا وَبِذِى ٱلْقُرْبَىٰ وَٱلْيَتَٰمَىٰ وَٱلْمَسَٰكِينِ وَٱلْجَارِ ذِى ٱلْقُرْبَىٰ وَٱلْجَارِ ٱلْجُنُبِ وَٱلصَّاحِبِ بِٱلْجَنۢبِ وَٱبْنِ ٱلسَّبِيلِ وَمَا مَلَكَتْ أَيْمَٰنُكُمْ ۗ إِنَّ ٱللَّهَ لَا يُحِبُّ مَن كَانَ مُخْتَالًا فَخُورًا ﴿ ٣٦ ﴾
16	لَن تَنَالُوا۟ ٱلْبِرَّ حَتَّىٰ تُنفِقُوا۟ مِمَّا تُحِبُّونَ ۚ وَمَا تُنفِقُوا۟ مِن شَىْءٍ فَإِنَّ ٱللَّهَ بِهِۦ عَلِيمٌ ﴿ ٩٢ ﴾

17	وَلْتَكُن مِّنكُمْ أُمَّةٌ يَدْعُونَ إِلَى ٱلْخَيْرِ وَيَأْمُرُونَ بِٱلْمَعْرُوفِ وَيَنْهَوْنَ عَنِ ٱلْمُنكَرِ وَأُوْلَٰئِكَ هُمُ ٱلْمُفْلِحُونَ ﴿١٠٤﴾
17	كُنتُمْ خَيْرَ أُمَّةٍ أُخْرِجَتْ لِلنَّاسِ تَأْمُرُونَ بِٱلْمَعْرُوفِ وَتَنْهَوْنَ عَنِ ٱلْمُنكَرِ وَتُؤْمِنُونَ بِٱللَّهِ وَلَوْ ءَامَنَ أَهْلُ ٱلْكِتَٰبِ لَكَانَ خَيْرًا لَّهُم مِّنْهُمُ ٱلْمُؤْمِنُونَ وَأَكْثَرُهُمُ ٱلْفَٰسِقُونَ ﴿١١٠﴾
18	۞ إِنَّ ٱللَّهَ يَأْمُرُ بِٱلْعَدْلِ وَٱلْإِحْسَٰنِ وَإِيتَآئِ ذِى ٱلْقُرْبَىٰ وَيَنْهَىٰ عَنِ ٱلْفَحْشَآءِ وَٱلْمُنكَرِ وَٱلْبَغْيِ يَعِظُكُمْ لَعَلَّكُمْ تَذَكَّرُونَ ﴿٩٠﴾
19	ثُمَّ جَعَلْنَٰكَ عَلَىٰ شَرِيعَةٍ مِّنَ ٱلْأَمْرِ فَٱتَّبِعْهَا وَلَا تَتَّبِعْ أَهْوَآءَ ٱلَّذِينَ لَا يَعْلَمُونَ ﴿١٨﴾
20	۞ شَرَعَ لَكُم مِّنَ ٱلدِّينِ مَا وَصَّىٰ بِهِۦ نُوحًا وَٱلَّذِىٓ أَوْحَيْنَآ إِلَيْكَ وَمَا وَصَّيْنَا بِهِۦٓ إِبْرَٰهِيمَ وَمُوسَىٰ وَعِيسَىٰٓ أَنْ أَقِيمُوا۟ ٱلدِّينَ وَلَا تَتَفَرَّقُوا۟ فِيهِ كَبُرَ عَلَى ٱلْمُشْرِكِينَ مَا تَدْعُوهُمْ إِلَيْهِ ٱللَّهُ يَجْتَبِىٓ إِلَيْهِ مَن يَشَآءُ وَيَهْدِىٓ إِلَيْهِ مَن يُنِيبُ ﴿١٣﴾
20	مَّا فَرَّطْنَا فِى ٱلْكِتَٰبِ مِن شَىْءٍ ثُمَّ إِلَىٰ رَبِّهِمْ يُحْشَرُونَ ﴿٣٨﴾
21	أَكْمَلْتُ لَكُمْ دِينَكُمْ وَأَتْمَمْتُ عَلَيْكُمْ نِعْمَتِى وَرَضِيتُ لَكُمُ ٱلْإِسْلَٰمَ دِينًا
21	ذَٰلِكَ ٱلدِّينُ ٱلْقَيِّمُ وَلَٰكِنَّ أَكْثَرَ ٱلنَّاسِ لَا يَعْلَمُونَ))
21	إِنَّ هَٰذَا ٱلْقُرْءَانَ يَهْدِى لِلَّتِى هِىَ أَقْوَمُ وَيُبَشِّرُ ٱلْمُؤْمِنِينَ ٱلَّذِينَ يَعْمَلُونَ ٱلصَّٰلِحَٰتِ أَنَّ لَهُمْ أَجْرًا كَبِيرًا ﴿٩﴾
25	وَإِنَّكَ لَعَلَىٰ خُلُقٍ عَظِيمٍ ﴿٤﴾
35	ذَٰلِكَ يُوعَظُ بِهِۦ مَن كَانَ مِنكُمْ يُؤْمِنُ بِٱللَّهِ وَٱلْيَوْمِ ٱلْأَخِرِ ذَٰلِكُمْ أَزْكَىٰ لَكُمْ وَأَطْهَرُ وَٱللَّهُ يَعْلَمُ وَأَنتُمْ لَا تَعْلَمُونَ

35	فَإِذَا بَلَغْنَ أَجَلَهُنَّ فَأَمْسِكُوهُنَّ بِمَعْرُوفٍ أَوْ فَارِقُوهُنَّ بِمَعْرُوفٍ وَأَشْهِدُوا۟ ذَوَىْ عَدْلٍ مِّنكُمْ وَأَقِيمُوا۟ ٱلشَّهَـٰدَةَ لِلَّهِ ذَٰلِكُمْ يُوعَظُ بِهِۦ مَن كَانَ يُؤْمِنُ بِٱللَّهِ وَٱلْيَوْمِ ٱلْأَخِرِ
40	. فَلَا تَجْعَلُوا۟ لِلَّهِ أَندَادًا وَأَنتُمْ تَعْلَمُونَ ﴿ ٢٢ ﴾
40	ٱعْبُدُوا۟ ٱللَّهَ وَلَا تُشْرِكُوا۟ بِهِۦ شَيْـًٔا ﴿ ٣٦ ﴾
40	إِنَّ ٱللَّهَ لَا يَغْفِرُ أَن يُشْرَكَ بِهِۦ وَيَغْفِرُ مَا دُونَ ذَٰلِكَ لِمَن يَشَآءُ وَمَن يُشْرِكْ بِٱللَّهِ فَقَدِ ٱفْتَرَىٰٓ إِثْمًا عَظِيمًا ﴿ ٤٨ ﴾
40	۞ قُلْ تَعَالَوْا۟ أَتْلُ مَا حَرَّمَ رَبُّكُمْ عَلَيْكُمْ أَلَّا تُشْرِكُوا۟ بِهِۦ شَيْـًٔا
40	وَإِذْ قَالَ لُقْمَـٰنُ لِٱبْنِهِۦ وَهُوَ يَعِظُهُۥ يَـٰبُنَىَّ لَا تُشْرِكْ بِٱللَّهِ إِنَّ ٱلشِّرْكَ لَظُلْمٌ عَظِيمٌ ﴿ ١٣ ﴾
41	ذَٰلِكَ وَمَن يُعَظِّمْ حُرُمَـٰتِ ٱللَّهِ فَهُوَ خَيْرٌ لَّهُۥ عِندَ رَبِّهِۦ وَأُحِلَّتْ لَكُمُ ٱلْأَنْعَـٰمُ إِلَّا مَا يُتْلَىٰ عَلَيْكُمْ فَٱجْتَنِبُوا۟ ٱلرِّجْسَ مِنَ ٱلْأَوْثَـٰنِ وَٱجْتَنِبُوا۟ قَوْلَ ٱلزُّورِ ﴿ ٣٠ ﴾ حُنَفَآءَ لِلَّهِ غَيْرَ مُشْرِكِينَ بِهِۦ وَمَن يُشْرِكْ بِٱللَّهِ فَكَأَنَّمَا خَرَّ مِنَ ٱلسَّمَآءِ فَتَخْطَفُهُ ٱلطَّيْرُ أَوْ تَهْوِى بِهِ ٱلرِّيحُ فِى مَكَانٍ سَحِيقٍ ﴿ ٣١ ﴾
47	أَرَءَيْتَ مَنِ ٱتَّخَذَ إِلَـٰهَهُۥ هَوَىٰهُ أَفَأَنتَ تَكُونُ عَلَيْهِ وَكِيلًا ﴿ ٤٣ ﴾ . أَمْ تَحْسَبُ أَنَّ أَكْثَرَهُمْ يَسْمَعُونَ أَوْ يَعْقِلُونَ إِنْ هُمْ إِلَّا كَٱلْأَنْعَـٰمِ بَلْ هُمْ أَضَلُّ سَبِيلًا ﴿ ٤٤ ﴾
53	مَا خَلَقْتُ ٱلْجِنَّ وَٱلْإِنسَ إِلَّا لِيَعْبُدُونِ ﴿ ٥٦ ﴾ مَآ أُرِيدُ مِنْهُم مِّن رِّزْقٍ وَمَآ أُرِيدُ أَن يُطْعِمُونِ ﴿ ٥٧ ﴾ إِنَّ ٱللَّهَ هُوَ ٱلرَّزَّاقُ ذُو ٱلْقُوَّةِ ٱلْمَتِينُ ﴿ ٥٨ ﴾
59	وَٱسْتَعِينُوا۟ بِٱلصَّبْرِ وَٱلصَّلَوٰةِ وَإِنَّهَا لَكَبِيرَةٌ إِلَّا عَلَى ٱلْخَـٰشِعِينَ ﴿ ٤٥ ﴾

59	وَٱلَّذِينَ صَبَرُواْ ٱبْتِغَآءَ وَجْهِ رَبِّهِمْ وَأَقَامُواْ ٱلصَّلَوٰةَ وَأَنفَقُواْ مِمَّا رَزَقْنَٰهُمْ سِرًّا وَعَلَانِيَةً وَيَدْرَءُونَ بِٱلْحَسَنَةِ ٱلسَّيِّئَةَ أُوْلَٰٓئِكَ لَهُمْ عُقْبَى ٱلدَّارِ ﴿٢٢﴾ جَنَّٰتُ عَدْنٍ يَدْخُلُونَهَا وَمَن صَلَحَ مِنْ ءَابَآئِهِمْ وَأَزْوَٰجِهِمْ وَذُرِّيَّٰتِهِمْ وَٱلْمَلَٰٓئِكَةُ يَدْخُلُونَ عَلَيْهِم مِّن كُلِّ بَابٍ ﴿٣٢﴾ سَلَٰمٌ عَلَيْكُم بِمَا صَبَرْتُمْ فَنِعْمَ عُقْبَى ٱلدَّارِ ﴿٤٢﴾
60	نِّى جَزَيْتُهُمُ ٱلْيَوْمَ بِمَا صَبَرُوٓاْ أَنَّهُمْ هُمُ ٱلْفَآئِزُونَ ﴿١١١﴾
60	إِنَّمَا يُوَفَّى ٱلصَّٰبِرُونَ أَجْرَهُم بِغَيْرِ حِسَابٍ ﴿٠١﴾
60	وَٱللَّهُ يُحِبُّ ٱلصَّٰبِرِينَ ﴿٦٤١﴾
61	وَلَنَبْلُوَنَّكُم بِشَىْءٍ مِّنَ ٱلْخَوْفِ وَٱلْجُوعِ وَنَقْصٍ مِّنَ ٱلْأَمْوَٰلِ وَٱلْأَنفُسِ وَٱلثَّمَرَٰتِ وَبَشِّرِ ٱلصَّٰبِرِينَ ﴿٥٥١﴾ ٱلَّذِينَ إِذَآ أَصَٰبَتْهُم مُّصِيبَةٌ قَالُوٓاْ إِنَّا لِلَّهِ وَإِنَّآ إِلَيْهِ رَٰجِعُونَ ﴿٦٥١﴾ أُوْلَٰٓئِكَ عَلَيْهِمْ صَلَوَٰتٌ مِّن رَّبِّهِمْ وَرَحْمَةٌ وَأُوْلَٰٓئِكَ هُمُ ٱلْمُهْتَدُونَ ﴿٧٥١﴾
61	وَٱصْبِرْ عَلَىٰ مَآ أَصَابَكَ إِنَّ ذَٰلِكَ مِنْ عَزْمِ ٱلْأُمُورِ ﴿٧١﴾
63	يَٰٓأَيُّهَا ٱلَّذِينَ ءَامَنُواْ لَا تَقُولُواْ رَٰعِنَا وَقُولُواْ ٱنظُرْنَا وَٱسْمَعُواْ وَلِلْكَٰفِرِينَ عَذَابٌ أَلِيمٌ ﴿٤٠١﴾
64	لَّا تَجْعَلُواْ دُعَآءَ ٱلرَّسُولِ بَيْنَكُمْ كَدُعَآءِ بَعْضِكُم بَعْضًا قَدْ يَعْلَمُ ٱللَّهُ ٱلَّذِينَ يَتَسَلَّلُونَ مِنكُمْ لِوَاذًا فَلْيَحْذَرِ ٱلَّذِينَ يُخَالِفُونَ عَنْ أَمْرِهِۦٓ أَن تُصِيبَهُمْ فِتْنَةٌ أَوْ يُصِيبَهُمْ عَذَابٌ أَلِيمٌ ﴿٣٦﴾

65	يَٰٓأَيُّهَا ٱلَّذِينَ ءَامَنُوا۟ لَا تَدْخُلُوا۟ بُيُوتَ ٱلنَّبِيِّ إِلَّآ أَن يُؤْذَنَ لَكُمْ إِلَىٰ طَعَامٍ غَيْرَ نَٰظِرِينَ إِنَىٰهُ وَلَٰكِنْ إِذَا دُعِيتُمْ فَٱدْخُلُوا۟ فَإِذَا طَعِمْتُمْ فَٱنتَشِرُوا۟ وَلَا مُسْتَـٔنِسِينَ لِحَدِيثٍ إِنَّ ذَٰلِكُمْ كَانَ يُؤْذِى ٱلنَّبِىَّ فَيَسْتَحْىِۦ مِنكُمْ وَٱللَّهُ لَا يَسْتَحْىِۦ مِنَ ٱلْحَقِّ وَإِذَا سَأَلْتُمُوهُنَّ مَتَٰعًا فَسْـَٔلُوهُنَّ مِن وَرَآءِ حِجَابٍ ذَٰلِكُمْ أَطْهَرُ لِقُلُوبِكُمْ وَقُلُوبِهِنَّ وَمَا كَانَ لَكُمْ أَن تُؤْذُوا۟ رَسُولَ ٱللَّهِ وَلَآ أَن تَنكِحُوٓا۟ أَزْوَٰجَهُۥ مِنۢ بَعْدِهِۦٓ أَبَدًا إِنَّ ذَٰلِكُمْ كَانَ عِندَ ٱللَّهِ عَظِيمًا ﴿٥٣﴾
66	وَمَا كَانَ لِمُؤْمِنٍ وَلَا مُؤْمِنَةٍ إِذَا قَضَى ٱللَّهُ وَرَسُولُهُۥٓ أَمْرًا أَن يَكُونَ لَهُمُ ٱلْخِيَرَةُ مِنْ أَمْرِهِمْ وَمَن يَعْصِ ٱللَّهَ وَرَسُولَهُۥ فَقَدْ ضَلَّ ضَلَٰلًا مُّبِينًا ﴿٣٦﴾
68	يَٰٓأَيُّهَا ٱلَّذِينَ ءَامَنُوا۟ لَا تَرْفَعُوٓا۟ أَصْوَٰتَكُمْ فَوْقَ صَوْتِ ٱلنَّبِىِّ وَلَا تَجْهَرُوا۟ لَهُۥ بِٱلْقَوْلِ كَجَهْرِ بَعْضِكُمْ لِبَعْضٍ أَن تَحْبَطَ أَعْمَٰلُكُمْ وَأَنتُمْ لَا تَشْعُرُونَ ﴿١﴾ إِنَّ ٱلَّذِينَ يَغُضُّونَ أَصْوَٰتَهُمْ عِندَ رَسُولِ ٱللَّهِ أُو۟لَٰٓئِكَ ٱلَّذِينَ ٱمْتَحَنَ ٱللَّهُ قُلُوبَهُمْ لِلتَّقْوَىٰ لَهُم مَّغْفِرَةٌ وَأَجْرٌ عَظِيمٌ ﴿٢﴾ إِنَّ ٱلَّذِينَ يُنَادُونَكَ مِن وَرَآءِ ٱلْحُجُرَٰتِ أَكْثَرُهُمْ لَا يَعْقِلُونَ ﴿٣﴾ وَلَوْ أَنَّهُمْ صَبَرُوا۟ حَتَّىٰ تَخْرُجَ إِلَيْهِمْ لَكَانَ خَيْرًا لَّهُمْ وَٱللَّهُ غَفُورٌ رَّحِيمٌ ﴿٤﴾
70	أَلَمْ تَرَ إِلَى ٱلَّذِينَ نُهُوا۟ عَنِ ٱلنَّجْوَىٰ ثُمَّ يَعُودُونَ لِمَا نُهُوا۟ عَنْهُ وَيَتَنَٰجَوْنَ بِٱلْإِثْمِ وَٱلْعُدْوَٰنِ وَمَعْصِيَتِ ٱلرَّسُولِ وَإِذَا جَآءُوكَ حَيَّوْكَ بِمَا لَمْ يُحَيِّكَ بِهِ ٱللَّهُ وَيَقُولُونَ فِىٓ أَنفُسِهِمْ لَوْلَا يُعَذِّبُنَا ٱللَّهُ بِمَا نَقُولُ حَسْبُهُمْ جَهَنَّمُ يَصْلَوْنَهَا فَبِئْسَ ٱلْمَصِيرُ ﴿٨﴾ يَٰٓأَيُّهَا ٱلَّذِينَ ءَامَنُوٓا۟ إِذَا تَنَٰجَيْتُمْ فَلَا تَتَنَٰجَوْا۟ بِٱلْإِثْمِ وَٱلْعُدْوَٰنِ وَمَعْصِيَتِ ٱلرَّسُولِ وَتَنَٰجَوْا۟ بِٱلْبِرِّ وَٱلتَّقْوَىٰ وَٱتَّقُوا۟ ٱللَّهَ ٱلَّذِىٓ إِلَيْهِ تُحْشَرُونَ ﴿٩﴾
71	فَٱلَّذِينَ ءَامَنُوا۟ بِهِۦ وَعَزَّرُوهُ وَنَصَرُوهُ وَٱتَّبَعُوا۟ ٱلنُّورَ ٱلَّذِىٓ أُنزِلَ مَعَهُۥٓ أُو۟لَٰٓئِكَ هُمُ ٱلْمُفْلِحُونَ ﴿١٥٧﴾

71, 204, 258	يَـٰٓأَيُّهَا ٱلَّذِينَ ءَامَنُوا۟ لَا تَخُونُوا۟ ٱللَّهَ وَٱلرَّسُولَ وَتَخُونُوٓا۟ أَمَـٰنَـٰتِكُمْ وَأَنتُمْ تَعْلَمُونَ ﴿ ٧٢ ﴾
72	إِنَّ ٱلَّذِينَ يُؤْذُونَ ٱللَّهَ وَرَسُولَهُۥ لَعَنَهُمُ ٱللَّهُ فِى ٱلدُّنْيَا وَٱلْءَاخِرَةِ وَأَعَدَّ لَهُمْ عَذَابًا مُّهِينًا ﴿ ٧٥ ﴾
75	لَّقَدْ كَانَ لَكُمْ فِى رَسُولِ ٱللَّهِ أُسْوَةٌ حَسَنَةٌ لِّمَن كَانَ يَرْجُوا۟ ٱللَّهَ وَٱلْيَوْمَ ٱلْءَاخِرَ وَذَكَرَ ٱللَّهَ كَثِيرًا ﴿ ١٢ ﴾
76	وَمَآ ءَاتَىٰكُمُ ٱلرَّسُولُ فَخُذُوهُ وَمَا نَهَىٰكُمْ عَنْهُ فَٱنتَهُوا۟ وَٱتَّقُوا۟ ٱللَّهَ إِنَّ ٱللَّهَ شَدِيدُ ٱلْعِقَابِ ﴿ ٧ ﴾
79	يَـٰٓأَيُّهَا ٱلَّذِينَ ءَامَنُوٓا۟ أَطِيعُوا۟ ٱللَّهَ وَأَطِيعُوا۟ ٱلرَّسُولَ وَأُو۟لِى ٱلْأَمْرِ مِنكُمْ فَإِن تَنَـٰزَعْتُمْ فِى شَىْءٍ فَرُدُّوهُ إِلَى ٱللَّهِ وَٱلرَّسُولِ إِن كُنتُمْ تُؤْمِنُونَ بِٱللَّهِ وَٱلْيَوْمِ ٱلْءَاخِرِ ذَٰلِكَ خَيْرٌ وَأَحْسَنُ تَأْوِيلًا ﴿ ٩٥ ﴾
80	لَقَدْ مَنَّ ٱللَّهُ عَلَى ٱلْمُؤْمِنِينَ إِذْ بَعَثَ فِيهِمْ رَسُولًا مِّنْ أَنفُسِهِمْ يَتْلُوا۟ عَلَيْهِمْ ءَايَـٰتِهِۦ وَيُزَكِّيهِمْ وَيُعَلِّمُهُمُ ٱلْكِتَـٰبَ وَٱلْحِكْمَةَ وَإِن كَانُوا۟ مِن قَبْلُ لَفِى ضَلَـٰلٍ مُّبِينٍ ﴿ ٤٦١ ﴾
83	يَوْمَ أَكْمَلْتُ لَكُمْ دِينَكُمْ وَأَتْمَمْتُ عَلَيْكُمْ نِعْمَتِى وَرَضِيتُ لَكُمُ ٱلْإِسْلَـٰمَ دِينًا
90	وَمَا قَدَرُوا۟ ٱللَّهَ حَقَّ قَدْرِهِۦٓ إِذْ قَالُوا۟ مَآ أَنزَلَ ٱللَّهُ عَلَىٰ بَشَرٍ مِّن شَىْءٍ قُلْ مَنْ أَنزَلَ ٱلْكِتَـٰبَ ٱلَّذِى جَآءَ بِهِۦ مُوسَىٰ نُورًا وَهُدًى لِّلنَّاسِ تَجْعَلُونَهُۥ قَرَاطِيسَ تُبْدُونَهَا وَتُخْفُونَ كَثِيرًا وَعُلِّمْتُم مَّا لَمْ تَعْلَمُوٓا۟ أَنتُمْ وَلَآ ءَابَآؤُكُمْ قُلِ ٱللَّهُ ثُمَّ ذَرْهُمْ فِى خَوْضِهِمْ يَلْعَبُونَ ﴿ ١٩ ﴾
90	وَمَا قَدَرُوا۟ ٱللَّهَ حَقَّ قَدْرِهِۦ وَٱلْأَرْضُ جَمِيعًا قَبْضَتُهُۥ يَوْمَ ٱلْقِيَـٰمَةِ وَٱلسَّمَـٰوَٰتُ مَطْوِيَّـٰتٌۢ بِيَمِينِهِۦ سُبْحَـٰنَهُۥ وَتَعَـٰلَىٰ عَمَّا يُشْرِكُونَ ﴿ ٧٦ ﴾

91	تَكَادُ ٱلسَّمَٰوَٰتُ يَتَفَطَّرْنَ مِن فَوْقِهِنَّ وَٱلْمَلَٰٓئِكَةُ يُسَبِّحُونَ بِحَمْدِ رَبِّهِمْ وَيَسْتَغْفِرُونَ لِمَن فِى ٱلْأَرْضِ أَلَآ إِنَّ ٱللَّهَ هُوَ ٱلْغَفُورُ ٱلرَّحِيمُ ۞ ٥
92	إِنَّ ٱلَّذِينَ يُؤْذُونَ ٱللَّهَ وَرَسُولَهُ لَعَنَهُمُ ٱللَّهُ فِى ٱلدُّنْيَا وَٱلْـَٔاخِرَةِ وَأَعَدَّ لَهُمْ عَذَابًا مُّهِينًا ۞ ٥
94	وَلَا تَسُبُّوا۟ ٱلَّذِينَ يَدْعُونَ مِن دُونِ ٱللَّهِ فَيَسُبُّوا۟ ٱللَّهَ عَدْوًۢا بِغَيْرِ عِلْمٍ كَذَٰلِكَ زَيَّنَّا لِكُلِّ أُمَّةٍ عَمَلَهُمْ ثُمَّ إِلَىٰ رَبِّهِم مَّرْجِعُهُمْ فَيُنَبِّئُهُم بِمَا كَانُوا۟ يَعْمَلُونَ ۞ ٨٠١
100	وَٱلَّذِينَ جَآءُو مِنۢ بَعْدِهِمْ يَقُولُونَ رَبَّنَا ٱغْفِرْ لَنَا وَلِإِخْوَٰنِنَا ٱلَّذِينَ سَبَقُونَا بِٱلْإِيمَٰنِ وَلَا تَجْعَلْ فِى قُلُوبِنَا غِلًّا لِّلَّذِينَ ءَامَنُوا۟ رَبَّنَآ إِنَّكَ رَءُوفٌ رَّحِيمٌ ۞ ٠١
101	وَٱلَّذِينَ ءَامَنُوا۟ وَهَاجَرُوا۟ وَجَٰهَدُوا۟ فِى سَبِيلِ ٱللَّهِ وَٱلَّذِينَ ءَاوَوا۟ وَّنَصَرُوٓا۟ أُو۟لَٰٓئِكَ هُمُ ٱلْمُؤْمِنُونَ حَقًّا لَّهُم مَّغْفِرَةٌ وَرِزْقٌ كَرِيمٌ ۞ ٤٧
101	لَٰكِنِ ٱلرَّسُولُ وَٱلَّذِينَ ءَامَنُوا۟ مَعَهُ جَٰهَدُوا۟ بِأَمْوَٰلِهِمْ وَأَنفُسِهِمْ وَأُو۟لَٰٓئِكَ لَهُمُ ٱلْخَيْرَٰتُ وَأُو۟لَٰٓئِكَ هُمُ ٱلْمُفْلِحُونَ ۞ ٨٨ أَعَدَّ ٱللَّهُ لَهُمْ جَنَّٰتٍ تَجْرِى مِن تَحْتِهَا ٱلْأَنْهَٰرُ خَٰلِدِينَ فِيهَا ذَٰلِكَ ٱلْفَوْزُ ٱلْعَظِيمُ ۞ ٩٨
102	وَٱلسَّٰبِقُونَ ٱلْأَوَّلُونَ مِنَ ٱلْمُهَٰجِرِينَ وَٱلْأَنصَارِ وَٱلَّذِينَ ٱتَّبَعُوهُم بِإِحْسَٰنٍ رَّضِىَ ٱللَّهُ عَنْهُمْ وَرَضُوا۟ عَنْهُ وَأَعَدَّ لَهُمْ جَنَّٰتٍ تَجْرِى تَحْتَهَا ٱلْأَنْهَٰرُ خَٰلِدِينَ فِيهَآ أَبَدًا ذَٰلِكَ ٱلْفَوْزُ ٱلْعَظِيمُ ۞ ٠٠١
102	نَ ٱلْمُؤْمِنِينَ رِجَالٌ صَدَقُوا۟ مَا عَٰهَدُوا۟ ٱللَّهَ عَلَيْهِ فَمِنْهُم مَّن قَضَىٰ نَحْبَهُ وَمِنْهُم مَّن يَنتَظِرُ وَمَا بَدَّلُوا۟ تَبْدِيلًا ۞ ٣٢
102	لِلْفُقَرَآءِ ٱلْمُهَٰجِرِينَ ٱلَّذِينَ أُخْرِجُوا۟ مِن دِيَٰرِهِمْ وَأَمْوَٰلِهِمْ يَبْتَغُونَ فَضْلًا مِّنَ ٱللَّهِ وَرِضْوَٰنًا وَيَنصُرُونَ ٱللَّهَ وَرَسُولَهُ أُو۟لَٰٓئِكَ هُمُ ٱلصَّٰدِقُونَ ۞ ٨

103	لَا يَسْتَوِي مِنكُم مَّنْ أَنفَقَ مِن قَبْلِ ٱلْفَتْحِ وَقَاتَلَ أُوْلَٰئِكَ أَعْظَمُ دَرَجَةً مِّنَ ٱلَّذِينَ أَنفَقُواْ مِنْ بَعْدُ وَقَاتَلُواْ وَكُلًّا وَعَدَ ٱللَّهُ ٱلْحُسْنَىٰ وَٱللَّهُ بِمَا تَعْمَلُونَ خَبِيرٌ ﴿١٠﴾
103	لَّقَدْ رَضِيَ ٱللَّهُ عَنِ ٱلْمُؤْمِنِينَ إِذْ يُبَايِعُونَكَ تَحْتَ ٱلشَّجَرَةِ فَعَلِمَ مَا فِي قُلُوبِهِمْ فَأَنزَلَ ٱلسَّكِينَةَ عَلَيْهِمْ وَأَثَٰبَهُمْ فَتْحًا قَرِيبًا ﴿١٨﴾
105	إِنَّ ٱلَّذِينَ ءَامَنُواْ ثُمَّ كَفَرُواْ ثُمَّ ءَامَنُواْ ثُمَّ كَفَرُواْ ثُمَّ ٱزْدَادُواْ كُفْرًا لَّمْ يَكُنِ ٱللَّهُ لِيَغْفِرَ لَهُمْ وَلَا لِيَهْدِيَهُمْ سَبِيلًا
105	إِنَّ ٱلَّذِينَ ٱرْتَدُّواْ عَلَىٰ أَدْبَٰرِهِم مِّنْ بَعْدِ مَا تَبَيَّنَ لَهُمُ ٱلْهُدَى
105	وَهُدُواْ إِلَى ٱلطَّيِّبِ مِنَ ٱلْقَوْلِ وَهُدُواْ إِلَىٰ صِرَٰطِ ٱلْحَمِيدِ
106	وَلَٰكِنَّ ٱللَّهَ حَبَّبَ إِلَيْكُمُ ٱلْإِيمَٰنَ وَزَيَّنَهُ فِي قُلُوبِكُمْ وَكَرَّهَ إِلَيْكُمُ ٱلْكُفْرَ وَٱلْفُسُوقَ وَٱلْعِصْيَانَ
112	وَكَيْفَ تَأْخُذُونَهُ وَقَدْ أَفْضَىٰ بَعْضُكُمْ إِلَىٰ بَعْضٍ وَأَخَذْنَ مِنكُم مِّيثَٰقًا غَلِيظًا ﴿٢١﴾
	وَٱلَّذِينَ هُمْ لِفُرُوجِهِمْ حَٰفِظُونَ ﴿٥﴾ إِلَّا عَلَىٰ أَزْوَٰجِهِمْ أَوْ مَا مَلَكَتْ أَيْمَٰنُهُمْ فَإِنَّهُمْ غَيْرُ مَلُومِينَ ﴿٦﴾ فَمَنِ ٱبْتَغَىٰ وَرَآءَ ذَٰلِكَ فَأُوْلَٰئِكَ هُمُ ٱلْعَادُونَ ﴿٧﴾
115	نِسَآؤُكُمْ حَرْثٌ لَّكُمْ فَأْتُواْ حَرْثَكُمْ أَنَّىٰ شِئْتُمْ وَقَدِّمُواْ لِأَنفُسِكُمْ وَٱتَّقُواْ ٱللَّهَ وَٱعْلَمُواْ أَنَّكُم مُّلَٰقُوهُ وَبَشِّرِ ٱلْمُؤْمِنِينَ ﴿٢٢٣﴾
121	وَيَسْأَلُونَكَ عَنِ ٱلْمَحِيضِ قُلْ هُوَ أَذًى فَٱعْتَزِلُواْ ٱلنِّسَآءَ فِي ٱلْمَحِيضِ وَلَا تَقْرَبُوهُنَّ حَتَّىٰ يَطْهُرْنَ فَإِذَا تَطَهَّرْنَ فَأْتُوهُنَّ مِنْ حَيْثُ أَمَرَكُمُ ٱللَّهُ إِنَّ ٱللَّهَ يُحِبُّ ٱلتَّوَّٰبِينَ وَيُحِبُّ ٱلْمُتَطَهِّرِينَ ﴿٢٢٢﴾
122	هُنَّ لِبَاسٌ لَّكُمْ وَأَنتُمْ لِبَاسٌ لَّهُنَّ ﴿١٨٧﴾

124	«وَلَهُنَّ مِثْلُ ٱلَّذِى عَلَيْهِنَّ بِٱلْمَعْرُوفِ وَلِلرِّجَالِ عَلَيْهِنَّ دَرَجَةٌ وَٱللَّهُ عَزِيزٌ حَكِيمٌ ﴿٢٢٨﴾»
124	وَعَاشِرُوهُنَّ بِٱلْمَعْرُوفِ فَإِن كَرِهْتُمُوهُنَّ فَعَسَىٰٓ أَن تَكْرَهُواْ شَيْـًٔا وَيَجْعَلَ ٱللَّهُ فِيهِ خَيْرًا كَثِيرًا ﴿١٩﴾
130	يَـٰٓأَيُّهَا ٱلنَّاسُ ٱتَّقُواْ رَبَّكُمُ ٱلَّذِى خَلَقَكُم مِّن نَّفْسٍ وَٰحِدَةٍ وَخَلَقَ مِنْهَا زَوْجَهَا وَبَثَّ مِنْهُمَا رِجَالًا كَثِيرًا وَنِسَآءً وَٱتَّقُواْ ٱللَّهَ ٱلَّذِى تَسَآءَلُونَ بِهِۦ وَٱلْأَرْحَامَ إِنَّ ٱللَّهَ كَانَ عَلَيْكُمْ رَقِيبًا ﴿١﴾
133	۞ هُوَ ٱلَّذِى خَلَقَكُم مِّن نَّفْسٍ وَٰحِدَةٍ وَجَعَلَ مِنْهَا زَوْجَهَا لِيَسْكُنَ إِلَيْهَا فَلَمَّا تَغَشَّىٰهَا حَمَلَتْ حَمْلًا خَفِيفًا فَمَرَّتْ بِهِۦ فَلَمَّآ أَثْقَلَت دَّعَوَا ٱللَّهَ رَبَّهُمَا لَئِنْ ءَاتَيْتَنَا صَـٰلِحًا لَّنَكُونَنَّ مِنَ ٱلشَّـٰكِرِينَ ﴿١٨٩﴾
134	وَٱللَّهُ جَعَلَ لَكُم مِّنْ أَنفُسِكُمْ أَزْوَٰجًا وَجَعَلَ لَكُم مِّنْ أَزْوَٰجِكُم بَنِينَ وَحَفَدَةً وَرَزَقَكُم مِّنَ ٱلطَّيِّبَـٰتِ أَفَبِٱلْبَـٰطِلِ يُؤْمِنُونَ وَبِنِعْمَتِ ٱللَّهِ هُمْ يَكْفُرُونَ ﴿٧٢﴾
134	وَمِنْ ءَايَـٰتِهِۦٓ أَنْ خَلَقَ لَكُم مِّنْ أَنفُسِكُمْ أَزْوَٰجًا لِّتَسْكُنُوٓاْ إِلَيْهَا وَجَعَلَ بَيْنَكُم مَّوَدَّةً وَرَحْمَةً إِنَّ فِى ذَٰلِكَ لَـَٔايَـٰتٍ لِّقَوْمٍ يَتَفَكَّرُونَ ﴿٢١﴾
142	ٱلرِّجَالُ قَوَّٰمُونَ عَلَى ٱلنِّسَآءِ بِمَا فَضَّلَ ٱللَّهُ بَعْضَهُمْ عَلَىٰ بَعْضٍ وَبِمَآ أَنفَقُواْ مِنْ أَمْوَٰلِهِمْ فَٱلصَّـٰلِحَـٰتُ قَـٰنِتَـٰتٌ حَـٰفِظَـٰتٌ لِّلْغَيْبِ بِمَا حَفِظَ ٱللَّهُ وَٱلَّـٰتِى تَخَافُونَ نُشُوزَهُنَّ فَعِظُوهُنَّ وَٱهْجُرُوهُنَّ فِى ٱلْمَضَاجِعِ وَٱضْرِبُوهُنَّ فَإِنْ أَطَعْنَكُمْ فَلَا تَبْغُواْ عَلَيْهِنَّ سَبِيلًا إِنَّ ٱللَّهَ كَانَ عَلِيًّا كَبِيرًا ﴿٣٤﴾
	وَإِنْ خِفْتُمْ شِقَاقَ بَيْنِهِمَا فَٱبْعَثُواْ حَكَمًا مِّنْ أَهْلِهِۦ وَحَكَمًا مِّنْ أَهْلِهَآ إِن يُرِيدَآ إِصْلَـٰحًا يُوَفِّقِ ٱللَّهُ بَيْنَهُمَآ إِنَّ ٱللَّهَ كَانَ عَلِيمًا خَبِيرًا ﴿٣٥﴾

143	وَإِنِ ٱمْرَأَةٌ خَافَتْ مِنۢ بَعْلِهَا نُشُوزًا أَوْ إِعْرَاضًا فَلَا جُنَاحَ عَلَيْهِمَآ أَن يُصْلِحَا بَيْنَهُمَا صُلْحًا وَٱلصُّلْحُ خَيْرٌ وَأُحْضِرَتِ ٱلْأَنفُسُ ٱلشُّحَّ وَإِن تُحْسِنُوا۟ وَتَتَّقُوا۟ فَإِنَّ ٱللَّهَ كَانَ بِمَا تَعْمَلُونَ خَبِيرًا ﴿١٢٨﴾
148	وَٱلَّٰتِى تَخَافُونَ نُشُوزَهُنَّ فَعِظُوهُنَّ وَٱهْجُرُوهُنَّ فِى ٱلْمَضَاجِعِ وَٱضْرِبُوهُنَّ فَإِنْ أَطَعْنَكُمْ فَلَا تَبْغُوا۟ عَلَيْهِنَّ سَبِيلًا إِنَّ ٱللَّهَ كَانَ عَلِيًّا كَبِيرًا ﴿٣٤﴾
158	إِنْ خِفْتُمْ شِقَاقَ بَيْنِهِمَا فَٱبْعَثُوا۟ حَكَمًا مِّنْ أَهْلِهِ وَحَكَمًا مِّنْ أَهْلِهَآ إِن يُرِيدَآ إِصْلَٰحًا يُوَفِّقِ ٱللَّهُ بَيْنَهُمَآ إِنَّ ٱللَّهَ كَانَ عَلِيمًا خَبِيرًا ﴿٣٥﴾
163	فَلَا جُنَاحَ عَلَيْهِمَآ أَن يُصْلِحَا بَيْنَهُمَا صُلْحًا وَٱلصُّلْحُ خَيْرٌ ﴿١٢٨﴾
164	إِن يُرِيدَا إِصْلَاحًا يُوَفِّقِ ٱللَّهُ بَيْنَهُمَا
169	يَٰٓأَيُّهَا ٱلنَّبِىُّ إِذَا طَلَّقْتُمُ ٱلنِّسَآءَ فَطَلِّقُوهُنَّ لِعِدَّتِهِنَّ وَأَحْصُوا۟ ٱلْعِدَّةَ وَٱتَّقُوا۟ ٱللَّهَ رَبَّكُمْ لَا تُخْرِجُوهُنَّ مِنۢ بُيُوتِهِنَّ وَلَا يَخْرُجْنَ إِلَّآ أَن يَأْتِينَ بِفَٰحِشَةٍ مُّبَيِّنَةٍ وَتِلْكَ حُدُودُ ٱللَّهِ وَمَن يَتَعَدَّ حُدُودَ ٱللَّهِ فَقَدْ ظَلَمَ نَفْسَهُ لَا تَدْرِى لَعَلَّ ٱللَّهَ يُحْدِثُ بَعْدَ ذَٰلِكَ أَمْرًا ﴿١﴾
171	واعلموا أن الله بكل شيء عليم"
171	واعلموا أن الله بما تعملون بصير
171	والله بما تعملون خبير
171	واعلموا أن الله غفور حليم
172	مَن يَتَّقِ ٱللَّهَ يَجْعَل لَّهُۥ مَخْرَجًا ﴿٢﴾
172	وَمَن يَتَّقِ ٱللَّهَ يَجْعَل لَّهُۥ مِنْ أَمْرِهِۦ يُسْرًا ﴿٤﴾
172	وَمَن يَتَّقِ ٱللَّهَ يُكَفِّرْ عَنْهُ سَيِّـَٔاتِهِۦ وَيُعْظِمْ لَهُۥٓ أَجْرًا ﴿٥﴾

173	وَإِذَا طَلَّقْتُمُ ٱلنِّسَاءَ فَبَلَغْنَ أَجَلَهُنَّ فَأَمْسِكُوهُنَّ بِمَعْرُوفٍ أَوْ سَرِّحُوهُنَّ بِمَعْرُوفٍ وَلَا تُمْسِكُوهُنَّ ضِرَارًا لِّتَعْتَدُوا وَمَن يَفْعَلْ ذَٰلِكَ فَقَدْ ظَلَمَ نَفْسَهُ وَلَا تَتَّخِذُوا ءَايَٰتِ ٱللَّهِ هُزُوًا وَٱذْكُرُوا نِعْمَتَ ٱللَّهِ عَلَيْكُمْ وَمَا أَنزَلَ عَلَيْكُم مِّنَ ٱلْكِتَٰبِ وَٱلْحِكْمَةِ يَعِظُكُم بِهِ وَٱتَّقُوا ٱللَّهَ وَٱعْلَمُوا أَنَّ ٱللَّهَ بِكُلِّ شَيْءٍ عَلِيمٌ ﴿١٣٢﴾
173	وَإِذَا طَلَّقْتُمُ ٱلنِّسَاءَ فَبَلَغْنَ أَجَلَهُنَّ فَلَا تَعْضُلُوهُنَّ أَن يَنكِحْنَ أَزْوَٰجَهُنَّ إِذَا تَرَٰضَوْا بَيْنَهُم بِٱلْمَعْرُوفِ ذَٰلِكَ يُوعَظُ بِهِ مَن كَانَ مِنكُمْ يُؤْمِنُ بِٱللَّهِ وَٱلْيَوْمِ ٱلْءَاخِرِ ذَٰلِكُمْ أَزْكَىٰ لَكُمْ وَأَطْهَرُ وَٱللَّهُ يَعْلَمُ وَأَنتُمْ لَا تَعْلَمُونَ ﴿٢٣٢﴾
174	وَءَاتُوا ٱلنِّسَاءَ صَدُقَٰتِهِنَّ نِحْلَةً فَإِن طِبْنَ لَكُمْ عَن شَيْءٍ مِّنْهُ نَفْسًا فَكُلُوهُ هَنِيئًا مَّرِيئًا ﴿٤﴾
174	يَٰٓأَيُّهَا ٱلَّذِينَ ءَامَنُوا لَا يَحِلُّ لَكُمْ أَن تَرِثُوا ٱلنِّسَاءَ كَرْهًا وَلَا تَعْضُلُوهُنَّ لِتَذْهَبُوا بِبَعْضِ مَا ءَاتَيْتُمُوهُنَّ إِلَّا أَن يَأْتِينَ بِفَٰحِشَةٍ مُّبَيِّنَةٍ وَعَاشِرُوهُنَّ بِٱلْمَعْرُوفِ فَإِن كَرِهْتُمُوهُنَّ فَعَسَىٰ أَن تَكْرَهُوا شَيْئًا وَيَجْعَلَ ٱللَّهُ فِيهِ خَيْرًا كَثِيرًا ﴿١٩﴾
175	يَٰٓأَيُّهَا ٱلنَّبِيُّ إِذَا طَلَّقْتُمُ ٱلنِّسَاءَ فَطَلِّقُوهُنَّ لِعِدَّتِهِنَّ وَأَحْصُوا ٱلْعِدَّةَ وَٱتَّقُوا ٱللَّهَ رَبَّكُمْ لَا تُخْرِجُوهُنَّ مِنۢ بُيُوتِهِنَّ وَلَا يَخْرُجْنَ إِلَّا أَن يَأْتِينَ بِفَٰحِشَةٍ مُّبَيِّنَةٍ وَتِلْكَ حُدُودُ ٱللَّهِ وَمَن يَتَعَدَّ حُدُودَ ٱللَّهِ فَقَدْ ظَلَمَ نَفْسَهُ لَا تَدْرِى لَعَلَّ ٱللَّهَ يُحْدِثُ بَعْدَ ذَٰلِكَ أَمْرًا ﴿١﴾
176	وَتِلْكَ حُدُودُ ٱللَّهِ وَمَن يَتَعَدَّ حُدُودَ ٱللَّهِ فَقَدْ ظَلَمَ نَفْسَهُ لَا تَدْرِي لَعَلَّ ٱللَّهَ يُحْدِثُ بَعْدَ ذَٰلِكَ أَمْرًا
176	طَلِّقُوهُنَّ لِعِدَّتِهِنَّ وَأَحْصُوا ٱلْعِدَّةَ» سورة الطلاق الآية ١

178	يَٰٓأَيُّهَا ٱلَّذِينَ ءَامَنُوٓاْ إِذَا نَكَحْتُمُ ٱلْمُؤْمِنَٰتِ ثُمَّ طَلَّقْتُمُوهُنَّ مِن قَبْلِ أَن تَمَسُّوهُنَّ فَمَا لَكُمْ عَلَيْهِنَّ مِنْ عِدَّةٍ تَعْتَدُّونَهَا فَمَتِّعُوهُنَّ وَسَرِّحُوهُنَّ سَرَاحًا جَمِيلًا ﴿٩٤﴾
181	"فَطَلِّقُوهُنَّ لِعِدَّتِهِنَّ وَأَحْصُواْ ٱلْعِدَّةَ» الطلاق
183	وَأُوْلَٰتُ ٱلْأَحْمَالِ أَجَلُهُنَّ أَن يَضَعْنَ حَمْلَهُنَّ» الطلاق ٤
183	وَٱلَّذِينَ يُتَوَفَّوْنَ مِنكُمْ وَيَذَرُونَ أَزْوَاجًا يَتَرَبَّصْنَ بِأَنفُسِهِنَّ أَرْبَعَةَ أَشْهُرٍ وَعَشْرًا" ﴿٢٣٤﴾
183	وَٱلْمُطَلَّقَٰتُ يَتَرَبَّصْنَ بِأَنفُسِهِنَّ ثَلَٰثَةَ قُرُوٓءٍ» البقرة ﴿٢٢٨﴾
183	"وَٱلَّٰٓئِى يَئِسْنَ مِنَ ٱلْمَحِيضِ مِن نِّسَآئِكُمْ إِنِ ٱرْتَبْتُمْ فَعِدَّتُهُنَّ ثَلَٰثَةُ أَشْهُرٍ وَٱلَّٰٓئِى لَمْ يَحِضْنَ» الطلاق ﴿٤﴾
187	وَإِذْ أَخَذْنَا مِيثَٰقَ بَنِىٓ إِسْرَٰٓءِيلَ لَا تَعْبُدُونَ إِلَّا ٱللَّهَ وَبِٱلْوَٰلِدَيْنِ إِحْسَانًا وَذِى ٱلْقُرْبَىٰ وَٱلْيَتَٰمَىٰ وَٱلْمَسَٰكِينِ وَقُولُواْ لِلنَّاسِ حُسْنًا وَأَقِيمُواْ ٱلصَّلَوٰةَ وَءَاتُواْ ٱلزَّكَوٰةَ ثُمَّ تَوَلَّيْتُمْ إِلَّا قَلِيلًا مِّنكُمْ وَأَنتُم مُّعْرِضُونَ ﴿٨٣﴾
187	وَٱعْبُدُواْ ٱللَّهَ وَلَا تُشْرِكُواْ بِهِۦ شَيْـًٔا وَبِٱلْوَٰلِدَيْنِ إِحْسَٰنًا وَبِذِى ٱلْقُرْبَىٰ وَٱلْيَتَٰمَىٰ وَٱلْمَسَٰكِينِ وَٱلْجَارِ ذِى ٱلْقُرْبَىٰ وَٱلْجَارِ ٱلْجُنُبِ وَٱلصَّاحِبِ بِٱلْجَنۢبِ وَٱبْنِ ٱلسَّبِيلِ وَمَا مَلَكَتْ أَيْمَٰنُكُمْ إِنَّ ٱللَّهَ لَا يُحِبُّ مَن كَانَ مُخْتَالًا فَخُورًا ﴿٣٦﴾
187	قُلْ تَعَالَوْاْ أَتْلُ مَا حَرَّمَ رَبُّكُمْ عَلَيْكُمْ أَلَّا تُشْرِكُواْ بِهِۦ شَيْـًٔا وَبِٱلْوَٰلِدَيْنِ إِحْسَٰنًا وَلَا تَقْتُلُوٓاْ أَوْلَٰدَكُم مِّنْ إِمْلَٰقٍ نَّحْنُ نَرْزُقُكُمْ وَإِيَّاهُمْ وَلَا تَقْرَبُواْ ٱلْفَوَٰحِشَ مَا ظَهَرَ مِنْهَا وَمَا بَطَنَ وَلَا تَقْتُلُواْ ٱلنَّفْسَ ٱلَّتِى حَرَّمَ ٱللَّهُ إِلَّا بِٱلْحَقِّ ذَٰلِكُمْ وَصَّىٰكُم بِهِۦ لَعَلَّكُمْ تَعْقِلُونَ ﴿١٥١﴾

199	وَمَن يُطِعِ ٱللَّهَ وَٱلرَّسُولَ فَأُوْلَٰئِكَ مَعَ ٱلَّذِينَ أَنْعَمَ ٱللَّهُ عَلَيْهِم مِّنَ ٱلنَّبِيِّـۧنَ وَٱلصِّدِّيقِينَ وَٱلشُّهَدَآءِ وَٱلصَّٰلِحِينَ وَحَسُنَ أُوْلَٰئِكَ رَفِيقًا ﴿ ٩٦ ﴾
202	قَالَ ٱللَّهُ هَٰذَا يَوْمُ يَنفَعُ ٱلصَّٰدِقِينَ صِدْقُهُمْ لَهُمْ جَنَّٰتٌ تَجْرِى مِن تَحْتِهَا ٱلْأَنْهَٰرُ خَٰلِدِينَ فِيهَآ أَبَدًا رَّضِىَ ٱللَّهُ عَنْهُمْ وَرَضُواْ عَنْهُ ذَٰلِكَ ٱلْفَوْزُ ٱلْعَظِيمُ ﴿ ١١٩ ﴾
203	يَٰٓأَيُّهَا ٱلَّذِينَ ءَامَنُواْ ٱتَّقُواْ ٱللَّهَ وَكُونُواْ مَعَ ٱلصَّٰدِقِينَ ﴿ ١١٩ ﴾
204	مِّنَ ٱلْمُؤْمِنِينَ رِجَالٌ صَدَقُواْ مَا عَٰهَدُواْ ٱللَّهَ عَلَيْهِ فَمِنْهُم مَّن قَضَىٰ نَحْبَهُ وَمِنْهُم مَّن يَنتَظِرُ وَمَا بَدَّلُواْ تَبْدِيلًا ﴿ ٢٣ ﴾ لِّيَجْزِىَ ٱللَّهُ ٱلصَّٰدِقِينَ بِصِدْقِهِمْ وَيُعَذِّبَ ٱلْمُنَٰفِقِينَ إِن شَآءَ أَوْ يَتُوبَ عَلَيْهِمْ إِنَّ ٱللَّهَ كَانَ غَفُورًا رَّحِيمًا ﴿ ٢٤ ﴾
204	إِنَّ ٱلْمُسْلِمِينَ وَٱلْمُسْلِمَٰتِ وَٱلْمُؤْمِنِينَ وَٱلْمُؤْمِنَٰتِ وَٱلْقَٰنِتِينَ وَٱلْقَٰنِتَٰتِ وَٱلصَّٰدِقِينَ وَٱلصَّٰدِقَٰتِ وَٱلصَّٰبِرِينَ وَٱلصَّٰبِرَٰتِ وَٱلْخَٰشِعِينَ وَٱلْخَٰشِعَٰتِ وَٱلْمُتَصَدِّقِينَ وَٱلْمُتَصَدِّقَٰتِ وَٱلصَّٰٓئِمِينَ وَٱلصَّٰٓئِمَٰتِ وَٱلْحَٰفِظِينَ فُرُوجَهُمْ وَٱلْحَٰفِظَٰتِ وَٱلذَّٰكِرِينَ ٱللَّهَ كَثِيرًا وَٱلذَّٰكِرَٰتِ أَعَدَّ ٱللَّهُ لَهُم مَّغْفِرَةً وَأَجْرًا عَظِيمًا ﴿ ٣٥ ﴾
205	يَٰٓأَيُّهَا ٱلَّذِينَ ءَامَنُواْ ٱتَّقُواْ ٱللَّهَ وَقُولُواْ قَوْلًا سَدِيدًا ﴿ ٧٠ ﴾ يُصْلِحْ لَكُمْ أَعْمَٰلَكُمْ وَيَغْفِرْ لَكُمْ ذُنُوبَكُمْ وَمَن يُطِعِ ٱللَّهَ وَرَسُولَهُ فَقَدْ فَازَ فَوْزًا عَظِيمًا ﴿ ٧١ ﴾
207	يَٰبَنِىٓ ءَادَمَ قَدْ أَنزَلْنَا عَلَيْكُمْ لِبَاسًا يُوَٰرِى سَوْءَٰتِكُمْ وَرِيشًا وَلِبَاسُ ٱلتَّقْوَىٰ ذَٰلِكَ خَيْرٌ ذَٰلِكَ مِنْ ءَايَٰتِ ٱللَّهِ لَعَلَّهُمْ يَذَّكَّرُونَ ﴿ ٢٦ ﴾ يَٰبَنِىٓ ءَادَمَ لَا يَفْتِنَنَّكُمُ ٱلشَّيْطَٰنُ كَمَآ أَخْرَجَ أَبَوَيْكُم مِّنَ ٱلْجَنَّةِ يَنزِعُ عَنْهُمَا لِبَاسَهُمَا لِيُرِيَهُمَا سَوْءَٰتِهِمَآ إِنَّهُ يَرَىٰكُمْ هُوَ وَقَبِيلُهُ مِنْ حَيْثُ لَا تَرَوْنَهُمْ إِنَّا جَعَلْنَا ٱلشَّيَٰطِينَ أَوْلِيَآءَ لِلَّذِينَ لَا يُؤْمِنُونَ ﴿ ٢٧ ﴾

208	يَـٰٓأَيُّهَا ٱلنَّبِىُّ قُل لِّأَزْوَٰجِكَ وَبَنَاتِكَ وَنِسَآءِ ٱلْمُؤْمِنِينَ يُدْنِينَ عَلَيْهِنَّ مِن جَلَـٰبِيبِهِنَّ ذَٰلِكَ أَدْنَىٰٓ أَن يُعْرَفْنَ فَلَا يُؤْذَيْنَ وَكَانَ ٱللَّهُ غَفُورًا رَّحِيمًا ﴿ ٥٩ ﴾
209	يَـٰٓأَيُّهَا ٱلَّذِينَ ءَامَنُوا۟ لَا تَدْخُلُوا۟ بُيُوتًا غَيْرَ بُيُوتِكُمْ حَتَّىٰ تَسْتَأْنِسُوا۟ وَتُسَلِّمُوا۟ عَلَىٰٓ أَهْلِهَا ذَٰلِكُمْ خَيْرٌ لَّكُمْ لَعَلَّكُمْ تَذَكَّرُونَ ﴿ ٢٧ ﴾
210	وَلَا يُبْدِينَ زِينَتَهُنَّ إِلَّا مَا ظَهَرَ مِنْهَا وَلْيَضْرِبْنَ بِخُمُرِهِنَّ عَلَىٰ جُيُوبِهِنَّ وَلَا يُبْدِينَ زِينَتَهُنَّ)
211	قُل لِّلْمُؤْمِنِينَ يَغُضُّوا۟ مِنْ أَبْصَـٰرِهِمْ وَيَحْفَظُوا۟ فُرُوجَهُمْ ذَٰلِكَ أَزْكَىٰ لَهُمْ إِنَّ ٱللَّهَ خَبِيرٌۢ بِمَا يَصْنَعُونَ ﴿ ٣٠ ﴾ وَقُل لِّلْمُؤْمِنَـٰتِ يَغْضُضْنَ مِنْ أَبْصَـٰرِهِنَّ وَيَحْفَظْنَ ﴿ ٣١ ﴾
214	وَسَارِعُوٓا۟ إِلَىٰ مَغْفِرَةٍ مِّن رَّبِّكُمْ وَجَنَّةٍ عَرْضُهَا ٱلسَّمَـٰوَٰتُ وَٱلْأَرْضُ أُعِدَّتْ لِلْمُتَّقِينَ ﴿ ١٣٣ ﴾ ٱلَّذِينَ يُنفِقُونَ فِى ٱلسَّرَّآءِ وَٱلضَّرَّآءِ وَٱلْكَـٰظِمِينَ ٱلْغَيْظَ وَٱلْعَافِينَ عَنِ ٱلنَّاسِ وَٱللَّهُ يُحِبُّ ٱلْمُحْسِنِينَ ﴿ ١٣٤ ﴾ وَٱلَّذِينَ إِذَا فَعَلُوا۟ فَـٰحِشَةً أَوْ ظَلَمُوٓا۟ أَنفُسَهُمْ ذَكَرُوا۟ ٱللَّهَ فَٱسْتَغْفَرُوا۟ لِذُنُوبِهِمْ وَمَن يَغْفِرُ ٱلذُّنُوبَ إِلَّا ٱللَّهُ وَلَمْ يُصِرُّوا۟ عَلَىٰ مَا فَعَلُوا۟ وَهُمْ يَعْلَمُونَ ﴿ ١٣٥ ﴾ أُو۟لَـٰٓئِكَ جَزَآؤُهُم مَّغْفِرَةٌ مِّن رَّبِّهِمْ وَجَنَّـٰتٌ تَجْرِى مِن تَحْتِهَا ٱلْأَنْهَـٰرُ خَـٰلِدِينَ فِيهَا وَنِعْمَ أَجْرُ ٱلْعَـٰمِلِينَ ﴿ ١٣٦ ﴾
215	﴿وَٱلْكَـٰظِمِينَ ٱلْغَيْظَ وَٱلْعَافِينَ عَنِ ٱلنَّاسِ﴾
215	﴿وَٱلْعَافِينَ عَنِ ٱلنَّاسِ﴾
215	وَلَا تَسْتَوِى ٱلْحَسَنَةُ وَلَا ٱلسَّيِّئَةُ ٱدْفَعْ بِٱلَّتِى هِىَ أَحْسَنُ فَإِذَا ٱلَّذِى بَيْنَكَ وَبَيْنَهُ عَدَٰوَةٌ كَأَنَّهُ وَلِىٌّ حَمِيمٌ ﴿ ٣٤ ﴾ وَمَا يُلَقَّىٰهَآ إِلَّا ٱلَّذِينَ صَبَرُوا۟ وَمَا يُلَقَّىٰهَآ إِلَّا ذُو حَظٍّ عَظِيمٍ ﴿ ٣٥ ﴾

218	فَبِمَا رَحْمَةٍ مِّنَ ٱللَّهِ لِنتَ لَهُمْ وَلَوْ كُنتَ فَظًّا غَلِيظَ ٱلْقَلْبِ لَٱنفَضُّواْ مِنْ حَوْلِكَ فَٱعْفُ عَنْهُمْ وَٱسْتَغْفِرْ لَهُمْ وَشَاوِرْهُمْ فِى ٱلْأَمْرِ فَإِذَا عَزَمْتَ فَتَوَكَّلْ عَلَى ٱللَّهِ إِنَّ ٱللَّهَ يُحِبُّ ٱلْمُتَوَكِّلِينَ ﴿ ١٥٩ ﴾
220	وَٱللَّهُ يُحِبُّ ٱلْمُحْسِنِينَ ﴿ ١٤٨ ﴾
220	وَإِن تُحْسِنُواْ وَتَتَّقُواْ فَإِنَّ ٱللَّهَ كَانَ بِمَا تَعْمَلُونَ خَبِيرًا ﴿ ١٢٨ ﴾
221	إِنَّ ٱلَّذِينَ ءَامَنُواْ وَعَمِلُواْ ٱلصَّٰلِحَٰتِ إِنَّا لَا نُضِيعُ أَجْرَ مَنْ أَحْسَنَ عَمَلًا ﴿ ٣٠ ﴾
221	وَٱصْبِرْ فَإِنَّ ٱللَّهَ لَا يُضِيعُ أَجْرَ ٱلْمُحْسِنِينَ ﴿ ١١٥ ﴾
221	إِنَّ ٱللَّهَ يَأْمُرُ بِٱلْعَدْلِ وَٱلْإِحْسَٰنِ وَإِيتَآئِ ذِى ٱلْقُرْبَىٰ وَيَنْهَىٰ عَنِ ٱلْفَحْشَآءِ وَٱلْمُنكَرِ وَٱلْبَغْىِ يَعِظُكُمْ لَعَلَّكُمْ تَذَكَّرُونَ ﴿ ٩٠ ﴾
221	هَلْ جَزَآءُ ٱلْإِحْسَٰنِ إِلَّا ٱلْإِحْسَٰنُ ﴿ ٦٠ ﴾

INDEX OF PROPHETIC NARRATIONS

Page	Index of Prophetic Narrations
16	«لاَ يُؤْمِنُ أَحَدُكُمْ حَتَّى يُحِبَّ لِأَخِيهِ مَا يُحِبُّ لِنَفْسِهِ»
23	«إِنَّمَا بُعِثْتُ لِأُتَمِّمَ صَالِحَ الأَخْلاقِ»
29	«إِنَّ مِنْ أَحَبِّكُمْ إِلَيَّ وَأَقْرَبِكُمْ مِنِّي مَجْلِسًا يَوْمَ الْقِيَامَةِ أَحَاسِنَكُمْ أَخْلاَقًا وَإِنَّ أَبْغَضَكُمْ إِلَيَّ وَأَبْعَدَكُمْ مِنِّي مَجْلِسًا يَوْمَ الْقِيَامَةِ الثَّرْثَارُونَ وَالْمُتَشَدِّقُونَ وَالْمُتَفَيْهِقُونَ». قَالُوا يَا رَسُولَ اللَّهِ قَدْ عَلِمْنَا الثَّرْثَارُونَ وَالْمُتَشَدِّقُونَ فَمَا الْمُتَفَيْهِقُونَ قَالَ: «الْمُتَكَبِّرُونَ»
29	«لا شيء أثقل في ميزان المؤمن يوم القيامة من حسن الخلق، وإن الله يبغض الفاحش البذئ»
30	«اكمل المؤمنين إيمانا أحسنهم خلقا»
30	«إِنَّ الْمُؤْمِنَ لَيُدْرِكُ بِحُسْنِ خُلُقِهِ دَرَجَةَ الصَّائِمِ الْقَائِمِ»
31	«قِيلَ لِلنَّبِيِّ ﷺ يَا رَسُولَ اللَّهِ إِنَّ فُلاَنَةَ تَقُومُ اللَّيْلَ وَتَصُومُ النَّهَارَ وَتَفْعَلُ وَتَصَدَّقُ وَتُؤْذِي جِيرَانَهَا بِلِسَانِهَا فَقَالَ رَسُولُ اللَّهِ صَلَّى اللَّهُ عَلَيْهِ وَسَلَّمَ«لا خَيْرَ فِيهَا هِيَ مِنْ أَهْلِ النَّارِ»
36	«لاَ يَزْنِي الزَّانِي حِينَ يَزْنِي وَهُوَ مُؤْمِنٌ وَلاَ يَشْرَبُ الْخَمْرَ شَارِبُهَا حِينَ يَشْرَبُهَا وَهُوَ مُؤْمِنٌ وَلاَ يَسْرِقُ السَّارِقُ حِينَ يَسْرِقُ وَهُوَ مُؤْمِنٌ وَلاَ يَنْتَهِبُ نُهْبَةً يَرْفَعُ النَّاسُ إِلَيْهِ فِيهَا أَبْصَارَهُمْ حِينَ يَنْتَهِبُهَا وَهُوَ مُؤْمِنٌ»

36	«مَنْ كَانَ يُؤْمِنُ بِاللَّهِ وَالْيَوْمِ الآخِرِ فَلْيَقُلْ خَيْرًا، أَوْ لِيَصْمُتْ، وَمَنْ كَانَ يُؤْمِنُ بِاللَّهِ وَالْيَوْمِ الآخِرِ فَلاَ يُؤْذِ جَارَهُ، وَمَنْ كَانَ يُؤْمِنُ بِاللَّهِ وَالْيَوْمِ الآخِرِ فَلْيُكْرِمْ ضَيْفَهُ»
36	«وَاللهِ لا يؤمن، واللهِ لايؤمن، واللهِ لا يؤمن!» قيل: من يا رسول الله؟ قال: «الذي لا يأمن جاره بوائقه». وفي رواية لمسلم:«لايدخل الجنة من لا يأمن جاره بوائقه»
42	«إِنَّ أَخْوَفَ مَا أَخَافُ عَلَيْكُمُ الشِّرْكُ الأَصْغَرُ: الرِّيَاءُ. وزاد أحمد: ” يقول الله -عز وجل- لهم يوم القيامة -إذا جزى الناس بأعمالهم-: اذهبوا إلى الذين كنتم تراءون في الدنيا فانظروا هل تجدون عندهم جزاء»
52	«يَا مُعَاذُ أَتَدْرِي مَا حَقُّ اللَّهِ عَلَى الْعِبَادِ» قَالَ اللَّهُ وَرَسُولُهُ أَعْلَمُ. قَالَ: «أَنْ يَعْبُدُوهُ وَلاَ يُشْرِكُوا بِهِ شَيْئًا، أَتَدْرِي مَا حَقُّهُمْ عَلَيْهِ» قَالَ اللَّهُ وَرَسُولُهُ أَعْلَمُ. قَالَ «أَنْ لاَ يُعَذِّبَهُمْ»
56	«إِنَّمَا الْأَعْمَالُ بِالنِّيَّاتِ وَإِنَّمَا لِكُلِّ امْرِئٍ مَا نَوَى فَمَنْ كَانَتْ هِجْرَتُهُ إِلَى اللَّهِ وَرَسُولِهِ فَهِجْرَتُهُ إِلَى اللَّهِ وَرَسُولِهِ وَمَنْ كَانَتْ هِجْرَتُهُ لِدُنْيَا يُصِيبُهَا أَوِ امْرَأَةٍ يَنْكِحُهَا فَهِجْرَتُهُ إِلَى مَا هَاجَرَ إِلَيْهِ»
56	قَالَ رَسُولُ اللَّهِ ﷺ «مَنْ أَحْدَثَ فِي أَمْرِنَا هَذَا مَا لَيْسَ فِيهِ فَهُوَ رَدٌّ» وفي رواية أخرى قال «مَنْ عَمِلَ عَمَلًا لَيْسَ عَلَيْهِ أَمْرُنَا فَهُوَ رَدٌّ»
78	«يُوشِكُ أَنْ يَقْعُدَ الرجلُ مُتَّكِئًا على أَرِيكَتِهِ، يُحَدَّثُ بحديثٍ مِنْ حديثي، فيقولُ: بينَنَا وبينَكُمْ كتابُ اللهِ، فما وجدنا فيه مِنْ حلالٍ اسْتَحْلَلْنَاهُ، وما وجدنا فيه مِنْ حرامٍ حرَّمنَاهُ، ألَا وإنَّ ما حرَّمَ رسولُ اللهِ مثلَ ما حرَّمَ اللهُ»
85	«مَنْ أَحْدَثَ فِي أَمْرِنَا هَذَا مَا لَيْسَ مِنْهُ فَهُوَ رد» وَفِي رِوَايَةٍ لِمُسْلِمٍ: «مَنْ عَمِلَ عَمَلًا لَيْسَ عَلَيْهِ أَمْرُنَا فَهُوَ رَدٌّ»

93	«قَالَ اللَّهُ: كَذَّبَنِي ابنُ آدَمَ وَلَمْ يَكُنْ له ذلكَ، وشَتَمَنِي ولَمْ يَكُنْ له ذلكَ، فأمَّا تَكْذِيبُهُ إيَّايَ فقَوْلُهُ: لَنْ يُعِيدَنِي، كما بَدَأَنِي، وليسَ أوَّلُ الخَلْقِ بأهْوَنَ عَلَيَّ مِن إعادَتِهِ، وأمَّا شَتْمُهُ إيَّايَ فقَوْلُهُ: اتَّخَذَ اللهُ ولَدًا وأنا الأَحَدُ الصَّمَدُ، لَمْ أَلِدْ ولَمْ أُولَدْ، ولَمْ يَكُنْ لي كُفُوًا أحَدٌ»
97	«أنَّ أَعمَى كانتْ لَه أُمُّ وَلَدٍ تَشتُمُ النَّبِيَّ ﷺ وتَقَعُ فيه، فينَهاها فلا تَنتَهِي، ويزَجُرُها فلا تَنزَجِرُ، فلمَّا كانَ ذاتَ ليلةٍ جَعَلَتْ تَقَعُ في النَّبِيِّ ﷺ وتَشتُمُه، فأخذَ المِعوَلَ فجَعَلَه واتَّكأَ عليها فقتَلَها، فلمَّا أصبَح ذُكِرَ ذلكَ للنَّبِيِّ ﷺ، فجَمَعَ النَّاسَ، فقال: أنشُدُ اللهَ رجُلًا فعَل ما فعَل، لي عَليه حقٌّ إلَّا قام، فقامَ الأَعْمى يَتخطَّى النَّاسَ، وهوَ يتدَلْدَلُ حتَّى قعَدَ بَينَ يَدَي النَّبِيِّ ﷺ، فقال: يا رَسولَ اللهِ ﷺ، أنا صاحِبُها، كانتْ تَشتُمُك وتَقَعُ فيكَ، فأنْهاها فلا تَنتَهِي، وأزجُرُها فلا تَنزَجِرُ، ولي مِنها ابنانِ مِثلُ اللُّؤلُؤَتَين، وكانت بي رَفيقةً، فلمَّا كان البَارحةَ جَعَلَت تَشتُمُك وتَقَعُ فيكَ، فأخَذْتُ المِعوَلَ فوَضَعْتُه واتَّكأْتُ عَليه حتَّى قتَلْتُها، فقال النَّبِيُّ ﷺ: ألَا اشْهَدوا أنَّ دَمَها هَدَر»
100	«آيَةُ الإيمانِ حُبُّ الأَنْصارِ، وآيَةُ النِّفاقِ بُغْضُ الأَنْصارِ»
101	«لا تَسُبُّوا أحَدًا مِن أصْحابِي، فإنَّ أحَدَكُمْ لو أنفَقَ مِثْلَ أُحُدٍ ذَهَبًا، ما أدرَكَ مُدَّ أحَدِهِمْ، ولَا نَصِيفَهُ»
110	«يا مَعشَرَ الشَّبابِ، مَنِ استَطاعَ مِنكُمُ الباءةَ فلْيتزَوَّجْ، فإنَّه أغَضُّ للبَصَرِ، وأحْصَنُ للفَرجِ، ومَن لَمْ يَسْتَطِعْ فعليه بالصَّومِ، فإنَّه له وِجاءٌ»
111	«إذا جاءكم مَن تَرضَونَ دِينَه وخُلُقَه فزَوِّجوه إلاَّ تَفْعَلوا تَكُنْ فِتْنَةٌ في الأَرْضِ وفَسادٌ كبير»
111	«تُنْكَحُ المَرأةُ لأربَعٍ لِمالِها ولِحَسَبِها وجَمالِها ولِدِينِها، فاظْفَرْ بذاتِ الدِّينِ تَرِبَتْ يَداكَ»

112	«حُبِّبَ إِلَيَّ مِن دُنياكم ثلاثٌ : الطِّيبُ، والنِّساءُ، وجُعِلَت قُرَّةُ عَيني في الصَّلاةِ»
116	«وفي بُضع أَحَدِكُم صَدَقَةٌ»، قالوا: يا رَسولَ اللهِ، أَيَأتي أَحَدُنا شَهوَتَه ويَكونُ له فِيها أَجرٌ؟ قالَ: «أَرَأَيْتُم لو وَضَعَها في حَرامٍ، أَكانَ عليه فِيها وِزرٌ؟ فكَذلكَ إذا وَضَعَها في الحَلالِ كانَ له أَجرٌ»
117	«تزوَّجوا الودودَ الوَلودَ فإنِّي مُكاثِرٌ بِكُمُ الأُمَمَ»
117	«أَمَا لو أَنَّ أَحَدَهُمْ يَقولُ حِينَ يَأتي أَهلَهُ: باسمِ اللهِ، اللَّهُمَّ جَنِّبني الشَّيطانَ، وجَنِّبِ الشَّيطانَ ما رَزَقتَنا، ثُمَّ قُدِّرَ بينَهما في ذلكَ، أَو قُضِيَ ولَدٌ؛ لَمْ يَضُرَّهُ شيطانٌ أَبَدًا»
117	«فإِنْ قضَى اللهُ بينَهما في ذلك ولَدًا، لم يضُرَّه الشيطانُ أَبدًا»
119	إذا أَتَى الرَّجُلُ امرأَتَه مِن دُبُرِها في قُبُلِها، كانَ الوَلَدُ أَحوَلَ، فنَزَلَت : ﴿نِسَآؤُكُمْ حَرْثٌ لَكُمْ فَأْتُواْ حَرْثَكُمْ أَنَّى شِئْتُمْ﴾ فقال رسول الله ﷺ : «مُقبِلةً ومُدبِرةً، إذا كان ذلك في الفرج»
120	«إِنَّ اللَّهَ لَا يَسْتَحْيِي مِنَ الْحَقِّ ثَلَاثَ مَرَّاتٍ لَا تَأْتُوا النِّسَاءَ فِي أَدْبارِهِنَّ»
120	«ملعونٌ مَن يأتي النِّساءَ في محاشِّهنَّ. يعني : أدبارَهنَّ»
120	«مَنْ أَتَى حائِضًا أَو امرأَةً في دُبُرِها أَو كاهِنًا، فقَدْ كَفَرْ بِمَا أَنْزِلَ عَلَى مُحَمَّدٍ ﷺ»
121	كان رسول الله ﷺ يأمرُ إحدانا إذا كانت حائضًا أن تتَّزِرَ ثُمَّ يُضاجِعُها زوجُها
123	«إِنَّ من شرِّ الناسِ عندَ اللهِ منزِلةً يومَ القيامةِ ، الرجلُ يُفضِي إلى امرأتِه وتُفضِي إليهِ ، ثُم يَنشُرُ سِرَّهَا»

123	«لَعَلَّ رجُلًا يقول ما يفعلُ بأهْلِهِ، ولعلَّ امرأةً تخبِر بما فعلَت مع زوجِها؟ ! فأرَمَّ القومُ، -أي سكتوا ولم يجيبوا- فقلتُ : إي واللَّهِ يا رسولَ اللَّهِ ! إنَّهنَّ ليفعَلْنَ، وإنَّهم ليفعَلونَ. قالَ : «فلا تفعَلوا، فإنَّما ذلِكَ مَثَلُ الشَّيطانِ لقيَ شيطانةً في طريقٍ فغَشِيَها والنَّاسُ ينظُرونَ»
128	«لا يفرَكُ مؤمن مؤمنة، إن كره منها خُلقًا رضي منها آخر أو قال غيره»
128	«استوصوا بالنساء، فإن المرأة خلقت من ضلع، وإن أعوج شيء في الضلع أعلاه، فإن ذهبت تقيمه كسرته، وإن تركته لم يزل أعوج، فاستوصوا بالنساء»
129	«الاَ وَاسْتَوْصُوا بِالنِّسَاءِ خَيْرًا، فَإِنَّمَا هُنَّ عَوَانٌ عِنْدَكُم. أَلاَ وَإِنَّ لَكُمْ عَلَى نِسَائِكُمْ حَقًّا، وَلِنِسَائِكُمْ عَلَيْكُمْ حَقًّا، فأَمَّا حَقّكُمْ عَلَى نِسَائِكُمْ فَلاَ يُوطِئْنَ فُرُشَكُمْ من تَكْرَهُونَ، وَلاَ يَأْذَنَّ في بُيُوتِكُمْ لِمَنْ تَكْرَهُونَ»
143	«كُلُّكُمْ رَاعٍ، وَكُلُّكُمْ مَسْئُولٌ عَنْ رَعِيَّتِهِ، وَالأَمِيرُ رَاعٍ، وَالرَّجُلُ رَاعٍ عَلَى أَهْلِ بَيْتِهِ، وَالْمَرْأَةُ رَاعِيَةٌ عَلَى بَيْتِ زَوْجِها وَوَلَدِهِ، فكُلُّكُمْ رَاعٍ وَكُلُّكُمْ مَسْئُولٌ عَنْ رَعِيَّتِه»
145	دَخَلَتْ هِنْدُ بنْتُ عُتْبَةَ امرأَةُ أَبِي سُفْيَانَ على رَسُولِ اللهِ ﷺ، فَقَالَتْ : يا رَسُولَ اللهِ، إنَّ أَبَا سُفْيَانَ رَجُلٌ شَحِيحٌ، لا يُعْطِينِي مِنَ النَّفَقَةِ ما يَكْفِينِي وَيَكْفِي بَنِيَّ إلّا ما أَخَذْتُ مِن مَالِهِ بغير عِلْمِه، فَهلْ عَلَيَّ في ذلكَ مِن جُنَاحٍ؟ فَقَالَ رَسُولُ اللهِ ﷺ : «خُذِي مِن مَالِهِ بالمَعروفِ ما يَكْفِيكِ وَيَكْفِي بَنِيكِ»
152	«أَلَا واسْتَوْصُوا بالنساءِ خيرًا، فإنهن عَوَانٌ عِندَكم، ليس تملكون منهن شيئًا غيرَ ذلك ؛ إلا أن يَأْتِينَ بفاحشةٍ مُبَيِّنَةٍ، فإن فعَلْنَ فاهجُرُوهُنَّ في المَضَاجِعِ، واضرِبُوهُنَّ ضَرْبًا غيرَ مُبَرِّحٍ، فإن أَطَعْنَكُمْ فلا تَبْغُوا عليهِن سبيلًا»

167	ان عليا رضي الله عنه بعث رجلين فقال لهما: أتريان ما عليكما؟ عليكما إن رأيتما أن تجمعا جمعتما, وإن رأيتما أن تفرقا فرقتما, فقال الرجل أما هذا فلا, فقال: كذبت والله لا تبرح حتى ترضى بكتاب الله عز وجل لك وعليك, فقالت المرأة : رضيت بكتاب الله
169	«أَبْغَضُ الْحَلَالِ إِلَى اللهِ الطَّلَاقُ»
169	«أَيُّما امرأةٍ سَأَلَتْ زَوجَها الطَّلاقَ في غيرِ ما بَأسٍ، فَحَرامٌ عليها رائحةُ الجنَّةِ»
177	«مره ليراجعها ثم يمسكها حتّى تطهر ثم تحيض فتطهر ، فان بدا له فليطلقها طاهرًا قبل ان يمسّها ، فتلك العدّه الّتى امرها الله تعالى ان يطلّق بها النّساء.»
179	اخبرني رسول الله ﷺ عن رجل طلق إمرأته ثلاث تطيقات جميعا فغضب وقال: «أيلعب بكتاب الله وأنا بين أظهركم ؟»
262	حدثنا رسول الله ﷺ، حديثين قد رأيت أحدهما، وأنا أنتظر الآخر: حدثنا أن الأمانة نزلت في جذر قلوب الرجال، ثم نزل القرآن فعلموا من القرآن، وعلموا من السنة، ثم حدثنا عن رفع الأمانة فقال: «ينام الرجل النومة فتقبض الأمانة من قلبه، فيظل أثرها مثل الوكت، ثم ينام النومة فتبض الأمانة من قلبه، فيظل أثرها مثل أثر المجل، كجمر دحرجته على رجلك، فنفط فتراه منتبرًا وليس فيه شيء » ثم أخذ حصاة فدحرجه على رجله »فيصبح الناس يتبايعون، فلا يكاد أحد يؤدي الأمانة حتى يقال:" إن في بني فلان رجلاً أمينًا، حتى يقال للرجل، ما أجلده ما أظرفه، ما أعقله! وما في قلبه مثقال حبة من خردل من إيمان . ولقد أتى علي زمان وما أبالي أيكم بايعت؛ لئن كان مسلمًا ليردنه علي دينه، ولئن كان نصرانيا أو يهودياً ليردنه علي ساعيه، وأما اليوم فما كنت أبايع منكم إلا فلانًا و فلانًا»

267	«عليكم بالصدق، فإن الصدق يهدي إلى البرِّ، وإن البر يهدي إلى الجنة، وما يزال الرجل يصدق ويَتَحَرَّى الصدق حتى يكتب عند الله صِدِّيقًا، وإياكم والكذب، فإن الكذب يهدي إلى الفجور، وإن الفجور يهدي إلى النار، وما يزال الرجل يكذب ويَتَحَرَّى الكذب حتى يكتب عند الله كذَّابا»
268	«آية المنافق ثلاث: إذا حدث كذب، وإذا وعد أخلف، وإذا اؤتمن خان» زاد في ((رواية لمسلم)): «وإن صام وصلى وزعم أنه مسلم»
269	«اضْمَنُوا لِي سِتًّا مِنْ أَنْفُسِكُمْ أَضْمَنْ لَكُمُ الْجَنَّةَ اصْدُقُوا إِذَا حَدَّثْتُمْ وَأَوْفُوا إِذَا وَعَدْتُمْ وَأَدُّوا إِذَا اؤْتُمِنْتُمْ وَاحْفَظُوا فُرُوجَكُمْ وَغُضُّوا أَبْصَارَكُمْ وَكُفُّوا أَيْدِيَكُمْ»
273	«الْبَيِّعَانِ بِالْخِيَارِ مَا لَمْ يَتَفَرَّقَا، فَإِنْ صَدَقَا وَبَيَّنَا بُورِكَ لَهُمَا فِي بَيْعِهِمَا، وَإِنْ كَذَبَا وَكَتَمَا مُحِقَتْ بَرَكَةُ بَيْعِهِمَا»
281	«الْإِيمَانُ بِضْعٌ وَسَبْعُونَ أَوْ بِضْعٌ وَسِتُّونَ شُعْبَةً فَأَفْضَلُهَا قَوْلُ لَا إِلَهَ إِلَّا اللَّهُ وَأَدْنَاهَا إِمَاطَةُ الْأَذَى عَنِ الطَّرِيقِ وَالْحَيَاءُ شُعْبَةٌ مِنَ الْإِيمَانِ»
281	«إِنَّ الْحَيَاءَ وَالْإِيمَانَ قُرِنَا جَمِيعًا، فَإِذَا رُفِعَ أَحَدُهُمَا رُفِعَ الْآخَرُ»
281	«دَعْهُ فَإِنَّ الْحَيَاءَ مِنَ الْإِيمَانِ»
281	«الْحَيَاءُ مِنَ الْإِيمَانِ وَالْإِيمَانُ فِي الْجَنَّةِ وَالْبَذَاءُ مِنَ الْجَفَاءِ وَالْجَفَاءُ فِي النَّارِ»
282	قَالَ النَّبِيُّ ﷺ: «إِنَّ مِمَّا أَدْرَكَ النَّاسَ مِنْ كَلَامِ النُّبُوَّةِ: إِذَا لَمْ تَسْتَحِ فَاصْنَعْ مَا شِئْتَ»
282	«الْحَيَاءُ لَا يَأْتِي إِلَّا بِخَيْرٍ»
282	«الْحَيَاءُ خَيْرٌ كُلُّهُ»

285	«لَيْسَ الشَّدِيدُ بِالصُّرَعَةِ، وَلَكِنَّ الشَّدِيدَ الَّذِي يَمْلِكُ نَفْسَهُ عِنْدَ الْغَضَبِ»
287	«أَتَتْكُمْ وُفُودُ عَبْدِ الْقَيْسِ» وَمَا يَرَى أَحَدٌ فَبَيْنَا نَحْنُ كَذَلِكَ إِذْ جَاءُوا فَنَزَلُوا فَأَتَوْا رَسُولَ اللَّهِ ﷺ وَبَقِيَ الْأَشَجُّ الْعَصَرِيُّ فَجَاءَ بَعْدُ فَنَزَلَ مَنْزِلاً فَأَنَاخَ رَاحِلَتَهُ وَوَضَعَ ثِيَابَهُ جَانِبًا ثُمَّ جَاءَ إِلَى رَسُولِ اللَّهِ ﷺ فَقَالَ لَهُ رَسُولُ اللَّهِ ﷺ: «يَا أَشَجُّ إِنَّ فِيكَ لَخَصْلَتَيْنِ يُحِبُّهُمَا اللَّهُ الْحِلْمَ وَالتُّؤَدَةَ» قَالَ يَا رَسُولَ اللَّهِ ﷺ «أَشَىْءٌ جُبِلْتُ عَلَيْهِ أَمْ شَىْءٌ حَدَثَ لِي قَالَ رَسُولُ اللَّهِ ﷺ «بَلْ شَىْءٌ جُبِلْتَ عَلَيْهِ»
290	«مَن كظم غيظاً ، وهو قادر على أن ينفذه، دعاه الله سبحانه وتعالى على رؤوس الخلائق يوم القيامة حتى يخيره من الحور العين ما شاء»
292	«أحب الناس إلى الله أنفعهم للناس ، وأحب الأعمال إلى الله عز وجل سرور تدخله على مسلم ، أو تكشف عنه كربة ، أو تقضي عنه دينا ، أو تطرد عنه جوعا ، ولأن أمشي مع أخي المسلم في حاجة أحبّ إليّ من أن اعتكف في هذا المسجديعني مسجد المدينة – شهرا ... ومن مشى مع أخيه المسلم في حاجة حتى يثبتها له أثبت الله تعالى قدمه يوم تزول الأقدام»

BIBLIOGRAPHY

1- BOOKS

'Abd al-Wahhāb, al-Qāḍī Abī Muḥammad. n.d. *al-Talqīn fī al-fiqh al-Mālikī*. Dār al-Kutub al-'Ilmiyyah.

Ibn Kathir, Ismā'īl b. 'Umar b. Kathīr al-Dimishqī. *Tafsīr Ibn Kathīr - Tafsīr al-Qur'ān al-'Aḍīm*. (Riyad: Darussalam, Dār al-Feyḥa, 2003)

al-Alūsī, Shihāb al-Dīn Abū Thanā' Muḥammad b. 'Abdallah. *Rūḥ al-Ma'ānī fī Tafsīr al-Qur'ān al-'Aẓīm wa Sab al-Mathānī*. (Beirut, Lebanon: Mu'assassat al-Risālah, 2010).

al-Baghawī, Abū Muḥammad al-Ḥussayn ibn Mas'ūd ibn Muḥammad al-Farrā'. *Sharḥ al-Sunnah*. (Damascus, Syria)

al-Bahrani, Sayyid Hashim. 1999. *Kitab al-Insaf fī an-Nas 'ala al-Aimmah al-Ithnay 'Ashar*. Tehran: Daftar-i Nashr-i Farhang-i Islami.

al-Bayḥaqī, Abū Bakr Aḥmad b. al-Ḥussayn. *Sunan al-Kubrā*. (Beirut, Lebanon: Dār al-Kutub al-'Ilmiyyah, 1994)

Al-Bukhari, Imam. 1996. *Ṣaḥīḥ Al-Bukhari*. Riyad: Maktaba Dar-us-Salam.

Al-dīn, Al-Albani Muḥammad Nasir. 2000. *At-Targheeb wat-Tarheeb*. Riyad: Dar Al Maarifah.

Al-dīn, Al-Albani Muḥammad Nasir. 2001. *Ṣaḥīḥ Al-Ādab al-Mufrad*. Darul Sadiqin.

—. 2004. *Silsilaat Al-Ahadith Al-Ṣaḥīḥah*. Riyad: Dar Al Maarifah.

Al-Ghazali, Abū Hamid. 2020. *Iḥyā ulūm al-dīn*. London: Turath Publishing.

AL-HAKIMI, HAFIDH. n.d. *MA'AARIJ AL-QABOOL*. Dar Ibn Al-Jawzy.

Al-Jawziyya, Ibn Qayim. 2020. *Madārij al-Sālikīn:" Ranks of the Divine Seekers*.

Al-Jawziyya, Ibn Qayyim. 2020. *Madārij al-Sālikīn:" Ranks of the Divine Seekers*.

AL-JAZA'IRY, SHAYKH ABU BAKR JABIR. 2001. *MINHAJ AL-MUSLIM*. Riyad: Darussalam publishers.

Al-Mawardi, Abūl Al-Ḥasan Bin Ali. 1994. *Al-Hawi Al-Kabeer*. Beirut: Darul Fikr.

al-Naysaburi, Muslim ibn al-Hajjaj. 1972. *Ṣaḥīḥ Muslim*. Beirut: Darul Ihya.

al-Qazvini, Muḥammad bin Yazid Ibn Majah. n.d. *Sunan ibn Majah*.

al-Qurtubi, Abū 'Abdallah Muḥammad ibn Aḥmad. n.d. *TAFSIR AL-QURTUBI - AL-JAMI' LI AHKAM AL-QURAN*. Darul Kitab Al-Ararabi.

Al-Razi, Imam Fakhr Al-din. n.d. *Al-Tafsir Al-Kabir Aw Mafatih al-Ghaib*. Dar Kotob al-Ilmiyah.

Al-Suyuti, Al-Mahalli and. 2010. *Tafsir Al-Jalalayn*. Al Bushra Library.

al-Zamakhshari, Abū al-Qasim Mahmud ibn Umar. n.d. *AL-KASHSHAF AN HAQAA'IQ AT-TANZEEL*. Beirut: Dar Al Maarifah.

Andlusi, Al qadi Iyad Al Yahsubi. 2009. *Al-Shifa - Healing through defining the rights of Prophet Muḥammad*.

an-Nasa'i, Abū 'Abdur Rahman. n.d. *Sunan An-Nasa'i*. Dar Al Maarifah.

AN-NAWAWI, IMAM. n.d. *AL-MAJMU' SHARH AL-MUHADDHAB*. Darul Fikr.

—. n.d. *AL-MINHAJ SHARH ṢAḤĪḤ MUSLIM*.

An-Nawawi, Imam. 1991. *Rawdatu Talibin*. Beirut: Al Maktab Al-Islami.

Ash-Shulhoob, Fu'ad Ibn "Abdul-'Azeez. 2003. *The Book of Manners*. Riyad: Darussalam Publishers & Distributors.

as-Saʿdi, 'Abd ar-Rahman ibn Nasir. 2018. *Taysir Al-Kareem Al-Raḥmān fii tafseer Al-Quran*. Dar Al-alamiyah.

as-Saʿdi, 'Abdur Rahman Nasir. n.d. *Tafsīr As-Saʿdi*.

AS-SHIRBIN, KHATIB. 1997. *Mughni al-Muhtaaj ila Maʿrifati Maʿani Alfaadh al-Minhaaj*. Beirut: Dar Al Maarifah.

as-Sijistan, Abū Dawud Sulayman ibn al-Ashʿath. n.d. *Sunan Abi Dawud*. Riyad: Dar Al Maarifah.

as-Suyūṭī, Imām Jalāl ad-Dīn. 1993. *Miftāḥ al-Jannah fi al-Iḥtijāj bi as-Sunnah*. Dar al-Nafa'is.

at-Tabari, Abū Jaʿfar Muḥammad ibn Jarir. n.d. *TAFSIR IBN JARIR AT-TABARI - JAMI' AL-BAYAN 'AN TA-WIL AL-QURAN*. Dar Kotob Al-Ilmiyah.

at-Tirmidhi, Muḥammad ibn 'Issa. 1978. *SUNAN AT-TIRMIDHI*. Beirut: Darul Fikr.

Az-Zuhayli, Wahbah. 2008. *Al-Fiqh Al-Shāfiʿi Al-Muyassar*. Damascus: Darul Fikr.

Guezzou, Mokrane. 2008. *Tafsir Ibn Abbas*. Louisville: Fons Vitae.

Ibn Hajar, Aḥmad Bin Ali Bin Hajar. n.d. *Fathul Bari Sharḥ Ṣaḥīḥul Bukhari*. Beirut: Dar Al Maarifah.

Ibn Taymiyah, Taqi Ad-Dīn Aḥmad, 1997. *majmual fatawa*. Riyad: Daeul Wafa.

Isfahani, Raghib. 1973. *Tafsil al-Nash'atayn wa-Tahsil al-Sa'adatayn.* Beirut: Al Hayat Library.

Majah, Ibn. n.d. *Sunan Ibn Majah.* Riyad: Darul Maarifah.

Mashood, Dr. Busari. 2017. "Iddat-talaq and iddat wafat: A reinterpretation of the phrase 'Hatta yada'na hamlahuna.'"

MAUDUDI, ABUL A'LA. n.d. *TAFHIM-UL-QURAN.*

Nawawi, Imam. 2003. *Riyad as-Salihin.* Darussalam.

Numani, Maulana Shibli. 1975. *Life of Umar Bin Khattab.* Karachi: Educational Press.

Philips, Dr. Abū Ameena Bilal. 2003. *Usool Al-Ḥadīth.* Riyad: International Islamic Publishing House

Qudā'ī, Muḥammad ibn Salāmah,. 2019. *Musnad Al-Shihab.*

Qutub, Sayid. 1986. *In the Shade of the Qur'an | Fi Dhilal al-Qur'ān.* Daru Al-Shuruq.

Ra'fat Al-Basha, 'Abdurahman. 2010. *Suwar Min Hayat Al-Sahabah.* Darul-Ādab Al-Islamy.

YA'LA, ABI. n.d. *Musnad.* Dar Al Maarifah.

2- ARTICLES

'Abdulsam, Dr. Sami. 2015. "ندب الحكمين في الخلع" "Empowering the arbitrators in the khula (divorce upon a settlement)." *London School of Economics and Political Science,* Juni 10.

Alaro, Dr. 'Abdul-Razzaq 'Abdul-Majeed. 2017. "Children Moral Upbringing: The Shariah Recipe." *Allawh Journal of Arabic and Islamic Studies, University of Maiduguri,* Juni 1.

Bakar, Naz. Abū. 1970. "Who represented the will of the people." *Council of Elders.*

Farooq, Sadaf. 2018. "Two Important Rules for a Blissful Marriage." August 22.

Hassan, Dr. Muḥammad Hanif. 2021. "Powerful conversations between a father and a son: lessons from Ibrahim and prophet Ismail as." July 19

Josh McDowell, Don Stewart. 1983. "Handbook of Today's Religions." *Handbook of Today's Religions.*

Judith Bennett, Ruth Karras. 2013. *The Oxford Handbook of Women and Gender in Medieval Europe.* New York: Oxford University Press.

Muslim Skeptic Team. 2022. "Wife-beating" in Judaism, Christianity, Hinduism, Buddhism, and Islam." *Muslim Skeptic Team*, August 7

Refaat, Ayman. 2002. "Pleasing Allāh through Taqwa. June." *AlJumuah Magazine*, June 27.

Reinhart, A. Kevin. 2017. "What We Know about Ma'rūf." *Journal of Islamic ethics.*

Shatibi, Ibrahim Ibn Musa Abū Ishaq Al. 2020. *Kitab Al-I'tisam.* Darul Affan.

Spiegel, James. 2010. "The Making of an Atheist." *The Making of an Atheist*, March 5.

Turner, Paul. n.d. "Finding your path arbitration sharia and the modern middle east."

Umm Mummad (Emily Assami), Mary Kennedy, Amatullah Bantley. 1997. *The Ṣaḥīḥ International translation.* The Publishing House (dar), dar Abūl Qasim.

Waggoner, Jarl. 2022. "Responding Biblically to Atheism." *Responding Biblically to Atheism*, Juni 22.

Wardle, Lynn D. 2008. "The Morality of Marriage and the Transformative Power of Inclusion." September 1.

3- ONLINE

https://www.emaanlibrary.com/wp-content/uploads/2017/12/
MuslimCharacter.pdf

https://researchspace.ukzn.ac.za/handle/10413/7512

https://www.alkitab.com/44240.html

https://alkitab.com/41973.html

https://archive.org/details/waq17714/page/n1/mode/2up

https://archive.org/details/alkafi_201601/AL-KAFI%20
VOLUME%203%20%28English%29/

https://archive.org/details/bedayt_almobtdy/page/n5/mode/2up

https://ahadith.co.uk/downloads/60sultaniyya.pdf

https://www.tibb.co.za/wp-content/uploads/2021/01/
Medicine-of-the-prophet.pdf

https://ukzndspace.ukzn.ac.za/bitstream/
handle/10413/7512/Ebrahim_Raḥīm_1996.
pdf?sequence=1&isAllowed=y

https://maktabahassunnahblog.file ordpress.com/2015/12/
the-explanation-of-the-three-fundamental-principles.
pdf

https://archive.org/details/StudiesInHadithMethodologyAnd
LiteratureByShaykhMuḥammadMustafa/mode/2up

https://archive.org/details/
IBNASAKIRSREPRESENTATIONSOF
SYRIAAND1/mode/2up

https://archive.org/details/waq3656/00_3656/

https://archive.org/details/in.ernet.dli.2015.431592/page/n3/
mode/2up

https://archive.org/details/musnadAhmadibnhanbal10/
MusnadAhmadIbnHanbal10/

https://www.alim.org/quran/tafsir/ibn-kathir/

https://myislam.org/surah-yusuf/ayat-70/

https://quran.com/12:70/tafsirs/en-tafisr-ibn-kathir

https://www.kalamullah.com/Books/Ranks%20of%20the%20Divine%20Seekers%20vol%201.pdf

file:///C:/Users/Bruker/Downloads/The_Unsheathed_Sword.pdf

https://archive.org/details/WAQ22583/00_22583/'

https://waqfeya.net/book.php?bid=3587

https://mahajjah.com/wp-content/uploads/2016/05/SWTQ-1.pdf

file:///C:/Users/Bruker/Downloads/Al_Khateeb_al_Baghdadi_and_His_Work_Tari.pdf

https://archive.org/details/FP5040/estzkar00/

https://quran.com/12:70/tafsirs/en-tafsir-maarif-ul-quran

http://www.englishtafsir.com/

https://archive.org/details/FPmfkmfk/mfk00/

file:///C:/Users/Bruker/Downloads/Sample_Kitab_At_Tawḥīd.pdf

https://d1.islamhouse.com/data/en/ih_articles/single2/en_The_Virtue_of_Truthfulness.pdf

Kalamullah.Com | In the Shade of the Qur'an | Fi Dhilal al-Qurān

Quran Tafsir | Tafsir Ibn Kathir - explanation of the Quran (alim.org)

SHIRK (Polytheism) IN ISLAM. The word shirk comes from an Arabic... | by The Sincere Seeker | Medium

Quranic Terminology: (Ilhad – Root: l/h/d) (ahl-alquran.com)

Blasphemy: Islamic Concept | Encyclopedia.com

The Moral Space of Marriage in The Holy Quran – مركز خُطوة للتوثيق والدراسات (khotwacenter.com)

What We Know about Ma'rūf in: Journal of Islamic Ethics Volume 1 Issue 1-2 (2017) (brill.com)

Marital Harmony And Conflict Resolution: The Quranic Paradigm - MuslimMatters.org

Islamic perspective on Chilhood & Child protectiom (darul-ilm. co.uk)

Kindness to Parents (All parts) - The Religion of Islam (islamreligion.com)

History of Atheism | Ligonier Ministries

Does the Quran let men beat their wives? (abuaminaelias.com)

The Three Meanings of Ihsan (yassine.net)

Analyzing the so-called 'Wife Beating Verse': 4:34 of the Holy Quran - The Muslim Vibe

The Noble Quran - Quran.com

Kalamullah.Com | Quran | Ma'ariful Quran

https://islam4u.pro/blog/parents-in-quran/

INDEX

Symbols

'Abdallah bin 'Umar 169
'Abd al-Raḥmān Ibn Kathīr 104
'Abd al-Wahhāb 318
'Abd ar-Rahman ibn Nasir 320
'Abdur Rahman Nasir 320
'Aqīdah 24, 37, 207, 210
'Ibādah ix, 24, 41, 55, 57, 113
'iddah 177, 178, 181, 182, 183, 184
   Definition of ix, 83, 181

A

Abū al-Qasim Mahmud ibn Umar 319
Abū Bakr 73, 105, 106, 318
Abū Bakr ﷺ 73
Abū Dawud 97, 123, 320, 328
Abū Dawud Sulayman ibn al-Ash'ath
   320
Abū Hamid 319
Abū Huraira 23, 29, 36, 111, 196, 209,
   213, 245, 259, 260, 263, 287
Abū Isḥāq Ibrāhīm b. Mūsā al-Shāṭibī
   22
Abūl Al-Ḥasan Bin Ali 319
Abū 'Abdallah (al Sadiq) 104, 105
Abū 'Abdur Rahman 319
Ādab 31, 38, 39, 120, 123, 196, 242,
   243, 247, 282, 318, 321
Ad-Dahhak 130, 261
Aḥmad Bin Ali Bin Hajar 320
'A'isha (ﷺ) 24, 26, 30
A. Kevin Reinhart 124, 125
Akhlāq 23, 24, 38
al-Alūsī 318

Al-Asmā' Wa-sifāt 42
Al-'Awaasim wa'l-Qawaasim 80
al-Baghawī 55, 318
al-Bahrani 318
al-Bayḥaqī 318
Al-Bukhari 31, 52, 93, 117, 119, 177,
   245, 262, 264, 268, 288
Al-Bukhari 100, 101, 177, 318
Al-dīn 318
Al-Ghazali 38, 193, 194, 205, 319
AL-HAKIMI 319
Al-Ḥasan 130, 261, 319
Al-Jawziyya 319
AL-JAZA'IRY 319
Al-Jurjānī 5
al-Khalifa' al-Rashida (Rightly Guided
   Caliphs) 73
Al-Mahalli 319
Al-Mawardi 319
Al-Mu'minūn 60, 112, 259, 260, 280
Al-Mu'minūn" (the believers) 280
Al-Munaawi 25
Al-Muqni Al-Muhtah 161
Al-Muslimūn 280
Al-Muslimūn" (the Muslims) 280
Al-Nawawi (ﷺ) 25
al-Naysaburi 319
Al qadi Iyad Al Yahsubi 319
al-Qazvini 319
al-Qurtubi 319
al-Raḥmān 91, 104
Al-Razi 153, 319
Al-ṣulḥ 164
Al-ṣulḥ (mediation) 164
Al-Suyuti 153, 277, 319

al-taṣawwuf 30
al-Zamakhshari 319
Amānah 205, 261, 262, 263
Amānah (the trust) 205, 262, 263
Anas ibn Mālik 16
an-Nasa'i 319
An-Nawawi 320
arḥam 239
Ark of Noah 80
Ar-Rabi 130
Ash-Shulhoob 320
as-Sa'di 320
AS-SHIRBIN 320
as-Sijistan 320
As-Suyooti, ﷺ 80
Atheism ix, 43, 44, 45, 46, 322, 325
at-Tabari 320
At-Tibb An-Nabawi 113
at-Tirmidhi 320
Az-Zuhayli 320

B

Beirut 5, 267, 318, 319, 320, 321
bid'ah 83, 85, 86
Bidayatul Mujtahid 161
Bidyat Al-mujtahid 177
bid'ah ḥasanah 86

C

Carl W. Ernst 88

D

Ṭā'ah 57
Damascus 318, 320
Dār al-Kutub al-'ilmiyyah 5
da'wa 219, 291
Da'wa 1, 4
Day of Judgment 15, 29, 73, 208, 209, 215, 269
dīn 112, 217, 318, 319
Dīn (religion) 210
Divine Names and Attributes of God 42
Don Stewart 44, 322
Dr. Abū Ameena Bilal Philips 75, 77

Dr. Ali Mohamed Salah 2
Dr. M. 'Abdalla Draz 13
du'ā 116
Du'ā 117

E

Ethics ix, 2, 5, 6, 7, 124, 293, 325

F

fā'ba'thū 161
faskh 156
faskh (marriage annulment) 156
fiṭrah 122
Fiṭrah 210
Fiṭrah (natural disposition) 210
fiṭrah (natural inclination) 122
Fizilal-Al-Quran 128

G

Genesis 146
ghayr mubarraḥ 151
ghayru mu'allim 152
ghayru mubarriḥ 152
ghusl 116
Guezzou, Mokrane 320

H

ḥadīth 74, 75, 80, 81, 85, 111
Ḥadīth x, 74, 75, 77, 78, 80, 254, 268, 280, 281, 321
ḥalāl 78, 86, 98, 121
Ḥanbali 97
ḥarām 78, 86, 98, 279
Hend Mustafa 115, 126, 132
ḥilm 283, 287
Ḥilm xi, 282, 284, 286, 287, 288, 289, 290
ḤILM (FORBEARANCE) 282, 284, 285
Honesty 26, 259
Humility 26

I

Ibn 'Abbas 97, 165
Ibn Abbas 67, 97, 130, 153, 166, 196, 320
Ibn al-Qayyim ﷺ 30
Ibn al-Wazir, ﷺ 80
Ibn Hajar 153, 320
Ibn Kathir 26, 53, 55, 67, 68, 95, 144, 153, 162, 318, 324
Ibn Kathir (ﷺ) 53
Ibn Qayim 319
Ibn Qayyim 319
Ibn Rajab 25
Ibn Taymiyah 96, 97, 98, 279, 320
Ibn Taymiyyah 49, 55, 81, 107
Ibnu Adiy 120
Ibn 'Umar 177, 208, 242, 281, 292
Ibnu Rushd 177
Ibnu Taymiyah 97
Ibrahim 130, 165, 199, 200, 223, 224, 225, 226, 227, 228, 322
iḥsān 124
Ijtihād 22
Ikrimah 130
Imam Al-Barbahārī 81
Imam Al-Ghazali 38
Imam Fakhr Al-din 319
Imam Is-haaq ibn Raahawayh, ﷺ 81
Imām Jalāl ad-Dīn 320
Imam Maalik ﷺ 80
Īmān 76, 104, 198, 207, 280
īmān (faith) 290
Isfahani, Raghib 321
ISLAM
    GOOD MORALS IN ix, 28
i'tikāf 293

J

Jamie' al-'Uloom wa'l-Hikam 25
Jannah 36, 81, 209, 210, 214, 320
Jarl Waggoner 45
Jennifer Gunner 7
Josh McDowell 44, 322

K

kāfir 42, 49, 50
khul' 156
khul' (divorce upon a settlement) 156
kufr 49, 86, 87, 88, 121

L

lawful (Ḥalāl) 206
Lebanon 5, 318
London 163, 319, 321

M

Ma'aarij al-Qubool 86
Madaarij as-Saalikeen 55
Madarij al-Salikeen 95
Majah, Ibn 321
Majmoo' Fataawa Ibn 'Uthaymeen 86
Majmoo'ul-Fataawaa 55
Majmuu'ul fatawa 81
Majmuu'ul Fatawaa 80
making supplications (du'ā) 116
Mālikī 97, 176, 277, 318
Marshall G.S. Hodgson 125
Mashood, Dr. Busari 321
mawaddah 135, 136, 137, 138
ma'rūf 156
Ma'rūf 123, 124, 125, 126, 127, 128, 138, 145, 149, 175, 322, 325
Miftah al-Jannah fi'l-Ihtijaaj bi's-Sunnah 81
Minor Shirk (Shirk Al-Asghar) 42
Modesty xi, 27, 273, 275, 281, 282
Morality x, xi, 5, 6, 10, 113, 114, 185, 250, 322
Moral Rebellion 45
Morals ix, x, 5, 7
MORALS
    PERFECTION OF ix, 19
    PRINCIPLES OF ix, 14
Mujahid 130, 261
Mujtahid 22, 161, 177
mushrik 49
Muslim ibn al-Hajjaj 319

Musnad Aḥmad 42, 43, 69, 269
muʿāmalāt 24

N

Nawawi, Imam 320, 321
New York 158, 322
Numani, Maulana Shibli 73, 321

O

observing ritual purification (ghusl) 116

P

Philips, Dr. Abū Ameena Bilal 321
pre-Islamic Persia 88
Prophet 72
    Abraham 19, 20, 200, 223, 224
    Ibrahim 130, 165, 199, 200, 223, 224,
        225, 226, 227, 228, 322
    Ismail xiii, 226, 227, 228, 322
    Jesus 19, 20
    Moses 19, 20, 90
    Muḥammad ix, 1, 5, 18, 19, 20, 23, 25,
        27, 28, 40, 52, 56, 68, 69, 72, 74,
        76, 79, 80, 83, 85, 89, 94, 96, 103,
        104, 107, 118, 143, 150, 151,
        155, 156, 165, 172, 186, 190,
        191, 194, 196, 202, 211, 212,
        216, 228, 233, 241, 242, 252,
        264, 270, 280, 287, 288, 289,
        318, 319, 320, 321, 322
    The character of 25
    Nuh 220–337, 221–337, 222–337
    Yakub 226–337, 229–337, 230–337

Q

Qadi Iyad 97
qawāmah 144, 145, 146
qiyāmul layl 30
Quḍāʿī, Muḥammad ibn Salāmah 321
Qutub, Sayid 321

R

Raʾfat Al-Basha, ʿAbdurahman 321

Raḥīm 63, 239, 323
Raḥīm Ebrahim 63
rahmah 136
riddah 88
Riyad 288, 318, 319, 320, 321
rubūbiyyah 42

S

ṣaḥīḥ 23, 25, 198, 208, 243, 245, 247,
    282
Ṣaḥīḥ al-Bukhari 85, 208
Ṣaḥīḥ al-Muslim 85
Ṣalāt 236, 268
Ṣalāt (prayer) 236, 268
Ṣawm 268
Ṣawm (fasts) 268
Sayyid Qutb 130, 131
Sayyid Quṭub 11, 12, 154
Shāfiʿi 97, 165, 166, 320
Sharḥ Al-sunnah 81
Sharḥ Muslim 25, 268
Sharḥ us-Sunnah 55
sharīʿa 236
Sharīʿa 95, 96
Sharīʿah 175
Shifa 97, 319
shirk 49, 95, 217, 218, 324
Shirk Al-Asghar 42
shirk (polytheism) 49, 95
Spiegel 46, 322
Stephen Nichols 44
Sunan al-Tirmidhī 120
Sunan ibn Mājah 119
Syria 318

T

Tafheemul Quran 71, 93, 155, 253
Tafsir al-Bagawi 144
Tafsīr al-Jalalayn 153
Tafsir al-Qurtubi 79
Tafsīr al-Qurtubi 95
Tafsir Ibn Kathir 53, 95, 144, 162, 324
talaq 35, 165, 171, 182, 321
Taqi Ad-Dīn Aḥmad 320

Taqwa 129, 138, 171, 207, 270, 272,
     273, 322
Taqwa (God-consciousness) 171, 207
tarbīyah 206, 221, 224, 225
Tarbīyah 204, 216, 218, 225, 226
tarbīyah (nurturing and upbringing)
     206
Tarikh Bagdad 80
Tawḥīd 39, 41, 42, 43, 50, 51, 52, 53,
     188, 217, 218, 221, 226, 324
Tawḥīd al-Rubūbiyyah 43
Tawḥīd al-Ulūhiyyah 43
Tirmidhi 29, 30, 78, 192, 194, 268, 320,
     329

U

Ubeidah 166

ulūhiyyah 42
Umar bin Khattab 56
unlawful (Ḥarām) 206

W

Wardle, Lynn D. 114, 322
West 1, 2, 4, 15, 146
without causing pain" (ghayru mu'allim)
     152
without severity" (ghayru mubarriḥ)
     152

Z

zandaqah 88
Zilalul Quran 66, 93